Globalization, Employment and the Workplace

The globalization of business is a relatively new process. Although its influence on work, employment, labour relations and management practices has become increasingly significant, little is known about these developments. In order to redress the imbalance, this book provides evidence of the nature and degree of significance that globalization holds for nation–states, cultures, trade unions, employees and business management. Underlying the various contributions is a focus on the varied and complex nature of globalization in the business world.

The work is wide-ranging, drawing on research from Africa, Australia, China, Europe, Latin America, the United Kingdom and the United States. Individual chapters cover diverse issues, including:

- Responses made by trade unions and their members to the pressures of globalization.
- The experiences and reactions of nation–states and geographical regions to the changes brought about in business performance and employment.
- The flow of cultural influences through transnational business developments.
- Discussion of the ways in which management often fail to grasp the new opportunities and benefits associated with globalization.

Academics and professionals working in international business, international management, human resource management, employment relations and associated areas will all find this a valuable and enlightening resource.

Yaw A. Debrah is a Senior Lecturer in Management at Cardiff Business School, Cardiff University, Wales, UK. He has published numerous articles and book chapters, and his current research interests include the impact of globalization on management, management in emerging/transition societies, international business, human resource management in the construction and hotel industries and age discrimination in employment.

Ian G. Smith is a Senior Lecturer in Human Resource Management at Cardiff Business School, Cardiff University, Wales, UK. He has published extensively on the subjects of employment in an international context, productivity and pay, reward management and wage and salary administration and benefits. His current research centres on the use of benefits in reward management and the impact of globalization on renumeration methods and practices.

Routledge Studies in International Business and the World Economy

Globalization, Employment and the Workplace

Diverse impacts

**Edited by Yaw A. Debrah
and Ian G. Smith**

London and New York

First published 2002 by Routledge
11 New Fetter Lane, London EC4P 4EE

Simultaneously published in the USA and Canada
by Routledge
29 West 35th Street, New York, NY 10001

Routledge is an imprint of the Taylor & Francis Group

Typeset in Baskerville by Keystroke, Jacaranda Lodge, Wolverhampton
Printed and bound in Great Britain by The Cromwell Press,
Trowbridge, Wiltshire

British Library Cataloguing in Publication Data
A catalogue record for this book is available from the British Library

Library of Congress Cataloging in Publication Data
Globalization, employment, and the workplace / edited by Yaw A. Debrah
and Ian G. Smith.
      p. cm.
Papers presented at the 1999 Employment Research Unit conference
at the Cardiff Business School.
Includes bibliographical references and index.
1. Foreign trade and employment–Congresses. 2. Globalization–
Economic aspects–Congresses. 3. International business enterprises–
Employees–Congresses. 4. International labour activities–Congresses.
5. Labor market–Congresses. 6. Free trade–Congresses.
I. Debrah, Yaw A., 1956– II. Smith, Ian G. III. Cardiff Business School.
Employment Research Unit.
HD5710.7 .G56 2001
337–dc21   2001031768

ISBN 0–415–25241–5

Contents

Tables

Contributors

Nicholas Bacon is Reader in Human Resource Mangement, University of Nottingham, Business School, UK.

Santina Bertone is Executive Director of the Workplace Studies Centre, Victoria University, Melbourne, Australia.

Andries Bezuidenhout is a researcher at the Sociology of Work Unit, University of Witwatersrand, South Africa.

Paul Blyton is Professor of Industrial Relations and Industrial Sociology, Cardiff Business School, University of Cardiff, Wales.

Yaw A. Debrah is a Senior Lecturer in Human Resource Management at Cardiff Business School, University of Cardiff, Wales.

Rick Delbridge is Professor of Organizational Analysis at Cardiff Business School, University of Cardiff, Wales, UK.

Tony Edwards is a Senior Lecturer in Human Resource Management at Kingston University.

Regina M.A.A. Galhardi is at the International Labour Organization (ILO), Geneva.

Rob Gearhart is at the Office of Distance Learning, Cornell University, Ithaca, New York, USA.

Larry Godfrey is at the General Motors University, Detroit, USA.

John Hassard is Professor of Organizational Behaviour at the School of Management, University of Manchester, Institute of Science and Technology (UMIST), Manchester, UK.

Edmund Heery is Professor of Human Resource Management at Cardiff Business School, University of Cardiff, Wales.

Peter Kidger is Senior Lecturer in Human Resource Management and Director of Postgraduate Programmes in the School of Management, University of Salford, UK.

Mary Leahy is a Research Fellow at the Workplace Studies Centre, Victoria University, Melbourne, Australia.

Marcie LePine is Assistant Professor of Human Resource Studies at the School of Industrial and Labor Relations, Cornell University, Ithaca, New York: USA.

Miguel Martinez Lucio is Senior Lecturer in Industrial and Labour Studies at the University of Leeds, UK.

John McGurk is Head of Research and Communications for the British Airline Pilots' Association, Heathrow, London.

Jonathan Morris is Distinguished Senior Research Fellow at Cardiff Business School, University of Cardiff, Wales.

George Milkovich is Professor of Human Resource Management at the School of Industrial Labor Relations, Cornell University, Ithaca, New York, USA.

John Salmon is a Lecturer in Industrial Relations and Japanese Management at Cardiff Business School, University of Cardiff, Wales.

Jackie Sheehan is Lecturer in Twentieth-Century Chinese History at the University of Nottingham, UK.

Melanie Simms is Research Associate at Cardiff Business School, University of Cardiff, Wales.

Dave Simpson is Lecturer in Industrial Relations at Cardiff Business School, University of Cardiff, Wales, and an Arbitrator for the Advisory, Conciliation and Arbitration Service.

Ian G. Smith is Senior Lecturer in Human Resource Management at Cardiff Business School, University of Cardiff, Wales.

Frederic Speidel is a doctoral research student at the University of Göttingen, Germany.

Ningyu Tang is at the Management School, Shanghai Tiao Tong University, China.

Ian M. Taplin is Professor of Sociology, International Studies and Management, Wake Forest University, Winston-Salem, North Carolina, USA.

Peter Turnbull is Professor of Human Resource Management and Labour Relations at Cardiff Business School, University of Cardiff, Wales.

Jonathan Winterton is Director of Research and Professor of Human Resource Management, Groupe ESC, Toulouse, France.

Yuxin Xiao is at Sunderland Business School, Sunderland University.

Preface

The nature of globalization and its influence on work, employment, the labour process and the management process forms the substance of this book. Authors from several nations and with varying perspectives approach globalization from different angles to provide evidence of the reality, character and the degree of significance globalization holds for nation–states, cultures, trade unions, employees and business management. Perhaps the greatest importance of these contributions derives from the focus they give to the varied and complex nature of internationalization in the business world, thus helping to fill gaps caused by the relatively little that is known about the problematic and unmeasured outcomes resulting from globalization.

In more detail the issues covered include the responses made by trade unions and their members to the new pressures exerted by globalization, particularly on working conditions and membership levels, in the national contexts of Australia, South Africa and the UK and in the airlines and iron and steel industry. The experiences and reactions of some nation–states and geographical regions to the changes brought about in the areas of business performance and employment are covered in the contexts of Europe, Latin America and China and reveal the difficulties involved in achieving the realization of business goals and forecasts. The flows of cultural influences through transnational business developments are analysed in terms of reverse diffusion in employment practices and the management of cultural diversity: additionally, the influence of internationalization on the structure of 'global' distance learning exercises lends reinforcement to the argument that cultural diversity requires management of 'connectedness' to ensure that diverse expectations are met. Finally, we may note that globalization presents as much in the form of new opportunities and challenges as it does in the form of problems, yet evidence in this work points out how management often fail to grasp the new opportunities and benefits because of their lack of precision in adapting practices which could ensure the efficiencies often demanded by the process of globalization.

What is perhaps ultimately revealing in all this work is the picture of a lack of cohesion which appears to characterize the internationalization of business and its influences, coupled with a lack of strategic focus and the presence of reactive behaviour. To understand globalization therefore requires analysis and debate in multiple areas and a comprehension of actions and reactions and this book adds to our knowledge of the globalization process and updates our understanding of the responses made by affected institutions, groups and individuals.

The papers which we have put together in this edited volume were presented at the 1999 Employment Research Unit Conference at the Cardiff Business School. We would like to thank, first, our contributors who have worked hard to meet the reviewers' high expectations. Second, we would like to express our appreciation to the reviewers for their thorough review of the manuscripts. Third, thanks are due to our colleagues at Cardiff Business School for their support. In particular, we would like to thank Julie Roberts for the excellent organization of the conference, and to Mandie Zalick and Jenny Firth for the efficient secretarial support.

Acknowledgements

The editors and publishers wish to thank Ashgate Publishing Limited for permission to use material from the following:

Ian M. Taplin and Jonathan Winterton (1997) *Rethinking Global Production: A comparative analysis of restructuring in the clothing industry*, Aldershot: Ashgate.

The editors and publishers also wish to thank:

Ravi Naidoo and the National Labour, Economic and Development Institute, South Africa (COSATU) for permission to reproduce tables 5.2, 5.3 and 5.4 from Naidoo R. (ed.) (1999) *Unions in Transition: COSATU in the New Millennium*, Johannesburg: Nadeli.

The International Institute of Labour Studies (ILO) for permission to reproduce material from Bezuidenhout, A. (2000) 'Towards Global Social Movement Unionism? Trade Union Responses to Globalization in South Africa', Geneva: ILO.

List of abbreviations

ABS	Australian Bureau of Statistics
ACTU	Australian Council of Trade Unions
ACTWU	American Clothing and Textile Workers Union
AEEU	Amalgamated Engineering and Electrical Union
AFL-CIO	American Federation of Labor – Congress of Industrial Organizations
AMF	Australian Multicultural Foundation
ANC	African National Congress
ANOVA	analysis of variance
AUT	Association of University Teachers
BA	British Airways
BALPA	British Air Line Pilots Association
BASSA	British Airlines Stewards and Stewardesses Association
BEP	Business Efficiency Programme
CAA	Civil Aviation Authority
CAWU	Construction and Allied Workers' Union
CCP	Chinese Communist Party
CEC	Central Executive Committee
CEDA	Committee for Economic Development
CEPPWAWU	Chemical, Energy, Paper, Printing, Wood and Allied Workers Union
CFDT	Confédération Française Démocratique du Travail
CGIL	Italian General Confederation of Labour
CMA	Communication Managers' Association
CMT	'cut, make and trim'
COCOSA	Coordinating Committee for South Africa
COSATU	Congress of South African Trade Unions
CUSA	Council of Unions of South Africa
CUT	Workers Centre of Brazil
CWIU	Chemical Workers Industrial Union
CWU	Communication Workers Union
DIMA	Department of Immigration and Multicultural Affairs (Australia)
ECA	European Cockpit Association

ECLAC	Economic Commission for Latin America and the Caribbean
EEFSU	Eastern Europe and the former Soviet Union
EEO	equal employment opportunity
EMA	Engineers and Managers Association
ENEU	National Urban Employment Survey
ETUC	European Trade Union Confederation
EWC	European Works Councils
FEDUSA	Federation of Unions of South Africa
FDI	foreign direct investment
FOFATUSA	Federation of Free African Trade Unions of South Africa
FOSATU	Federation of South African Trade Unions
FSG	financial services group
FTO	full-time officer
GATT	General Agreement on Tariffs and Trades
GCS	group company system
GDP	gross domestic product
GPMU	Graphical Paper and Media Union
HRM	human resource management
HSD	honest significant difference
ICEM	International Federation of Chemical, Energy, Mine and General Workers' Union
ICFTU	International Confederation of Free Trade Unions
ICS	importing-competing sectors
ICU	Industrial and Commercial Workers' Union of South Africa
IFALPA	International Federation of Airline Pilots Associations
ILO	International Labour Organization
IMF	International Monetary Fund
IPMS	Institution of Professionals, Managers and Specialists
IR	industrial relations
ISTC	Iron and Steel Trades Confederation
IT	information technology
ITF	International Transport Workers Federation
ITGLWF	International Textile, Garment and Leather Workers' Federation
ITS	International Trade Secretariat
IUF	International Union of Food, Agriculture, Hotel, Restaurants, Catering, Tobacco and Allied Workers' Association
IUHS	Independent Union of Halifax Staff
ISI	importing-substitution-industrialization
JIT	just in time
KFAT	National Union of Knitwear, Footwear and Allied Trades
KMU	Kilosang Mayo Uno (May 1st Movement) of the Philippines
LDCs	less developed countries
MDL	multidistance learning
MES	modern enterprise system

MFA	Multi-Fibre Agreement
MNCs	multinational corporations
MNE	multinational enterprise
MSF	Manufacturing, Science, Finance
MUA	Maritime Union of Australia
NAAWU	National Automobile and Allied Workers' Union
NACTU	National Council of Trade Unions
NAFTA	North American Free Trade Association
NCOH	National Council for Occupational Health
NEDLAC	National Economic, Development and Labour Council
NICs	newly industrializing countries
NIE	newly industrializing economies
NESB	non-English-speaking background
NUM	National Union of Mineworkers
NUTW	National Union of Textile Workers
OATUU	Organization for African Trade Union Unity
OECD	Organization for Economic Cooperation and Development
OLS	ordinary least squares
OPT	outward processing trade
PAC	Pan Africanist Congress
PCS	Public and Commercial Services Union
PMV	passenger motor vehicle
PPWAWU	Paper, Printing, Wood and Allied Workers Union
QR	quick response
RC	radio communication
SACP	South African Communist Party
SACTU	South African Congress of Trade Unions
SACTWU	Southern African Clothing and Textile Workers' Union
SADC	Southern African Development Community
SAPs	structural adjustment programmes
SATUCC	Southern Africa Trade Union Coordinating Council
SCER	State Commission for Economic Restructuring
SCTU	Swaziland Congress of Trade Unions
SEP	safety equipment procedures
SET	skill-enhancing trade
SIGTUR	Southern Initiative on Globalization and Trade Union Rights
SME	small and medium-sized enterprise
SOE	state-owned enterprise
TGWU	Transport and General Workers' Union
TSSA	Transport Salaried Staffs Association
TUC	Trades Union Congress
TUCSA	Trade Union Congress of South Africa
UAW	United Auto Workers
WFTU	World Federation of Trade Unions
WTO	World Trade Organization

1 Globalization, employment and the workplace

Diverse impacts?

Yaw A. Debrah and Ian G. Smith

Introduction

It is now conventional wisdom that, barring any insurmountable difficulties, the globalization trend which achieved much prominence towards the end of the last century is set to gather pace, to transform the workplace, to change employment relations and, indeed, our way of life. With the recent advances and innovations in technology, we seem to be racing down an unpaved road towards a globalized world. The unpaved nature of the road implies that the journey will not always be smooth and comfortable and there are bound to be some rough rides along the way. These rough rides signify the unforeseen problems, challenges, or opportunities ahead in the management of people but for now these do not seem to deter businesses in their quest for global reach. If these unforeseen problems become insurmountable, they will halt the race towards globalization but as yet this has not happened and there seems to be no shortage of organizations willing to travel down the road to the 'global village'. Hence, the impression we get from the mass media and from fund managers is: 'at the dawn of our new millennium the globalization of business is set to continue at breakneck pace with rapid integration of the world economy' (Peel, 1999).

Globalization, then, has become something of a buzz word and politicians, journalists and academics have jumped on the bandwagon. As Kelly and Olds (1999) succinctly put it, a preoccupation with the 'global' has become one of the emblematic – almost obsessive characteristics of our time. This obsession is partly due to the realization that globalization is transforming the world at a rapid pace and it is changing the traditional workplace, employment practices and the way organizations are managed.

As organizations play a crucial role in contemporary society a worthwhile task for scholars is to research the varying ways in which globalization impacts on organizations and employees. However, any meaningful research requires a clear understanding of the concept of globalization. While most commentators seem to accept that the globalization process is underway, there is much controversy surrounding its definition, main components and characteristics. This, then, leads to the question, what is globalization?

The management literature abounds with various definitions of globalization. It is now very much 'in vogue' for writers to apply the concept of globalization to any topic under the sun. The numerous publications on globalization in the various academic disciplines and practitioner journals reveal the range of definitions of the concept; see Pieterse (1995), Kelly and Olds (1999).

According to Kogut and Gittelman (1999), globalization is the process of increasing integration between world civilizations. Waters (1995) adds that it is a social process in which the constraints of geography on social and cultural arrangements recede and in which people become increasingly aware that these constraints are receding. In a sense, globalization implies a borderless world (Ohmae, 1995). Giddens (1990: 4) also describes globalization as the intensification of world-wide social relations which link distant localities in such a way that local happenings are shaped by events occurring many miles away and vice versa. These few definitions of globalization point to the trend towards the global village (Ohmae, 1990).

Exploration of these definitions reveals that globalization impacts on several areas of social life. These include: (a) the economy; (b) the polity; and (c) the culture (Waters, 1995). This implies that the definition of globalization adopted by a particular author depends on the focus of the study. But it is known that globalization is the product of both exogenous and endogenous forces as governments, firms and groups all interact to effect significant political, economic and social changes (Kogut and Gittelman, 1999).

While it is not possible for us to study the totality of the impact of globalization on society as a whole, we can examine some aspects of the economic impacts of globalization. However, Wiseman (1998) argues that while it is important for us to focus on the economic aspects of globalization, an adequate understanding of the diverse processes of globalization requires a more integrated approach, which illuminates the overall landscape of economic, social, cultural, environmental and political relationships. Hence, it is advisable that while investigating the economic impacts of globalization one does not gloss over its political and social antecedents. In this book we intend to deal principally with economic globalization.

Following Hill (2001), we use the term globalization in an economic sense to refer to the shift towards a more integrated and interdependent world economy. This is in line with the debates in the literature on the increasing interdependence of regional and national economies and the fundamental shift occurring in the global economy. In Hill's view, we are witnessing the end of an era when national economies were pretty well isolated from each other by barriers to international trade and investment, by time zones, distance, language, by national differences in government regulations, culture, and business systems. In its place we are witnessing the movement towards a more integrated and interdependent global economic system.

Lee (1996) sees the main manifestations of this form of economic globalization primarily in terms of the rapid growth in international trade, foreign direct investment (FDI) and cross-border financial flows in recent years. This process has been associated with a world-wide wave of economic liberalization – including the lowering of tariff and non-tariff barriers to international trade, the encouragement of FDI, and the deregulation of financial markets. Running concurrent with this development are technological developments that have reduced the cost of transportation and communications, hence making it possible for goods and services to be internationally traded in unprecedented scope and volume. These processes have myriad impacts on organizations and the people who work in them. Discussion of these processes is one of the aims of this book.

In spite of the recent popularity of the concept of economic globalization in academic debates, there is a dearth of research on its implications on work, the workplace, employment and trade unions. This book attempts to provide empirical evidence to shed light on some of the views and debate in the literature on the impacts of economic globalization on the workplace and employment. It attempts to contribute to the debate by bringing together research from the UK, the USA, Africa, Latin America, Australia, Continental Europe and East Asia to illuminate our understanding of what is actually happening to organizations, workforces, employee groupings/representatives and individual employees as a result of economic globalization.

In this regard, this chapter provides a broad overview of the concept of economic globalization, the factors that account for the move towards economic globalization, the issues pertaining to the impacts of economic globalization on employees particularly, on employment, incomes and labour relations. This chapter also provides the key themes of the book. In relation to this it reviews the important issues examined in the various chapters. These include:

1   the pressures facing both local and global firms in a globalized era and the various ways in which they are responding to the human resource management (HRM) challenges brought about by globalization;
2   the impact of reverse diffusion on the nature of employment relations in the domestic workplaces of multinational corporations (MNCs);
3   effects of economic liberalization on employment, wages, skills and other labour issues;
4   the implications of globalization for industrial relations, trade union organizing and campaigns;
5   an assessment of the debate on the impact of globalization on labour, work and employment in some specific industrial sectors.

Upon examination of issues presented in this book it is argued that the influence of globalization on work and employment, and on the labour process and the management process is inexorable and at the same time imperfectly understood. International business activity is at the same time complex in nature and pressurizing nation–states and cultures in novel ways, with little known as yet about medium to long-term outcomes. Hence, revealing the reality, the nature, extent and significance of economic globalization remains a learning process involving the expansion of a body of knowledge and understanding on the subject. In this regard, the following chapters represent substantial contributions to this learning process and better understanding from the perspective of the nation–state, and employee and business/ management.

Factors accounting for the move towards economic globalization

Many factors account for the increased economic globalization. Knight (1998) asserts that the driving forces behind economic globalization include (a) technological advancement, particularly advances in communication technology; (b) the pervasive adoption of free market ideology worldwide; (c) the economic expansion and the associated world-wide wave of economic liberalization in developing countries; and (d) the increase in free trade including the lowering of tariff and other barriers to international trade, e.g., the provision of services across borders and the movement of capital.

As noted by Levitt (1983: 92), technological progress has been at the forefront of the push towards a globalized world. In particular, the recent significant developments in communications and information processing, including developments in the mobile telephony, e-mail, the Internet and the World-Wide Web and transportation technologies, it is argued, have advanced the cause of economic globalization. In real terms, developments in microprocessors, satellites, optical fibre and wireless technologies have had the effect of reducing the cost of global communication and with it the cost of co-ordinating, controlling, planning and managing a global organization (Hill, 2001).

Equally, innovations in shipment (containerization) have made it possible for products to be shipped more economically to any part of the world. These cost reductions have intensified competition in the global marketplace. In particular, these advancements provide opportunities for far-flung business interactions to create more global business opportunities (Parker, 1998). Consequently, it is possible for small, previously unknown, local companies to tap into both national and international markets.

Economic globalization has also been accelerated by the decline in barriers to investment and free trade – including the lowering of tariffs and other barriers to international trade. Beginning in the mid-twentieth century, declining tariffs and advances in air and freight transport paved the way for a great expansion in global trade. This gave rise to the greater interdependence of national markets for goods and services, particularly financial services, resulting in the integration of capital and financial markets.

According to Kogut and Gittelman (1999), the global integration of financial markets has been made possible by a confluence of supply and demand factors. The supply side factors include deregulation of currency controls, innovations in financial instruments, and advances in communications and IT that allow transactions to be executed instantaneously across national boundaries. The demand-side factors include the increase in corporate restructuring that created demand for new sources of financing, rapid growth in foreign investment and trade, and the adoption of free market principles in a number of previously regulated economies.

Another force behind the rapid globalization trend has been the increase in foreign direct investment (FDI). In recent years many countries, particularly those in the developing world, have opened their economies to FDI by liberalizing FDI regulations and hence made it easier for foreign companies to enter their markets. Governments in many developing countries have created opportunities through the liberalization of their economies for firms in their countries to attract FDI and this in turn has opened the doors to MNCs to expand their network of operations in developing countries. Budhwar and Debrah (2001) show that since the early 1980s many developing countries have initiated economic liberalization programmes which have as their essential elements privatization and the attraction of FDI. Countries worthy of mention here include China, India, South Africa, Brazil and Russia but equally such regions as Latin America, Sub-Saharan Africa, Eastern Europe and South Asia are also involved.

In Sub-Saharan Africa, the end of apartheid in South Africa has given rise to a fundamental restructuring of the economy and concerted efforts on the part of the government to attract FDI and to persuade those MNCs which pulled out of South Africa as a result of the anti-apartheid campaign to return. Elsewhere in Sub-Saharan Africa the end of the Cold War ushered in a wind of change which is blowing all over the region. One clear manifestation of this is the adoption of structural adjustment programmes.

These economic restructuring programmes initiated by the International Monetary Fund (IMF) and the World Bank focused on:

1   the liberalization of the economies by subjecting them to both local and international competition;
2   liberalization of domestic trade and commerce;
3   reform of fiscal policy;
4   reform of the financial sectors;
5   reform of agriculture; and
6   reduction of budget deficits.

Countries such as Ghana and Uganda have been at the forefront of such reforms but by and large the majority of Sub-Saharan African countries have introduced the reforms partially or in their entirety (Debrah, 2000; Debrah, 2001; Budhwar and Debrah 2001).

In other parts of the world, the changes taking place in Eastern and Central Europe including the former states of the USSR as a result of the collapse of communism as well as the economic liberalization in China (see, Pollert, 2000; Sadher *et al.*, 1999; and Warner, 2001) have all accelerated the pace of economic globalization. Similarly, in Latin America, democratic and free market reforms initiated in countries such as Brazil, Argentina and Chile among others have been powering ahead. In many instances the trade barriers and free market restrictions imposed by previous Latin American governments have been removed.

In yet another part of the world, Budhwar (2001) succinctly discusses the Indian economic liberalization programme which began in 1991. He asserts that the pre-1992 centralized economic planning system brought India to its knees and this galvanized the forces of change. It is reported that by 1991, India had a double digit rate of inflation, decelerated industrial production, fiscal indiscipline, an astronomically high ratio of borrowing to the GNP and abysmally low level of foreign exchange reserves. By any economic indicator or measure, India had effectively been plunged into an economic crisis.

Enter the World Bank and the IMF. These institutions agreed to bail out India but only on condition that it introduced free market reforms. In accordance with this agreement, the Indian government initiated a series of economic liberalization policies which included the devaluation of the currency (the Rupee), and the introduction of new industrial, fiscal and trade policies. The public sector along with trade, exchange policy, the banking sector and foreign investment policies were reformed.

In summary, then, the liberalization of the economies in the developing world coupled with democratization policies, the relatively prudent management of debt and the tackling of inflationary pressures have now turned the table round in both the investment and FDI arenas. In a sense, better management of the investment environment in many developing countries is encouraging foreign investment. Equally, with debt and inflation down in many developing countries, their governments are busy privatizing public enterprises and going all out to attract FDI as their economies gather steam. These developments have increased the attractiveness of some developing countries as destinations for FDI.

One measure of economic globalization is the growth in FDI. In light of the current global surge in FDI, Horton (1998) asserts that we are witnessing the ascendancy of the transnational economy. The predominant view here is that economic globalization was initially facilitated by the growth of MNCs, particularly large Western MNCs, but the trend is changing.

A brief analysis of the history of international trade reveals that prior to the First World War, MNCs were the main players in FDI and many of the powerful MNCs were from the USA. During this era, UK companies were also actively engaged in FDI but their involvement heightened in the period up to the Second World War. Other European companies were also involved and this reduced the dominant role of the USA. The post-war period witnessed the reassertion of the dominance of US companies in the area of FDI. Vaupel and Curhan (1973) have shown that from 1939 to the mid-1970s, US MNCs were responsible for two-thirds of the increase in FDI and the growth in the number of overseas affiliates. However, changes in the world economy and economic order in the early 1970s made the USA a more attractive location for investment. Consequently, by the late 1980s inward investment in the USA had more than double the outflows as this period witnessed a phenomenal increase in Japanese direct (inward) investment to the USA. During this period, Japanese companies began to set up subsidiaries world-wide.

In recent years, with the continuing trend in economic liberalization around the world, there has been a sharp increase in FDI overall. There is some evidence that world-wide outflows of FDI are growing at a faster rate than both exports and gross domestic products (GDP). Thus, it is asserted that FDI has replaced trade as the engine of international economic integration (Kogut and Gittelman, 1999).

One interesting aspect of the growth in FDI is the concomitant growth/rise in non-Western MNCs, particularly East Asian MNCs. As mentioned earlier, the ascendancy of MNCs from Japan has been matched by others from countries such as South Korea, Taiwan, other newly industrializing economies (NIEs) and in some cases developing countries in Latin America, South Asia and South Africa. Hill (2001) refers to these MNCs as the mini-MNCs (medium-sized and small MNCs) and argues that they play important roles in international business as they have global operations and are seriously involved in international trade and investment. This view is reinforced by Yeung (1999) who has shown that MNCs from developing countries, particularly in East Asia and Latin America, have a significant presence in the global market, many have become global players in international business and are becoming significant competitors in the global economy.

Although globalization has intensified FDI flows to developed countries, flows of FDI by MNCs to developing countries have equally been on the increase. In 1998 flows of FDI by MNCs to Latin America and the Caribbean Islands increased by 5 per cent over that of the previous year to reach US$28.7 billion. In particular, the FDI went into new business opportunities created by privatization in Brazil, Venezuela, Columbia, Argentina, Mexico, El Salvador and Guatemala. Equally, more traditional FDI investments in export-oriented industries went to companies in Jamaica, Costa Rica and the Dominican Republic (UNCTAD, 1999a).

Similarly, FDI inflows to Africa have been increasing significantly since the early 1990s. With the transition to democratic rule and liberalization of the economies of some African countries, the prospects for FDI flow into Africa have improved. Countries such as Nigeria, South Africa, Ghana, Mozambique, Uganda, Botswana, Namibia and Tunisia have improved their business environment to enhance their chances of attracting FDI and it appears that some MNCs are responding positively to these policies. FDI inflows into Africa in 1998 amounted to US$8.3 billion (UNCTAD, 1999b).

FDI is also flowing to some of the oil-producing countries in the Middle East. Countries such as the Yemen, Kuwait, Oman, the United Arab Emirates and Qatar have been able to attract investments from MNCs with the opening of their economies to foreign investors (UNCTAD, 1999c). The Pacific Islands attracted US$175 million of FDI investment from MNCs in 1998. These investments came from MNCs based mainly in Australia, New Zealand and Japan although some European and North American MNCs were important sources of FDI investment in the region. In 1998 Fiji received US$91 million, Papua New Guinea US$30 million, and Vanuatu US$28 million (UNCTAD, 1999c).

In spite of the recent financial crisis in East Asia, FDI continues to flow into the region. In 1998, FDI to the Asia-Pacific region was US$85 billion. FDI inflow by MNCs to China in 1998 was US$45.5 billion. China received more than half of the total FDI flow to the region and was the third largest recipient of FDI in the world after the USA and the UK (UNCTAD, 1999c). Countries such as Malaysia, the Philippines, Thailand, Singapore and Indonesia continue to be attractive destinations for FDI.

Central and Eastern European countries have, since the introduction of liberalization policies following the disintegration of the USSR, been important destinations for FDI. In 1998, FDI by MNCs in this region were heavily concentrated in Poland, the Czech Republic, Romania, Hungary and the Russian Federation. According to UNCTAD (1999d), many countries in Central and Eastern Europe are doubling their efforts to attract foreign investment and in this respect they are catching up with the rest of the world in their capacity to attract FDI (UNCTAD, 1999d).

FDI provides a means for MNCs to exert considerable influence on work and employment as they introduce new working practices which often filter down to local firms. Technology transfer through MNCs also has the ability to transform work practices, social relations in the workplace, and employment practices. In particular, MNCs develop employment strategies which tend to follow their global strategies. Hence more and more innovations in working practices developed in one part of the world are being implemented in other parts of the world by means of the diffusion of MNCs' policies. Advances in Information Technology and Communications make such diffusion possible.

Seen from this perspective, it is conceivable that local firms can learn from MNCs' HRM practices. Hence, globalization has made it possible for MNCs to become the main stimulus for changes and innovations in the management of HRs and this has a multifaceted impact on work and employment in organizations.

The impact of economic globalization on employees

With the shift towards a more integrated and interdependent world economy, the emergence of a global marketplace where firms compete fiercely is apparent. This globalization of markets has facilitated the globalization of production which makes it possible for firms to source goods and services from dispersed global locations. Globalization of production enables firms to buy the highest quality product at the lower cost. Both of these processes have significant implications for work and employment.

As Frenkel and Peetz (1998) point out, economic globalization initiates competitiveness both at the firm and national level. At the national level, governments all over the world are under pressure to internationalize their economies to satisfy the requirements of MNCs and foreign investors. Liberalization of economies creates competitiveness for local firms. With intensified competition organizations are making efforts to meet international competitive standards on the three Ps – price, productivity and profits – and this has implications for work and employment (Bryan and Rafferty, 1999).

To tackle the competitive issues, organizations tend to adopt strategies aimed at increasing both organizational and labour effectiveness, particularly on productivity and quality (Kuruvilla, 1996). In the view of Frenkel and Peetz (1998), these strategies initiated by economic globalization encourage management rationalization and greater emphasis on competing more effectively. Hence, firms put more emphasis on cost reduction and quality enhancement while at the same time removing or curtailing job security.

At another level, increased competitiveness leads to an increase in management unilateralism in the workplace, where union demands for recognition, collective bargaining, and more job security are often ignored (Bryan and Rafferty, 1999). Under global competitive pressures, employers are more likely to resort to the hiring of employees on fixed-term (temporary) contracts, contracting out and casualization, rather than lifetime employment. In both developed and developing countries, more and more employees now work in an environment where permanent and secure employment contracts are being replaced by less stable, less secure and 'non-standard' forms of employment (Cooper, 2000; Heery and Salmon, 2000).

Faced with the imperative of globalization, management constantly seek greater wage flexibility, functional and numerical flexibility. Thus, the competitive pressures associated with economic globalization induce shifts in workforce composition, labour demand and the inter-temporal deployment of workers. In short, as the idea of a permanent job disappears, we see an increase in short-term contracts or part-time work (de Ruyter and Burgess, 2000).

One consequence of this trend is the erosion of the psychological contract between employer and employee in terms of reasonable permanent employment for competent work effort. Cooper (2000) cites a survey of working conditions in seventeen European countries to show that the employment security of workers declined considerably between the mid-1980s and late 1990s: the UK, from 70 per cent to 48 per cent; Germany, from 83 per cent to 55 per cent; France, 64 per cent to 50 per cent; Netherlands, from 73 per cent to 61 per cent; Belgium, from 60 per cent to 54 per cent; and Italy from 62 per cent to 57 per cent.

Equally, in many Sub-Saharan African countries, economic restructuring and privatization in response to economic globalization pressures have resulted in significant job losses. In Ghana, for instance, since the initiation of the privatization programme in 1989, 132 state-owned enterprises have been sold off and have become 232 privately owned companies. A further 168 are being prepared for privatization (Knipe, 2000). This has resulted in significant job losses as over 100,000 workers in public enterprises were made redundant prior to privatization and in some cases public enterprises which were deemed to be not viable or impossible to privatize were liquidated (Debrah, 2001).

Globalization is also accelerating the pace of international migration of workers and creating skill shortages in both developed and developing countries. In developed countries the advances in IT have created acute skill shortages and some governments have responded by relaxing restrictions on immigration and work permit rules on foreign professionals. It is well known that many North American and European companies have been recruiting IT workers from India. Similarly, the skills shortages facing the IT industry globally have prompted Western companies to outsource IT work to Indian companies (Lamb, 2000).

In the UK, it was recently announced that the government is relaxing its restrictions on work permits to attract high-flyers with key skills to tackle skills shortages in areas such as information technology. This change of heart arises from the government's determination to ensure that the UK leads in e-commerce and the Internet and can compete for scarce labour in the global economy (Taylor, 2000). Countries such as Germany and Sweden are also relaxing their work permit regulations to attract skilled IT personnel globally.

Both UK public and private sector organizations have recruited health care, IT, and teaching personnel from many developing countries including South Africa, Ghana, Nigeria, the Philippines, and the English-speaking West Indian countries (Johnson, 2001). The skills shortages in the UK railway industry have forced firms to recruit skilled staff from India. Indian railway workers are providing a solution to the growing recruitment problems in the industry in the UK, e.g., firms have gone to India to recruit signal engineers – a skill which is in short supply world-wide (*People Management*, 2000).

The sourcing of talents globally creates a diversified workforce. As Lewis *et al.* (2001) point out, this creates challenges for managers in coping with the increasing cultural diversity in the workplace, and, as the global trend continues – even accelerates – in the new millennium, the development of skills in managing people from diverse cultural backgrounds will become more and more of a priority for managers in advanced industrialized societies.

It is also now well known that economic globalization has a significant impact on industrial relations systems. Chaykowski and Giles (1998) assert that there is evidence of erosion in traditional patterns of bargaining and in workplace norms and, in addition, many countries are seeing a decline in unionism and collective bargaining. The changing nature of global labour markets has also posed new challenges for IR. Baecherman and Chaykowski (1996) assert that changes in work systems and the loosening of the customary spatial ties of workers to worksites are fundamentally changing the traditional concept of the workplace. It is argued that this poses challenges to unions with regard to the organizing of employees.

According to Chaykowski and Giles (1998), the advancements in technology in a globalized era have transformed production processes, facilitated the mobility of goods and services, and factors of production, and provided a basis for new forms of economic activity. Also, the rise of the information economy has resulted in the shift from manufacturing to service industries with profound implications for workers, unions, management and work in general. This shift has resulted in the decline in union membership in developed countries, and in developing countries privatization has done away with many unionized jobs and hence created a decline in union membership. The decline in mass production has also ushered in new production systems characterized by smaller scales of production, greater flexibility in the organization of work, a leaner, less labour-intensive workforce, increased emphasis on employing more highly skilled workers, and flatter hierarchies (Cappelli *et al.*, 1997; Hollingsworth *et al.*, 1997).

As Chaykowski and Giles (1998) succinctly explain, economic globalization is undermining the traditional concept of the workplace in so far as the physical location of production and employment is concerned. In their view, globalization assisted by technological changes has encouraged the spatial transformation of both production and work. Consequently, production sites and economic activity are now more dispersed globally and new activities start up in previously undeveloped sites as production sites are more easily relocated. Firms seek competitive advantage by selecting physical sites that are regulated by advantageous labour policies, 'competitive' labour costs and cheaper taxes (Horton, 1998). Consequently, both large and small firms are combing the world for the best price, technology, delivery and quality (Pyke, 1998).

This task has been made easier by the advent of the e-economy as companies are now scanning the globe for the best materials and services at the lowest possible price. The e-economy enables the purchaser to directly negotiate with suppliers and also to outsource from the global market much more easily. Thus many firms now concentrate their efforts and resources on core competencies and outsource nearly everything else. It is perceived that these sorts of practices result in job losses, work intensification, increased income inequality and consequent anxiety for both skilled and unskilled workers and unions (Lee, 1996, 1997).

These anxieties have generated interesting debates in the literature. The debates revolve around the impact of FDI on jobs and incomes in both industrialized and developing economies. It is believed that the export of low-wage, labour-intensive and low-skilled jobs to low-wage economies through FDI destroys jobs and creates unemployment for low-skilled workers in industrialized countries.

At another level, it is perceived that the import of manufactured goods from low-wage countries to industrialized countries can have the potential to destroy labour-intensive manufacturing jobs in high-wage industrialized countries as the prices of products of firms from high-wage countries become uncompetitive in the market, leading to the closure of such firms. Accompanying the demise of labour-intensive jobs is the increase in wage inequalities in industrialized countries because of the lack of demand for unskilled workers relative to the skilled (Lee, 1996).

In developing countries in particular, it is feared that economic globalization which has fuelled economic liberalization and the desire to attract FDI may lead to high transitional unemployment and increase wage and income inequality. However, there are patterns of diversity in the experiences of developing countries. While this is true of some Latin American countries (Robbins, 1995), the same cannot be said about the NIEs in East Asia which have been able to achieve rapid economic growth while reducing inequality. In East Asia impressive economic growth has been achieved in spite of the fact that the NIEs liberalized their economies and focused on the export of manufactured goods (Lee, 1996).

Some writers have attempted to explain why the NIEs have been able to achieve rapid growth and low inequality at the same time but this has eluded some developing countries (see Robbins, 1995; Wood, 1994). However, after an extensive review of these reasons, Lee (1996) contends that it still remains unclear why there is rising wage inequality in some developing countries after trade liberalization.

At another level, it is advocated that globalization can potentially have negative consequences on labour standards leading to the possibility of a 'race to the bottom' in so far as labour standards are concerned (Lee, 1997). The central argument here is that barring international cooperation to stamp out 'unethical' practices, increasing economic integration and its consequent fierce competition have the potential to cause a downward spiral on labour standards in developing countries (Bhagwati and Hudec, 1996).

It is argued that the reduction in trade barriers and increasing free trade would serve as a source of encouragement to firms in advanced industrialized societies to 'export' their manufacturing operations to developing countries without the strict enforcement of health and safety regulations, environmental policies, labour standards, etc. (Goldsmith J., 1996). Such a move is often precipitated by the perceived injustices in the regulatory environment as firms in advanced industrialized societies have to adhere to strict regulations in the aforementioned areas while those in developing nations do not (Batra, 1993). Hence, firms in advanced industrialized societies attempt to correct the imbalance in costs and competitiveness by moving their manufacturing operations to developing countries that do not enforce the labour standard regulations (Choate, 1993).

In assessing these views, Lee (1996) comments that there is very little empirical evidence in the literature to confirm that this is actually happening. Furthermore, he questions the view that the 'export' of low-skilled jobs to low-wage countries through relocation has increased competition in imports and consequently resulted in a decline in demand for low-skilled workers in the industrialized countries. Arguably, there may be other factors that account for the increase in unemployment and wage inequality.

After reviewing the empirical evidence, Lee (1996) concludes that both trade and FDI have contributed in a minor way to the rise in unemployment and wage inequality in industrialized countries (see Lawrence and Slaughter, 1993; Sachs and Shatz, 1994; Krugman, 1994; Bhagwati, 1994). Lee (1996) also casts doubt on the view that an increase in FDI, the removal of barriers to capital flows and the consequent creation of a global labour market have negative consequences on the wages of employees. This scepticism is based on the evidence that MNCs for various reasons do not easily relocate production from one country to another. In other words, MNCs are not as 'footloose' as they are generally thought to be (Hirst and Thompson, 1996; Wade, 1996).

Finally, it is also pointed out that there is no consensus in the literature as to the inevitability of this race to the bottom. After a careful review of the arguments on both sides of this debate, Lee (1996) asserts that with regard to the 'race to the bottom' thesis, there is no clear evidence that economic globalization has caused the lowering of labour standards in industrialized countries. He adds that the rather inconclusive balance of *a priori* argument makes it important to resolve the issue through direct empirical evidence, but this hardly exists in any systematic way. The chapters in this book provide empirical evidence shedding light on some of the debates on the diverse impacts of economic globalization on work, the workplace, employment, workers/managers and organizations.

The structure and overview of the book

From the kaleidoscope of material contained in the twelve empirical chapters in this book there emerges a picture of occasionally well-informed and more often ill-informed responses to globalization spread liberally among company boards and managements, governments and trade unions. Within this maelstrom of imprecise decision-making, groups and individual employees can often only survive and make 'the best of it'. And here we find one of the greatest paradoxes attached to economic globalization – the small-scale process of 'muddling through' which dominates the management of and response to the global developments. Strategy and long-termism are as divorced from the process of economic globalization as they are from the many more established facets of business and national life and events.

The outcomes of this uncoordinated and incohesive internationalization are, to say the least, varied. The process is like a 'juggernaut' attacking on several fronts at once. Therefore the arguments contained in this book are trained on or aimed at many fronts pertaining to the impacts of economic globalization on work and employment.

The essential variety of economic globalization issues forces the debate on the subject into a similar degree of variety or diversity. Consequently, a significant variety of outcomes deriving from economic globalization have been extensively evaluated within this book, resulting in a significant amount of material which has implications for the academic discussion of economic globalization, and equally for corporate main board directors and their managers, trade unions, employee groups and individuals, nation–states, their cultures and governments.

Four chapters: i.e., those by Blyton *et al.*, Heery *et al.*, Bacon and Blyton, and Bezuidenhout (Chapters 2, 3, 4 and 5 respectively) are concerned with various responses made by trade unions and labour to the pressures and influences brought about by economic globalization. From these initial chapters we run into the issue of variety in these responses with no clear consistency or pattern emerging from research in airlines and the iron and steel industry, and in South Africa and the UK. Several varying but focused pictures of organized labour's anticipative and reactionary behaviour to cope with the internationalization of business and the outcomes, particularly as they affect labour markets, emerged. Not least in these responses, however, is a seemingly confused and complex mix of opportunism and strategic choice particularly in the northern hemisphere.

Chapters by Hassard *et al.*, Galhardi and Speidel and Simms (Chapters 6, 7 and 8 respectively) reveal elements of some national experiences and reactions to the pressures on business performance, industrial relations and employment in China, Europe, and Latin America. At the same time, real difficulties in formulating responses by governments, managers and trade unions are revealed against the background of a complex mix of compromises, unrealized commercial ambitions and the failure of economic predictions in the managing and forecasting of international trade and business.

At another level, it is shown that globalization confronts managements with many issues requiring new and particular responses. The requirements for such developments and the forces pressurizing them are the focus of Chapters 9 and 10 by Edwards and by Kidger respectively. The challenges of reverse diffusion in employment practices and the need to integrate the efforts of culturally diverse workforces are not readily dealt with by managements, often to the disadvantage of the enterprise. These issues of cultural diversity and the management of cultural capital or assets are thoroughly investigated in the Australian context by Bertone and Leahy in Chapter 11 and the potential for misunderstanding between cultures, particularly in the workplace, is revealed as a very real concern. That it is not managed sensitively through non-discriminatory and cohesive HRM policies and practices and has simultaneously undermined social justice and equity in the Australian labour markets and robbed international companies of many of the claimed benefits of internationalization including enhanced corporate performance is emphasized.

In Chapter 12 by LePine *et al.* the focus turns to internationalization in an educational context and they study the relationship between regional effectiveness in learning outcomes in the local classroom and the 'global' lecture presented in the global classroom. In a globalized business world, new initiatives to enhance the benefits of a globalized distance learning venture are required. The global distance learning approach ensures that learning copes with diversity in cultures and the expectations of world-wide students in a manner which parallels the issue of cultural diversity management in business.

The issue of enterprises failing to grasp the opportunities and benefits deemed to derive from globalization is interestingly underpinned in Chapter 13 by Taplin and Winterton which is based on experiences in the clothing industry. There is a definitive lack of certainty among managements in this industry about the type of production management and employment practice responses which should be made to the pressures of internationalization in order to lower costs, improve efficiency and improve value added. Interestingly, managements experience the same difficulties as trade unions in interpreting and responding to the process of economic globalization.

A plurality of issues

In assembling the four broad themes presented above, some licence has been taken in simplifying the contents of the various chapters. The themes therefore represent an outline or skeleton framework to help guide the reader in locating particular issues. The reality is of course more complex and the chapters raise a plurality of issues and arguments which appear in many areas. At the least we should recognize that all the above themes represent some type of change which is brought into the organization's (of whichever type) environment with substantial implications for the exercise of power and influence, the management of change in general and cultural change in particular and associated cultural diversity. Such issues flow through all of the following chapters and affect a plurality of industries, firms, nations, cultures, people and institutions. Some of these issues are elaborated below.

Globalization and labour

Globalization often presents radical changes to the local labour market. Blyton *et al.* raise the spectre of deteriorating terms and conditions for labour and the weakened role of trade unions in the face of internationally based decisions on capital which impact negatively on labour. Bacon and Blyton refer to the 'race to the bottom' for employment conditions, although they find no common pattern to support a universal state of improvement and maintenance or degradation for such conditions.

Additionally, these two writers reveal the relative inability of trade unions to influence events and outcomes in the globalization process. This last point may be partially explained by Heery *et al.*'s work on the response of UK unions to the US-inspired 'organizing model' of trade unions, a response which has been patchy and limited to a few 'cash-rich' unions which have adopted the membership campaign approach. The inability of many British trade unions to overcome the obstacles to the adoption of the organizing model may have a negative impact on membership growth and representational power in the battle to influence globalization and its impacts on the employment experience of existing union members.

Bezuidenhout's review of South African trade union responses to economic gobalization shows that the traditional use of collective power has been useful in blocking the development of unjust and inequitable structures in employment and in society more generally. Notable in this process has been the integration of local and workplace activities with the work of overseas trade unions which have members employed in the same transnational company, an interesting and as yet rare example of a strategic international trade union response to the pressures brought about by globalization. This places South African trade union activity (at least historically) above the 'muddling through' approach of trade unions elsewhere. Unfortunately the momentum and essential nature of the global campaigns have become more symbolic as unions have become divided in the face of greater global pressures in recent years. Consequently, many of the previous gains are now being eroded.

The case for an international multi-level trade union response to globalization is 'writ large' in the chapter by Bezuidenhout, yet such responses are rare. Only the stronger unions with high membership and the financial resources to support campaigns as revealed in the airline and iron and steel industries seem able to resist the degradation of membership employment. Where such strength does not exist, as in the clothing industry, wage depression, insecurity and exploitation are the more likely outcomes.

For many workers, therefore, globalization has so far come to mean changes in operations and workplace relations which in turn weaken unions, bring about non-unionism and the decline of collective bargaining. The final outcomes are the insecure workforce (Heery and Salmon, 2000), the loss of established working patterns (Chaykowski and Giles, 1998), and the intensification of work. These continue to be matters urgently requiring trade union attention as the successes of the strong alongside the problems of the weak make for an uncomfortable comparison. The need for a strategic integrated response to economic globalization is as strong for unions and their staff as it is for corporate directors and managers.

National and regional experiences

If transnational and national trade union policies and actions are currently found wanting, the chapters by Hassard *et al.*, Galhardi, and Speidel and Simms reveal similar problems on national and regional scales affecting many institutions in addition to trade unions. For instance, the iron and steel industry in China is unable to develop the entrepreneurship model of management to help better exploit the more liberal yet competitive South East Asian markets because of domestic political constraints. In addition, neither government nor industry has proved capable of establishing a fully appropriate and cohesive response to the new conditions arising from internationalization and liberalization of markets in the region.

In the context of Latin America, Galhardi points to the relationship which exists between economic growth, currency appreciation and the increasing use of capital to reduce costs. The labour markets of the region have been profoundly affected by this process with a slowing down of job creation and rising unemployment. Additionally, the influence of trade liberalization on capital utilization has resulted in higher wages for the skilled groupings of manpower while depressing unskilled wage levels. This experience aligns with the view that globalization often works through the structures and institutions of the labour market, threatening the vulnerable and disadvantaged members of that market (Lee, 1996).

In contributing to the debate on effects of globalization on employees, Bacon and Blyton assert that there is no universal 'race to the bottom' for employment conditions. Latin America, however, may provide an exceptional example of one area where it is difficult to halt the decline in unskilled employment because of local and specific characteristics. Certainly, Latin American countries have not benefited from any competitive advantage in trade which stimulates demand and remuneration for the unskilled. The recommended response to this is greater focus and effort on the training of the unskilled to enhance the quality and productivity of human resources in Latin America and to provide a better 'underpinning' for high value and high growth industries, thus ensuring better integration of Latin American economies with the global economy. Galhardi admits that this will be a difficult challenge for Latin American nations, perhaps not least because, as Blyton *et al.* point out in Chapter 2, labour representation is not significant in decisions made about capital and its utilization and the effect on labour. More optimistically Bacon and Blyton point to greater training as a positive outcome of economic globalization; yet a question remains on whether this can gain priority over capital utilization in Latin America.

The situation discussed in connection with the iron and steel industry in China (and Latin American difficulties on a regional scale) reveals that the forces of economic globalization can be insensitive to local, nation–state and industry issues, preferences and aspirations. Perhaps the organizations and structures within such nations are incapable of challenging this insensitivity and more positively influencing outcomes.

So far there is no definitive assessment of whether there is convergence to some new world order, because of the difficulty in identifying harmonization patterns and their achievements. In the chapters discussed so far, more positive outcomes might have been achieved by the harmonization of global and national aspirations, as discussed in the case of South Africa; certainly, this contrasts with globalization operating as a unitary process of convergence. Indeed, we may go further and note that divergence is now influencing the globalization debate; Katz and Darbishire (2000) have identified more variety and flexibility in the approach taken by multinational organizations towards the local host nation's labour process and institutions than has previously been assumed.

Convergence and divergence are both questioned by Speidel and Simms in their analysis of the impact of economic globalization on industrial relations in France and Germany. The fresh dimension for globalization determined by these authors revolves around the differences in what globalization actually means for the two nations. In suggesting 'contextual divergence' as a model to explain differences, our understanding of globalization is now enhanced by a clearer picture of local details fuelling local responses, for example, different starting points in the globalization process and different adjustment processes for the industrial relations responses to globalization. Thus France and Germany have experienced globalization operating in two 'opposite' roles because of different existing industrial relations frameworks. Thus neither convergence nor divergence adequately help us understand the impact of globalization at the local host nation level, at least in the case of France and Germany.

Diversity, diffusion and HRM

Traditionally, as we have noted, globalization has more often than not been seen as a process of convergence to some new state of being. We have also noted that latterly it has been seen by some as a process of divergence which is rather more sensitive to local factors than has hitherto been accepted in the academic debate. The attractiveness of divergence becomes clear if we consider that business methods, which appear to work well in one culture, may lead to disaffection, grievance and dispute in another. A major issue in this context is the management of cultural diversity which has been studied by Bertone and Leahy in the Australian business world.

The findings support the argument that international businesses require skills in cross-cultural communication and the management of cultural diversity. The authors assert that their findings indicate that businesses benefit in terms of performance, particularly employee contributions and market growth – if a diverse workforce is valued, yet few businesses are aware of such benefits and rarely make the issue of cultural diversity a management priority. Thus, diversity is rarely managed effectively. Studies in Australia hint at a 'darker side' of racial and ethnic discrimination which sees 'cultural capital' undervalued by managers and business performance suffering as a result.

Cultural diversity and its management are at the heart of a very problematic aspect of globalization – the potential for conflict between the local 'host' (and culture), on the one hand, and international 'convergence', on the other. The 'crucible' out of which any approaches to deal with this in a more positive manner as defined by Bertone and Leahy involves management – HRM in particular, and trade unions. The latter have been seen to demonstrate a 'patchy' ability to deal effectively with the matter.

In this regard, Blyton *et al.* have revealed the lack of any transnational union response or consistent behaviour across different employee groupings; rather, the power of unions, where it exists, is the constraint on degradation of the employment experience. Although labour responses have differed from nation to nation, hinting at more divergence than convergence in the process of globalization in the airline industry, it is the power differentials between occupational groupings that cause differences in the 'race to the bottom'. The overall picture provided by Blyton *et al.* and Bacon and Blyton is that economic globalization's impact on employment reveals that divergence may be no more encouraging in terms of outcomes than convergence. Indeed, Bezuidenhout's findings on South African union activity present a convergence model of such activity in the face of internationalization of business and its impact on social justice and equity.

Bertone and Leahy's findings on cultural diversity and its management may reveal better exploitation of cultural capital, but the question remains on the role of trade unions in recognizing and working with such diversity to the benefit of racially and ethnically different employee groups. Indeed, little if anything is known of the position and role of trade unions in the context of diversity, nor its relationship to union activities and campaigns for membership.

This last point of union membership campaigns is, however, discussed in its own right by Heery *et al.* with little evidence of systematic approaches to membership maintenance or growth either within or across culturally diverse working populations. Furthermore, transnational trade union activity in the northern hemisphere at least is revealed as *ad hoc* and opportunistic and often operates on a personal level. It seems that the attitudes of members and union officials represent real obstacles to more sophisticated union policies and methods in the face of internationalization. If not within and across trade unions, we must continue to ask how diversity across workforces is to be better handled and by whom.

It is from the boardroom and the human resource decisions of the international enterprise that the most evidence on positive (and more often) negative approaches to managing diversity derives. The chapters by Kidger and Edwards reveal perplexing trends. Kidger's study of UK firms reveals a positive approach taken by human resource specialists to develop 'cross-national' HR principles but is frustrated by centralist corporate policies. Thus, for HRM to achieve the goals of common understanding and collaboration across culturally diverse employee groupings may require informed methods somewhat outside the multinational corporation's formal arrangements. Indeed, the role of HRM in overcoming conflict in diversity has been emphasized by Veersma (1995) and within the process of globalization may allow the multinational company to forge a link with, and even understanding of, the culture and industrial relations structures of the host nation–state (De Nijs, 1992). Kidger finds that this HR activity takes an informal form, and therefore the formal structures for some universal approach to HRM do not appear to exist. Thus cross-national HRM policies within multinationals have not appeared in any tangible form (De Nijs, 1995).

New directions

An added complication in the debate on effective formal HRM policies and practices within multinationals derives from the phenomenon of 'reverse diffusion' of employment practices studied by Edwards. This poses a twist to the discussion of globalization and employment by looking at the influence of international employment practices on those employed at the multinational enterprises' domestic places of work. Within the process of reverse diffusion, Edwards identifies the role played by multinational organization structures in the competitive environment of multinationals, bringing about product market standardization which in turn enhances the power of the headquarters over employment practices across divisions and various national locations. The outcome of this is reduced power over employment practices at the level of the local domestic plants as headquarters assigns key strategic roles to overseas plants. Diversity in Edwards' vision presents us with a new twist – rather than the traditional view of multinationals forcing convergence on overseas plants, we have overseas plants (and cultures and conditions of their host countries) forcing convergence on plants located in the multinational corporation's home nation. The HRM responses to this are not readily identifiable but might at least reinforce the provision of equal treatment for different national and cultural groups while avoiding a feeling of reduced value on the part of domestic workers. At worst we may ask the question of whether reverse diffusion threatens to 'drag' employment conditions down in the home states of the multinationals. At best, reverse diffusion might enable equity in the face of diversity.

Edwards contends that globalization and reverse diffusion are closely linked where multinational headquarters are able to exert increased pressure on employment practices across the enterprise. In an interesting parallel with this, Kidger identifies a more positive opportunity for multinational managements through what might be termed the connectedness enabled by world-wide learning, transnational approaches to management development and cross-cultural integration. In both cases there are clear instances of HRM responses to the processes and outcomes of globalization. In essence, globalization confronts HRM with the real challenge of gaining workforce acceptance of the multinational's objectives. Edwards and Kidger present two opposite ways of forging an HRM response.

Kidger's notion of shared understanding might be termed connectedness, an issue raised by LePine *et al.* in the context of multi-media distance learning. The provision of education from a central classroom in the United States to the 'outlier' classrooms in overseas locations with vastly different institutions, cultures and values may re-visit the issue of diversity raised by Bertone and Leahy. Not least of the requirements to underpin the effectiveness of distance learning is the full and open criss-crossing of interaction and communication which is necessary in the process of ensuring transnational and cross-diversity connectedness. Vital in this process is the encouragement in each national (local) cultural student grouping of positive perceptions of other national cultural student groupings (located anywhere in the world) within the distance learning network and of the instructors at the central classroom in the United States. In particular, the research by LePine *et al.* reveals that the virtual team of instructors in America needs to maintain close and ongoing communication with the local instructors playing 'host' to the multimedia learning network. Such requirements raise echoes of the collaboration and common understanding required of effective HRM policies and practices in the managing of diversity in multinational enterprises. In the pursuit of effectiveness in transnational distance learning may be found reminders of why, how and where connectedness and cross-boundary integration are vital components of an effective global organization.

Response or reaction

When considering the pressures created by globalization the commentator must allow for the reality of confusion and incohesion in the behaviour and approaches of players such as companies and trade unions. Managing cultural diversity may be desirable and union campaigns are vital in the face of globalization but, as we have discovered, little such activity has actually been undertaken. Quite often responses to market and economic environment changes are clearly discernible as measured exercises to cope with events usually outside the control of the company and its management.

Once this strategic analysis of the market is completed, however, there then follow the 'knee jerk' reactions which characterize the next phase of decisions to be taken – usually about the workforce. Such is the situation revealed by Taplin and Winterton in the clothing industry; the responses by management to a contracting market and shrinking market shares include such strategic moves as evaluation of a shift into high value added products (and production), improvements to the supply chain and the re-design of work methods and arrangements.

But this is where strategy ends and perhaps where short-termism begins as the implications of strategy (assuming that this is the term to describe the actions of managers) work through to what the two authors found in the clothing industry – sub-contracting, the depression of remuneration and exploitation of ethnic and racial minorities. Once again outcomes from globalization are removed from any 'connectedness', rather, they might be called 'disconnected reactiveness'.

Yet the problematic nature of the reactive responses is overshadowed by Taplin and Winterton's revelations on management lack of clarity about where economic globalization is taking the industry, leading to a lack of precision in the definitions of new production structures. Depressingly, the authors indicate that manager's responses are no more sophisticated an arrangement than reconfigured Taylorism.

The discoveries made by Taplin and Winterton may indicate the current response to a new world context from clothing manufacturers. There may be a 'settling down' process here or a period of adjustment where managers find their feet in a new globalized market environment. New responses are still needed and the globalization debate might provide them by questioning universalism and standardization and overcoming unproductive conformity with flexible management styles tuned to the reality of internationalism and the characteristics of effective management of human and cultural capital. In the vacuum created by what has largely been the absence of such a style, weaker trade unions have failed to counter the disadvantageous pressures of globaliztion while stronger unions have exploited their power to prevent the 'race to the bottom' for their members.

At the same time management are missing out on the bottom-line contributions of our proposed more sensitive management style. The aim of such a style would not be to eradicate standardization where it is appropriate, but would introduce more connectedness for diversity. That this will happen is not at all clear, but as a first step managerial (and trade union) reactions to globalization could usefully give way to strategic measured responses. Globalization remains an emerging subject for research to be undertaken for many years ahead. The current need is for even more new work on the benefits accruing to and losses experienced by the various interested and involved parties.

References

Batra, R. (1993) *The Myth of Free Trade*, New York: Touchstone Books.

Betcherman, G. and Chaykowski, R. (1996) 'The Changing Workplace: Challenges for Public Policy', *Human Resources Development Canada*, Research Paper R-96-13E, Ottowa: HRDC.

Bhagwati, J.N. (1994) 'Free Trade: Old and New Challenges', *Economic Journal*, 104(423): 231–46.

Bhagwati, J.N. and Hudec, R.E. (eds) (1996) *Fair Trade and Harmonization: Prerequisites for Free Trade?*, vol. 1, *Economic Analysis*, vol. 2, *Legal Analysis*, Cambridge, MA: MIT Press.

Bryan, D. and Rafferty, M. (1999) *The Global Economy in Australia*, Sydney: Allen and Unwin.

Budhwar, P.S. (2001) 'Human Resource Management in India', in P.S. Budhwar and Y.A. Debrah (eds) *Human Resource Management in Developing Countries*, London: Routledge, pp. 75–90.

Budhwar, P.S. and Debrah, Y.A. (2001) 'Introduction: Dynamics of Human Resource Management in Developing Countries', in P.S. Budhwar and Y.A. Debrah (eds) *Human Resource Management in Developing Countries*, London: Routledge, pp. 1–15.

Cappelli, P., Bassi, L., Katz, H., Knoke, D., Osterman, P. and Useem, M. (1997) *Change at Work*, York, Oxford.

Chaykowski, R. and Giles, A. (1998) 'Globalization, Work and Industrial Relations', *Relations Industrielles – Industrial Relations*, 53(1): 3–12.

Choate, P. (1993) *Jobs at Risk: Vulnerable US Industries and Jobs under NAFTA*, Washington, DC: Manufacturing Policy Projects.

Cooper, C.L. (2000) 'Job Insecurity Goes Hand in Hand with Flexible Working', *The Sunday Times*, 4 June, p. 3.

Debrah, Y.A. (2000) 'Management in Ghana', in M. Warner (ed.) *Management in Emerging Countries*, London: Thomson Learning, pp. 189–97.

Debrah, Y.A. (2001) 'Human Resource Management in Ghana', in P.S. Budhwar and Y.A. Debrah (eds) *Human Resource Management in Developing Countries*, London: Routledge, pp. 190–208.

De Nijs, W. (1992) 'Patterns of Industrial Relations, and Personnel Management in Three European Countries', in J. Dijck and A. Wentink (eds) *Transnational Business in Europe: Economic and Social Perspectives*, Tilberg: Academic Press, pp. 27–90.

De Nijs, W. (1995) 'International Human Resource Management and Industrial Relations: A Framework for Analysis', in A. Harzing and J. Van Russeyveldt (eds) *International Human Resource Management*, London: Sage, pp. 271–90.

De Ruyter, A. and Burgess, J. (2000) 'Part-time Employment in Australia: Evidence for Globalization?', *International Journal of Manpower* 21(6): 452–63.

Frenkel, S. and Peetz, D. (1998) 'Globalization and Industrial Relations in East Asia: A Three Country Comparison', *Industrial Relations* 37(3): 282–310.

Giddens, A. (1990) *The Consequences of Modernity*, Cambridge: Polity Press.

Goldsmith, E. (1996) 'Global Trade and the Environment', in J. Mander and E. Goldsmith (eds) *The Case Against the Global Economy*, San Francisco: The Sierra Book Club.

Goldsmith, J. (1996) 'The Winners and the Losers', in J. Mander and E. Goldsmith (eds) *The Case Against the Global Economy*, San Francisco: The Sierra Book Club.

Heery, E. and Salmon, J. (2000) 'The Insecurity Thesis', in *The Insecure Workforce*, London: Routledge, pp. 1–24.

Hill, C.W.L. (2001) *International Business: Competing in the Global Market Places: Postcript 2001*, New York: Urwin–McGraw-Hill.

Hirst, P. and Thompson, G. (1996) *Globalization in Question: The International Economy and the Possibilities of Governance*, Cambridge: Polity Press.

Hollingsworth, J.R. and Boyer, R. (eds) (1997) *Contemporary Capitalism: The Embeddedness of Institutions*, Cambridge: Cambridge University Press.

Horton, R.J. (1998) *Globalization and the Nation-State*, London: Macmillan.

Johnson, R. (2001) 'Import Duty', *People Management*, 8 March, pp. 25–9.

Katz, H.C. and Darbishire, O. (2000) *Converging Divergences: Worldwide Changes in Employment Systems*, Ithaca, NY: ILP Press, Cornell University Press.

Kelly, P.E. and Olds, K. (1999) 'Questions in a Crisis: The Contested Meanings of Globalization in the Asia-Pacific', in K. Olds, P. Dickens, P.F. Kelly, L. Kong and H.W. Yeung, *Globalization and the Asia Pacific: Contested Territories*, London: Routledge, pp. 1–15.

Knight, R. (1998) 'Global Finance: The Great Equaliser', in *Mastering Global Business: Navigating the Tides of Global Finance*, London: Financial Times.

Knipe, M. (2000) 'The Nation Giving Hope to the Rest of Africa', *The Times*, Focus on Ghana, 8 April, p. 1.

Kogut, B. and Gittelman, M. (1999) 'Globalization', in R. Tung (ed.) *The IEBM Handbook of International Business*, London: International Thomson, pp. 200–14.

Krugman, P. (1994) 'Does Third World Growth Hurt First World Prosperity?, *Harvard Business Review* 72(4): 113–21.

Kuruvilla, S. (1996) 'Linkages Between Industrialisation Strategies and Industrial Relations/Human Resource Policies: Singapore, Malaysia, the Philippines and India', *Industrial and Labour Relations Review* 49, July: 635–57.

Lamb, J. (2000) 'Recruiters Turn to India for IT Expertise as Skills Crisis Bites', *People Management*, 24 August, pp. 12–13.

Lawrence, R.S. and Slaughter, M.J. (1993) 'International Trade and American Wages in the 1980s: Giant Sucking Sound or Small Hiccup?', *Brookings Papers on Economic Activity* 2: 161–210.

Lee, E. (1996) 'Globalization and Employment: Is Anxiety Justified?', *International Labour Review* 135(5): 485–97.

Lee, E. (1997) 'Globalization and Labour Standards: A Review of Issues', *International Labour Review* 136(2): 173–89.

Levitt, T. (1983) 'The Globalization of Markets', *Harvard Business Review* May–June, pp. 92–102.

Lewis, D., French, E., Phetmany, T. (2001) 'Cross-Cultural Diversity, Leadership and Workplace Relations in Australia', in Y.A. Debrah and I.G. Smith, (eds) *Work and Employment in a Globalized Era: An Asia Pacific Focus*, London: Frank Cass, pp. 105–24.

Ohmae, K. (1990) *The End of the Nation State*, New York: Free Press.

Ohmae, K. (1995) *The Borderless World: Power and Strategy in the Interlinked Economy*, London: HarperCollins.

Parker, B. (1998) *Globalization and Business Practice: Managing Across Boundaries*, London: Sage.

Peel, Q. (1999) 'Walls of the World Come Tumbling Down', *Financial Times* Survey: The Millennium II, 6 December, p. 16.

People Management (2000) 'News in Brief – Indian Railway Workers Providing Solution to Growing Recruitment Problems in the UK', 28 December, p. 8.

Pieterse, J.N. (1995) 'Globalization and Hybridization', in M. Featherstone, S. Lash and R. Robertson (eds) *Global Modernities*, London: Sage, pp. 45–68.

Pollert, A. (2000) *Transformation at Work*, London: Sage.

Pyke, D. (1998) 'Strategies for Global Sourcing', in *Mastering Global Business: Creating the Global Organisation, Financial Times* Survey, January, pp. 2–4.

Robbins, D.J. (1995) *Trade, Trade Liberalization and Inequality in Latin America and East Africa: Synthesis of Seven Country Studies*, Cambridge, MA: Harvard University Press.

Sachs, J.D. and Shatz, H.J. (1994) 'Trade and Jobs in US Manufacturing', *Brookings Papers on Economic Activity* 1: 1–69.

Sadher, K., Vinnicombe, S. and Tyson, S. (1999) 'Downsizing and the Changing Role of HR', *International Journal of Human Resource Management* 10(5): 906–23.

Taylor, R. (2000) 'Rules to be Relaxed to Attract Overseas IT Skills', *Financial Times*, 22 March, p. 4.

UNCTAD (1999a) *Foreign Investment Gains in Latin America* September, Geneva: UN.

UNCTAD (1999b) *Significant Investment Opportunities in Africa Exist*, UNCTAD Survey for the World Investment Report, September, Geneva: UN.

UNCTAD (1999c) *Foreign Investment Flows into Developing Asia*, Geneva: UN.

UNCTAD (1999d) *Foreign Investment Flows into Central and Eastern European Countries*, September, Geneva: UN.

Vaupel, J.W. and Curhan, J.P. (1973) *The World's Largest Multinational Enterprises*, Cambridge, MA: Harvard University Press.

Veersma, O. (1995) 'Multinational Corporations and Industrial Relations', in A. Harzing and J. Van Russeyveldt (eds) *International Human Resource Management*, London: Sage, pp. 318–36.

Wade, R. (1996) 'Globalization and its Limits: Reports of the Death of the National Economy are Greatly Exaggerated', in S. Berger and R. Dore (eds) *National Diversity and Global Capitalism*, Ithaca, NY: Cornell University Press, pp. 60–88.

Warner, M. (2001) 'Human Resource Management in China', in P.S. Budhwar and Y.A. Debrah (eds) *Human Resource Management in Developing Countries*, London: Routledge, pp. 19–33.

Waters, M. (1995) *Globalization*, London: Routledge.

Wiseman, J. (1998) *Global Nation: Australia and the Politics of Globalisation*, Cambridge: Cambridge University Press.

Wood, A. (1994) *North–South Trade, Employment and Inequality: Changing Fortunes in a Skill-Driven World*, Oxford: Clarendon Press.

Yeung, H.W. (1999) 'Introduction: Competing in the Global Economy: The Globalisation of Business Firms From Emerging Economies', in H.W. Yeung (ed.) *The Globalisation of Business Firms from Emerging Economies*, vol. 1. Cheltenham: Elgar, pp. xii–xlvi.

2 Globalization, restructuring and occupational labour power

Evidence from the international airline industry

Paul Blyton, Miguel Martinez Lucio, John McGurk and Peter Turnbull

Introduction – globalization in civil aviation

The globalization strategies that have been evident in the international civil aviation sector in recent years are predicated on two other changes characterizing the industry over that period: the reduction in national state regulation of civil aviation and the widespread privatization of former state-owned airlines (see Button *et al.*, 1998; ITF, 1992; Kassim, 1997; Lyth, 1997). The effects of these new operating conditions have been visible in several developments within the industry, of which three are most prominent. First, there has been a rapid growth in new operators (and new subsidiaries of established operators) entering the passenger airline market, primarily providing a 'low-cost' service via less heavily congested airports, but increasingly extending their activities to more established routes (AEA, 2000: 6; *Air Transport World*, 2000: 47). Second, a more general increase in competition has been experienced by established carriers, giving rise to major organizational restructuring to improve productivity and efficiency (Morrell and Lu, 2000). Third, among the major operators an accelerated search has taken place for a global presence in the passenger airline market, reflecting the greater profitability and growth potential of long haul compared to short haul traffic. Prominent in the last of these developments has been the development of strategic alliances between carriers located in different geographical regions. By mid-2000, over 570 alliances of one form or another existed in the industry, though of these just five[1] global alliances accounted for over 57 per cent of the total world market in civil aviation (*Airline Business*, 2000).

In both the responses to increased competition and in the related development of global alliances, the cost and performance of labour represent a key focus for airline management. In searching for more efficient cost structures, for example, labour costs are not only the largest single operating cost (ranging from 25 to 35 per cent of total operating costs in different airlines) but also represent a cost more directly under management's control than various other operating costs (such as the price of aircraft, fuel and airport charges) which are less open to modification by airline companies, at least in the short term. As a result, labour costs have become a focus of broader cost reduction strategies as airlines seek to restructure in order to bolster their position in a more open market. At the same time, the quality of labour performance lies at the heart of any strategy based on enhancing competitiveness through improved service quality, a key component of which is the passenger's experience of the service she or he receives from customer contact staff such as check-in staff or cabin crew personnel (Carlzon, 1987). This twin position of labour – as a key cost and a critical factor in service quality – has placed it at the centre of airline restructuring initiatives throughout the last decade.

Labour cost and utilization also represent an important focus in the developing strategy of airline alliances. The major gains from strategic alliances are likely to be secured not from the increased revenue generated by additional customers (which to date has been comparatively modest) but rather from the potential cost savings available to alliances as a result of their stronger collective purchasing power and their scope for reducing and rationalizing duplicate services. Such rationalization and pooling of services have particular implications for labour, not only in terms of the job losses that could be expected to ensue from the removal of activities, but also from the possibility that remaining services would, wherever feasible, be provided by alliance members whose costs (including labour costs) were the lowest.

If this global search for lowest labour costs among alliance members develops as anticipated, it will mirror developments already advancing within individual airline companies, where labour cost reduction has been effected partly by locating a greater proportion of activity in low labour cost countries. This is demonstrated, for example, in the switching of various administrative functions by British Airways (BA) and other western European carriers to India, and the development of aircraft maintenance activities by Lufthansa, Air France, Swissair and Cathay Pacific among others, in China, Morocco, Ireland and elsewhere (*Airline Business*, 1999a, 1999b; Oum and Yu, 1998: 64).

This sourcing of labour on a global rather than solely on a national basis encapsulates both a primary feature of globalization and a key potential danger in globalization for labour. Globalization can be defined as the integration of spatially separate locations into a single international market. Such a definition highlights the removal of time and space as barriers to international markets, barriers removed or reduced both by economic factors (such as a reduction in the cost of transportation) and political factors (such as the introduction of free trade agreements and industry deregulation). However, an important aspect of this definition of globalization is that the 'integration of markets' relates not only to product but also to labour markets. Further, central to understanding the effects of globalization is the recognition that it is first and foremost a management strategy rather than a developing feature of the context in which organizations operate (as at least some discussions of globalization have implied). As such, globalization must be analysed on the same basis as any other management strategy is ultimately judged: that is, in terms of the value it secures for the organization's shareholders via the maximization of revenue and the minimization of costs.

The threat from globalization for labour is seen to stem from the greater choice over location options that opens up for capital. The availability of alternative locations, for both goods and service production, can further increase the relative power of capital over labour, allowing capital to drive down the cost of labour in any one geographical area by threatening to shift its activities to lower labour cost areas elsewhere within its global operations, unless costs are equated. The result of this leverage exerted by capital is feared by many labour analysts and others to be an international 'race to the bottom' on employees' terms and conditions of employment (see, for example, Brecher and Costello, 1994; Wiseman, 1996) as labour is forced either to accept lower terms and conditions to maintain jobs in any one location, or relinquish those jobs to regions where terms and conditions of employment are significantly lower.

However, though appealing in its simplicity, this argument suffers from several empirical and theoretical problems in its portrayal of an omnipotent capital and an impotent labour. Three of these problems are particularly relevant to the argument put forward in the remainder of this chapter. First, there is no clear evidence that globalization *per se* has caused a lowering of labour standards in industrialized countries (Lee, 1997: 182–3). It is widely accepted that globalization has exerted an adverse effect on less skilled workers in labour-intensive industries (e.g. textiles) in many developed countries (see, for example, Wood, 1995), but at best the evidence is contradictory (Bacon and Blyton, 2000 and this volume; and Breitenfellner, 1997: 534–5). At worst, there is simply no systematic empirical evidence on workers' pay and conditions of employment in many industrial sectors (Lee, 1997: 182).

Second, the argument assumes that capital is indeed footloose and can therefore act on its threats if labour refuses to yield. Yet in practice the options facing capital are likely to be restricted in many if not most cases, not least by the need for adequate return on capital investment made in any particular location. Further, capitalist firms still have strong socio-economic, political and legal roots in particular national economies (see, for example, Ferner, 1997). States still control their own borders and exercise sovereign powers within those borders, especially their national air space. Thus, at least for the present, states and national institutions remain significant influences on the behaviour of capitalist organizations and their dealings with, among other groups, labour.

Third, the argument for the omnipotence of capital under globalization assumes a lack of ability by labour to contest capital's power to dictate terms and conditions. Yet, we have already noted the centrality of labour in a sector such as civil aviation – a centrality revolving around not just the cost of labour but crucially also around the service delivery by customer contact staff. In addition, account must also be taken of the role of national systems of labour regulation in specific countries that specify the rights and obligations of both parties to the employment relationship, and thereby provide labour with further potential to offset capital's greater bargaining power deriving from globalization. Further, labour's potential for coordinating activity at different levels from the workplace to the international labour confederation must also be factored in to the equation, particularly in an industry such as civil aviation where union density levels are high and organized labour is comparatively well coordinated at the international level by the International Transport Workers Federation (see for example, Breitenfellner, 1997: 545). Given the existence of these factors, it would be premature to write off labour's options by conferring an all-embracing power upon an increasingly globalized capital.

The study reported here sought to respond to these weaknesses in the current debate on globalization and labour. To contribute more detailed, sector-level findings on the impact of globalization and other industry changes on aspects of employment and work, the present authors undertook a study in the late 1990s of the international civil aviation industry. This comprised several elements including a global survey of trade unions with members in the civil aviation sector; a survey of European pilots' associations; and four national case studies, each assessing change as experienced by different groups of airline personnel.

The findings reported to date have sought to contribute in three ways to the 'globalization and labour' debate. First, considerable evidence was gathered which pointed to a widespread deterioration in terms and conditions in the industry, as airline companies have sought both to reduce total labour costs and increase labour effort (Blyton *et al.*, 1998a, 2001b). Second, trade unions in different countries have demonstrated markedly different patterns of response to management restructuring initiatives. Different national, corporate and trade union circumstances have given rise to a range of responses, from outright resistance to negotiated change and partnership approaches. The range of responses has underlined the importance of specific national contexts for assessing developing relations between capital and labour in the industry, rather than seeking to 'read off' capital's power and labour's response from the abstract powers that globalization reputedly vests in one and diminishes in the other (Martinez Lucio *et al.*, 2001). Third, the importance of international trade union coordination in the sector has been underlined. This has highlighted the ITF's ability to coordinate industrial action and communication internationally, and 'match' corporate developments such as the growth of global alliances by fostering the parallel networks of trade unions that have been initiated in recent years (see also Gill, 1998). At the same time, this research has noted the significant obstacles that remain to the development of powers that effectively constrain international capital's ability to take labour-related decisions without due consideration of the bodies representing labour's interest (Blyton *et al.*, 2001a).

The aim of this chapter is to begin to consider the evidence for the impact of airline restructuring on different occupational groups, and the differential ability of those groups to respond to management initiatives towards labour. This focus is a response to a tendency in the growing debate on labour and globalization to overlook the importance of occupational differences and to present labour (and indeed capital) as relatively undifferentiated phenomena, both in terms of how globalization is impacting (or will impact) on labour and the scope for the latter's response to the pressures arising from globalization (see, for example, Leisink, 1999; Moody, 1997; Munck and Waterman, 1999; O'Brien, 2000; Waddington, 1999). To explore this, we use examples from two occupational groups – pilots and cabin crew – that have important aspects of their occupational role in common (namely that both are involved in flight activities) but in other respects are clearly differentiated. What the analysis of both survey and case study evidence reveals is that while subject to common restructuring pressures, which feed through into a number of shared experiences of restructuring, the marked differences in the ability of the two groups to contest management's restructuring objectives underline the power differences held within the different occupational groups, which in turn shape the ways in which they are able to respond to management restructuring initiatives in an increasingly globalized industry.

To this end, the rest of the chapter is divided into four sections. We begin with a brief review of occupational differentiation, drawing on the work of Batstone (1988). Following this, survey evidence relating to the employment and work experience of cabin crew and pilots is considered, before looking in more detail at case study material on how these groups have experienced and have responded to the pressures for change in the cost and utilization of flying personnel within the industry.

Sources of occupational power

One of the most useful frameworks to consider the power resources of different occupational groups is that developed by Eric Batstone (1988). Batstone identifies three principal power resources of labour in relation to capital: the extent of an occupation's scarcity value in the labour market; the disruptive capacity of that group in the production process; and the level of its political influence within the political arena. On the first, the scarcity value of any particular occupational group depends on the skills held by that group and the availability of other (substitutable) sources of labour. This availability of alternative labour is in turn influenced not only by the degree of control that the occupational group has over its skill formation (for example, through trade union or professional association control over occupational entry and/or qualification) but also by the complexity of the skill formation (the length of time taken to train, the difficulty in successfully completing the training, the requirement for periodic re-training, and so on).

The disruptive power of labour is related to its scarcity (or more specifically its substitutability), but also depends on a range of factors pertaining to the occupational group – in particular how well it is organized, and thus how effectively its disruptive power can be mobilized. Also important here is a range of factors relating to the production process, including the perishability of the product, the interdependencies between stages in the production process, and the centrality of particular groups to the overall production of a service or good.

The third resource, the political power of the occupational group, primarily represents the political leverage of the group's union or association (reflected, for example, in its ability to sway the opinion of political leaders and/or influence public opinion). Also significant here could be the political power gained through the level of involvement in international as well as national policy-making bodies (Blyton and Turnbull, 1998: 111).

Pilots and cabin crew display both similarities and differences in the power resources that they may be expected to command. In terms of scarcity value in the labour market, for example, the skill formation of both groups is based on a period of training to operate different types of aircraft safely. However, pilot training and the acquisition and maintenance of a pilot's licence are a far lengthier and more complicated skill formation process, compared to the much shorter safety training on evacuation and other procedures required by cabin crew (weeks rather than the years required by pilots). Nevertheless, while some cabin crew training is generalized (for example, the efficient dispensing of food and beverages), other cabin crew training is more specialized in that safety training (and qualification) are aircraft specific, thereby limiting the employer's scope for substitutability.

In terms of disruptive power, the two occupational groups hold three features in common. First, flight regulations require that aircraft cannot depart without a full complement of cabin and flight crew. Second, the common product that the two groups are dealing with – seats on aircraft – is highly perishable: it is not possible for employers to 'stockpile' the product in any way, nor can they offer substitute products. Even the threat of disruption to the service will have an effect on demand as passengers book with other companies as a hedge against possible flight cancellations (Turnbull *et al.*, 2000). Thus, the possible disruptive effect held by both groups is considerable. The potential to mobilize this disruptive power is also enhanced by the third factor held in common by the two groups: their high rate of trade union membership. One difference here, however, is that while in the UK, pilots in companies such as British Airways (BA) are organized by a single representative organization, the British Air Line Pilots Association (BALPA), a significant minority of cabin crew belong not to the British Airlines Stewards and Stewardesses Association (BASSA), but to the more moderate breakaway union Cabin Crew 89.

The political power of the two groups appears comparatively similar, though this is harder to quantify. BASSA's political power derives in important part from its status as a section within the large Transport and General Workers Union (TGWU), and also its prominence within the civil aviation section of the International Transport Workers Federation (ITF). BALPA's political power, on the other hand, derives partly from its prominence within several international bodies (such as the European Cockpit Association (ECA) and the International Federation of Airline Pilots Associations – IFALPA) and the lobbying role of these organizations at the supra-national level.

The global picture of airline restructuring

Two separate surveys conducted by the authors in the late 1990s shed light on the overall impact of globalization and airline restructuring on the working conditions of airline personnel. The first was a global survey of civil aviation unions affiliated to the (ITF). Some 52 unions completed the survey (a response rate of 36 per cent) representing half a million airline workers in twenty-nine countries (see Blyton *et al.*, 1998a). The largest occupational group represented by these responding unions was cabin crew personnel, followed by ground services and maintenance. A small number of respondent unions also represented flight deck personnel (pilots and flight engineers). However, since many pilot associations are not affiliated to the ITF, this group of airline employees was captured by a separate survey conducted among pilot associations affiliated to the ECA. This survey gained a response from thirteen of its fifteen member associations, together representing over 30,000 pilots in Europe.

The surveys covered many areas of employment and work change, together with developments in industrial relations and attitudes towards the role of the state and regulatory policy in the civil aviation industry (for more details, see Blyton *et al.*, 1998b). We have reported the overall findings of these surveys elsewhere (Blyton *et al.*, 1998a, b, 1999, 2001b) and here we wish to focus on the responses of the two occupational groups comprising the flying personnel, namely cabin crew and flight deck staff.

In terms of employment change, the growth in industry passenger traffic in the 1990s was widely reported to have brought about an increase in cabin crew staff. Thus, three-fifths of unions representing cabin crew reported an increase in employment during the previous five years; a further 25 per cent reported stable employment and 14 per cent reported a decrease over that period (this pattern was in marked contrast to those unions representing services such as cleaning and catering staff who were far more likely to report declining employment levels in the preceding five years; see Blyton *et al.*, 2001b for details). Similarly, among the pilots' associations, two-thirds reported an increase in the number of captains and first officer posts over the previous five years.

There were also similarities – and some important differences – between cabin crew and pilots in terms of reported changes in the experience of work. Among cabin crew there was widespread evidence of a negative impact of restructuring on many aspects of work, including levels of work intensity, job security, job satisfaction and the quality of management–staff relations. Further, cabin crew unions were more likely than their counterparts representing other occupational groups to report a deterioration in these areas, and were also more likely to report an increase in hours of work and a reduction in earnings over the five-year period. On hours of work, the negative developments were the result of longer and/or more frequent shifts or an overall increase in working hours. The vast majority (88 per cent) of unions representing cabin crew reported increases in hours over the previous five years. Among flying staff, temporal flexibility has assumed a much greater importance in recent years as management has sought to increase staff utilization and maximize the use of newer aircraft that allow longer stage lengths (length of flying without the need for refuelling). As part of this, airline companies have been increasing hours of cabin and flight crew and pressing for the relaxation of regulations on flight and cabin crew duty limitations established at national and supra-national levels. Morrell and Lu (2000: 81) report that between 1988 and 1998, average pilot/co-pilot hours in Europe increased by 17 per cent, and by 1998 were almost 12 per cent higher than their North American counterparts and over 15 per cent higher than pilots in the Asia-Pacific region.

Similarly, among the national pilots' associations, more than four out of five reported increases in work intensity over the previous five years and all the thirteen national associations reported increased hours of work, either as a result of reductions in rest periods or duty breaks, or as a result of increases in shift duration and/or frequency of shifts. Like their cabin crew counterparts, clear majorities of the pilots' associations also felt that restructuring had led to a deterioration in job satisfaction and the quality of management–staff relations. Unlike the cabin crew representatives, however, a majority of the pilots' associations felt that restructuring had had a positive impact on the possibilities of career progression among their members (reflecting particularly the expansion of airline fleets) and were less likely than cabin crew representatives to identify a negative effect on job security.

A further significant difference between the two survey samples was that, unlike the pilots, cabin crew unions reported a negative impact on earnings over the previous five years stemming from either wage reductions or pay freezes, the withdrawal of cost of living agreements or the introduction of two-tier wage rates with a lower second tier rate (typically for new recruits) and much slower salary progression. No equivalent negative impact on earnings was reported, however, among the pilots.

Overall, then, the surveys pointed to a number of similar experiences of restructuring among cabin crew and flight deck personnel, with the work of flight and cabin crew becoming both more intensive and – reflecting the increase in hours – more extensive, with resulting implications for job satisfaction and other work variables. However, the two surveys also highlighted areas such as job security, pay and career progression where the experiences of the two groups significantly diverged. We now turn to the case study evidence using data gathered from cabin crew and pilots working for BA in the UK, to examine these areas of similarity and difference in more detail. This will then allow us to draw some conclusions in the final section regarding the relative ability of the two groups to successfully contest management's restructuring programme.

The national picture of airline restructuring

Cabin crew

As part of the project, the researchers attended trade union meetings and interviewed over twenty union representatives and individual cabin crew employees at different occupational grades (cabin service directors, pursers and cabin crew grade) working for BA on both short- and long-haul routes and stationed at Gatwick or London Heathrow. One focus of this research came to be the cabin crew strike which took place during the research period in protest at management's cost-cutting proposals for cabin services (see Turnbull *et al.*, 2000). Central to BA's restructuring programme in the late 1990s was the company's Business Efficiency Programme (BEP) designed to identify savings of £1 billion over the 1997–2000 period. This included a cost reduction of £42 million from the short-haul cabin crew services from Heathrow, traditionally seen as a union stronghold of the main cabin crew trade union, BASSA. Objecting to the absence of negotiations over the proposed changes, and exacerbated by the company signing an agreement on the restructuring plan with the minority union Cabin Crew 89, the resulting antagonism culminated in a damaging three-day strike in mid-1997, reputed to have cost the company over £125 million in lost sales (Turnbull *et al.*, 2000). The resulting compromise settlement enabled BA to secure the required cost savings but it did not secure agreement to restructure key conditions of employment at Heathrow.

However, these agreements on employment conditions notwithstanding, subsequent interviews with cabin crew at different levels highlighted a number of important changes experienced in the job. Most notable among these was the changes in hours reported and changes in pay that have taken place. On hours, the picture is one of both increased work intensification and extensification with management deploying hours more flexibly and using longer shift lengths to maximize labour utilization. Most of those interviewed commented that their working pattern had deteriorated, especially on short-haul operations (on short haul, earnings have traditionally been lower but still preferred by many – particularly those with families – because the work involves fewer overnight stopovers compared to long-haul operations, and overall a more conducive work pattern). Management were seen to be using agreed flexibility over the working period to roster more intensive shift patterns and using longer shift lengths to accommodate additional flights. Typical comments from cabin crew included the following:

> They [the company] have much tighter rosters, you are working much harder. They use you to the full now . . . we have flight time limitations set by the CAA [Civil Aviation Authority] and the union, but they are now using these [limits] more effectively to get more out of them, and as a result we've got a lot of really tough schedules. (cabin services director, Heathrow short haul)

> The hours are longer. You have a lot of turns [flights] now which carry the minimum rest, a lot of multi-sector jobs. Out of a six-day block you might have three or four 12-hour days. (purser, Heathrow short haul)

> We are pushed much more, it's very high intensity, more rotations . . . My job has got much harder and more intensive. (purser, EuroGatwick)

> We are flying longer rotations with more stopovers, doing more hours in the air . . . You are doing more trips, working with smaller crews, doing more night stops and working longer hours . . . There are many more early starts and later finishes. (cabin crew, Heathrow short haul)

> The big thing really is the length of the working day . . . They can roster you for 12.5 hours but in an emergency even that goes out of the window . . . The other thing is the amount of stopovers we are doing now. [The company] are using more stopovers. It of course helps them to get the first flight out in the morning from a lot of European cities, but it plays havoc with your home life. (cabin services director, Heathrow short haul)

As well as the increased scope for rostering flexibility obtained by management, changes in the system of allowances for unsocial hours were seen to have encouraged working time changes – particularly allowances paid for use of employees' own car out of hours. This ending of own car allowances was part of a broader change in reward structure for cabin crew which entailed the consolidation of various allowances into salary. Though this was organized so as not to lead to reduced earnings, a widespread feeling among cabin crew interviewed was that they were working harder for no additional reward.

> We used to get a motor transport allowance . . . you got this if you finished after 2100 and before 0830. It meant on your last Amsterdam's and first Frankfurt's which you do a lot, you were getting this allowance for the use of your own car. No longer – they've scrapped it. Now that's had two effects. They brought in more early starts and late finishes and they have no real incentive to get you finished because they are not paying anything. (cabin services director, London Heathrow)

However, in terms of cabin crew wage structure the more far-reaching change introduced by management has been the introduction of a two-tier wage system with far lower (around £8k) starting salaries for new recruits. This has been seen to have had various consequences, not least encouraging a lower calibre intake (higher calibre individuals seen as being able to secure higher paid employment elsewhere) which, coupled with a shortening of the training period, was judged to have created considerable additional workload for more experienced crew in the form of informal supervision:

> The speed they are churning people out of cabin service training . . . It's down now to three weeks from five and a half weeks. When I did the course it was ten weeks . . . Without a word of a lie, you are getting people who don't know one end of a trolley from the other. (cabin services director, London Heathrow)

> I am working with far less experienced crews. I am nursemaiding a lot of people who have been taken, in my opinion, simply as cheap labour. (cabin services director, London Heathrow)

> We have a great deal more unpaid supervision . . . some of the new starts are very good but 50–60 per cent are absolutely useless. I was on a Nice trip with a B767 . . . There was an emergency. We had six junior crew, four of which had less than four months experience. As we went through the SEP [Safety Equipment Procedures – the procedures adopted when the captain has indicated an emergency situation] they were like headless chickens. They were asking us openly in front of passengers what was happening and they were looking terrified. When we got the alert call telling us it wasn't so serious, we still had to have a good talk with one of the new crew, she was terrified. (cabin crew, London Heathrow, short haul)

The introduction of less well-trained and much less rewarded cabin crew was seen to be affecting morale among the established cabin crew personnel:

> They [the company] are determined to restructure cabin crew and turn it from a professional safety-based job into a half-baked waiter-type job. (cabin crew, London Heathrow short haul).

> The people [the new recruits] know they have a raw deal. They are serving with us doing the same job and earning less than half of what we are earning. That affects their morale and ours. (cabin crew, London Heathrow, short haul)

Summarizing the reported effects of recent restructuring, the implications of changing rosters, consolidation of allowances into basic earnings, the ramifications of a two-tier earnings structure and reduced training have brought about an intensification of work for cabin crew, with no felt commensurate increase in reward. The cabin crew strike may have mitigated the effects of some of the changes that management were seeking (notably, a substantial change to the work/rest day ratio), but nevertheless many of management's demands for change had been implemented. One of the most visible outcomes of the changes was a fall in morale among employees after the strike – a fall acknowledged by BA management as a major obstacle to maintaining levels of customer service (Lebrecht, 1999).

Pilots

As the survey evidence revealed, pilots and cabin crew representatives identified a number of common experiences in recent years as companies have sought to restructure working patterns and terms and conditions of employment to create a higher performing and lower cost workforce. In the interviews with pilots, the strongest point of similarity with their cabin crew counterparts was in relation to the increased tempo of work.

> The main problem . . . is definitely the increase in schedule and the frequency of turnarounds. You are dashing from aircraft to aircraft, coming in one pier and being expected to be at another instantaneously . . . we are chasing all over in crew buses trying to make unrealistic connections. By the time you get on the flight deck, kick the tyres [walk round visual pre-flight inspection] you are flying into pre-flight [pre-flight checks of equipment and systems]. Then you are warming the engines and pushing back still talking to the co-pilot about the briefing and to the crew about exits and stuff. It's pretty hectic.

> The significant changes have been in terms of the frequency of operation and the intensity of flying. It's been like a treadmill the last couple of years. Obviously as the airline builds in more through connections in its hubbing strategy you end up with many more flights. More flights to places like Geneva, Cologne, Budapest, which have all grown up recently . . . with scheduling changes it means sometimes on turnaround you barely have time for a cup of tea.

All in all . . . we are facing much more of a grind in the day-to-day job, you have less and less time to yourself, less briefing less prep[aration] time, less time to take a co-pilot aside and say 'Look, sonny, that was a bit of a hairy approach, or let's try and get that RT [radio communication] a bit more distinct', that sort of thing. So it's not desperately bad but it's a kind of chipping away . . . There is more pressure, and I am starting to notice it.

We will continue to work harder as they push more and more of these new routes onto us, and it is becoming more stressful on the ground and in the air. Deregulation with all these new carriers entering the market is leading to a crowding of airspace and increased pressure on slots.

90 per cent of our discussions with management involve rostering. We have the problem that management . . . are always trying to throw things into the roster, that bit more flying time or less briefing time, for example, . . . management want you up in the air as much as possible.

A further similarity between pilots and cabin crew is the intensification of work that pilots have experienced. As part of the agreement following the 1996 pilots' dispute (see below), flying hours for some pilots were increased from 650 to 700 hours per annum, an increase which brought them closer to the permitted maximum under prevailing flight and duty time limitations.

However, in other key respects the recent experience of the two occupational groups has been substantially different. These relate both to substantive aspects of terms and conditions of employment – notably pay and allowances – but also to process issues regarding both industrial relations and more generally the different ways in which the two groups have experienced and responded to management's Business Efficiency Programme. First, on terms and conditions, pilots over several years have faced demands by BA management to agree cuts in various non-wage costs, for example, by accepting lower grade accommodation on overnight stops. Much more significant, however, was the attempt by management in 1996 to impose changes in the pay and conditions of pilots. The central issue was a pay restructuring which threatened core terms and conditions by seeking to reduce the pay entitlements for flying some larger aircraft to levels applying to smaller craft.

This action by management resulted in BALPA balloting its members and obtaining an overwhelming majority in support of industrial action. The threat of widespread strike action was sufficient for management to withdraw the demand. Further, subsequent negotiations over pay structures were widely regarded as a victory for the pilots. In particular, not only was the pay restructuring removed, but pilot negotiators subsequently established a common 'flying hour rate' within BA which effectively extended pay parity among pilots, significantly improving the position of short-haul pilots who previously had not received the reward for their greater intensity of operations compared to their counterparts in long haul who enjoyed extra payments for their longer duties. Where pay concessions were made by the pilots' representatives – for example, regarding lower starting salaries for flight cadets – these have been on a much smaller scale than the two-tier wage system introduced for cabin crew. Overall, the outcome of the threatened industrial action and subsequent negotiations over pilots' pay and conditions was far more favourable than the outcome achieved by cabin crew following their strike action the following year.

In terms of differences in employee relations between the two groups, the significance for management of the breakdown in relations with pilots (and symbolized in the strength of pilots' support for industrial action) was subsequently demonstrated in their (and BALPA's) attempts to improve industrial relations. BA management and the pilots' association signed a 'guiding principles' agreement (a form of partnership agreement) as a basis for improved dialogue. The parties also sought assistance from a consultancy firm to facilitate meetings. Several interviewees referred to this arrangement as akin to 'marriage guidance' which was seen by many to be at least partly (though not entirely) successful. As one pilot negotiator put it, 'As we cannot get a divorce we have to solve things in a way which doesn't disadvantage one partner over another. That's why we are reaching settlement on a range of issues.' A major source of continued tension was identified as arising from management's frustration in failing to secure significant changes to pilots' terms and conditions.

The influence that the pilots enjoyed in negotiations with management was evident in their discussions with management over the Business Efficiency Programme measures. Overall, BEP was regarded by the pilots interviewed as a 'two-way process' to a much greater extent than was evident among cabin crew negotiators interviewed. Among the pilots, the *quid pro quo* for agreeing the increased work rate and longer hours was seen to be the changes in the flying hour rate system and an unwillingness to countenance further management proposals for welfare reductions, reduced annual leave and a future wage freeze. Overall, the outcome of the threatened industrial action and subsequent negotiation of efficiency changes was seen to be gains in some areas, matched by concessions in others, and a refusal to concede on a range of other issues.

This successful contesting of BEP by the pilots contrasts with the experience of cabin crew and the outcomes of their industrial action and negotiations over BEP. Here the picture appears more one of certain concessions being won by the union (for example, over the work/rest day ratio) but at the expense of more fundamental changes to work patterns and payment and allowance systems – changes which fed through into widespread reported reductions in morale among cabin crew personnel in the period following the strike (Turnbull *et al.*, 2000).

In accounting for the different experiences of the two occupational groups, we can return to Batstone's (1988) discussion of sources of occupational power. First, in terms of power deriving from scarcity value in the labour market, the wide variation in training requirements for pilots and cabin crew have already been commented upon. In addition, the stronger labour market position of the pilots was further underlined by the occurrence of widespread rest day working evident throughout the period of the research. The expansion of operations, coupled with a shortage of highly qualified pilots, had resulted in a management reliance on substantial rest day working by pilots. This shortage had been exacerbated by the poorer reward structures for many pilots on the shorter domestic and European routes, particularly those based at Gatwick, which in turn had not only encouraged an increased interest in transferring to long haul when positions became available, but also left harder-to-fill vacancies in parts of the domestic and European operation. This picture of labour shortage contrasts with the successful expansion of cabin crew personnel through additional recruitment, and tellingly, an expansion achieved despite the lower starting salaries on offer following the introduction of the two-tier wage system.

Second, the difference in degree of disruptive power held by the two groups is suggested by several aspects. First, there is the general point that the pilots achieved significant concessions from management by simply threatening industrial action, whereas cabin crew were required to actually engage in strike action in order to gain concessions from management. Further, the presence of the minority Cabin Crew 89 union, whose members continued to work during the strike, reduced the degree of overall solidarity displayed by those cabin crew taking action. In addition, while management were faced with no alternative but to concede to the pilots' demand when faced with industrial action, in the cabin crew dispute, alternative courses of action that were pursued not only included management undertaking cabin crew duties, but also formulating contingency plans to train an alternative cabin crew workforce should the strike persist.

If anything, the broader political influence achieved by the cabin crew was greater than among the pilots, and represented in particular by the degree of support and publicity that the cabin crew strike received internationally, following campaigning activities by BASSA and the ITF (ITF, 1997). At the same time, it could be argued that because of the high degree of 'local' power held by the pilots, they did not need to secure the 'global' power that BASSA were required to seek during their industrial action. In any event, this mobilization of international cabin crew solidarity notwithstanding, a comparison of the two occupational groups indicates that the pilots overall demonstrated a much stronger ability to contest management restructuring than was achievable by their cabin crew counterparts.

Conclusion

The developments taking place within civil aviation – privatization, globalization and restructuring – have led airline managers to put much greater emphasis on reducing labour costs and improving labour's performance. The ways in which this has fed through to the work of pilots and cabin crew was evidenced in reported higher levels of work intensity, longer work hours and various other work-related changes. Both the surveys and the case study evidence highlighted important changes that have taken place both on the flight deck and particularly among cabin crew in the recent period.

What the survey and particularly the more detailed case evidence also revealed was an ability by both cabin crew and pilots to contest management's restructuring objectives, partly via in one case threatened industrial action, and in the other, actual strike action. However, what the study also demonstrated was a much greater ability among one of the groups, the pilots, to successfully contest management's restructuring agenda. Their stronger labour market position gave the pilots an occupational power far in excess of that of the cabin crew. A differential also existed in the respective disruptive power of the two groups, reflected by one being able to secure major concessions from management through the threat of industrial action, while for the other actual strike action was required and even then management ultimately secured much (though not all) of its restructuring agenda. Even though cabin crew gained some additional power from international supportive action, this was insufficient to provide it with a degree of leverage to enable them to wrest the level of concessions from management that pilots were able to secure.

Note

1   The biggest of the global alliances, with over 21 per cent of world passenger traffic in June 2000, is the Star Alliance centred on Lufthansa and United Airlines in combination with eleven other carriers in Europe, North and South America, Asia and Australasia. The **one** world alliance, with over 16 per cent of world passenger traffic, comprises eight airlines including BA, American Airlines, Qantas, Cathay Pacific and Iberia. The alliance around Air France and Delta, established in 1999, carries just under 10 per cent of world passenger traffic, while the alliance based on Northwest Airlines and KLM accounts for over 6 per cent of total passenger traffic. The smallest of the big five alliances is the Qualiflyer alliance, centred on Swissair and Sabena, and accounts for 3.6 per cent of world passenger traffic (*Airline Business*, 2000).

References

AEA (2000) *Yearbook 2000*, Brussels: Association of European Airlines.
Airline Business (1999a) 'Special Report Maintenance: Asia Faces Fallout', *Airline Business* March: 57–8.
Airline Business (1999b) 'Special Report Maintenance: Europe's Big Three', *Airline Business* March: 52–4.
Airline Business (2000) 'Motivated Mergers', *Airline Business* July: 46–51.
Air Transport World (2000) 'World Airline Report 2000', *Air Transport World* 7: 47–64.
Bacon, N. and Blyton, P. (2000) *Meeting the Challenge of Globalisation: Steel Industry Restructuring and Trade Union Strategy*, Geneva: International Metalworkers' Federation.
Batstone, E. (1988) 'The Frontier of Control', in D. Gallie (ed.) *Employment in Britain*, Oxford: Blackwell, pp. 218–47.
Blyton, P., Martinez Lucio, M., McGurk, J. and Turnbull, P. (1998a) *Contesting Globalisation: Airline Restructuring, Labour Flexibility and Trade Union Strategies*, London: International Transport Workers' Federation.
Blyton, P., Martinez Lucio, M., McGurk, J. and Turnbull, P. (1998b) *Globalisation, Deregulation and Flexibility on the Flight Deck*, report prepared for the European Cockpit Association, Cardiff Business School, Cardiff University.
Blyton, P., Martinez Lucio, M., McGurk, J. and Turnbull, P. (1999) *Employment Relations under Deregulation: A Study of European Airlines*, End of Award report, London: Leverhulme Trust.
Blyton, P., Martinez Lucio, M., McGurk, J. and Turnbull, P. (2001a) 'Globalisation and

Trade Union Strategy: Evidence from the International Civil Aviation Industry', in R. Munck (ed.) *Labour and Globalization*, Liverpool: Liverpool University Press, in press.

Blyton, P., Martinez Lucio, M., McGurk, J. and Turnbull, P. (2001b) 'Globalisation and Trade Union Strategy: Industrial Restructuring and Human Resource Management in the International Civil Aviation Industry', *International Journal of Human Resource Management* 12(3): 455–63.

Blyton, P. and Turnbull, P. (1998) *The Dynamics of Employee Relations*, 2nd edn, Basingstoke: Macmillan.

Brecher, J. and Costello, T. (1994) *Global Village or Global Pillage: Economic Reconstruction from the Bottom Up*, Boston: South End Press.

Breitenfellner, A. (1997) 'Global Unionism: A Potential Player', *International Labour Review* 136(4): 531–55.

Button, K., Haynes, K. and Stough, R. (1998) *Flying into the Future: Air Transport Policy in the European Union*, Cheltenham: Edward Elgar.

Carlzon, J. (1987) *Moments of Truth*, New York: Harper and Row.

European Commission (1997) *Air Transport*, report prepared by Cranfield University, London: Kogan Page.

Feldman, J.M. (1998) 'Making Alliances Work', *Air Transport World* 6: 25–35.

Ferner, A. (1997) 'Country of Origin Effects and Human Resource Management in Multinational Companies', *Human Resource Management Journal* 7(1): 19–37.

Gill, T. (1998) 'Flexing Muscles', *Airline Business* October: 46–8.

ITF (1992) *The Globalisation of the Civil Aviation Industry and its Impact on Aviation Workers*, London: International Transport Workers' Federation.

ITF (1997) *1997 Civil Aviation Review*, London: International Transport Workers' Federation.

Kassim, H. (1997) 'Air Transport and Globalization: A Sceptical View', in A. Scott (ed.) *The Limits of Globalization*, London: Routledge, 202–22.

Lebrecht, D. (1999) 'Effects on Airline Employees of Growing Competition', paper presented at Airline Industrial Relations Conference, SMi Group, 25–26 October, London.

Lee, E. (1997) 'Globalization and Labour Standards: A Review of Issues', *International Labour Review* 136(2): 173–89.

Leisink, P. (ed.) (1999) *Globalization and Labour Relations*, Cheltenham: Edward Elgar.

Lyth, P. (1997) 'Experiencing Turbulence: Regulation and Deregulation in the International Air Transport Industry 1930–1990', in J. McConville (ed.) *Transport Regulation Matters*, London: Pinter, 154–74.

Martinez Lucio, M., Turnbull, P., Blyton, P. and McGurk, J. (2001) 'Using Regulation: An International Comparative Study of the Civil Aviation Industry in Britain and Spain', *European Journal of Industrial Relations* 7(1): 49–70.

Moody, K. (1997) *Workers in a Lean World: Unions in the International Economy*, London: Verso.

Morrell, P. and Lu, C. H-Y. (2000) 'Ahead of the Game', *Airline Business* February: 80–3.

Munck, R. and Waterman, P. (eds) (1999) *Labour Worldwide in an Era of Globalization*, Basingstoke: Macmillan.

O'Brien, R. (2000) 'Workers and the World Order: The Tentative Transformation of the International Union Movement', *Review of International Studies* 26: 533–55.

Oum, T. and Yu, C. (1998) *Winning Airlines: Productivity and Cost Competitiveness of the World's Major Airlines*, Boston: Kluwer.

Turnbull, P., Blyton, P., McGurk, J. and Martinez Lucio, M. (2000) *Strategic Choice and Industrial Relations: A Case Study of British Airways*, mimeo, Cardiff: Cardiff Business School.

Waddington, J. (ed.) (1999) *Globalization and Patterns of Labour Response*, London: Mansell.

Wiseman, J. (1996) 'A Kinder Road to Hell? Labor and the Politics of Progressive Competitiveness in Australia', in L. Panitch (ed.), *The Socialist Register 1996: Are There Alternatives?* London, Merlin Press.

Wood, A. (1995) 'How Trade Hurt Unskilled Workers', *Journal of Economic Perspectives* 9(3): 57–80.

3 Global labour? The transfer of the organizing model to the United Kingdom

Edmund Heery, Rick Delbridge, John Salmon, Melanie Simms and Dave Simpson

Introduction

Globalization is rightly regarded as a threat to the labour movements of developed economies in at least three senses. First, the transfer of jobs to low-wage economies overseas threatens to erode union membership (Jacoby, 1995: 12). Second, the exposure of domestic markets to foreign competition threatens to undermine the rent-seeking behaviour of unions (Brown, 2000: 313). And, third, the growth of regime competition between nation–states seeking inward investment threatens the national industrial relations settlement, which in many countries has afforded unions influence over economic and social policy (Hyman, 1997; Streeck, 1991). However, globalization may also present opportunities to trade unions and the chance to develop new union forms, access new resources and develop a new agenda, aimed at regulating the international economy. Globalization is not a single, determinate process, therefore, but embraces a range of developments, some of which are inimical to the interests of trade unions and their members and some of which may prove relatively benign (Murray *et al.*, 2000; Waddington, 1999).

According to Crouch (1999: 43), globalization 'conveys a sense of the interdependence of the entire world, and of the interchangeability of many elements in it'. It is this sense of globalization that informs the present chapter. We are concerned with the extent to which labour is becoming global, such that contact between national labour movements is increasing and norms of good union practice are being transferred from one country to another. Specifically, we are interested in the diffusion of the 'organizing model', an approach to union organizing that emerged in the USA in the 1980s and which has since influenced union activity in other countries, including Australia, Canada, New Zealand, and the UK. In what follows we examine the transfer of the organizing model to the latter and consider three issues in detail.

First, we identify the factors that have made UK unions receptive to learning from overseas, both by comparing the UK with other national cases and identifying the features of those UK unions that have been particularly receptive to the organizing model. Research on the diffusion of business practices has indicated that their transfer is mediated by the 'socio-economic settlements between social agencies and institutions operating on a national terrain' (Elger and Smith, 1994: 33) and that adoption within countries is often highly variable. In the light of these findings, our aim is to establish the aspects of the institutional settlement that have made UK labour receptive to the organizing model and the characteristics of those national unions with a peculiar susceptibility to learning from outside.

Second, we review the processes through which transfer has occurred and the role of different agents and institutions in promoting learning. With regard to the diffusion of business practices, foreign direct investment by transnational corporations, the control of practice in supplier firms and the roles of exemplars, champions and propagandists have been identified as significant mechanisms (Elger and Smith, 1994: 45–9; Pfeffer, 1994: 205–14). Only the latter of these has a direct parallel within the labour movement and our focus is on the role of central labour confederations, like the Trades Union Congress (TUC), in promoting the organizing model. Accordingly, we review the nature and efficacy of the deliberate attempt by the TUC to act as a conduit for the diffusion of trade union best practice in the field of organizing. In addition, we examine diffusion processes within individual unions and seek to identify the structural and other characteristics of unions that permit a relatively broad acceptance of an organizing approach.

Finally, we examine the extent to which the diffusion of the 'organizing model' has encountered resistance within unions. Again, parallels can be drawn with the diffusion of business practice, where studies reveal a piecemeal and incomplete transfer of production systems and techniques at the level of the individual company, which is often explained by reference to worker resistance (Elger and Smith, 1994: 51). Our object is to identify the forces of opposition within unions to the new emphasis on organizing. Any process of organizational change has the potential to disrupt established relations and threaten established interests. The aim is to isolate those interests within trade unions that are threatened by new organizing initiatives and which, consequently, have failed to support or actively opposed that bundle of changes that can be referred to loosely as the 'organizing model'.

In carrying out the empirical examination we have drawn upon a number of original data sources. The authors have attended virtually all meetings of the TUC's New Unionism Task Group, which has overseen the attempt to learn from Australian and US organizing practice. Other qualitative research has included an extensive programme of interviews with senior officers of the TUC and individual unions and with organizers being trained at the TUC's Organizing Academy. In addition, quantitative methods have been used and we draw upon the results of two questionnaire surveys. The first is a national survey of all TUC unions and all non-TUC unions with more than 3,000 members that was conducted in 1998. This survey was completed by senior union officers and sought information on the level and form of union policy with regard to organizing, including receptiveness to the 'organizing model'. A total of sixty-four responses were received, equivalent to 67 per cent of the population. The second survey was administered to each of the first two cohorts of organizers graduating from the TUC's Organizing Academy. A total of fifty-four responses were gathered from the sixty-six trainees who completed the programme (82 per cent) and the data provide a unique record of the characteristics, activities and difficulties of UK union organizers who have been trained in the techniques of the 'organizing model'.[1]

The organizing model

The contrast between an organizing and a servicing model of trade unionism has become an established feature of debate on trade union strategy in the USA, the UK and other countries in recent years (Carter, 2000; Hurd, 1998; Oxenbridge, 1997; Waddington and Kerr, 2000). At its most basic, the distinction refers to the difference between a form of unionism in which the union as an institution acts on behalf of its members, who are conceived of as clients or customers, and one in which members actively participate and 'become' the union through their collective organization and activity. Thus, Waddington (2000: 320) notes that 'the servicing model relies on trade union activities external to the workplace to support trade unionists at their place of work . . . [while] [t]he organising model . . . places emphasis on union organisation and activity at the workplace'. As such, the distinction re-expresses the tension between worker mobilization and routine representation that is as old as the labour movement itself.

The distinction is important in the current context, however, because it has been used to launch a programme for the revitalization of organized labour that is deemed equally applicable to all national cases and for all types of union. This programme originated in the USA – the term 'organizing model' was first coined in 1988 in a manual for US labour organizers (Hurd, 1998: 23) – and has attracted adherents elsewhere, partly because US supporters have actively exported it overseas. The programme, which is variably labelled the 'organizing model', the 'organizing approach' or 'organizing unionism', contains both broad statements of principle and priority and specific recipes for action, in a manner akin to programmes for business reform, such as total quality management, lean production and business process re-engineering.

Among the broad principles, the most basic is that unions must commit themselves to organizing the unorganized as their first priority. Applying the organizing model, in the first instance, means committing greater effort and resource to the task of recruiting workers into membership and in the USA the American Federation of Labor–Congress of Industrial Organisations (AFL-CIO) has tried to commit its members to ambitious expenditure targets for union organizing. Particular stress is laid on organizing relatively marginal workers in secondary labour markets, that is on extending union organization downwards to those who require it most but who, like immigrants, young workers and minorities, have often been neglected by unions in the past. Membership is to be created and sustained, however, through the development of self-sustaining collective organization among workers. In the US, organizers speak of identifying workplace leaders, while in the UK they refer to activists and the need to attract and retain membership around an activist core. Organization is itself to emerge from a planned campaign that mobilizes workers and draws them into a series of meetings, actions, and protests. Such a campaign may be directed at establishing union organization for the first time, though equally it may be deployed to support collective bargaining, industrial action or even political protest. Central to the process, however, is the concept of mobilization and adherents of the organizing model refer frequently to the re-creation of labour as a social movement: putting the 'move' back in the labour movement.

A feature of this emphasis on mobilization is the use of a particular moral discourse to frame union activity, which uses the language of 'dignity, justice and respect' at work. This framing language not only legitimates union joining and activity, it also presents the union as a counter to the employer. Organizing unionism is generally adversarial or militant (Kelly,1996) in its assumptions and seeks to organize workers against the employer. Indeed, the emphasis on collective organization arises from a conviction that workers must generate their own power resources if they are to secure concessions from employers whose interests are fundamentally opposed. Given the weak labour market position of unorganized workers, however, it is recognized that there are limits to their internal capacity to organize and confront employers. Additional resources are to be garnered therefore through developing alliances with other progressive movements and institutions beyond the workplace and the final core principle of the organizing model is that union activity should be extended into the wider community. In organizing workers the union should broaden its concerns to embrace the wider needs of 'working families', while drawing on the support of religious, community, political and other institutions which can pressure employers into making concessions (Nissen, 1999).

While the organizing model is based on these core assumptions about union activity, it is also associated with a set of specific techniques that can be deployed in union recruitment and organizing campaigns. These 'union-building' techniques (Bronfenbrenner, 1997) include the following:

- Reliance on planned organizing campaigns, in which the union proactively identifies and researches targets and sets clear and timed objectives that are subject to periodic review.
- Reliance on paid 'lead organizers' to oversee organizing campaigns and foster activism among the target workforce.
- Involvement of activists in the development and running of campaigns through a representative 'organizing committee'.
- The use of 'mapping' techniques to identify all members of the workforce and rank them systematically in terms of their propensity to become active in the union.
- The identification of current issues and grievances around which a campaign can be developed.
- The use of 'actions' to mobilize the workforce that can range from badge-wearing and the signing of a petition through to street theatre and protest strikes.
- Use of 'one-to-one' or 'person-to-person' recruitment, in which trained volunteer organizers seek to persuade non-members to join the union either at the workplace or through 'house calls'.

- Reliance on the principle of 'like-recruits-like', such that recruiters have the same demographic and occupational identity to those being recruited.
- The demonstration of union effectiveness in the course of campaigns by publicizing concessions from the employer.
- 'Inoculating' workers against anti-union propaganda through continuous communications through the course of the campaign and the rapid rebuttal of accusations or criticism stemming from the employer.
- The identification of 'levers', allies and pressure points that can be used to discourage employer opposition and press for union recognition.
- The development of media and community support, so that the campaign extends beyond the workplace to embrace community, political and consumer organizations.

Research in the USA indicates that this set of practices is used, albeit in only a minority of organizing campaigns, and is effective even in the face of employer opposition (Bronfenbrenner, 1997; Bronfenbrenner and Juravich, 1998). Moreover, like human resource management (MacDuffie, 1995), the techniques appear to have added value when they are bundled and reinforce one another rather than being used piecemeal or in isolation. Much of the diffusion of the organizing model from the USA to the UK and other countries has involved attempts to transfer these techniques and our next purpose is to consider why particular national labour movements and particular unions have been receptive to the organizing message.

Receptiveness: national labour movements

Despite repeated critique, convergence theses continue to exert influence in the field of employment relations. Thus, the common challenge of globalization has been claimed to stimulate the emergence of a new unionism across the developed economies though opinions differ sharply on the direction of change, with some identifying a qualitative step towards partnership while others see the revival of union militancy (cf. Brown, 2000; Kelly, 1998). The corollary of convergence in theory is best practice in policy (Smith and Meiksins, 1995: 242). The organizing model is a recipe for best practice but what is notable about its international diffusion is the degree of unevenness. National labour movements face a common problem of decline and common challenges emanating from the global economy but there has been variable take-up of the best practice model.

In the UK the organizing model has attracted considerable interest and stimulated experiment. The TUC has conducted fact-finding visits to the USA and Australia to learn about organizing practice and in 1998 opened an Organizing Academy to train a new generation of union organizers in the philosophy and methods of the organizing model (Heery *et al.*, 2000b). This is based on similar programmes launched by the AFL-CIO and the Australian Council of Trade Unions (ACTU) and is an initiative that is shot through with the assumptions and terminology of organizing unionism. Individual unions have followed suit and, while practice has often fallen short of prescription, a number have tried to re-create themselves as 'organizing' unions. Unions, such as Connect, Graphical, Paper and Media Union (GPMU), the Iron and Steel Trades Confederation (ISTC), Manufacturing, Science and Finance (MSF), Transport Salaried Staffs Association (TSSA) and UNISON, have invested more heavily in organizing, in part by sponsoring trainees at the Organizing Academy, and have tried deliberately to apply aspects of the organizing model (Carter, 2000; Heery *et al.*, 2000a; Waddington and Kerr, 2000).

Similar attempts to learn from the USA and apply the organizing model have occurred in Australia and New Zealand (Cooper, 2000; Oxenbridge, 2000). In Canada, moreover, international unions, based in the USA, have carried organizing unionism across the border. Elsewhere interest in the organizing model is less apparent. In Western Europe there are recent reports that unions are attaching greater priority to member recruitment though with the partial exception of France, where the Confédération Française Démocratique du Travail (CFDT) has sought to apply US organizing methods (Daly, 1999: 204), there are no reported attempts to apply the organizing model. The main methods that have been used to rebuild membership include improvements in member services and union communications and attempts to appeal to women, the young, white-collar workers and workers on contingent contracts by changing union government systems and bargaining policy (Daly, 1999: 200–1; Mahon, 1999: 146–50; Silvia, 1999: 113–14; Waddington, 2000: 320–2). The situation in Japan is similar with largely indigenous attempts to rebuild membership through improved services and the extension of enterprise unionism to subsidiary firms and sub-contractors (Fujimura, 1997).

Why has the union movement in the UK proved relatively receptive to the organizing model? Part of the explanation may be cultural and it is notable that it is the Anglophone countries that have shown most appetite for learning from the USA. It is also the case that UK labour has declined further and faster than the trade union movement in most other countries and therefore may have a particularly acute incentive to experiment with new ways of organizing.[2] Australia and New Zealand are also countries where there has been a sharp fall in union density since the 1980s. There are additional incentives for unions in these countries to experiment with the organizing model, however, which arise from the institutional structure of their industrial relations systems.

Two features of the institutional structure of industrial relations appear to have most relevance: the level of collective bargaining and the arrangements in place to provide for 'union security', that is the provisions to allow unions to secure and retain recognition from employers. Like the USA and Canada, the UK has a decentralized system of collective bargaining, in which unions mainly negotiate with employers at enterprise or workplace levels (Brown *et al.*, 2000: 615). Australia and New Zealand have also moved towards this pattern in recent years as a result of government programmes of industrial relations reform (Boxall and Haynes, 1997: 568; Katz and Darbishire, 2000: 138). Devolved bargaining arguably encourages interest in organizing, first of all, because union bargaining power within companies is dependent on the level of membership and degree of collective organization among the workforce to an extent that is less apparent where bargaining is centralized. In the UK a union wage mark-up is generally only attained at high levels of density (Brown *et al.*, 1997: 78). Second, devolved bargaining renders unions dependent on the activities of volunteers and activists because it is impossible to service members across a dispersed system of bargaining through external, full-time officers. Public service unions in the UK that have invested in organizing, such as the Public and Commercial Services Union (PCS) and the Institution of Professionals, Managers and Specialists (IPMS) give as a prime motive their need to develop a representative capacity and enhance bargaining power in a context of increasingly devolved bargaining. The same is true of unions like Connect and TSSA that have had to cope with privatization and the break-up of state enterprises into separate businesses.[3]

Interest in the organizing model has risen in the UK and other Anglophone countries against the background of a 'neo-liberal environment' in which 'the state no longer underwrites union survival' (Boxall and Haynes, 1997: 568).[4] The TUC's New Unionism policy, which gave rise to the Organizing Academy, was adopted under the Conservatives whose programme of labour law had withdrawn all of the main props to union security (Brown *et al.*, 1997). In a series of measures the Conservative government had abolished the pre-entry and post-entry closed shops, outlawed contract compliance and secondary industrial action to promote union recognition, allowed employers to discriminate against union members in setting terms and conditions of employment, imposed restrictions on the collection of union dues at source and abolished the statutory route to trade union recognition. The period from the great miners' strike of 1984–85 to the return of Labour to power in 1997 also witnessed increasingly militant action by employers and a rising trend of union avoidance, marginalization and derecognition (Brown *et al.*, 1997; Claydon, 1996). In this context the organizing model, with its emphasis on union self-reliance and the identification of new sources of power in community alliances, has proved attractive. For unions like the GPMU, which has had to contend with the collapse of the closed shop in the printing industry, or for Natfhe and Connect, which have been faced with more assertive employers, it has promised to restore membership when traditional supports of union organization are no longer available.

Since Labour's return to power, UK unions have faced a more benign environment. A statutory recognition procedure was instituted in June 2000 and other legal measures have served to bolster union security. There is also evidence that UK employers have taken their lead from government and have become more receptive to union requests for recognition (Gall, 2000). The effects of these changes have been mixed. On the one hand, they have encouraged the TUC and some member unions to place increasing emphasis on the theme of social partnership and in 2001 a Partnership Institute was launched alongside the Organizing Academy. As public policy has changed and supports for union security have been strengthened, therefore, there has been the accentuation of alternative themes in union policy which rest on very different assumptions to those of the organizing model (Heery, 1998). On the other hand, the creation of a statutory recognition procedure has provided a fresh incentive for unions to engage in organizing. Unions believe that there is a limited window of opportunity during which the legislation can be used to restore recognition where it has collapsed and extend it to new areas. Moreover, the need to demonstrate majority support among the workforce and the opportunities afforded by the recognition procedure for employer opposition and delay (Wood and Godard, 1999) have confirmed the commitment to the organizing model of unions like the GPMU and the ISTC. In the USA where equivalent 'certification' procedures exist, they have been used effectively by employers to block union recognition and relatively sophisticated 'union-building' approaches to organizing have evolved in response. For at least sections of the UK trade union movement this has implied that the switch in public policy should lead to an intensification rather than a reduction in organizing effort.

While structural features of the industrial relations system have provided an incentive for UK unions to accept the organizing model, elements of the indigenous tradition of trade unionism have also been important. UK unions are less well resourced and more dependent on the voluntary work of activists than many of their counterparts overseas. There is also an established tradition of fostering lay organization and encouraging self-reliant trade unionism at workplace level (Heery and Kelly, 1990). For a number of unions that have tried to apply elements of the organizing model, the experiment represents a reaffirmation of an established practice and a return to basic principles of union-building. In the Transport and General Workers' Union (TGWU) the organizing model has informed a 'lay organizer' training programme and has been linked explicitly to the union's tradition of active shopfloor organization; in the GPMU the organizing model has been presented as a way of renewing chapel organization; and in UNISON it conforms to the tradition of promoting workplace trade unionism in its founding unions that dates back to the early 1970s. While some of the methods and language associated with the organizing model are novel, therefore, its basic objectives and principles conform to an established, if attenuated, tradition of active workplace trade unionism. As such, it can more easily be accommodated, and provide a source for innovation, without being seen as an alien imposition.

To summarize, therefore, the receptiveness to organizing unionism of UK labour lies partly in the experience of decline that has been shared with most other labour movements in the developed world and partly in the tradition of workplace organization that characterizes UK trade unionism. Over and above these factors, however, are institutional features of the system of industrial relations that have predisposed UK trade unionism to reach for the organizing model as part of a solution to its problems. These are the devolved structure of bargaining, which puts a premium on effective workplace organization, and the weak, albeit recently strengthened, system of union security, which puts a premium on union self-reliance. These characteristics are shared with other national labour movements that have turned to the organizing model, most notably Australia and New Zealand and they are also shared with the USA, the society that gave birth to the model. It is institutional distinctiveness, therefore, that appears to underlie the variable diffusion of union best practice. It is wrong to reify institutional structures, however, and over-emphasize their fixed and enduring nature. Devolved bargaining and a lack of union security are structural features that have been strengthened in recent years through state reform of industrial relations and the actions of employers. Interest in the organizing model within the TUC and its affiliated unions has emerged against a dynamic background of 'union exclusion'. Its very attractiveness derives from this situation in that it offers a route to the renewal of the labour movement that is dependent on its own efforts and the re-creation of internal resources of power and capacities for collective action.

Receptiveness: individual unions

Just as there are differences in the receptiveness of national labour movements to organizing unionism, so there are differences between individual unions. Even among unions that have sponsored trainees at the TUC's Organizing Academy there is notable variation in the extent to which they have been influenced by the organizing model, have attempted to apply its associated techniques and have reinforced the training delivered centrally by the TUC's New Unionism Unit (Heery *et al.*, 2000b). Table 3.1 provides further evidence of variation and indicates that UK unions differ in the extent to which they report learning new methods of organizing from abroad, agree that lessons can be learnt from organizing tactics overseas and state that they have been influenced by the organizing model. It indicates that while most unions accept that there are useful lessons to be learnt from organizing practice in other countries, only a minority (less than 20 per cent) report they have been strongly influenced by the organizing model.

Table 3.2 presents further data on receptiveness to organizing unionism. It shows the percentages of UK unions that report using a series of techniques that are commonly regarded as elements of an organizing approach. Table 3.2 indicates

Table 3.1 The receptiveness of UK unions to the organizing model (%)

Statement	Opinion				
	Very true	True	True to some extent	Not true	
We have learnt new methods of recruiting from unions in other countries	10.2	18.6	28.8	42.4	
	Strongly agree	Agree	Neither	Disagree	Strongly disagree
British trade unions can learn a lot from organizing tactics used overseas	12.5	42.9	37.5	5.4	1.8
My union has been strongly influenced by the organizing model current in Australia and the United States	7.1	10.7	35.7	26.8	19.6

Source: Survey of UK unions 1998
Note: N = 59, 56, 56

Table 3.2 Reliance on the organizing model (%)

Organizing technique	Used frequently	Used occasionally or rarely	Not used
Person-to-person recruitment at the workplace	69.4	25.8	4.8
Raising the union profile in the workplace (e.g. through petitions, surveys, displays, demonstrations)	45.2	50.0	4.8
Identification of employee grievances as a basis for organizing	33.9	59.6	6.5
Establishing membership targets at workplace or company level	29.0	41.9	29.0
Reliance on principle of 'like-recruits-like' in recruitment (e.g. young recruiters for young workers)	26.2	47.5	26.2
Establishing an organizing committee or team within workplaces for targeted recruitment	21.0	46.8	32.3
Systematic rating of non-members in terms of their propensity to join	6.6	47.5	45.9
Public campaigns against anti-union employers	4.9	42.7	52.5
Link-up with community organizations (e.g. ethnic groups)	3.3	44.3	52.5
House calls to non-members' homes	1.6	12.9	85.5

Source: Survey of UK unions 1998
Note: N = 61–64.

that, while aspects of UK union practice conform to or have been influenced by the organizing model, take-up has been patchy. Most unions report frequent use of person-to-person recruitment and just under half use petitions, surveys and demonstrations to raise the union profile in the workplace. More distinctive features of the model, however, such as target-setting and the use of organizing committees are confined to a minority of unions and those aspects of the model that extend union organizing into the community are reported in only a handful of cases. There are unions, like the GPMU and the ISTC, that have been heavily influenced by the organizing model but, at present, these constitute a small vanguard within UK trade unionism.

The data in each of these tables comprise a statistically reliable scale and these can be used to provide formal tests of the characteristics of unions that are receptive to the organizing model. To execute these tests a limited number of separate dimensions of union organization, context and behaviour were identified as follows:[5]

- *Union structure*. Two structural variables were identified: union size, measured by union membership in 1998, and membership composition. The latter was a dummy variable with unions with a largely managerial or professional membership taking the value of '1'. It was hypothesized that unions with a membership of this kind would be less receptive to the 'organizing model', as collective organization might be more difficult to establish among more individualistic and dispersed employees in senior roles (Batstone *et al.*, 1977) and because these employees may identify more strongly with their employer. Larger unions, in contrast, might be more susceptible, essentially because their greater size and greater resources allow them to monitor their external environment more readily.

- *Union incentive.* Innovation in unions, as in other organizations, may be driven by crisis and therefore receptiveness to the organizing model may be a function of the incentive unions face to restore lost membership (Ross and Martin, 1999: 387–8). The incentive measures used were the percentage decline in union membership in the period immediately prior to the survey (1994–98) and union funds per member, a crude measure of union wealth derived from the annual financial return registered unions are required to make to the Certification Officer.
- *Union context.* Innovation in organizations may be a function of membership of an 'institutional field' and access to the organizational forms and practices that circulate among field members (DiMaggio and Powell, 1991). To provide an initial test of this institutional hypothesis we divided the unions in our sample between those that were affiliated to the TUC and those that were independent, on the assumption that TUC members would have greater access to the organizing model by virtue of the TUC's own commitment to its diffusion. A further test was obtained by including a measure of union involvement in the Organizing Academy. Unions were scored on the number of times they had sponsored a trainee organizer at the Academy (maximum score '3') and it was hypothesized that those with most involvement would display most commitment to the organizing model.
- *Union strategy.* A pronounced theme in recent writing on trade unions declares that union leaders have scope for strategic choice (Boxall and Haynes, 1997; Kelly, 1997). The choices that were isolated for examination were those relating directly to union organizing. The organizing model has been advanced as a means to 'organize the unorganized' and, accordingly, we developed a measure of union commitment to extending membership beyond established bargaining groups. This measure, 'expansion', is a scale derived from a series of four questions in the 1998 survey that asked respondents to gauge the level of their union's commitment to recruiting in non-union firms, in new companies (e.g. inward investors) and among suppliers and contractors to organizations where membership was already established. A second scale measure, 'diversity', was also developed. This was based on items in the questionnaire that asked respondents to report on commitment to recruiting women, young workers and members of minority groups. Advocates of the organizing model stress the need to attract 'non-traditional' groups into membership and it was hypothesized that unions with this orientation would therefore be receptive to learning from the model.

The results of a linear regression analysis of the data are shown in Table 3.3. This reveals that, in combination, the independent variables explain a relatively high proportion of variation in the two measures of union receptiveness. It also provides a picture of which union characteristics are associated with a propensity to adopt the organizing model. Perhaps the clearest finding is that seeming incentives to engage in organizing provide no stimulus to adopting the organizing model: neither union decline nor union penury are associated with the measures of union receptiveness. In individual cases these factors may have stimulated attempts to learn from overseas. MSF is a union with financial difficulties which was prompted to experiment with the organizing model, at least in part, by a need to boost subscription income. Similarly, the GPMU turned to the organizing model because the union was faced with the prospect of extinction if it did not take action to reverse membership decline: 'We looked over the edge' was how the sense of crisis was described. However, while financial and membership decline may prompt unions to innovation, it does not follow that innovation will take the form of experiment with the organizing model. There are other options available to union leaders, including retrenchment, merger and attempts to reverse decline through 'organizing the employer' and the availability of these other responses probably explains the lack of association.[6] It is also the case that the absence of crisis may allow experiment. The most prominent organizing union in the UK, the ISTC, is relatively wealthy and has opted to invest a proportion of its wealth in organizing. In other cases growing unions, such as the Association of University Teachers (AUT), have developed an interest in the organizing model in order to maintain momentum and help spread membership to areas where they have previously been absent, which for the AUT is within the new universities.

The situation with regard to union structure is more complex. It is clear though that, once other factors are controlled for, union size is not associated with receptiveness to the organizing model. Further evidence of this can be seen in the unions that have sponsored trainees at the TUC's Organizing Academy, which have included some of the largest (e.g. the AEEU, MSF, UNISON) together with several relatively small unions (e.g. Connect, ISTC, IUHS, MPO, TSSA). The other measure of union structure, managerial or professional membership, is associated positively with interest in overseas methods but not with their application. The positive association is the reverse of what was anticipated.

A possible explanation can be found in the interviews with senior officers in unions such as AUT, CMA, Connect, EMA, IPMS and MPO. These were all unions that had increased their organizing activity and which stressed the possibility of learning from American and Australian experience. All of them emphasized the need to strengthen workplace organization, and several commented positively on the use by US unions of dedicated organizing staff and planned organizing campaigns. There was a degree of scepticism with regard to the more mobilizing, social movement elements within the organizing model, however, which it was felt would bemuse if not alienate the kinds of worker some of these unions were seeking to recruit. 'They're not chicken pluckers from Arkansas' was how one officer described his membership, while another said that wearing a colourful tie was as close to

Table 3.3 Union characteristics and receptiveness to the organizing model

Variables	Descriptive statistics			Regression 1 Receptiveness to organizing model[6]		Regression 2 Use of organizing techniques[7]	
	Mean	SD	Alpha	Standardized coefficients[6]	T value	Standardized coefficients[7]	T value
Union membership	104,022	229,197	—	.037	(.325)	.085	(.764)
Membership composition[1]	—	—	—	.389***	(3.416)	.033	(.291)
Membership decline 1994–98	−7.39	18.67	—	.129	(1.149)	−.008	(−.071)
Funds per member	£110.69	£143.62	—	.114	(1.002)	−.077	(−.670)
TUC affiliate[2]	—	—	—	.180	(1.528)	.032	(.281)
Involvement in Academy[3]	0.59	1.09	—	.449***	(3.911)	.206*	(1.763)
Expansion in organizing	9.00	3.28	.80	.384***	(3.137)	.527***	(4.402)
Diversity in organizing	15.89	4.76	.87	.103	(.903)	.182	(1.510)
Receptiveness[4]	8.17	2.70	.85				
Organizing methods[5]	24.02	6.10	.84				

Source: Survey of Unions 1998

Notes on variables:

[1] 22 unions (34.4 per cent) had a primarily managerial or professional membership.

[2] 52 unions (81.3 per cent) were affiliated to the TUC.

[3] A total of 17 unions had sponsored a trainee at the Academy; five in one year (7.8 per cent); three in two years (4.7 per cent) and nine in one year (14.1 per cent).

[4] Scale derived from the items in Table 3.1.

[5] Scale derived from the items in Table 3.2.

[6] F = 7.269; sig.000

   R^2 = .599

   Adj R^2 = .516

[7] F = 6.355; sig.000

   R^2 = .530

   Adj R^2 = .447

N = 47, 53; significance: *p < .10, ***p < .01

rebellion as many of his members were likely to get. This ambivalence may explain the pattern in the data. These unions were anxious to organize and were appreciative of those elements in the organizing model that emphasize systematic and professional recruitment. In some cases there was a desire to correct an inherited situation of relatively weak workplace organization. Several were less attracted to the adversarial and mobilizing elements in organizing unionism, however, with the result that receptiveness to learning has not been accompanied by any marked experiment with organizing model techniques.

The pattern of association with the union context variables was as anticipated: receptiveness to the organizing model and the use of organizing techniques were associated positively with membership of the TUC and involvement in the Organizing Academy. It is only the associations with the Academy that are statistically significant, however, and it has seemingly been exposure to this particular aspect of the TUC's activities that has been decisive in prompting experiment. However, a note of caution must be sounded. The direction of association could well flow the other way with unions that have independently acquired an appetite for the organizing model joining the Academy to satisfy it. Indeed, several unions within the Academy, including Connect, Communication Workers Union (CWU), GPMU and ISTC had had separate contact with their sister organizations in the USA before the Academy opened. This is not to minimize the role of the Academy in disseminating the message of organizing but it is likely that there has been a reciprocal influence with unions that are committed to organizing perceiving value in Academy involvement.

Of the strategy variables, it is only commitment to expansion that is associated with interest in the organizing model and application of its techniques. It is primarily unions that are seeking to enter new territory that have been attracted to the organizing model. The ISTC provides a graphic example in that it has used the techniques of organizing unionism to re-launch itself as a 'community union', committed to developing membership across manufacturing industry in the old steel making areas. To do this it has invested heavily in the Organizing Academy and sought to apply US organizing techniques in fairly direct fashion in an organizing programme directed largely at light manufacturing companies though a number of call centre and distribution firms have also been targeted. Other unions, such as CWU, GPMU and National Union of Knitwear, Footwear and Allied Trades (KFAT) have acted in a similar fashion and have drawn upon US and Australian experience in developing a programme of 'greenfield' organizing. Of course the nostrums and techniques of organizing unionism are not only of relevance to greenfield organizing. They can equally be applied to restoring membership and organization in companies where unions are recognized (Heery *et al.*, 2000a) and in the USA and Australia an organizing approach has been applied to generate member support in collective bargaining and political campaigns (Cooper, 2000: 584–6). In the UK, however, it seems that the organizing model has been deemed to have most relevance to situations where unions are seeking to expand into new territory.

A general lesson that can be taken from Table 3.3 is that, with the exception of the propensity of professional unions to learn from overseas, the structural dimensions of unions and their environments are not strong predictors of receptiveness to the organizing model. Rather, it is involvement in the Organizing Academy and a commitment to expansion that have inclined unions to experiment with organizing methods developed overseas. The results support the arguments of strategic choice theorists first because they point to the role of the TUC in shaping union behaviour through deliberate innovation in the form of the Organizing Academy. They also underscore the importance of strategic choice within individual unions and the fact that ambition in union organizing strategy is associated with innovation in union organizing practice. While the propensity of the UK trade union movement to adopt the organizing model seems to be related to structural features of UK industrial relations, the propensity of individual unions to experiment appears to derive from the strategic choices of union leaders. Union strategies, as well as the formal institutions of industrial relations, seemingly make a difference to the way unions behave.

Processes of diffusion

So far we have considered why trade unions may be receptive to the diffusion of the international organizing model. Now we want to consider how diffusion has occurred by analysing the process of transfer. The first thing to note about the latter is that it has not involved international trade union organizations and agencies. Neither at regional level, in the form of the European Trade Union Confederation (ETUC), nor at global level, in the form of the International Confederation of Free Trade Unions (ICFTU), have the institutions of international trade unionism contributed significantly to the diffusion of the organizing model. Rather, diffusion has occurred through bilateral contact between sister unions in the UK, Australia, New Zealand and the USA and between central trade union confederations, like ACTU, AFL-CIO and the TUC.

The involvement of union confederations has been particularly striking. Central labour organizations have tended to attract academic attention with respect to their role as social partners in the context of neo-corporatist exchange. In states where this pattern of interaction is absent (the UK, the USA, New Zealand) or has recently collapsed (Australia), it is often assumed that confederations will be confined to residual functions and that these may themselves be threatened through the process of union merger and the emergence of large super-unions. Somewhat against the grain, however, central union confederations have re-launched themselves in the past decade and have become active proponents of organizing unionism. This is true of the USA, Australia and, more recently New Zealand, as well as the UK (Cooper, 2000; Heery, 1998; Hurd, 1998; Oxenbridge, 2000). Coordinating and promoting union organizing activity has emerged as a new function for confederations in situations where coordinating union wage bargaining or political activity has become less significant.

The attempt by the TUC to promote the organizing model has embraced a range of activities. Some of these correspond to the work of state agencies and business organizations in trying to promote new management techniques (cf. Pfeffer, 1994:

207–17), while others involve an elaboration of established TUC activities. Examples of the former include organizing fact-finding visits of senior union officers to the USA and Australia to learn about new organizing techniques and see them in operation. It also includes arranging conferences, seminars and away-days for union officers and activists to enable them to hear accounts of organizing, consider research evidence and exchange experiences. Top billing at a number of these events has been given to charismatic organizers from other countries who have served to inspire and legitimize organizing innovation in the manner of management gurus. The effect of much of this work may be transitory and undoubtedly it has elicited a sceptical response from a proportion of those exposed to it. It has nevertheless exposed a substantial segment of the activist and officer cadre of UK unions to the notion of an organizing model and its language, techniques and assumptions. In interview several national organizers referred to the 'Road to Damascus' moment they had experienced on visits to the USA and the bilateral contacts between the TUC and other national centres undoubtedly have aided diffusion.[7]

That aspect of the TUC's traditional repertoire that has been elaborated to promote organizing is union training. The central initiative here is the Organizing Academy, a twelve-month training programme for 'lead organizers' that is based on classroom sessions interspersed with prolonged periods of placement with a sponsoring union. The programme is based explicitly on the organizing model and seeks to develop a series of organizing competencies among trainees that will equip them to initiate and lead both greenfield and in-fill organizing campaigns on graduation. To help development, sponsoring unions supply coaches who mentor and assess the progress of Academy Organizers and who are themselves offered training by the TUC in the principles and practice of organizing, as well as coaching. Since its inception in 1998, the Academy programme has been extended to include an optional second year's training and a parallel short course, Winning the Organised Workplace, has been launched, which is targeted at lay activists and general full-time officers. Moreover, there are proposals to reformulate the basic shop steward and full-time officer training courses that are offered by the TUC to incorporate elements of the organizing model. To date, more than 100 trainee organizers have entered the Academy, and the majority of these have completed the programme and found employment either in their sponsoring unions or in organizing positions elsewhere in the UK trade union movement (Heery *et al.*, 2000b).

A feature of the Organizing Academy that is truly innovative is direct employment of organizers by the TUC. All trainees are employed jointly by the TUC and their sponsoring union and the members of the TUC New Unionism Unit are involved directly in their management. This is itself a practice imported from the Organising Works programme in Australia. It has two primary objectives. The first is to use the Academy to attract an identifiably new workforce to the trade union movement, who can be trained in organizing techniques and work for their diffusion in their sponsoring unions. In this the Academy has been reasonably successful. Its graduates are majority female and much younger on average than the typical full-time officer and a significant proportion have brought with them experience of activism in non-labour settings (Heery *et al.*, 2000b). Evidence from the Academy Organizer survey indicates that they graduate with a strong commitment to the organizing model – more than 90 per cent agree that 'the organizing model is the best way to build membership' – though over time this may attenuate as organizers become socialized into their employing unions.

The second objective has been to create a distinctive cohort of organizers that can provide the basis of an inter-union network for the diffusion of organizing practice and experience. A term that has been used by the TUC to encapsulate this notion is 'pan-unionism'. The aim appears to be to create ties between organizers in different unions that are grounded in their common experience of the Organizing Academy and common commitment to organizing unionism. How successful this initiative has been it is difficult to gauge. At the point of graduation more than two-thirds of Academy Organizers agree that the Academy 'has generated a cross-union network of organizers' and it has undoubtedly helped generate an 'organizing current' among union officers and activists.[8] Attempts to institute a more formal network of organizers have come to naught, however, and, again, over time it may be that pressures to conform and to develop careers lead to the employing union, rather than fellow organizers, becoming the primary focus of identification.

The goal of the TUC has been to transfer the organizing model to the UK and ensure that as many UK unions as possible are exposed to and influenced by its elements. It is also possible to talk of diffusion within individual unions where it is the union's own leadership, or elements within it, which is promoting the organizing cause. 'Internal' diffusion of this kind has taken two main forms. The first can be labelled 'mainstreaming' and involves an attempt to spread a commitment to and knowledge of organizing broadly across the union's officers and activists. This can embrace communication and training initiatives and unions that have sponsored trainees at the Academy have generally reinforced their involvement through training programmes for full-time officers and shop stewards (Heery *et al.*, 2000b). It has also involved the use of performance management techniques. In a number of unions these have been targeted at the generalist full-time officer workforce which has been encouraged to identify organizing targets, formulate objectives and report results. Performance management can extend beyond the appraisal of individual officers, however, and in its most ambitious form has involved the development of planning and review procedures that are designed to promote organizing activity at each level of union organization. In UNISON, for example, recruitment targets have been formulated at the national, service, regional and branch levels of organization and at the lowest level there is an emphasis on identifying lay activists and stimulating participation (Waddington and Kerr, 2000: 250–4). 'Managed activism' of this kind is also apparent in GPMU, IPMS, ISTC and other unions, where branch and workplace audits are encouraged as a basis for strengthening membership and organization. The voluntary and formally democratic nature of unions as organizations means that performance management techniques of this kind are peculiarly dependent on willing cooperation and so are likely to be implemented unevenly across the union branch network. They represent an attempt, however, to translate the core element of the organizing model, reliance on collective organization as a basis for union membership, right across the union in a systematic fashion.

The second method of diffusion is specialization, which can be seen in the appointment and training of dedicated union organizers and the setting up of organizing units or departments. Involvement in the Academy is an example of this kind of initiative but several Academy unions have gone beyond sponsorship and have retained graduates in employment and appointed additional organizers, in some cases from Australia. The AEEU, Connect, CWU, GPMU, MSF, IPMS, ISTC, KFAT and TSSA are all unions that have established or expanded specialist organizing units in recent years. In some cases they have also created specialist lay organizer roles. The purpose of specialist units has been to allow the concentration of union resources for dedicated organizing campaigns, particularly where the union is seeking to extend membership to non-union employers. They have also served to shield organizers from the demands and, even hostility, of the remainder of the organization in order to ensure that they are not distracted from organizing work into routine servicing.

The use of specialist units has permitted experiment with an organizing approach and there is evidence from the Academy Organizer survey that, where trainee organizers have been placed in a specialist unit, their work has corresponded most closely to the organizing model. This can be seen in Table 3.4, which reports regression tests using the survey data. The tests employed two measures of organizing unionism. These were scale variables based on the organizers' reports of the methods they had used on organizing campaigns and the range of activities in which they were engaged during the twelve-month traineeship. The scales were designed to measure the application of organizing model techniques and the extent to which the trainees' work corresponded to a 'lead organizer' role, as opposed to that of a generalist full-time officer or a recruiter engaged in the direct recruitment of individual union members. The independent variables included placement in a specialist unit plus a number of controls relating to the individual characteristics (sex and age) and experience (background in union and non-labour activism) of Academy Organizers. Also included were measures of union organizing strategy and the extent to which the trainee had been involved in campaigns to extend union organization to non-union sites (expansion) and to women, the young and minorities (diversity).

The results indicate that organizer characteristics and union strategy are associated with application of the organizing model, the latter result confirming the findings in Table 3.3. Over and above these effects, however, placement in a specialist unit is associated at a statistically significant level, both with the use of organizing techniques and approximation to a lead organizer role. The latter association is particularly strong and it seems that Academy Organizers are most likely to get involved in identifying and researching organizing targets, planning campaigns, and recruiting, training and supporting activists where they work within the kind of specialist unit established by Connect, GPMU and ISTC. Elsewhere, their role tends to be narrower and they are used more as recruitment officers,

Table 3.4 Specialist organizing units and the diffusion of the organizing model

Variables	Descriptive statistics			Regression 1 Use of organizing techniques[10]		Regression 2 Lead organizer role[11]	
	Mean	SD	Alpha	Standardized coefficients[10]	T value	Standardized coefficients[11]	T value
Specialist unit[1]	–	–	–	.337***	(3.085)	.402***	(3.015)
Sex[2]	–	–	–	.016	(.150)	-.101	(.801)
Age[3]	2.39	1.09	–	-.124	(-1.156)	-.100	(-.767)
Union experience[4]	2.33	1.19	–	.271***	(2.471)	.096	(.713)
Non-union experience[5]	2.02	1.47	–	.025	(.229)	.092	(.701)
Expansion[6]	5.72	2.16	.90	.449***	(4.031)	.241*	(1.774)
Diversity[7]	17.66	3.81	.78	.385***	(3.610)	.276**	(2.117)
Organizing techniques[8]	4.91	2.38	.67				
Lead organizer role[9]	6.33	2.27	.73				

Source: Academy Organizer Survey

Notes on variables:

1   A dummy variable with placement in a specialist unit taking the value '1'; 63 per cent of trainees worked in a unit of this kind.
2   A dummy variable with female taking the value '1'; 57 per cent of trainees were women.
3   An ordinal variable with the following values: 1 (aged below 25), 2 (26–30), 3 (31–35), 4 (36–40), 5 (41+); 63 per cent of employees were aged 30 or less.
4   A count of the number of union roles (e.g. member, shop steward, full-time officer) each organizer had occupied before entering the Academy.
5   A count of the number of non-union social movements (e.g. womens' movement, community action) organizers had been involved in before entering the Academy.
6   A scale based on two items that gauge the extent to which organizers have been directed at the organizing of non-union sites.
7   A scale based on six items that measure the priority attached to organizing women, the young, part-timers, agency workers, temps and members of minorities.
8   A scale based on reports of the frequent use of thirteen techniques associated with the organizing model. These techniques are: setting membership targets; mapping the workplace; person-to-person recruitment; like-to-like recruitment; house calls; social events; grievance-based organizing; equality-based organizing; organizing committees; raising the union profile through 'actions'; link up with community organizations; corporate campaigns; media involvement.
9   A scale based on nine activities that constitute the 'lead organizer' role. The activities are: identifying organizing targets; researching targets; planning campaigns; preparing recruitment material; direct recruitment of members; recruitment of activists; encouraging activists to recruit; training activists in recruitment; promoting workplace organization.
10 F = 8.499; sig.000
    R² = .575
    Adjusted R² = .507
11 F = 3.632; sig.004
    R² = .366
    Adjusted R² = .265

N = 51; significance: * p < .10; ** p < .05; *** p < .01.

visiting workplaces, setting up in canteens and persuading individuals directly to join the union (Heery *et al.*, 2000b). Mainstreaming and specialization may work together, for example, where specialist organizers are used to develop greenfield campaigns while generalist officers and branches apply organizing techniques to strengthening membership and organization at sites where the union is established. Where mainstreaming is incomplete, however, the value of a specialist unit may be to preserve and sustain the experiment with organizing unionism.

Constraints on organizing

The diffusion of management practices is often incomplete, at least in part because they elicit resistance from workers, and even from managers themselves, whose interests are challenged (Yong and Wilkinson, 1999: 147–9). Change in trade unions is equally likely to generate opposition and, in addition, unions face a further obstacle in implementing strategic change; they are secondary organizations and successful innovation is in part dependent on their securing the cooperation of the employers of their members. In this section the response of employers to union organizing is not considered and, instead, there is a focus on the internal sources of opposition to organizing. The data, once again, are taken mainly from the TUC's Academy Organizers. These are a group of union officers charged with applying and largely committed to the organizing model and in our interviews and survey we tried to identify the main internal sources of opposition to organizing that they had encountered.

Three potential sources of internal opposition were considered: existing members and lay representatives, union full-time officers and the leadership of the union. The responses to survey items covering these sources of opposition are shown in Table 3.5, which also shows the responses to general questions on the level of union support for organizing. What is immediately striking in Table 3.5 is the fact that substantial percentages of Academy Organizers report a 'lack of support' or 'limited commitment' from each of the three groups specified. It is only union leaders who are not identified as an important problem faced in organizing by a majority of those surveyed. Moreover, while two-thirds agree that their sponsoring union is committed to organizing, only a minority of Academy Organizers deny there is a lack of support for organizing or that their sponsor places more emphasis on direct recruitment than on strengthening workplace organization. The latter is often seen as a litmus test of commitment to the organizing model among organizers themselves.

Why do lay activists, union officers and union leaders fail to support organizing, at least on occasion? The answer, suggested by the research, was that a strong commitment to organizing could contradict some of the primary interests of these groups. Those interests, and the response to organizing, varied, however, depending on the group examined. With regard to lay members and activists, there appeared to be two types of problem. The first arose from members whom Academy Organizers were seeking to draw into active participation in organizing campaigns. There could be striking success in this and we gathered numerous accounts of workers being drawn into activism in the manner proposed in the organizing model.

Table 3.5 Academy Organizers' reports of opposition to organizing

Statement	Opposition (%)		
Problem encountered while engaged in organizing activity in sponsoring union	Very important	Fairly important	Not important
Difficulty in identifying activists	15.4	51.9	32.7
Lack of commitment/experience of activists	30.8	55.8	13.5
Lack of support from lay officers	21.2	46.2	32.7
Lack of support from full-time officers	21.2	34.6	44.2
Limited commitment to organizing from the union leadership	21.2	21.2	57.7
Statement about sponsoring union	Agree/Str agree	Neutral	Disagree/ Str disagree
My sponsoring union is committed to organizing	65.4	21.2	13.2
There is a lack of support for organizing in my sponsoring union	22.6	34.0	43.4
My union emphasises recruitment not organizing	32.1	32.1	35.9

Source: Survey of Academy Organizers
Note: N = 52.

For a significant proportion of Academy Organizers, however, there were difficulties in identifying activists or securing anything but perfunctory participation: 'They're not willing to do stuff. They won't do very much, only so much', was how one organizer described his contacts in a campaign directed at airline workers. The reason for this was that activism can impose significant costs on workers, particularly where there is no established union tradition or where the employer is hostile. These costs include giving up free time, exposing oneself to possible hostility from co-workers and the risk of victimization. The latter should not be minimized and while the ruthless response of many US employers to union organizing has not been reproduced in the UK we gathered plentiful examples of victimization, up to and including summary dismissal. A significant constraint on the application of the organizing model, therefore, which is neglected in much of the organizing literature, is the limited enthusiasm of workers for activism.

The second type of problem associated with lay members was the lack of support for organizing among lay union officers who were not themselves directly involved in campaigns but who controlled resources. In a number of cases union branches and other lay committees blocked, undermined or simply failed to endorse union organizing activity involving Academy Organizers. Opposition arose for a number of reasons, including factional competition and resistance to interference by the wider union.[9] At its heart, however, lay the fact that for many lay officers from well-organized establishments the organizing of new groups of workers was just not a priority. Their focus was the union's internal political system and the needs of existing members and these had first claim on scarce resources. We encountered some impressive examples of solidarity with lay activists getting involved in organizing campaigns away from their own place of work. Activism in UK unions, however, is mainly directed inwards towards existing members at organized establishments and the result can be a lack of engagement with organizing: 'They tend to be conservative and concentrate on the existing members' one senior lay representative remarked of his colleagues.

Opposition was also reported from local full-time officers (FTOs) and a number of Academy Organizers complained that their coaches provided little support and had little knowledge and less sympathy with the norms of organizing unionism. For a number of senior union officers, too, local FTOs were something of a *bête noire* and were accused of resisting organizing because it threatened their prerogatives and members' dependence on their expertise. This is a common critique of union officers made by theorists of union bureaucracy (Smith, 1987: 295). However, earlier research has indicated that local FTOs generally encourage self-servicing workplace organization (Heery and Kelly, 1990) and the lack of support for the 'organizing model' appeared to originate in other factors. These included a belief that there was implied criticism of officer performance in the appointment of a fresh cohort of specialist organizers and resentment at increased management control and work intensification as a result of pressure to organize (see also Carter, 2000). There was also a mismatch between the skills and priorities of many local FTOs, which were directed at servicing the existing membership, and those of the new organizing agenda. While many FTOs have supported organizing, therefore, their primary accountability to existing members and their responsibility for operating the machinery of mature industrial relations have proved problematic for the diffusion of the organizing model.[10]

According to Academy Organizers the top leadership is the group that has been least opposed to organizing, contrary to the common assumption that this is the least innovative group within unions. Nevertheless a considerable proportion report that the commitment of senior union officers has been low. A possible explanation of this could be that senior union officers are wary of the militant, mobilizing current within 'organizing unionism' and its capacity to disrupt existing relationships with employers and government (Hyman, 1989: 85). There was some evidence for this. At least two unions withdrew from the Organizing Academy after its first year because they were out of sympathy with the style of organizing that was being promoted and a number of senior officers noted a potential tension between organizing and the TUC's espousal of labour–management partnership. A much stronger explanation, however, was the pressure on union leaders from their executives to ensure that investment in Academy Organizers was recouped relatively quickly through increased member subscriptions. The need to demonstrate relatively short-term success had led in some unions to the deployment of organizers as travelling recruiters, directly recruiting individual members with only limited regard to the encouragement of workplace activism. An associated response was to concentrate recruitment at recognized sites and neglect greenfield organizing. This was not a majority pattern and most Academy Organizers denied that they had been allocated fixed recruitment targets (78 per cent) and reported involvement in greenfield campaigns (85 per cent). Nevertheless the interest of union leaders in maintaining the finances of their organizations could lead to a less than full application of the organizing model.

Of course, not all lay activists, local FTOs or union leaders were out of sympathy with the organizing model and the shared interest of all groups in the renewal of unions provided fairly broad-based support. Analysis of the problems encountered by Academy Organizers, however, points to real constraints on the revitalization of the labour movement through application of the organizing model. The latter involves a shift in union resources from existing to potential members, from generalist servicing officers to specialist organizing officers and from short-term to long-term investment. As such, it is likely to be resisted, either covertly or openly, by those groups within unions who carry the costs. One implication is that if unions are to continue to pursue an organizing agenda they must insulate the policy from those who are likely to resist. This could be, and seemingly is being, achieved through the development of a specialist organizing function within unions. More controversially perhaps it might also require centralization so that resources can be concentrated and re-allocated from representing workers with an established union tradition to organizing the unorganized.

Conclusion

In the field of employment relations globalization tends to be viewed as an external, economic force that undermines established national systems of worker representation (Giles, 2000). The response of trade unions that has attracted the interest of researchers has been the development of international trade unionism as a means of countering the global reach of business and securing an element of international regulation of the employment relationship. Researchers differ in their assessment of the effectiveness of this response but they have shared a common object of study, the institutions of the international labour movement and cross-national union cooperation within large multinational enterprises (Ramsay, 1999). However, globalization has another meaning to do with time–space compression and the increasing interconnectedness of different national societies. It is this meaning that has informed our research. We have been concerned with the interconnection of national labour movements and the diffusion of an international model of good union practice, the organizing model that has circulated via bilateral contact between national union centres. This aspect of international trade unionism has been largely neglected in the past and in our opinion this is regrettable. Attempts to learn deliberately from overseas appear to be a pronounced feature of the union scene in a number of countries at present and are a relatively benign feature of the process of globalization.

The empirical research on the transfer of the organizing model to the UK has generated a number of findings that parallel results from research into the diffusion of business practices. Trade unions in the UK have proved to be relatively receptive to the organizing model, partly because they face a particularly acute problem of decline but also because the institutional structure of industrial relations provides a powerful incentive for unions to organize. These structural features include the decentralization of collective bargaining, which puts a premium on effective workplace organization, and an absence of strong institutional supports for trade unionism, which requires unions to generate internal sources of power. Within the UK labour movement, however, it is not structural features that appear to explain receptiveness to the organizing model. Rather, it is aspects of the strategy of individual unions. Where unions are committed to expanding their job territory, they have been anxious to learn and apply new methods and have become involved in networks established for the diffusion of new organizing techniques.

With regard to the process of diffusion the research has generated two main findings. The first is the identification of the key role played by the TUC and its sister organizations in other countries, in facilitating the transfer of the organizing model. In national systems characterized by an absence of, or weak, arrangements for social partnership, the promotion of organizing seems to have become a new distinctive competence for central union confederations. The second is the role played by organizational change and the setting up of specialist units in diffusing organizing within individual unions. Practice on the ground appears to conform most closely to the organizing model where organizers are concentrated in a specialist unit and can draw upon the support and expertise of co-workers who are similarly committed to and trained in the norms of organizing unionism.

The importance of specialization is underlined by our final set of results. While there is broad support in UK unions for the new emphasis on organizing, there is also opposition. This can come from members wary of the costs of activism, lay officers whose priority is the existing membership, paid officers whose skills and systems of accountability stress member servicing and union leaders under pressure to deliver rapid results from investment. At the heart of this opposition lies a pressing problem for UK trade unions: how to invest in organizing and extend membership to the growing population of non-union establishments when there is pressure to represent and improve servicing of the existing membership. Balancing competing pressures in this way is particularly difficult for representative, formally democratic institutions like trade unions, especially for those in the UK that are loosely structured and have a tradition of relatively autonomous branch and workplace organization. The solution suggested by the research is to bifurcate union structure and develop a specialist organizing function. Organizational change and the commitment and concentration of specialist resources are seemingly the precondition for the further diffusion of the organizing model in the UK.

Notes

1 The research was funded in the first place by a small grant from the Nuffield Foundation and subsequently by a larger grant from Cardiff University. The authors would like to thank both providers of finance for their support and acknowledge the unrivalled cooperation received from the TUC and those unions that have participated in its Organizing Academy.

2 Between 1980 and 1995 the UK experienced an 18 per cent decline in union density, the third heaviest amongst the OECD countries and, in Europe, only Portugal registered a sharper drop (34 per cent). Despite this decline the UK's rank order for union density dropped from only 10th to 11th within the OECD (Brown *et al.*, 1997: 74).

3 In countries with centralized systems of bargaining, union effectiveness is less dependent on levels of membership in individual enterprises and in Germany, France and other European countries there is a notable divergence between the level of union density and coverage by collective bargaining (Adams, 1995: 78). The movement towards bargaining decentralization in these countries, however, may prompt greater interest in organizing unionism in the future. Turner (1998) gives the example of Digital in Germany, a company which does not abide by industry agreements, and where union influence has been developed through the kind of rank and file organizing strategy advocated by supporters of the organizing model. There is no indication in this case, however, of the German union involved, IG Metall, deliberately seeking to apply US organizing tactics.

4 This is a notable contrast with the countries of Western Europe where state support for trade unions remains generally high and where industry bargaining, extension procedures and statutory works councils provide for a high level of union security.

5 The number of cases and the need to keep to a minimum the number of missing values limits the number of independent variables that can be included in the model.

6 We witnessed a policy meeting at the TUC where this very point was described. The subject under discussion was the need to further diffuse organizing unionism in the face of union apathy. One person described the situation in the GPMU and said that the presentation of 'scary graphs' to union officers showing the consequences of continuing decline had been vital in promoting change. This was countered, however, by the argument that people rapidly became inured to warnings of disaster and that a more sophisticated diffusion strategy was necessary.

7 An organizer from the ISTC described a visit to an organizing campaign in the USA where he saw a young Latino woman, 'a young lass', who had 'big, hairy-arsed steelworkers eating out of her hand'. He was persuaded at this point that the same organizing methods, using the same kind of dedicated lead organizer, ought to be applied in the UK.

8 This is particularly apparent at large organizing events, such as the TUC's Organize 2000 conference, which in certain respects take the form of a gathering of the organizing clan within the UK union movement.

9 The results of a statistical analysis not reported here indicated that, after controlling for a range of variables, women and younger organizers were more likely to report an absence of lay support. Those who do not conform to traditional expectations of what a union officer should be like are seemingly most likely to encounter membership opposition (see also Pocock, 1998).

10 It was notable that Academy Organizers with coaches who were themselves specialist organizers were significantly less likely to report a lack of officer support for organizing.

References

Adams, R.J. (1995) *Industrial Relations under Liberal Democracy*, Columbia, South Carolina: University of South Carolina Press.

Batstone, E., Boraston, I. and Frenkel, S. (1977) *Shop Stewards in Action: The Organization of Workplace Conflict and Accommodation*, Oxford: Basil Blackwell.

Boxall, P. and Haynes, P. (1997) 'Strategy and Trade Union Effectiveness in a Neo-liberal Environment', *British Journal of Industrial Relations* 35(4): 567–91.

Bronfenbrenner, K. (1997) 'The Role of Union Strategies in NLRB Certification Elections', *Industrial and Labor Relations Review* 50(2): 195–212.

Bronfenbrenner, K. and Juravich, T. (1998) 'It Takes More than House-calls; Organising to Win with a Comprehensive Union-building Strategy', in K. Bronfenbrenner, S. Friedman, R.W. Hurd, R.A. Oswald and R.I. Seeber (eds) *Organizing to Win: New Research on Labor Strategies*, Ithaca, NY: ILR Press.

Brown, W. (2000) 'Putting Partnership into Practice in Britain', *British Journal of Industrial Relations* 38(2): 299–316.

Brown, W., Deakin, S., Nash, D. and Oxenbridge, S. (2000) 'The Employment Contract: from Collective Procedures to Individual Rights', *British Journal of Industrial Relations*, 38(4): 611–29.

Brown, W., Deakin, S. and Ryan, P. (1997) 'The Effects of British Industrial Relations Legislation 1979–97', *National Institute of Economic and Social Research Review* 161: 69–83.

Carter, B. (2000) 'Adoption of the Organising Model in British Trade Unions: Some Evidence from Manufacturing, Science and Finance (MSF)', *Work, Employment and Society* 14(1): 117–36.

Claydon, T. (1996) 'Union Derecognition: A Re-examination', in I. Beardwell (ed.) *Contemporary Industrial Relations: A Critical Analysis*, Oxford: Oxford University Press.

Cooper, R. (2000) 'Organise, Organise, Organise! ACTU Congress 2000', *Journal of Industrial Relations* 42(4): 582–94.

Crouch, C. (1999) *Social Change in Western Europe*, Oxford: Oxford University Press.

Daly, A. (1999) 'The Hollowing Out of French Unions: Politics and Industrial Relations after 1981', in A. Martin and G. Ross (eds) *The Brave New World of European Labor*, New York and Oxford: Berghahn Books.

DiMaggio, P.J. and Powell, W.W. (1991) 'The Iron Cage Revisited: Institutional Isomorphism and Collective Rationality', in W.W. Powell and P.J. DiMaggio (eds) *The New Institutionalism in Organizational Analysis*, Chicago: University of Chicago Press.

Elger, T. and Smith, C. (1994) 'Global Japanization? Convergence and Competition in the Organization of the Labour Process', in T. Elger and C. Smith (eds) *Global Japanization? The Transnational Transformation of the Labour Process*, London: Routledge.

Fujimura, H. (1997) 'New Unionism: Beyond Enterprise Unionism?', in M. Sako and H. Sato (eds) *Japanese Labour and Management in Transition*, London: Routledge.

Gall, G. (2000) 'In Place of Strife?', *People Management* 14 September: 26–30.

Giles, A. (2000) 'Globalization and industrial relations theory', *Journal of Industrial Relations* 42(2): 173–94.

Heery, E. (1998) 'The Re-launch of the Trades Union Congress', *British Journal of Industrial Relations* 36(3): 339–60.

Heery, E. and Kelly, J. (1990) 'Full-time Officers and the Shop Steward Network: Patterns of Co-operation and Interdependence', in P. Fosh and E. Heery (eds) *Trade Unions and their Members*, Basingstoke and London: Macmillan.

Heery, E., Simms, M., Simpson, D., Delbridge, R. and Salmon, J. (2000a) 'Organising Unionism Comes to the UK', *Employee Relations* 22(1): 38–57.

Heery, E., Simms, M., Delbridge, R., Salmon, J. and Simpson, D. (2000b) 'The TUC's Organizing Academy: An Assessment', *Industrial Relations Journal* 31(5): 400–15.

Hurd, R.W. (1998) Contesting the Dinosaur Image: The Labor Movement's Search for a Future', *Labor Studies Journal* 23(4): 5–30.

Hyman, R. (1989) *Strikes*, 4th edn, Basingstoke and London: Macmillan.

Hyman, R. (1997) 'Trade Unions and Interest Representation in the Context of Globalization', *Transfer* 3: 515–33.

Jacoby, S.M. (1995) 'Social Dimensions of Global Economic Integration', in S.M. Jacoby (ed.) *The Workers of Nations: Industrial Relations in a Global Economy*, Oxford: Oxford University Press.

Katz, H. and Darbishire, O. (2000) *Converging Divergences: Worldwide Changes in Employment Systems*, Ithaca, NY and London: ILR Press.

Kelly, J. (1996) 'Union Militancy and Social Partnership', in P. Ackers, C. Smith and P. Smith (eds) *The New Workplace and Trade Unionism*, London: Routledge.

Kelly, J. (1997) 'Challenges to Trade Unionism in Britain and Europe', *Work, Employment and Society* 11(2): 373–6.

Kelly, J. (1998) *Rethinking Industrial Relations: Mobilization, Collectivism and Long Waves*, London: Routledge.

MacDuffie, J.P. (1995) 'Human Resource Bundles and Manufacturing Performance: Organizational Logic and Flexible Production in the World Auto Industry', *Industrial and Labor Relations Review* 48 (2): 197–221.

Mahon, R. (1999) 'Yesterday's Modern Times Are No Longer Modern: Swedish Unions Confront the Double Shift', in A. Martin and G. Ross (eds) *The Brave New World of European Labor*, London and New York: Berghahn Books.

Murray, G., Lévesque, C. and Vallée, G. (2000) 'The Re-regulation of Labour in a Global Context: Conceptual Vignettes from Canada', *Journal of Industrial Relations* 42(2): 234–57.

Nissen, B. (1999) 'Introduction', in B. Nissen (ed.) *Which Direction for Organized Labor?*, Detroit: Wayne State University Press.

Oxenbridge, S. (1997) 'Organising Strategies and Organising Reform in New Zealand Service Sector Unions', *Labor Studies Journal* 22(3): 3–27.

Oxenbridge, S. (2000) *Trade Union Organising among Low-wage Service Workers: Lessons from America and New Zealand*, ESRC Centre for Business Research, Working Paper 160, Cambridge: University of Cambridge.

Pfeffer, J. (1994) *Competitive Advantage through People: Unleashing the Power of the Workforce*, Boston: Harvard Business School Press.

Pocock, B. (1998) 'Institutional Sclerosis: Prospects for Trade Union Transformation', *Labour and Industry* 9(1): 17–36.

Ramsay, H. (1999) 'In Search of International Union Theory', in J. Waddington (ed.) *Globalisation and Patterns of Labour Resistance*, London and New York: Mansell.

Ross, G. and Martin, A. (1999) 'Through a Glass Darkly', in A. Martin and G. Ross (eds) *The Brave New World of European Labor*, New York and Oxford: Berghahn Books.

Silvia, S.J. (1999) 'Every Which Way but Loose: German Industrial Relations Since 1980', in A. Martin and G. Ross (eds) *The Brave New World of European Labor*, London and New York: Berghahn Books.

Smith, C. (1987) *Technical Workers: Class, Labour and Trade Unionism*, Basingstoke and London: Macmillan.

Smith, C. and Meiksins, P. (1995) 'System, Society and Dominance Effects in Cross-national Organisational Analysis', *Work, Employment and Society* 9(2): 241–67.

Streeck, W. (1991) 'More Uncertainties: German Unions facing 1992', *Industrial Relations* 30(3): 317–49.

Turner, L. (1998) 'Rank-and-file Participation in Organising at Home and Abroad', in K. Bronfenbrenner, S. Friedman, R.W. Hurd, R.A. Oswald and R.L. Seeber (eds) *Organizing to Win: New Research on Union Strategies*, Ithaca, NY and London: ILR Press.

Waddington, J. (1999) 'Situating Labour within the Globalization Debate', in J. Waddington (ed.) *Globalization and Patterns of Labour Resistance*, London: Mansell.

Waddington, J. (2000) 'Towards a Reform Agenda? European Trade Unions in Transition', *Industrial Relations Journal* 31(4): 317–30.

Waddington, J. and Kerr, A. (2000) 'Towards an Organising Model in UNISON? A Trade Union Membership Strategy in Transition', in M. Terry (ed.) *Redefining Public Sector Unionism: UNISON and the Future of Trade Unions*, London: Routledge.

Wood, S. and Godard, J. (1999) 'The Statutory Recognition Procedure in the Employment Relations Bill: A Comparative Analysis', *British Journal of Industrial Relations* 37(2): 203–45.

Yong, J. and Wilkinson, A. (1999) 'The State of Total Quality Management: A Review', *International Journal of Human Resource Management* 10 (1): 137–61.

4 The impact of ownership change on industrial relations, jobs and employees' terms and conditions

Nicholas Bacon and Paul Blyton

Introduction

The increasing globalization of production raises potentially profound issues for workers and trade unions. At both company and workplace level managers are translating the pressures of globalization into programmes aimed at changing terms and conditions, industrial relations and work organization. When confronted by these changes and the underlying rapid increases in trade and technological change, traditional institutions such as national governments and trade unions often appear unable to influence events. For workers increasingly concerned over their incomes and job security, the central issue is to what extent globalization is exerting a downward pressure on their terms and conditions in what has been termed 'a race to the bottom' (Lee, 1996, 1997). Although the International Labour Organization generally takes a positive view of globalization as promoting efficiency and enabling high productivity, high wage jobs (ILO, 1998), as yet it is difficult to assess whether a 'race to the bottom' is occurring and there have been calls for more empirical evidence on changing working conditions (Lee, 1997: 182). For trade unions seeking to represent these workers, the challenge is to maintain or establish effective industrial relations structures to influence increasingly global companies. Trade unions also face the prospect of negotiating the introduction of new working methods as globalization also involves the potential for an increased rate of transfer of the most productive forms of working.

The aim of this chapter is to contribute some empirical evidence by exploring whether the iron and steel industry is witnessing a 'race to the bottom' on employees' terms and conditions as a result of globalization. We report systematic evidence on how aspects of globalization are affecting terms and conditions, industrial relations and work organization. In particular, we consider the impact of ownership and recent changes in ownership in the industry, including the increased ownership of facilities by foreign companies.

Globalization and labour relations

'Globalization' is generally measured subjectively (Makhija *et al.*, 1997) and encapsulates many different aspects of change, notably: structural changes in trade, economics, products and technology; the decline of national and regional state regulation, often involving privatization; the emergence of international or global companies; and different recipes for restructuring organizations. In this way, globalization is a summary term for a set of inter-related changes rather than a single development. The multi-faceted character of the changes occurring under the label of globalization makes it difficult to unravel the precise effects of the different elements for trade unions and their members. One outcome has been that it has become commonplace to assume that the changes taking place lie beyond the influence of individual companies, governments or trade unions, and to attribute almost any change to 'globalization'. Furthermore, authors who have been termed 'globalization sceptics' (Radice, 1999) argue that the extent of globalization has been overplayed (Hirst and Thompson, 1996) and others maintain that regional internationalization is a more accurate description than globalization (Kleinknecht and terWengel, 1998).

There is widespread apprehension that globalization will result in a continued shake-out of jobs (especially in higher wage economies) downward pressure on terms and conditions and attacks on collective bargaining. In addition, there is evidence that aspects of globalization such as trade liberalization fuel increasing wage inequalities by reducing the relative wage of unskilled workers in developed countries who find themselves in direct competition with workers in low-wage economies (Dinopoulos and Segerstrom, 1999). International companies can drive this process by organizing production facilities on an increasingly international scale, and thereby gain new opportunities to transfer production (or at least threaten to do so) from less to more profitable sites. Companies are also in a stronger position to make direct comparisons between plants and make plant survival and new investment dependent upon trade unions accepting certain new demands, such as restricting wage claims or guaranteeing greater effort and flexibility.

In studies of specific sectors, for example civil aviation, there is evidence that globalization exerts 'an adverse effect on terms and conditions of employment and the experience of work' (Blyton *et al.*, 1998: 25). However, in general, even where cheap labour is an important factor, it is not the only factor that companies consider when locating production. One study of globalization of the footwear industry, for example, revealed that although companies in this sector are thought to be involved in a 'ceaseless search for cheap and amenable labour', successful performance depended upon a wide range of features (Lowder, 1999). A further study across a range of economic sectors discovered trade and direct investment had little impact on income distribution (Mahler *et al.*, 1999).

The extent to which these fears over employees' terms and conditions will be realized is not yet clear and there may be countervailing tendencies. For example, globalization also involves an increasing pace of technological change with technology transfer from foreign-owned firms (Barrell and Pain, 1997). This involves not just equipment change but also new developments in how work is organized. Although such changes make many demands upon workers, wages in those industries characterized by higher rates of technological change are also traditionally higher (Bartel and Sicherman, 1999). Additionally, in a comparative study of Mexico, Venezuela and the United States, Aitken *et al.* (1996) discovered that higher levels of foreign direct investment (FDI) were associated with higher wages, although there was no evidence of wage spill-over leading to higher wages in domestic firms in two of these countries.

The industrial relations implications of globalization are equally difficult to unravel, though it is generally assumed that companies will be increasingly reluctant to let trade unions affect major change. It is suggested that world market integration reduces union power (Boswell and Stevis, 1997) with national unions increasingly competing directly with each other for capital investment from global companies (Haworth and Ramsay, 1986). In the main, we might also expect companies investing abroad to seek low-wage and union-free regions. One recent study that focused on the effects of FDI on industrial relations discovered that investment was lower where government restrictions on laying off workers were stronger, union density was higher and collective bargaining was centralized at industry level (Cooke and Noble, 1998). Similarly, Zhao (1998) has argued that FDI reduces the negotiated wage when labour–management bargaining is industry-wide. However, Cooke and Noble (1998) also discovered that FDI was greater in high-skill high-wage countries, countries that ratified ILO standards and those that had works councils. In a comparison of three countries, Frenkel and Peetz (1998) argue that although globalization generated a general pressure for labour flexibility, the outcome depended upon societal factors including the influence trade unions were able to exert. Similarly, Levesque and Murray (1998) maintain that local unions can still influence management under favourable conditions. In their study of 210 local unions in Quebec, unions with both high and low exposure to the international economy could influence workplace change, although they conclude that 'exposed' unions also need to draw upon support and expertise from a wider labour movement.

The impact of other features of globalization, for example privatization which has reduced both the political regulation and the national focus of companies, also indicate a more complex mixture of effects than that portrayed by a 'race to the bottom'. In some countries, for example the UK, privatization has certainly included explicit industrial relations aims involving reducing public sector pay settlements and encouraging a shake-out of labour that suggest a downward path. Evidence to date, however, indicates that although privatization has involved reduced employment, it also involves rising average incomes and little fundamental change to industrial relations institutions albeit with some decentralization of collective bargaining (D'Souza and Megginson, 1999; Pendleton, 1997).

In sum, the evidence reviewed thus far raises more questions than it provides satisfactory answers. To explore these issues further we address several questions in this chapter using the iron and steel industry as a sectoral focus. First, what are the main trends in terms and conditions, industrial relations and work organization in the iron and steel sector as it becomes a global industry? Second, are there significant differences according to the ownership of steel plants? Third, what is the effect of privatization? And fourth, what impact does foreign ownership have? Before we examine the findings of the study we will discuss globalization in the iron and steel industry and outline our research methods.

Globalization in the iron and steel industry

A major feature of globalization in the steel industry is the changing ownership of steel facilities. This can take such forms as privatization, acquisition or joint ventures. The changes also involve a reduction in the domestic ownership of the steel industry and the (albeit gradual) rise of international steel companies. Traditionally, steel companies have not invested heavily overseas nor relocated in large numbers to low-wage locations. Such moves were deterred by widespread state ownership, high transportation costs and the enormous sunk capital costs involved that made it difficult to exit from existing operations (Aylen, 1988). All three of these factors have become less important in recent years. First, privatization has become widespread in the steel industry. State-owned companies controlled one-quarter of world crude steel capacity in 1986; by 1995 this had shrunk to 15 per cent and has continued to fall subsequently. Privatization has been particularly prevalent in Latin America, Western and Eastern Europe. The public sector share in developing countries fell from two-thirds in 1986 to 45 per cent in 1995. In Latin America, for example, 95 per cent of steelworks have been privatized since 1990. Such dramatic changes might be expected to have a significant impact upon steel trade unions and their members as state subsidies for the protection of terms and conditions are removed. Privatization also releases companies from operating within national borders and enables future cross-national mergers and alliances.

Second, falling transport costs for intermediate steels between plants now make up only a fraction of the sale price. For example, the stainless steel manufacturer, Avesta, transfers steel between processes from plants in Sweden to the UK at a return cost of only around £12 per tonne (approximately 1 per cent of its sale value).

Third, technological changes are making steel a less capital-intensive industry and are accelerating the pace of geographical and structural change (D'Costa, 1999). 'Mini-mills' have taken over one-third of the US steel market away from larger integrated steel producers. Mini-mills are small efficient steel producers that use electric arc furnaces to melt scrap and have significant advantages in terms of lower labour and capital construction costs (Crandall, 1996). Although the European Community's Manifest Crisis policies of production quotas in the 1980s hindered the growth of mini-mills (Moore, 1998) such powers will be lost with the end of the Treaty of Paris in 2002. A widely held belief is that, compared to integrated plants, mini-mills combine greater workforce flexibility, lower pay rates, decentralized decision-making and are more likely to be non-union (Konzelmann Smith, 1995). Not only are these features of mini-mills of direct concern to trade unions representing mini-mill workers but they also threaten to drag down terms and conditions in integrated sites. The threat to trade unions – that some of these features will spread beyond the mini-mill sector – appears likely as an increasing number of senior executives of steel companies gain their formative experience in non-union mini-mills. For example, by 1989, almost half (47 per cent) of the total output of the Italian steel industry was managed by former mini-mill entrepreneurs. Mini-mill entrepreneurs heading companies such as Riva and Lucchini have built up companies to rank among the largest steel producers in the world.

Steel-makers are likely eventually to reflect the approach of the motor industry with a reduced number of manufacturing groups and production on a world-wide scale. Already, steel companies are pursuing innovative trans-national alliances, aggressive purchasing, increased overseas investment and mergers to create a less nationally-based steel industry. The pace of these trends should not be exaggerated, however. The steel industry is not yet truly global. There are as yet no significant steel companies operating fully on a multinational basis, and national steel companies continue to largely dominate and supply home markets (Bacon and Blyton, 1996). Nevertheless, the strategies being adopted by leading steel companies are acting to reduce the traditional role of national governments and the responsibilities felt by steel companies towards traditional steel areas. The implications of these developments are central to trade union responses to globalization.

Methodology

To gather the necessary information, a series of questionnaire surveys were dispatched during 1998 with the final returns in early 1999. The surveys were designed by the authors of this chapter but were translated, dispatched and returned to the International Metalworkers Federation (IMF) in Geneva. In total, the survey involved three different questionnaires, aimed separately at national unions, together with samples of both integrated steel plants (where steel-making involves the conversion of steel from iron) and mini-mills (where scrap steel is the feedstock for steel production) represented by each IMF affiliate. The use of employee representatives as respondents is a useful counter-weight to potential employer-response bias in surveys where access is controlled by management and thus participating firms are 'probably better-than-average employers' (Appelbaum *et al.*, 2000: 21).

Data from thirty countries were collected.[1] A total of thirty-nine national trade unions completed questionnaires along with responses from ninety-two integrated sites and forty-eight mini-mills. Due to the way the samples were created (affiliates to the International Metalworkers' Federation) and the nature of the respondents to the survey (national union officials and local union representatives), all sites in the survey recognized trade unions. While this excludes responses from those parts of the sector which remain non-union (particularly part of the mini-mill sector) overall, the iron and steel industry remains a highly unionized one, thereby minimizing the bias effects of collecting data solely from unionized plants.

The surveys covered a number of areas including markets, production, ownership structure, technological change, industrial relations and work organization. Though the final picture is inevitably incomplete, nevertheless these surveys represent the largest and most detailed of their kind ever undertaken in this sector. We begin by describing the overall findings in respect to changes in terms and conditions, industrial relations and work organization.

Results

Changes in terms and conditions

The main threat posed by globalization for labour is that it will act to drive down the basic terms of workers' contracts and lead to a deterioration in work conditions (Lee, 1996). A useful place to begin the analysis therefore is to explore reported recent changes in the terms and conditions of steelworkers. Table 4.1 provides an overall assessment of changes in terms and conditions by union officers within national unions and at plant level over the previous five years. The picture is a mixed one and does not support a simple 'race to the bottom' interpretation. For while there are widespread reports of increased workloads, subcontracting, redundancies, job insecurity and to a lesser extent job dissatisfaction, there are also reported increases in training and skills. At the same time, many terms and conditions, such as holiday and pension provisions appear largely unchanged.

Nature of industrial relations

The overall industrial relations trends are presented in Table 4.2. Respondents indicate that the structural integration of unions into a partnership with management has developed in many plants (for a description see Mangum and McNabb, 1997) although for significant minorities of sites there are signs that trade unions are less secure (reflected, for example in those reporting threats to de-recognize or reduce the union's health and safety role).

Table 4.1 The changing experience of work reported by national unions and plant-level unions over the previous five years (%)

	National (N = 39)			Plant level (N = 140)		
	Increased	*Same*	*Decreased*	*Increased*	*Same*	*Decreased*
Work loads	83	11	6	66	16	16
Subcontracting of jobs	73	19	8	47	37	16
Skills levels	70	27	3	62	33	5
Training	43	38	19	58	32	10
Number of redundancies	46	31	23	35	32	33
Earning power	30	38	32	46	27	27
Pension provision	28	66	6	22	57	21
Accidents	31	30	39	29	25	46
Occupational illness	25	44	31	23	48	29
Job satisfaction	22	40	38	17	51	32
Hours of work	19	65	16	26	56	18
Job security	14	35	51	29	38	33
Holidays	8	92	0	13	84	3

Table 4.2 Industrial relations practices and climate reported by plant-level unions

Industrial relations practice	%
Managers attach a lot of importance to agreements with unions	78
Unions involved strategically at plant level	77
Management value employees	65
Unions trust management	65
Co-operation rather than conflict typifies union–management relations	53
Change depends on agreement	42
Threat of union de-recognition a problem	36
Worker representatives on main board	29
Attempts to reduce role of unions in health and safety	25
More agreements reached at plant level than five years ago	18*

Notes: N = 140
*Figure for this item represents integrated sites only.

Changes in work organization

As global integration increases, the search for the most productive working practices becomes a world-wide phenomenon. In response to unstable market conditions and as a further attempt to cut costs, many employers have sought increased flexibility in the numbers of workers they employ through a greater use of non-standard contracts. As Table 4.3 indicates, seven out of ten of all plants surveyed reported increases in the last five years of employees on fixed term contracts and contract employees.

Table 4.3 Percentage of plants reporting numbers of employees increasing by contract type in past five years

Contact type	Yes	No
Workers on fixed-term contracts	72	28
Number of contractors	70	30
Part-time employees	26	74
Casual workers	14	86

Note: N = 140

To assess further the extent to which working practices have been restructured, a number of 'high involvement' work practices were examined (Table 4.4). High involvement work practices are those designed to increase the flexibility and commitment of employees to their work and there is some debate as to whether they are also associated with increased levels of effort and stress (Appelbaum *et al.*, 2000). Twelve high involvement work practices were measured to assess the extent to which these had spread deeply into workplaces (taken to be whether these work practices applied to over 50 per cent of the employees they would affect). The resulting picture is one of a high level of adoption of the various practices

Table 4.4 Percentage of plants reporting high involvement work practices applied to over 50 per cent of employees

Work practice	Proportion of plants with the practice (%)
Responsibility for quality resting with the shop-floor	73
Foremen or team leaders working in production	72
Employee job descriptions that are flexible and not fixed to one specific task	70
Smaller unit crews with larger activity ranges	61
A just in time production system	59
Employees organized into teams to solve problems and discuss performance, sometimes called quality circles	57
Employees organized into work groups or teams to supervise their own work	56
Maintenance tasks integrated into production jobs	56
Production teams including skilled maintenance workers	53
Reduction in the layers of management	52
Employee participation schemes	50
Operators involved in decisions regarding major changes in process technology or equipment	41

Note: N = 140

across the steel plants and countries studied. Only one of the practices fell below the level of half the establishments having adopted the practice for a majority of employees.

The impact of ownership

If ownership matters, it should be possible to detect different trends in steel plants according to the nature of their ownership. In assessing the impact of ownership and ownership change we will concentrate on the sample of integrated plants. Among the present sample of integrated plants: 16 per cent were state-owned; 47 per cent were privately owned by one domestic company; 15 per cent were privately owned by one overseas company; 5 per cent were privately owned not quoted; 17 per cent were part-state and part-privately owned; 10 per cent were joint ventures between domestic companies; 14 per cent were joint ventures between domestic and overseas companies; and 2 per cent were joint ventures between overseas companies.[2]

Making a simple assessment by comparing the extent to which terms and conditions had improved or deteriorated in integrated sites under different ownership conditions suggests no marked variation due to ownership (Table 4.5). Four common trends were most prominent, with a significant majority of plants in each ownership category reporting increases occurring in: training, skills, workloads and the amount of subcontracting. From this evidence, it appears no longer the case that state ownership provides any particular benefit to terms and conditions that is not equally likely to be found (or be absent) under other ownership conditions.

Table 4.5 Changes to terms and conditions at integrated sites reported by ownership (means and standard deviations)

	State owned N = 14	Domestically owned N = 42	Overseas owned N = 11	State/ private N = 15	Joint venture domestic cos. N = 9	Joint venture domestic/ overseas N = 13
Earning power	2.0 (1.04)	2.33 (.79)	2.09 (.83)	2.13 (.83)	.44 (.88)	2.15 (.80)
Hours of work	1.93 (.48)	2.02 (.64)	2.0 (.82)	2.13 (.62)	2.25 (.47)	1.92 (.49)
Holidays	2.07 (.27)	2.09 (.43)	2.09 (.7)	2.06 (.25)	2.11 (.33)	1.85 (.36)*
Accidents	2.14 (.95)*	1.54 (.83)	2.09 (.94)	2.13 (.89)	1.56 (.88)	1.15 (.38)*
Occupational illness	2.14 (.86)	1.95 (.8)	1.64 (.51)	1.93 (.70)	1.56 (.73)	1.46 (.66)*
Training	2.5 (.76)	2.47 (.67)	2.73 (.47)	2.69 (.48)	2.44 (.53)	2.62 (.65)
Pension provision	2.0 (.56)	2.19 (.66)	2.09 (.54)	2.07 (.59)	2.22 (.67)	2.09 (.54)
Redundancies	1.85 (.8)	2.22 (.88)	2.09 (.7)	2.0 (.79)	2.33 (.87)	1.69 (.86)
Job security	2.15 (.69)	1.77 (.81)	1.91 (.83)	1.87 (.52)	1.67 (.71)	1.92 (.76)
Skill levels	2.43 (.51)	2.55 (.71)	2.91 (.3)	2.5 (.52)	2.44 (.73)	2.83 (.39)
Work loads	2.39 (.65)	2.81 (.55)*	2.55 (.82)	2.47 (.74)	2.44 (.88)	2.77 (.60)
Job satisfaction	2.0 (.79)	1.72 (.7)	1.82 (.75)	1.93 (.59)	1.89 (.6)	1.77 (.60)
Subcontracting	2.21 (.7)	2.47 (.74)	2.18 (.75)	2.07 (.7)	2.11 (.93)	2.31 (.75)

Notes: All terms and conditions measured on a three-point scale (increased = 3, same = 2, decreased = 1).
* p < 0.05, t-test comparison of means (single ownership category compared to the combined remainder).
N = 140

There were few statistically significant differences between plants according to ownership on most aspects of industrial relations, all forms of flexible contracts and the incidence of high involvement work practices. The aspect of industrial relations that did vary was level of bargaining. In a detailed question about the main level for negotiating agreements on a range of thirteen terms and conditions, the most distinct plants were state-owned and domestic joint ventures (Tables 4.6 and 4.7). State-owned plants were more likely to negotiate earnings, job guarantees, investment and new technology at local levels. Domestic joint ventures were more likely to negotiate holidays, pensions and a minimum wage at local levels, but negotiate health and safety and training at a higher level.

Table 4.6 Ownership and level of negotiations at integrated plants: the impact of state ownership

| | State-owned (N = 11) | | Not state-owned (N = 50) | | |
	mean	*SD*	*mean*	*SD*	*t-test*
Earnings	1.73	1.0	2.62	1.51	−1.86*
Job guarantees	1.22	1.09	2.25	1.45	−2.44**
Investment	1.18	1.08	2.0	1.44	−2.7**
New technology	0.9	0.98	1.75	1.28	−2.37**

Notes: Not covered by agreements = 0, plant level = 1, business/division of company = 2, company = 3, region = 4, national industry = 5.
*$p < 0.1$ **$p < 0.05$ ***$p < 0.01$ (due to the small sub-sample sizes, 10 per cent confidence levels are reported in addition to 5 and 1 per cent levels)

Table 4.7 Ownership and level of negotiations at integrated plants: the impact of domestic joint ventures

| | Domestic joint ventures (n = 8) | | Not domestic joint venture (n = 53) | | |
	mean	*SD*	*mean*	*SD*	*t-test*
Holidays	1.75	1.04	2.57	1.8	−1.85*
Health and safety	2.88	1.73	1.8	1.18	2.24**
Training	2.75	1.39	1.73	1.19	2.21**
Pensions	0.89	1.37	2.59	2.0	−3.18***
Minimum wage	1.13	1.25	3.08	1.87	−3.79***

Notes: Not covered by agreements = 0, plant level = 1, business/division of company = 2, company = 3, region = 4, national industry = 5.
*$p < 0.1$ **$p < 0.05$ ***$p < 0.01$

The impact of ownership change

More than three out of every five plants (62 per cent) reported a change in ownership during the previous fifteen years. The most consistent finding relating to ownership change was the general differences reported between plants with no change and those with ownership change. As Table 4.8 indicates, any change in ownership

Table 4.8 The effects of ownership change on terms and conditions at integrated sites

Terms and conditions[1]	No change in ownership (N = 29)		Any change in ownership (N = 29)		
	mean	SD	mean	SD	t-test
Hours of work	2.0	0.89	2.44	0.79	−2.17**
Holidays	2.17	0.38	2.0	0.34	1.97*
Accidents	1.91	0.92	1.51	0.82	1.92*
Occupational illness	2.0	0.74	1.69	0.8	1.7*
Skill levels	2.46	0.7	2.74	0.45	−1.97*
Subcontracting of jobs	2.57	0.66	2.27	0.75	1.81*

Notes: *p < 0.1 **p < 0.05
[1] All terms and conditions scored on a three point scale from increased (= 3) to decreased (= 1).

generally was more associated with increases in hours and skills levels. Plants with no change in ownership were more likely to report increases in holidays, accidents and occupational illness, and subcontracting of jobs.

Thus, overall, the information provided by integrated plants on changes to terms and conditions reveals a significant finding – that *any* change in ownership appears to bring about certain improvements to terms and conditions. Overall, the plants with more negative than positive changes in terms and conditions were those that had experienced *no* change in ownership. However, unions overall appeared to fare better where there had been no change in ownership. Plants that had undergone a change in ownership reported less union involvement in strategic company decisions and the threat of union de-recognition was higher (Table 4.9).

Table 4.9 Industrial relations and training in integrated sites by change of ownership (%)

	Privatized	Floated	Became a joint venture	Acquired	No change
Unions involved strategically at plant level	47	21	12	29	58
Worker representatives on main board	64	17	12	35	32
Attempts to reduce role of unions in health and safety	30	25	17	29	19
Threat of union de-recognition a problem	59	50	50	44	29
Change depends on agreement	35	55	57	50	50
Unions trust management	48	42	43	50	49
Designated training budgets	49	14	7	10	72
Extensive on-job training	44	15	8	17	50
Management value employees	72	67	86	63	58

Privatization

Our survey of integrated plants included over a third that had been privatized during the previous fifteen years. More of these plants reported workforce reductions and increased redundancies (t = 2.3, p < 0.05) compared to the remainder of integrated sites. In addition, more privatized sites reported managers had linked pay to company profitability and quality targets. However, privatization was not all bad news for trade unions in those plants that survived closure. A large majority of union representatives in privatized plants reported managers still regarding as important agreements reached with unions, and more privatized companies have a workers' representative on the Board of Directors of the company, together suggesting that public ownership bestows a pro-union legacy that survives privatization. However, this may be changing as a greater proportion of respondents at privatized plants, compared to other plants, also reported the threat of union de-recognition and attempts to reduce the role of unions in health and safety, although these latter differences did not reach statistical significance. Plants that were privatized did not report a greater decentralization of bargaining than other plants. Also, work organization practices did not differ significantly between privatized and other plants.

The reduced benefits of state ownership in protecting employee terms and conditions described above have occurred alongside the privatization of much of the world steel industry in recent years. There is strong evidence that in the eyes of the national unions, privatization (and the process leading up to privatization) decreases the number of jobs, threatens pension provision, reduces job security, increases workloads, leads to fewer steel plants and diminishes the role and influence of trade unions (Table 4.10). Privatization was also seen to be widely associated with companies opening plants overseas (thereby driving further internationalization) and increased plant investment. To a lesser extent, privatization was also linked (by around two in five national unions) to increased training; however, the sample was fairly evenly divided on the effect of privatization on employee earnings.

Table 4.10 The effects of privatization reported by national steel unions (%)

	Increased	*Stayed the same*	*Decreased*
Work loads	68	20	12
Investment in plant	58	38	4
Companies opening overseas plants	48	52	0
Education and training	39	50	11
Employee earnings	31	42	27
Pension provision	19	66	55
Employment security	11	50	39
Role and influence of trade unions	8	48	44
Number of plants	8	36	56
Number of jobs	12	8	80

Note: N = 39

Foreign ownership of steel facilities

The declining proportion of plants owned by domestic companies is a key feature of globalization in the steel industry. National unions were asked to indicate the effects of foreign ownership of steel companies in their country. Table 4.11 reveals that foreign ownership was more likely to be associated with absence of union recognition, inferior basic terms and conditions, higher workloads, less job guarantees and greater use of temporary employees and contractors. Yet at the same time those plants were also seen as more likely to operate innovative work organization policies, involve employees in quality improvement, provide good training and improve skill levels. Overall, foreign ownership of steel companies appears to be an important factor in threatening to reduce terms and conditions, while simultaneously diffusing new working practices.

Data from the survey of integrated sites indicate that foreign ownership as part of a joint venture was significantly associated with increases in the number of

Table 4.11 Sites with foreign investment compared to domestically owned sites (%)

	More likely	*Same*	*Less likely*
Introduce innovative working practices	53	42	5
Use more contractors	48	47	5
Use more temporary employees	48	47	5
Involve employees in quality improvement	40	60	0
Improve skill levels	37	47	16
Provide good training	35	55	10
Provide good terms and conditions	14	53	33
Establish a partnership with unions	11	26	63
Operate reasonable workloads	10	55	35
Limit redundancies	5	57	38
Recognise unions	5	59	36
Provide good pensions	0	72	28
Offer job guarantees	0	63	37

Note: N = 39; table shows % of national steel unions reporting

Table 4.12 Changes to terms and conditions over the past five years in integrated sites (t-tests) according to overseas involvement in joint ventures

Terms and conditions[1]	*Overseas involvement in joint venture (N = 12)*		*Others (N = 57)*		
	mean	*SD*	*mean*	*SD*	*t-test*
Holidays	1.83	0.39	2.11	0.36	−2.33*
Accidents	1.17	0.39	1.83	0.91	−4.00***
Occupational illness	1.42	0.67	2.0	0.81	−2.33*
No. of redundancies	1.58	0.79	2.20	0.83	−2.35**
Skill levels	2.91	0.3	2.51	0.66	3.18**

Notes: *$p < 0.05$ **$p < 0.01$ ***$p < 0.001$
[1] All terms and conditions scored on a 3 point scale from increased (= 3) to decreased (= 1).

redundancies, accidents and occupational illness (Table 4.12). As the results in Table 4.12 on page 81 show, however, it was also associated with increased holidays and skill levels.

Conclusion

These findings highlight a number of important developments, but at the same time warn against any tendency simply to 'read off' consequences for labour from the developing globalization within the international iron and steel industry. It is evident that widespread changes have taken place in terms and conditions and the nature of work. Within this, the findings indicate a widespread deterioration in certain aspects of labour's position within the industry – not least in the areas of continued redundancies, increased workloads, greater job insecurity and a growth in non-standard contracts. At the same time, however, various other terms and conditions appear largely unchanged, while in some aspects of work – such as skill levels and the amount of training – the picture is generally one of improvements in labour's position.

Overall, then, there is no consistent evidence of a 'race to the bottom' in respect of employees' terms and conditions within this industry. The same is true in regard to the structural position of trade unions and the developing nature of industrial relations within the industry. As regards ownership change, privatization and the foreign ownership of facilities, the picture for labour in the iron and steel industry is again a mixed one. It is clear that ownership change and foreign investment can bring benefits to extant workforces as well as costs. Overall, individual features of globalization were seen as exerting a differentiated impact on labour, rather than equating simply with a diminished position for labour.

Further work to overcome limitations within the data will hopefully allow a fuller picture to be drawn on the impact of globalization on labour. First, more investigation of international trade data will highlight those parts of the industry where globalization is more intense, and where the overall effects on labour may be more clear-cut. Second, the origins of the present sample mean that non-union firms are not represented in the findings and again their inclusion via additional data collection may highlight areas of particular development in labour-related aspects. These current limitations notwithstanding, however, the present findings do underline the need for a more careful assessment of the influence of globalization on labour than some accounts to date might suggest.

Acknowledgement

The authors would like to express their thanks to Len Powell at the International Metalworkers' Federation for his help with the data collection.

Notes

1   The countries taking part in the surveys were Argentina, Austria, Australia, Belgium, Brazil, Canada, Colombia, Czech Republic, Ecuador, Finland, France, Germany, Greece, Hungary, India, Italy, Japan, Malaysia, Netherlands, Norway, Philippines, Portugal, Romania, Spain, Sweden, Taiwan, Tunisia, Turkey, the UK, the USA.
2   The percentages sum to more than 100 due to a small proportion fitting into more than one category.

References

Aitken, B., Harrison, A. and Lipsey, R. (1996) 'Wages and Foreign Ownership – A Comparative Study of Mexico, Venezuela and the United States', *Journal of International Economics* 40(3–4): 345–71.

Appelbaum, E., Bailey, T., Berg, P. and Kallenberg, A. (2000) *Manufacturing Advantage*, Ithica, NY: Cornell University Press.

Arthur, J. (1994) 'Effects of Human Resource Management Systems on Manufacturing Performance and Turnover', *Academy of Management Journal* 37: 670–87.

Aylen, J. (1988) 'Privatisation of the British Steel Corporation', *Fiscal Studies* 9(3): 1–25.

Bacon, N. and Blyton, P. (1996) 'Re-casting the Politics of Steel in Europe: The Impact on Trade Unions', *West European Politics* 19(4): 770–86.

Barrell, R. and Pain, N. (1997) 'Foreign Direct Investment, Technological Change, and Economic Growth within Europe', *Economic Journal* 107: 1770–86.

Bartel, A. and Sicherman, N. (1999) 'Technological Change and Wages: An Interindustry Analysis', *Journal of Political Economy* 107(2): 285–325.

Blyton, P., Martinez Lucio, M., McGurk, J., and Turnbull, P. (1998) *Contesting Globalisation: Airline Restructuring, Labour Flexibility and Trade Union Strategies*, London: International Transport Workers' Federation.

Boswell, T. and Stevis, D. (1997) 'Globalisation and International Labor Organizing: A World System Perspective', *Work and Occupations* 24(3): 288–308.

Cooke, W. and Noble, D. (1998) 'Industrial Relations Systems and US Foreign Direct Investment Abroad', *British Journal of Industrial Relations* 36(4): 581–609.

Crandall, R. (1996) 'From Competitiveness to Competition: The Threat of Mini-mills to Large National Steel Companies', *Resources Policy* 22(1–2): 107–18.

D'Costa, A. (1999) *The Global Restructuring of the Steel Industry*, London: Routledge.

Dinopoulos, E. and Segerstrom, P. (1999) 'A Schumpeterian Model of Protection and Relative Wages', *American Economic Review* 89(3): 450–72.

D'Souza, J. and Megginson, W. (1999) 'The Financial and Operating Performance of Privatised Firms During the 1990s', *Journal of Finance* 54(4): 1397–438.

Frenkel, S. and Peetz, D. (1998) 'Globalization and Industrial Relations in East Asia: A Three-country Comparison', *Industrial Relations* 37(3): 282–301.

Haworth, N. and Ramsey, H. (1986) 'Matching the Multinationals: Obstacles to International Trade Unionism', *International Journal of Sociology and Social Policy* 6(2): 55–82.

Hennart, J., Roehl, T. and Zeitlow, D. (1999) '"Trojan Horse" or "Work Horse?": The Evolution of US-Japanese Joint Ventures in the United States', *Strategic Management Journal* 20(1): 15–29.

Hirst, P. and Thompson, G. (1996) *Globalisation in Question*, London: Polity.

ILO (1998) *World Employment, 1996–7*, Geneva: International Labour Organization.

Kleinknecht, A. and terWengel, J. (1998) 'The Myth of Economic Globalisation', *Cambridge Journal of Economics* 22(5): 637–47.

Konzelmann Smith, S. (1995) 'Internal Co-operation and Competitive Success: The Case of the US Steel Mini-mill Sector', *Cambridge Journal of Economics* 19: 277–304.

Lee, E. (1996) 'Globalization and Employment: Is Anxiety Justified?', *International Labour Review* 135(5): 485–97.

Lee, E. (1997) 'Globalization and Labour Standards: A Review of Issues', *International Labour Review*, 136(2): 173–89.

Lévesque, C. and Murray, G. (1998) 'Globalisation and the Joint Regulation of Workplace Change', *Relations Industrielles* 53(1): 90–122.

Lowder, S. (1999) 'Globalisation of the Footware Industry: A Simple Case of Labour?', *Tijdschrift Voor Economische en sociale geografie* 90(1): 47–60.

MacShane, D. (1996) *Global Business: Global Rights*, Fabian Pamphlet 575, London: Fabian Society.

Mahler, V., Jesuit, D. and Roscoe, D. (1999) 'Exploring the Impact of Trade and Investment on Income Inequality: A Cross-national Sectoral Analysis of the Developed Countries', *Comparative Political Studies* 32(3): 363–95.

Makhija, M., Kim, K. and Williamson, S. (1997) 'Measuring Globalisation of Industries Using a National Industry Approach', *Journal of International Business Studies* 28(4): 679–710.

Mangum, G.L. and McNabb, R.S. (1997) *The Rise, Fall, and Replacement of Industrywide Bargaining in the Basic Steel Industry*, New York: M.E. Sharpe.

Moore, M. (1998) 'European Steel Policies in the 1980s: Hindering Technological Innovation and Market Structure Change', *Review of World Economics* 134(1): 42–68.

Otto, K.P. and Wachter, H. (1996) 'Saarland Steel: Restructuring and Managing redundancy', in J. Storey (ed.) *Blackwell Cases in Human Resource and Change Management*, Oxford: Blackwell, pp. 106–23.

Pendleton, A. (1997) 'What Impact Has Privatisation Had on Pay and Employment? A Review of the UK Experience', *Relations Industrielles* 52(3): 554–82.

Piore, M. and Sabel, C. (1984) *The Second Industrial Divide: Prospects for Prosperity*, New York: Basic Books.

Radice, H. (1999) 'Taking Globalisation Seriously', *Socialist Register 1999: Global Capitalism versus Democracy*, London: Merlin Press, pp. 1–28.

Smith, S.K. (1995) 'Internal Co-operation and Competitive Success: The Case of the US Steel Mini-mill Sector', *Cambridge Journal of Economics* 19(2): 277–304.

Werner Franz, H. (1995) 'Do it Right First Time: Quality as the Crucial Change Agent in the European Steel Industries', *International Journal of Human Factors in Manufacturing* 5(2): 211–24.

Wills, J. (1998) 'Taking on the CosmoCorps? Experiments in Transnational Labor Organization', *Economic Geography* 74(2): 111–30.

Zhao, L. (1998) 'The Impact of Foreign Direct Investment on Wages and Employment', *Oxford Economic Papers* 50(2): 284–301.

5 'What we do' or 'Who we are'?

Trade union responses to globalization and regionalization in South Africa[1]

Andries Bezuidenhout

Introduction

In April 2000 the International Confederation of Free Trade Unions (ICFTU) held its 17th World Congress in Durban, South Africa. The theme of the gathering was Globalising Social Justice: Trade Unionism in the 21st Century. Several speakers commented on the significance of the ICFTU holding its congress in South Africa, where the labour movement was instrumental in ridding the society of its apartheid regime, and debated issues such as social clauses to trade agreements and the merits of reforming global institutions such as the World Trade Organization, the International Labour Organization, the International Monetary Fund and the World Bank. A document proposing a 'Millennium Review' argued:

> Unions are increasingly looking to their international structures for effective, coherent and co-ordinated action to transform the institutions that govern the global economy, to achieve sustainable development, to counter-balance the power of multi-national enterprises, and to channel practical and effective solidarity among national trade union organizations.
>
> (ICFTU, 2000: 2)

This vision of collective action from the global labour movement to reform globalized capitalism diverges starkly from some influential strands in current sociological theory. In his three volumes on *The Information Age: Economy, Society and Culture*, Manuel Castells argues that the way in which capitalism operates has fundamentally been altered by a technological revolution. He equates the significance of this 'information technology revolution' with the historical significance of the Industrial Revolution. As bureaucracy has been tied to industrial society, the network is fast becoming the social form of organization prevalent in the information society. For the first time in history, capitalism as a global system is integrated through financial markets operating in real time. This process fundamentally alters the role of states and other social actors in the global economy, as the global network, operating through its many nodes in the 'space of flows' and 'timeless time', challenges historical logics. This process is innovative, creative and flexible, while at the same time being highly exclusionary. The social consequences can potentially be devastating, especially for the emerging 'Fourth World' (Castells, 1996).

In his second volume, *The Power of Identity*, Castells (1997) considers the role of social movements in the context of the information/network society. To summarise his argument:

> Social movements tend to be fragmented, localistic, single-issue oriented, and ephemeral, either retrenched in their inner worlds, or flaring up for just an instant around a media symbol. In such a world of uncontrolled, confusing change, people tend to regroup around primary identities: religious, ethnic, territorial, national . . . People increasingly organise their meanings not around what they do but on the basis of what they are, or believe they are.
>
> (Castells 1996: 3)

In the context of changes taking place in the patriarchal family, as well as an increased environmental awareness, Castells sees the women's and environmental movements potentially as the most prominent forces of contestation:

> [O]ld and new cleavages of class, gender, ethnicity, religion, and territoriality are at work in dividing and sub-dividing issues, conflicts, and projects. But this is to say that embryonic connections between grassroots movements and symbol-oriented mobilizations on behalf of environmental justice bear the mark of alternative projects. These projects hint at superseding the exhausted social movements of industrial society, to resume, under historically appropriate forms, the old dialectics between domination and resistance, between *realpolitik* and utopia, between cynicism and hope.
>
> (Castells, 1997: 133)

Hence, the labour movement, the most prominent 'old social movement', is by implication described as 'exhausted', since workplace identities, constructed around 'what we do', will be superseded by 'who we believe we are'. Apart from changes in subjectivity, and hence the diminished possibility for constructing solidarities around a shared class identity, the nature of global network capitalism alters the relationship between labour and capital fundamentally. As Castells argues:

> [W]hile capitalist relationships of production still persist . . . capital and labour increasingly tend to exist in different spaces and times: the space of flows and the space of places . . . Thus they live by each other, but do not relate to each other. Capital tends to escape in its hyperspace of pure circulation, while labour dissolves its collective entity into an infinite variation of individual existences . . . The struggle between diverse capitalists and miscellaneous working classes is subsumed into more fundamental opposition between the bare logic of capital flows and the cultural values of human experience.
>
> (Castells, cited in Waterman, 1999: 366)

Thus, for the time being, trade unions are still 'influential political actors in many countries' and remain 'tools for workers to defend themselves against the abuses from capital and from the state'. However, argues Castells,

> the labour movement does not seem fit to generate by itself and from itself a project identity able to reconstruct social control and to rebuild social institutions in the Information Age. Labour militants will undoubtedly be part of new, transformative social dynamics.

Notwithstanding, Castells feels 'less sure that labour unions will' (ibid.).

In contrast to Castells' pessimistic view of the ability of labour movements to engage with globalization, several authors have chosen to focus on the opportunities opened up by new terrains of contestation in a globalizing economy. Some of these authors draw on the new labour studies, which were sparked by the resounding successes of labour movements such as those in Brazil and South Africa (see Munck, 1988). As workers across the globe are becoming increasingly interconnected, either through common employers, or through the threat of factories relocating to areas where labour is docile and cheap, trade unions themselves have increasingly become aware of the need for a different approach to union campaigns. Also, certain recent events, such as the prominence trans-national industrial action had in the Australian dock worker strike, and the involvement of the International Confederation of Free Trade Unions (ICFTU) in social clause campaigns during the Seattle talks of the World Trade Organization, have all indicated that there is an increased realization among organized labour that national responses alone to the effects of globalization are not adequate (Taylor, 1998).

More recently, the work of Kim Moody (1997), but especially the concept of 'global social movement unionism', has sparked renewed interest in the role of organized labour as a significant global player. Indeed, Richard Hyman argues: 'Rather than a crisis of trade unionism, what has occurred is a crisis of a specifically narrow based type of trade unionism' (cited in Munck, 1999: 12). Ronaldo Munck also points out:

> [W]orkers of the 'world-market factories' are more than just a passive component of a global reserve army of labour. Like women, the once excluded and peripheralized Third World workers are now playing a key role in revitalizing the strategies of the traditional model of trade unionism. Whether it is Brazil, the Philippines, or South Africa it is this 'new' working class which is helping develop adequate answers to the dilemmas posed by global capitalism in the 1990s.
>
> (ibid.: 7–8)

In this regard, Rob Lambert (1998: 73) argues that South African trade unions turned towards social movement unionism, which involved alliances with civil society, and also entailed global action in attempts to win workplace and broader campaigns. These campaigns paid off, insofar as the apartheid state capitulated and gave rise to a constitutional democracy. However, on an economic level, the new state is still conservative and embraces neoliberal globalization. It is here where social movement unionism, based on national campaigns only, cannot begin to respond to the pressures of globalization.

Lambert (1998) argues that many unions have been responding to globalization through a form of business unionism. This approach is 'characterised by a narrow workplace focus' and a 'failure to engage community organisations'. Also, in this case, there is an absence of 'a vision of social transformation'. Business unionism becomes global business unionism when unions 'accept the logic of globalization as a reason for their engagement'. This form of unionism is bound to be unsuccessful, since it does not address one of the core reasons why the position of workers in the world economy has been weakened. It takes a narrow national focus on an economy that is in practice not only a national one, but also globalized.

However, Lambert argues that an alternative form of unionism has been emerging, that of global social movement unionism:

> Global social movement unionism arises when unions are conscious of the linkage between workplace, civil society, the state and global forces and develop a strategy to resist the damaging pressures of globalization through creating a movement linking these spheres.
>
> (1998: 73)

He argues:

> Union leaders in South Africa who were active in the 1970s and 1980s are likely to have a deep understanding of this approach. They became conscious that the apartheid state could not be brought to its knees through a narrow workplace focus, no matter how militant that focus might have been.
>
> (ibid.: 73–4)

As with the relationships between trade unions and other social movements, such as the environmental movement and consumer groups, the relationships between trade unions and trade union centres in different parts of the world are by no means unproblematic or without contradictions. Indeed, trade unions are located in different parts of the world under conditions of global economic inequality. Also, trade unions operate under different local political regimes. Hence, unions globally have followed different paths of development. Unions in Western Europe, for example, went through stages of mobilization in the 1960s and early 1970s, corporatism in the late 1970s and early 1980s, and then decentralization, flexibility and decline after that (Regini, 1992). This usually happened in the context of social or liberal democracies. Many trade unions from the South, however, were involved in broader struggles for the democratization of their societies under labour repressive regimes. As argued earlier, this form of unionism took on a social movement character. The labour movements in South Africa and Brazil were examples of this (see Seidman, 1994; Webster, 1985).

But as some of these campaigns paid off, the resulting process of democratization took place in an economic environment that was hostile to trade unions and labour rights. COSATU, which traditionally operated as a social movement union federation, then faced a new challenge: to defend existing rights under globalization.

This forced some of the unions in the South to turn their attention outwards, and, like unions in the North, to assist other social movement unions in their struggles for recognition and political democratization through acts of solidarity. While the end of the Cold War provides a more favourable context for the labour movement to build global unity and to forge new links, older questions of unequal relationships between trade unions in different parts of the world remain relevant (see Silver and Arrighi, 2001; Stevis, 1998).

The first part of this chapter considers historical examples of trans-national forms of trade union action in the South African context. It is argued that labour internationalism is nothing new, and that it is shaped by various social processes. However, a global realignment in labour politics took place in the 1990s, and COSATU has been an active player in this.

Globally, the traditional industrial membership base of trade unions has been threatened by a trend towards the casualization of labour. These trends take on different patterns and contours in different parts of the world. In the South African context, a labour market, which was historically segmented, is now re-segmented by the introduction of a layer of casual employment, be it in the form of subcontracting, the use of various arrangements that institutionalize casual work as a permanent condition, temporary work through fixed-term contracts, as well as the use of provisions for so-called independent contractors in labour legislation to avert defining *de facto* contracts of employment as *de jure* contracts of employment, in order to circumvent labour legislation. However, the casualization of work has also forced trade unions to take cognisance of the gender (and sometimes 'ethnic' and 'citizenship') bias brought about by just organizing industrial workers in stable jobs. Hence, the second part of the chapter considers trade union campaigns dealing with the issue of casualization. In order to do so, an overview in changes in membership campaigns is provided.

The ability of unions and union federations to organize global campaigns depends on the ability to mobilize resources and the support of membership. The third part of the chapter therefore focuses on changes in COSATU and its affiliates in order to assess whether current organizational dynamics might contribute to global campaigns.

Historical overview of COSATU's involvement in regional and global action

All three of the major trade union federations, COSATU, the Federation of Unions of South Africa (FEDUSA), and the National Council of Trade Unions (NACTU), are affiliated to the International Congress of Free Trade Unions (ICFTU). Also, several other trade unions, are affiliated to the ICFTU's International Trade Secretariats. Apart from involvement in these various international bodies, both

COSATU and NACTU are involved in the continent, as well as the region, through the Organization for African Trade Union Unity (OATUU), as well as the Southern Africa Trade Union Coordinating Council (SATUCC).

But trans-national trade union involvement is not something new to the South African labour movement which is a result of recent trends in globalization. The nature of campaigns may be changing, or may be increasing in terms of frequency and intensity, but South African unionism, as will be shown, has always been tied to international dynamics. However, the union movement's engagement with organized workers and bodies set up by or 'for' them, has certainly not been unproblematic. At times, it has been characterized by immense levels of solidarity, but also by suspicion and animosity. Significantly, the relationship between South African trade unions and global players, such as the ICFTU and the World Federation of Trade Unions (WFTU) was shaped by both the internal struggle against apartheid, as well as global Cold War politics. Roger Southall (1995) argued that COSATU was able to draw on resources from unions in the North while maintaining its independence through its policy of non-alignment. However, now that COSATU has achieved many of the campaign goals of the 1980s, its position as a recipient of assistance is changing to one where it is forced to become more outward-looking and to contribute to the struggles of other social movement unions in the Southern African and Asian context.

Concerning the early years of industrialization, following the discovery of gold and diamonds in South Africa and the trade unions that resulted from this, Hyslop (1999: 2) has convincingly argued that an analysis of the emergence of the earliest artisan unions in South Africa and their policies of 'white labourism' should not be analysed as '"nationally" discrete entities'. Instead, any analysis should recognize that, during the height of colonialism, workers of European origin 'were bound together into an imperial working class, by flows of population which traversed the world'.

In the 1920s, Clements Kadalie's ICU sought affiliation with the British Trade Union Council (TUC), but was referred to the International Federation of Trade Unions instead. After the expulsion of communists in the union, the ICU's application was accepted in 1927. Even after considerable opposition from the South African government, Kadalie attended an ILO conference as an unofficial delegate in the same year. According to Harold Grimshaw, then the ILO's 'colonial section' head, Kadalie's visit prepared the way for a favourable reception for delegates from Africa at future ILO conferences (Simons and Simons, 1983: 362; Southall, 1996: 6).

The involvement of South African trade union federations in international forums from the 1950s onwards was very much shaped by a global campaign against apartheid. This campaign was again, in turn, shaped by the Cold War politics of international labour and the schism which existed between the WFTU and the ICFTU. In the late 1950s and the early 1960s, SACTU, even though not formally affiliated with the WFTU, used its connection with that federation to lobby in the ILO against the representation of TUCSA, which was seen as a racially based federation. Following this and several other campaigns, South Africa was expelled from the ILO in 1963. SACTU also campaigned against the ICFTU's support in South Africa for federations such as the Federation of Free African Trade Unions of South Africa (FOFATUSA), a federation which was basically set up by themselves in an attempt to organize black workers, and TUCSA. In the context of the decolonization of Africa at the time, SACTU successfully lobbied against the affiliation of trade unions to the ICFTU in Africa, resulting in the federation losing many of its African affiliates (ibid.: 8–9).

However, when the AFL-CIO withdrew from the ICFTU in 1969, the way was opened up for the ICFTU to play a much more active role in campaigning against apartheid. However, this role was initially overshadowed by SACTU in exile, who, with the support of the WFTU, organized an International Trade Union Conference against apartheid in 1973. But, resulting from the 1973 Durban strike wave, 'the international as well as the South African landscape was . . . transformed' (ibid.: 9).

When small industrial unions emerged after a strike wave in 1973, several trade unions from across the globe, mostly unions affiliated to the ICFTU, offered assistance. The ICFTU itself became more involved in the assistance of the emerging independent trade union movement. In 1974, it set up the Coordinating Committee for South Africa (COCOSA), which, according to Southall, became involved in industrial action to boycott South African goods, assisting the emerging trade unions with legal costs, pressurizing trans-national corporations to recognize South African trade unions, and channelling and coordinating financial assistance from ICFTU affiliates to South African trade unions (which amounted to more than US$6.6 million from 1976 to 1984) (ibid.: 10–11).

The ICFTU and its affiliates provided funding to a broad spectrum of the emerging black unions – to FOSATU (later COSATU), unions affiliated to what became known as NACTU, as well as a range of other independent unions (Fraser, 1991: 27). However, in the context of the Cold War, COSATU actively pursued an approach of non-alignment. Likewise, NACTU was not formally affiliated to the ICFTU, even though its predecessor, CUSA was (Southall, 1996: 10–11; Naidoo, 1991: 16–21; Ngcakuna, 1991: 22–6). Also, SACTU in exile was not only suspicious of the ICFTU's role in South Africa, but was originally also hostile towards the emerging independent trade union movement. SACTU insisted that it was the sole representative of the South Africa working class abroad and that funding to South African unions had to be channelled through it. However, the ICFTU and its affiliates maintained direct links with South African trade unions. In fact, South African trade unionists formed networks with many of the unionists abroad through attending short educational courses. Southall argued that this resulted in 'a formidable network of personal, sectoral and professional contacts which proved of inestimable value during particular industrial struggles or when unions became subject to political attack' (1996: 15).

These networks supported campaigns of South African trade unions in various ways:

- Especially in the 1970s, when trade unions campaigned for recognition, South African unions organizing workers in subsidiaries of multinational corporations linked up with trade unions representing workers at factories in home countries. From 1977 to 1978, for instance, pressure from unions organizing Smith and Nephew factories in Britain contributed to the local subsidiary renewing its recognition of the National Union of Textile Workers (Southall, 1996: 15). The National Union of Textile Workers (NUTW) (and later SACTWU) also built up an impressive network with the American Clothing and Textile Workers Union (ACTWU). This relationship took on the form of joint campaigns against common employers. In 1987, South African workers supported a campaign of the ACTWU against Courtaulds, a British textile multinational through an overtime ban. Later, the ACTWU undertook an international pressure campaign and raised US$25 000 in support of a negotiation process by South African workers with another company, Hextex (Hudson, 1991: 40).

• A second form of linkage involved South African trade unions calling on trade unions organizing in the same trans-national corporations abroad for more generalized campaigns. Southall mentions a campaign by the National Union of Textile Workers in Canada through the Canadian Labour Congress to get trans-nationals to abide by a Code of Investment (1996: 16).

• A third form of linkage was, according to Southall (1996: 16–17), a more successful form of solidarity. Many South African trade unions linked up with International Trade Secretariats. In 1980, the International Metalworkers Federation, through contributing to a strike fund and through pressure from its affiliate in Germany (IG Metal), contributed to a resounding victory for the National Automobile and Allied Workers' Union (NAAWU) for a 'living wage' at the Volkswagen plant in South Africa. NACTU unions also used the ITSs successfully, particularly in negotiating with Unilever, a British multinational, it used its links to the British unions through the IUF to put pressure on the company (Ngcukana, 1991: 24).

It is important to note that these examples of international solidarity became prominent especially in industries where production had become globalized, such as the steel and motor manufacturing industries, and industries that were specifically vulnerable to trade tariff cuts, such as the clothing and textile industries.

In the case of the NUTW and the ACTWU, unionists had first established personal contacts through international meetings. ACTWU vice-president John Hudson pointed out that his union members were particularly interested to get involved with the NUTW because of 'a desire to further contribute to the fight against apartheid'. Through their involvement, the unions provided each other with support on different matters, such as health and safety training and an exchange of research materials on companies operating in both countries. When the NUTW merged with another union to form the SACTWU, they also drew on the experiences of the ACTWU, who had gone through a merger previously. Hudson (1991: 41) mentioned specifically that his union learnt a lot from the NUTW's organizing strategies.

In some instances, these 'direct links' were successful in campaigns, and in others they were less successful. Southall argued that South African unions formed closer links with trade unions generally affiliated to the ICFTU more so than the WFTU, since they were interlinked through trans-national corporations. The unions organizing in former socialist countries could not really offer the level of assistance that their counterparts in the capitalist world could. Towards the end of the 1980s, SACTU 'quietly [buried]' its opposition to direct links, and in the context of the British anti-apartheid movement, had a much more harmonious relationship with the TUC (Southall, 1996: 15, 17).

Of course, the collapse of the Soviet Union, as well as the unbanning of the ANC, the SACP, the PAC, and other liberation organizations in 1990 changed the landscape considerably. Politically, South Africa entered a process of nego-tiations around the nature of a post-apartheid society. Internally, COSATU played an important role, now in formal alliance with the ANC and the SACP. In 1990, COSATU put the issue of international relationships on its agenda. Jay Naidoo, then the general secretary of the federation, pointed out that this was for very specific reasons, mentioning 'particularly the world restructuring of the economy, and the loosening of the political climate internationally with the formal ending of the Cold War and the collapse of Eastern European regimes'. In this context, Naidoo felt that 'workers are going to begin sharing common problems, particularly where there is an unbridled move to free market systems, where the lives and jobs of workers, the benefits they have gained, are being jeopardised' (1991: 17).

In terms of its relationships with international bodies such as the ICFTU and the WFTU, COSATU entered into a process of re-evaluation. In October 1990, COSATU sent its first formal political delegation to the Soviet Union, however, already then, it was clear that COSATU was leaning towards a more engaging approach with the ICFTU (Mather, 1991: 13; Naidoo, 1991: 18). In December 1990, COSATU had its first meeting with the Executive Council of the ICFTU in Tokyo. COSATU also attempted to 'normalize' its relationship with the AFL-CIO. Having already established strong links with affiliates of the AFL-CIO, such as the ACTWU and the UAW, Naidoo pointed out:

> [T]here is more that unites than divides us. We should not pretend that there are not differences – there will always be differences – but we should cooperate around the issues common to us. Whether you are an American worker, or a worker in the Soviet Union, Europe, Asia or Africa, the world restructuring of the economy is going to undermine your rights in the interests of increased profits for the capitalists.

> (ibid.: 18)

In 1991, Jay Naidoo told the *South African Labour Bulletin*:

> International policy has never been high on COSATU's agenda. We did not feel that it was a priority compared with building a strong internal labour movement. Also, we wanted to avoid the situation where conflicts in the international trade union movement . . . could divide us.

He also pointed out, though, that COSATU unions had developed links with unions in Scandinavia, the Netherlands and Canada, when in need of international solidarity when dealing with multinationals. He pointed out that these unions were affiliated to the ICFTU (1991: 18).

On 15 March 1991, COSATU appointed its first international officer, in the person of Mcebisi Msizi, who had worked for the exiled union federation SACTU. At this time, COSATU also increased its activities in the African, as well as the Southern African, region. In 1990, COSATU for the first time attended the congress of the Organization of African Trade Union Unity (OATUU). Naidoo pointed out:

> In 1987, the first real debate took place, over the question of affiliation to OATUU. None of us really knew what OATUU stood for, but it was a symbolic thing of wanting to identify with Africa. The consensus at the end was that we should develop a working relationship and get to know what OATUU did, the value of it could be both to us building internally and also to establish relations across the region.
>
> (ibid.: 17)

Apart from establishing relations with OATUU, COSATU had also been building links with unions in the Southern African region, through the Southern African Trade Union Coordinating Committee (SATUCC). The federation was involved in a process of setting up a social charter for worker's rights. Naidoo described the move: 'Our common interests with Southern African workers will be shared, particularly as borders open up, with industry relocating, or manufacturing industry in the Frontline States being wiped out by South Africa' (ibid.: 18).

In the 1980s NACTU had already established links with OATUU and was actively involved in SATUCC. It affiliated to OATUU even before COSATU did in 1991. Concerning his affiliate's involvement in Southern Africa, Cunningham Ngcukana, general secretary of NACTU pointed out:

> The Southern African region is economically integrated. We have a lot of migrant labour from neighbouring countries and we should develop a social charter to protect their rights. Most South African employers in industries including construction, mining, and forestry, are taking people from outside because they do not have to make social security payments . . . Also, once the political question is resolved in South Africa, there are possibilities that South African companies will move into neighbouring states and exploit workers there . . . Cooperation amongst Southern African trade unions is very important to tackle employers in the whole region.
>
> (1991: 26)

Here one can see a process of re-evaluation taking place. Where COSATU and NACTU traditionally drew on support from unions in the North, there was already a realization in the early 1990s that they had to engage with other unions in Africa, and Southern Africa in particular. South African unions, in the relative context of the Southern African region, increasingly occupy a position similar to unions of Western Europe and the United States globally.

In July 1991, the ICFTU hosted a conference for African trade unions in Gaborone, Botswana. Exchanges at this conference between African trade unionists and the ICFTU showed that the relationship between the international federation and unions on the continent was still an extremely complicated one. Some African unionists accused the ICFTU of paternalism and 'Euro-centrism', while Enzo Friso, then Assistant General Secretary of the ICFTU, criticized OATUU's clause prohibiting affiliates from affiliating with other international trade union federations and called on African trade unions to join the ICFTU. Representatives from both COSATU and NACTU attended this conference (Keet, 1991: 70–81).

Also in the early 1990s, COSATU was involved in other international initiatives, mainly through conferences with labour movements from elsewhere. The following are two examples:

- One initiative was the Indian Ocean Regional Initiative, which held its first meeting in Perth, Western Australia in May 1991. Apart from Australian unions, unions from the Philippines, Pakistan, Sri Lanka, Malaysia, Indonesia and Papua New Guinea attended (Lambert, 1992: 66–73). The second meeting was held in December 1992 and was attended by COSATU, as well as the Zimbabwean Congress of Trade Unions. Unionists agreed to implement an exchange programme and to work collectively towards a Social Code of Conduct, which set out basic trade union rights. The Code called for targeted boycott campaigns against companies which did not comply with labour standards set out (Von Holdt, 1993: 76–9). In November 1994, the Initiative held another meeting, and COSATU 'played a key role in the meeting' (Lambert, 1995: 91–2).
- The second was joint conferences held with the Italian General Confederation of Labour (CGIL) and the Workers Centre of Brazil (CUT). Issues such as globalization and union responses to globalization were discussed at these seminars (Von Holdt, 1993a: 72–9).

In February 1993, in the context of an increase in violence in South Africa, specifically in the KwaZulu-Natal province, COSATU and NACTU hosted a delegation from the ICFTU, including the federation's General Secretary and the chair of the ICFTU's human rights committee. The delegation also included unionists from the Scandinavian countries, the Netherlands, Britain, the USA, Italy, Japan, and Zambia. The Coordinating Committee on South Africa (COCOSA) met in Johannesburg, the first time in South Africa since it was founded in 1976. Representatives from the ITSs were also present. In an interview with the *South African Labour Bulletin*, Enzo Friso from the ICFTU indicated that the confederation would welcome a progressive input from COSATU. He also acknowledged that funds from the ICFTU had in the past gone 'into the pockets' of certain African and South East Asian dictators, and that this would come to an end. Significantly, he was critical of structural adjustment programmes, saying that these programmes had 'no principles'. He also said that it was possible to put pressure on the IMF and the World Bank to 'listen and not only impose' (Von Holdt and Zikalala, 1993: 67–71; for an opinion on the significance of these statements, see Waterman, 1993: 82–4). These statements seemed to indicate that the ICFTU was willing, at least on a symbolic level, to confront some of its Cold War legacies.

But these 'concessions' took place in the context of a considerable critique of the ICFTU's role in Asia. Through the Indian Ocean Regional Initiative, COSATU had become involved with many of the 'independent' unions in Asia who were very critical of the ICFTU's membership base in the so-called 'yellow' unions – unions which were set up by governments to pre-empt the establishment of independent trade unions. Consequentially, COSATU's potential affiliation with the ICFTU became a hotly debated topic. A group of unionists from Asia expressed their satisfaction with the above statements from the ICFTU when in South Africa, but were 'concerned that these view points be translated into practical policy in Asia'. According to them, 'such a change would necessitate a dramatic transformation of the ICFTU's role in Asia, its affiliation base and its organisational structures'. They argued:

> If COSATU affiliates to the ICFTU without bargaining and negotiating the issue of the character of the ICFTU in Asia, an historic opportunity will have been lost. The pressure for an organizational transformation of the ICFTU in Asia will be dramatically reduced because the ICFTU will be able to gain enormous credibility from COSATU's affiliation, without having to transform its Asian operations.
>
> (Meecham *et al.*, 1993: 76–81)

The KMU (1993: 60–5) from the Philippines wrote an open letter to COSATU, calling on COSATU not to affiliate, since the ICFTU was 'tainted with blood and bribe money' in the Philippines.

Towards the end of the 1990s trade unions became more aware of the need for global cooperation. Both NACTU and COSATU formalized their involvement with the ICFTU and its members by affiliating formally, NACTU in 1994, and COSATU in 1997. In 1998, FEDUSA, the other major South African trade union federation, also affiliated to the ICFTU.

COSATU's involvement in OATUU and SATUCC led to more active campaigns in the region. COSATU's role in these fora led to the federation taking on the role of supporting campaigns of other unions, rather than being supported. One interesting example is COSATU's campaign in support of the Swaziland Congress of Trade Unions (SCTU). In 1997, the SCTU went on a two-day strike to support its demands for democratization and the recognition of labour rights by the Swaziland government. COSATU supported the strike by calling on its affiliates to embark on a 'go slow' in handling goods delivered to and from Swaziland during the strike. The Swaziland government lodged a compliant with the South African government, arguing that COSATU's actions amounted to interference by the South African government in its domestic affairs. COSATU pointed that it was independent from the South African government.

On the first day of the strike, 31 January 1997, the Swaziland government imprisoned twenty-three members of the pro-democracy movement, including the SCTU general secretary, Jan Sithole. In response, COSATU threatened to block the delivery of goods to Swaziland at the border. When, twelve days after the general strike began, the union leaders had not been released, a delegation from SATUCC, including representatives form COSATU and NACTU, met with the Swaziland government to attempt to negotiate for the release of the detained leaders. The leaders were later released.

In March 1997, COSATU, in consultation with SATUCC and the SCTU, organized a blockade of the border posts between South Africa and Swaziland in order to keep up the pressure on the Swazi government to meet worker and political demands, bringing the transport of goods between the two countries to a standstill. While still not resulting in major reforms in Swaziland, the action shows how SATUCC became involved in a coordinating capacity in struggles for labour rights and democratization in Southern Africa.[2]

But individual unions have also been involved in trans-national campaigns, especially in the clothing and textile industries. Also in 1997, while South Africa was negotiating a bilateral trade agreement with Zimbabwe, the Southern African Clothing and Textile Workers' Union wrote a letter to the Southern African Customs Union, demanding that it prevent Zimbabwe from importing textiles into South Africa until workers who had been dismissed as a result of a strike were reinstated. The Zimbabwe Congress of Trade Unions strategically used the letter in its public campaigns for labour rights.

The result of a recent campaign, also in the clothing and textile industry, is the Maputo Declaration on the Textiles, Clothing and Leather Industries, signed on the 9th of May 1999. Several unions organizing workers in these related industries, including unions from countries such as South Africa, Lesotho, Malawi, Mauritius, Mozambique, Zambia, Tanzania and Zimbabwe, met in Maputo to discuss the state of the industry in the region.

The participants identified common problems, such as the erosion of labour standards, the impact of Structural Adjustment Programmes (SAPs) on their economies, export processing zones eroding labour standards, the impact of tariff reductions as well as large-scale smuggling of goods on the industry, and the trading of second-hand clothing intended as donations. In the declaration, the unions jointly called for, among other things, more appropriate macro-economic policies, the promotion of worker rights, linking trade and labour rights, a more careful consideration of the reduction of import tariffs on specific industries, and the integration of export processing zones into the national economies of countries.

The unions committed themselves to use their resources to 'build strong, financially independent organisations, controlled by members and run in a democratic manner' and to 'share information and build a comprehensive database on every company in the region, and on wages and working conditions applicable in every country and every workplace'. Unions also agreed to meet as a regional structure at least twice a year and to build the structures of the International Textile, Garment and Leather Workers' Federation (ITGLWF) in Africa. Also, unions committed themselves to 'convene meetings of shop stewards in the region from the same companies, and undertake campaigns to be run across national frontiers'.

The involvement of SACTWU in this initiative illustrates the point that, whereas SACTWU (and earlier the NUTW) drew on international support for recognition struggles in the 1970s and the 1980s from other unions, it is now in a position where it has to contribute to the struggle for basic rights of other unions in the region. The approach of the Maputo Declaration to trade unionism reflects COSATU's and its predecessors' model of unions controlled by workers and strong shop stewards committees, linked up to broader campaigns for democratization, i.e. social movement unionism.

Another initiative involves two of the unions who attended the SIGTUR conference. The Maritime Union of Australia (MUA) and the Transport and General Workers' Union (TGWU) signed a statement of intent that committed the leaderships present at the SIGTUR conference to 'advancing a process of linking the ports of Fremantle in Western Australia and Durban in South Africa organisationally'. This follows several examples of trans-national union campaigns, including the refusal of TGWU members to offload Australian ships during the 1998 dock worker dispute in Australia. The statement of intent will be discussed by the memberships of the two unions, upon which appropriate organizational steps are to be taken. The process is at an early stage, but provides an example of how unions are attempting to set up organizational structures to concretize global campaigns.

Currently, the 'new internationalism' is on COSATU's broader agenda. Although losing its international officer to the government when he became the new ambassador in Nigeria, the Federation hosted several high profile conferences and congresses in South Africa in 1999 and 2000. The first was the 7th Ordinary Congress of OATUU, which was held in Johannesburg in September. The second took place in October 1999, when COSATU hosted a conference of the Southern Initiative on Globalization and Trade Union Rights (SIGTUR). The theme of the conference is Trade unionism in the 21st century – vision and strategy, and the specific focus is on 'the impact of globalization on trade unions'. Topics addressed specifically included the following:

- workplace restructuring through 'lean production', resulting from economic liberalization, privatization, downsizing, outsourcing and casualization;
- forms of union resistance, including the Korean workers' campaigns against casualization and the conflict on the Australian waterfront;
- sector level strategies on recruiting workers, building strong unions, and new approaches to casualization.

Unionists from South Africa, South Korea, Australia, Pakistan, India, Indonesia and the Philippines attended the conference.

The third congress, that of the International Federation of Chemical, Energy, Mine and General Workers' Union (ICEM), was held in Durban from 3 to 5 November. At this conference, the NUM used the opportunity to lobby support from unions in Canada and Australia to put pressure on the multinational mining company Placer Dome for their campaign to get 3,000 retrenched workers reinstated at Western Areas gold mine. The fourth was the general congress of the ICFTU, mentioned in the introduction, which took place in Durban.

Hence, the independent trade unions which emerged in the 1970s drew on international networks in several of their campaigns for recognition, through industrial action and campaigns. They also received financial assistance from unions in the North. In the 1980s, when this union movement consolidated its structures, and in the context of the Cold War, these unions pursued an active policy of non-alignment. However, it continued to draw on international networks. During the transition process starting in the 1990s, and in the context of the collapse of the Cold War, there was a process of international realignment. COSATU entered into talks with the ICFTU, but also with unions in the South which were critical of the ICFTU.

Towards the end of the 1990s, however, all three major trade union federations in South African formally affiliated to the ICFTU, and are, as a result, attempting to shape the direction of the federation to also represent the interests of union in developing countries. A good example of this is the awareness of South African unionists of the lobbying campaign focusing on the WTO Seattle negotiations. But COSATU is also retaining other links with unions in the South on both sides of the ocean – in Asia, Australia through SIGTUR, as well as Brazil. But these links now include a working relationship with the ICFTU's ITSs. In the context of political democratization under conditions of economic liberalization, COSATU is taking on a new role in international campaigns. It increasingly has to take on the role of not only acting as host to conferences on a symbolic level, but of supporting the struggles of the other social movement unions of the South through real campaigns.

The casualization of work and membership campaigns

The ability to engage in effective campaigns depends on a solid membership base, and requires a level of identification of union members with these campaigns. Castells is not the first to comment on the impact of the changing nature of work and labour markets on trade union membership and organization.[3] For instance, Guy Standing argues that globalization leads to a segmentation of labour markets. This has to do with new opportunities opening up globally for skilled professionals, but also with the casualization of work at the 'lower' end of the labour market (Standing, 1997). No reliable quantitative data based on official statistics is available to provide evidence on the extent of casualization in the South African context, but indications from several studies point towards a process of rapid casualization in several industries, including mining, retail, construction, transport and manu-facturing (Kenny and Bezuidenhout, 1999a).

It has to be noted that in South Africa this process of casualization is taking place in the context of a labour market that is already historically segmented (Kenny and Webster, 1999), as well as the absence of a comprehensive social security system that can alleviate the social impact of underemployment (Kenny and Bezuidenhout, 1999b; Barchiesi, 2000).

However, since the early 1970s, trade union membership as well as trade union density has increased as a result of successful membership campaigns. In 1976, 673,000 workers were members of trade unions (see Table 5.1). In 1998, this number increased to 3.8 million union members. Of these union members, more than 1.7 million were members of COSATU. Union density in the non-agricultural formal sector of the economy increased from 18 per cent in 1985 to 51 per cent in 1998 (see Table 5.2).

According to Jane Barrett (1993: 45–50), this growth in membership can be attributed to the successful organization of three major sectors in the economy. First, the earliest successful membership campaigns were based on the organization of workers based in the manufacturing sector following the historical strike wave in 1973. Throughout the 1970s and the 1980s, unions that are now affiliated to COSATU successfully organized workers into various manufacturing unions. These unions currently account for 30.2 per cent of COSATU's total membership.

Second, the formation of the National Union of Mineworkers (NUM) from 1982 onwards, and the affiliation of NUM with COSATU when it was formed in 1985, provided the federation with a considerable injection of well-organized members. Currently, NUM is still the largest union affiliated to COSATU, even though its membership reduced drastically following a rapid decline in the gold price especially since late 1997 and a reduction of employment levels in the gold mining industry

Table 5.1 Membership of registered trade unions, 1976–95

Year	Number of registered unions	Number of union members
1976	173	673,000
1977	174	677,000
1978	174	698,000
1979	167	727,000
1980	188	781,000
1981	200	1,054,000
1982	199	1,226,000
1983	194	1,288,000
1984	193	1,406,000
1985	196	1,391,000
1986	195	1,698,000
1987	205	1,879,000
1988	209	2,084,000
1989	212	2,130,000
1990	209	2,459,000
1991	200	2,750,000
1992	194	2,905,000
1993	201	2,890,174
1994	213	2,470,481
1995	248	2,690,727

Source: Department of Manpower (later Department of Labour) Annual Reports, 1976–1995

Table 5.2 Union membership and union density, 1985–98

	1985	1987	1989	1991	1993	1996	1998
Union membership	1,391,423	1,887,940	2,130,117	2,750,400	3,272,768	3,016,933	3,801,388
COSATU membership	400,000	712,231	924,499	1,205,307	1,205,244	1,639,865	1,713,533
Non-COSATU members	991,423	1,175,709	1,205,618	1,545,093	2,067,524	1,377,068	2,087,855
Nonunionized workers	6,451,277	6,128,560	6,026,583	5,237,100	4,484,897	4,573,067	3,746,612
Total employment	7,842,700	8,016,500	8,156,700	7,987,500	7,757,665	7,590,000	7,548,000
Total employment (excluding agriculture)	6,090,900	6,265,500	6,454,500	6,315,600	6,115,365	5,238,572	4,922,029
Union density (excluding agriculture)	18%	24%	26%	34%	43%	40%	51%

Source: Naidoo (1999: 16–17)

that resulted from this, as well as large-scale casualization through subcontracting (Bezuidenhout, 1999; Kenny and Bezuidenhout, 1999a). Currently, NUM accounts for 14.9 per cent of COSATU's membership.

Third, from the late 1980s to the early 1990s, several COSATU unions conducted successful membership campaigns in the public sector. Public sector unions currently account for 36.4 per cent of COSATU's total membership.

These three categories of unions account for almost 82 per cent of all COSATU's members. The rest is made up of unions organizing construction workers, agricultural and plantation workers, and workers in the service sectors in general (see Table 5.3).

One reason for the rapid growth in public sector union membership is the fact that the public sector is undergoing a process of large-scale restructuring. Although workers felt secure in their jobs in the past, the public sector is currently undergoing retrenchments, as well as processes of outsourcing, contributing to insecurity among workers. Also contributing to insecurity is the privatization of certain sectors. It should be noted here that FEDUSA, the second largest union federation, has a strong membership base among white-collar workers, but mostly in the civil service and the public sector in general.

Hence, membership campaigns have been successful in sectors such as manufacturing and the public sector, where workers seem to have relatively stable jobs. However, unions have been less successful in 'vulnerable' sectors – specifically the service, construction and agricultural sectors. Included in the service sector is the large number of African women who work as domestic workers. This inability of unions to organize 'vulnerable' sectors is reflected in the fact that men make up 71 per cent of union membership, while women, who are mostly employed in the informal sector and casual jobs, only constitute 29 per cent of union membership. However, of men in formal sector employment, 37 per cent are union members. Of all women in formal sector employment, 32 per cent are members of unions. This implies that women who are in formal employment are more readily organized into unions than women in casualized jobs and the informal sector (Naidoo, 1999: 18). Unions have also not been able to attract younger workers. Only 7 per cent of those between the ages of 15 and 24 are members of trade unions, whereas 35 per cent of those between the ages of 25 and 34 are members. This may also relate to the high levels of youth unemployment in South Africa, but when one takes into account only those who are in formal employment, the proportion of young workers who are members of unions still is significantly lower than older workers (see Table 5.4).

Apart from workers in vulnerable sectors, the increased trend towards the casualization of employment contracts also has the potential to erode the membership base of unions in well-organized sectors. The September Commission expressed a clear concern about the COSATU's record of not organizing the 'growing layers of "flexible" workers'. It pointed out that, if the Federation continued 'with no change', 'subcontracting, casualizing [and] labour brokering [may] become more common . . . Ultimately COSATU could end up being based in a shrinking section of the working class, as happened to trade unions in a number of countries'

Table 5.3 COSATU union membership by sector, 1987–99

	1987	1989	1991	1993	1994	1995	1996	1997	1998	1999
Mining										
NUM	261,901	212,000	269,622	267,630	310,596	305,937	300,430	290,216	277,718	265,355
Manufacturing										
NUMSA	130,769	188,013	220,000	180,000	169,598	185,750	182,592	177,845	173,754	169,258
SACTWU	30,538	177,908	185,740	160,000	156,500	157,450	155,005	150,355	145,844	127,000
FAWU	65,278	77,507	129,480	121,534	124,576	139,810	138,755	133,250	122,500	100,000
PPWAWU	23,310	31,151	42,962	32,000	36,630	61,463	53,900	47,468	49,422	43,000
CWIU	29,859	35,151	45,147	44,500	43,321	41,462	43,000	45,198	45,850	45,000
Construction										
CAWU	26,291	21,000	30,123	28,304	25,461	26,718	39,000	31,606	31,606	28,000
Services										
SACCAWU	56,000	72,823	96,628	102,234	102,234	105,301	108,460	111,714	115,065	118,417
SASBO						74,145	72,786	70,324	67,788	
SADWU	9,402	14,525	16,462	16,652	24,149	25,149				
Public service										
SADTU				40,000	59,470	59,427	106,209	160,000	166,309	210,509
NEHAWU	9,197	14,295	18,110	44,058	63,835	96,000	120,348	179,231	190,527	230,000
POTWA/CWU		16,842	21,162	24,162	23,400	23,081	34,550	38,750	39,582	40,398
SAMWU	16,967	23,638	60,304	71,191	103,846	112,063	108,738	120,109	116,524	116,524
SAPSA							14,318	14,318	14,318	14,318
IPS						13,055	8,527			
POPCRU						40,186	43,520	47,538	44,999	44,999
Agriculture										
SAAPAWU						29,000	29,000	33,000	29,000	29,000
Transport										
SARHWU/ SATAWU	34,411	16,400	36,243	34,957	35,398	35,221	35,573	34,808	37,150	45,000
TGWU	18,281	23,182	33,324	38,022	38,482	38,270	38,653	37,822	55,438	55,438
Total	712,231	924,499	1,205,307	1,205,244	1,317,496	1,569,488	1,633,365	1,723,552	1,725,841	1,750,004

Source: Naidoo (1999: 9)

Table 5.4 Unions and age, 1995 (%)

	15–24	25–34	35–44	45–54	55–64
Share of union membership	7	35	33	18	6
Proportion of formally employed in unions	22	36	39	37	34

Source: Naidoo (1999: 18)

(COSATU, 1997: 125). The Commission proposed measures essentially around six themes to organize casual workers:

1 National office bearers in affiliates responsible for organizing workers had to take responsibility for the development of 'campaigns and strategies for recruiting members . . . in vulnerable sectors'. Proposed strategies included an annual campaign to organize vulnerable workers.
2 The formation of 'complaints services'. These services were to be located in affiliates 'affected by . . . non-standard labour' and affiliates that organize vulnerable sectors. The 1999 COSATU National Congress took a resolution to go ahead with the setting up of advice services.
3 Statutory bodies, such as bargaining councils, wage boards and the National Council for Occupational Health (NCOH) had to be used to regulate 'the working life of vulnerable workers'. Other institutions, such as courts, the constitutional court and the media were also mentioned as possible terrains of advocacy.
4 Education courses offered to address existing 'practices and attitudes' in unions which hinder the possibility of organizing casualized layers of workers effectively. The Commission argued that some 'officials and shopstewards do not take the problems and grievances of non-standard workers in their workplaces seriously, and even regard them as second-class workers'.
5 Another strategy revolved around an existing campaign of COSATU for centralized collective bargaining in the industrial sectors of the economy to institute minimum labour standards on a national level, in order to ensure that 'all industries and workplaces are governed or regulated by minimum standards and rights via national legislation, bargaining councils or wage determinations, and that adequate instruments exist to monitor and police such regulations'.
6 Influencing tendering procedures followed by parastatals and the public sector. The Commission proposed that COSATU had to 'fight for representation on . . . tender boards . . . [and] insist that guidelines for winning a tender include compliance with the relevant minimum standards' (COSATU, 1997: 131–4).

Apart from proposing certain strategies to organize casual workers in relatively well-organized sectors, the September Commission also recommended certain strategies to organize 'vulnerable' workers in 'vulnerable' sectors.

On the recommendation of the September Commission, in 1997 the 6th National Congress of COSATU took a resolution to set a process in motion to form trans-industrial 'super unions'. This touches on one of the core principles on which the founding of COSATU was based in 1985, namely 'one industry, one union'. The resolution taken on this at the 6th National Congress therefore adapted the COSATU model of industrial unionism to a form of trans-industrial unionism.

Since the 1997 National Congress, several unions have merged into larger unions, notably the merger of the Chemical Workers Industrial Union (CWIU) and the Paper, Printing, Wood and Allied Workers Union (PPWAWU) into the Chemical, Energy, Paper, Printing, Wood and Allied Workers Union (CEPPWAWU), as well as the South African Transport and Allied Workers' Union (SATAWU), itself the result of a merger, with the Transport and General Workers' Union (TGWU). Mostly, these mergers did not involve the merging of unions operating in 'vulnerable' sectors into strong industrial unions. One exception is the National Union of Mineworkers (NUM) that has recently merged with the Construction and Allied Workers' Union (CAWU) – it remains to be seen whether this leads to a more effective organizing strategy for the building and construction industries, or whether it means that the COSATU union for these workers merely disappears into the NUM.

Hence, the September Commission proposals dealing with the casualization of work in well-organized sectors of the economy, such as manufacturing and mining, can be accommodated within the existing union structures. Proposals focus on advocacy within existing regulatory frameworks, such as bargaining councils, wage boards and agreements between unions and individual firms. The introduction of advice centres for casual workers is a movement in the direction of a different approach to the servicing of a certain layer of workers. Unions will have to link up more closely with advice centres, community-based organizations and other organizations based in civil society if they want to succeed in representing these workers. Another traditional practice will also have to be adapted; union member-ship fees are subtracted from salaries by stop orders. This way of union financing is based on the assumption that workers have a permanent and consistent flow of income. This is very often not the case with casual and/or subcontract workers. Unions will therefore have to rethink their approach to signing up members and collecting union dues.

The fact that the September Commission put these issues on the agenda does not, however, mean that the labour movement is engaging effectively to address these issues. As the Commission itself acknowledges, responses in general are piecemeal. Attempts to deal with casualization and workers in vulnerable sectors remain rhetorical to large extent.

Changes in union structures: bureaucratization?

Since the early 1990s, COSATU as a federation has undergone substantial structural changes, partly as a response to the challenges posed by globalization, but also as a result of engagement in various national institutions, such as NEDLAC. These changes also result from the fact that the coming of parliamentary democracy opened up other avenues for the labour movement to influence policy-making.

As a result, COSATU is losing some of its characteristics as a social movement union. As indicated in the previous section, the 1997 COSATU National Congress adopted resolutions on the functioning of the union federation, as well as unions themselves. One of the resolutions adapts one of the founding principles of COSATU so as to enable unions in different industrial sectors to merge into 'union cartels' or 'super-unions'.

There has always been a tension in trade unions between 'democracy' and 'efficiency'. This tension plays out on many levels – between members and officials, between members and elected representatives, and between the different structures at different levels (local, regional and national) (Buhlungu, 1999a, 1999b). In the context of this, the 'independent' trade union movement in South Africa is largely based on the organization of trade unions at workplace level based on shop stewards. These shop stewards have always been central to plant, local, regional and national structures. Keeping in line with the principle of worker control, COSATU and its unions have maintained the principle that the number of representatives on executive committees who are shop stewards, i.e. actual wage workers, should be more than the number of union officials, i.e. people who are employed by trade unions or federations. Shop stewards and officials were also not allowed to take decisions on behalf of workers without proper mandates.

But the tradition of 'worker control' seems to have undergone changes in the past decade. These changes should not only be seen in the context of the labour movement's involvement in more structures, such as originally the National Manpower Commission and the National Economic Forum, and later on the National Economic, Development and Labour Council (NEDLAC), but also in the context of the rapid growth of trade unions from the late 1980s until recently. The average size of a trade union affiliated to COSATU is just over 100,000 members, with structures spread geographically across the whole country. This massive growth of trade unions had certain implications for trade union structures:

- The influx of a large number of new members put pressure on the existing traditions of worker control. Many new shop stewards were appointed, who did not necessarily share the collective memory of the post-1973 model of organization (Marie, 1992: 21). A survey conducted in 1991 found that 28 per cent of COSATU shop stewards were in their twenties. This implied that many were not experienced and also did not share the 'union traditions of democratic workers control' (Collins, 1994: 30).
- The increase in membership 'necessitated complex nationally centralised structures'. This resulted in a 'greater division of labour and responsibilities between structures and among staff' (Marie, 1992: 21).
- A large membership body demands a greater focus on servicing, which led to a shift from an organizing model of trade unionism, towards a servicing model (Marie, 1992). Apart from more demands for effective servicing, shop stewards were required to attend more and more meetings on different levels. Many unions responded to these demands on shop stewards by reducing the

frequency of branch meetings, to enable shop stewards to engage in regional and national structures (Collins, 1994: 31).

- To deal with the increased workload of shop stewards, the number of full-time shop stewards has been expanding, enabling elected representatives to play a more central role in the day-to-day running of union matters. This practice has been criticized for removing shop stewards from the day-to-day experiences of the workers they are supposed to represent. (Collins, 1994: 33–4)

However, several surveys have found that members of unions affiliated to COSATU elect shop stewards still regularly, usually by secret ballot (Collins, 1994; Wood, 1999). A survey conducted in 1994 found that 84 per cent of shop stewards were elected by membership, 13 per cent appointed by union leadership, and 1 per cent appointed by management. In a 1998 survey, the number of workers who reported that shop stewards were elected by membership increased to 92 per cent. Only 3 per cent reported that shop stewards were appointed by leadership, with management appointments remaining constant at 1 per cent. These figures actually imply an expansion of shop-floor democracy in terms of the election of shop stewards. Indeed, 93 per cent of workers interviewed in 1998 pointed out that shop steward elections are held at least every three years (Wood, 1999: 10–12). The 1999 COSATU National Congress took a resolution that mandated the federation to coordinate shop steward elections for all the affiliates on an annual basis. In future, these elections will take place at the same time, giving the election process a higher profile.

A major shift, which occurred from 1994 to 1998, is how workers view the role of shop stewards. In 1994, 26 per cent of workers felt that shop stewards 'had the right to represent workers' interests as they saw fit, or that they had discretion within a broad mandate'. In the 1998 survey, this number increased to 50 per cent. Wood argues that this could reflect changes in the 'increased complexity of the bargaining environment', where 'industrial relations are increasingly institutionalised'. The proportion of workers who felt that shop stewards should be dismissed when they failed to do what their constituencies desired remained constant at 93 per cent in both surveys. Wood concludes: 'It is evident that an increasing number of workers are willing to trust shop stewards to engage with management on their behalf, as long as they report back from time to time' (1999: 13). However, 71 per cent of the workers interviewed in the 1998 survey said that they attended union meetings at least once a month. This number declined from 77 per cent in 1994 (ibid.: 9).

There also seemed to be a generational shift taking place in terms of worker opinions on the roles of shop stewards. Younger workers were more likely to give shop stewards broad mandates, or treat shop stewards as a form of indirect democracy. The views of older workers, however, conformed much more to the militant form of direct participation based on worker control, as Table 5.5 illustrates. The data confirm the view that the role of shop stewards as 'simple bearers of the mandate' (Marie, 1992: 23), is changing towards a role as an active representative with more discretion.

Apart from changes in the relationships between members and shop stewards, there also seems to be a shift taking place in terms of the role of full-time union

Table 5.5 Age variations by views on mandates issued to shop stewards (%)

When you elect a shop steward, s/he . . . Age	. . . can represent your interests as s/he sees fit	. . . can only do what the membership tells them to do	. . . has the discretion within a broad mandate	Total
18–25	47.2	27.8	25	100
26–35	35.3	42.2	22.4	100
36–45	28.1	53.8	18.1	100
46–55	22.1	56.6	21.3	100
56–65	14.3	85.7		100
Total	30.2	49.7	20.1	100

Source: Wood (1999: 27)

officials. This has to do with the range of complex challenges posed by the rapid transformation process. Unions tend to rely more on a specialized division of labour and experts to respond to pressing deadlines, leading in turn to what is described as 'bureaucratization' (Buhlungu, 1997: 34). A new generation of officials 'are coming in at a phase in which there is an increasing tendency for officials to lead office bearers than the other way round' (Collins, 1994: 37). Concerns were also expressed about the 'brain drain' from COSATU. Experienced union leaders were lost to parliament, the structures of the governing African National Congress and, ironically, big business and some of the unions' own new investment corporations. According to Baskin (1996: 15), COSATU lost about 80 of its 1,450 officials employed by affiliates in 1994 alone. In 1999, six of COSATU's four national office bearers left the labour movement, some to pursue careers as parliamentarians, and one to be a provincial premier.

In the 1970s and the 1980s, many unions had the policy of not paying their officials more than the highest paid workers in the industries in which they organized (Buhlungu, 1997: 17). However, in response to the so-called 'brain drain' of union officials (Buhlungu, 1994: 26–32), COSATU and its affiliates have been moving towards higher remuneration structures in an attempt to retain experienced officials. Standard union packages include benefits such as car allowances, housing allowances, medical aid and provident funds (Buhlungu, 1997: 17).

A consequence of this may be a move of union officials further away from the class position of their members. Internally, the movement have also seen an increased wage gap between officials at different levels. Packages are generally linked to grading systems. Table 5.6 provides a breakdown of remuneration packages of trade union officials from Buhlungu's survey. The survey also showed that 63.2 per cent of employed officials did not see themselves as working in the union movement in five years' time (see Table 5.7). Furthermore, it indicated that 'a majority of [union] officials (57 per cent)' had only been working in the union for four years or less (see Table 5.8). This implies a careerist attitude among a large proportion of union officials, as well as inexperience resulting from a rapid staff turnover. This, according

Table 5.6 Salaries in COSATU and its affiliates, 1997

Salary range	Officials	Percentage
R1 – 1,000	2	0.4
R1,001 – 2,000	31	5.8
R2,001 – 3,000	167	31.3
R3,001 – 4,000	223	41.8
R4,001 – 5,000	57	10.7
R5,001 – 6,000	27	5
R6,001 – 7,000	10	1.9
R7,001 – 8,000	9	1.7
R8,001 – 9,000	3	0.6
R9,001 – 10,000	2	0.4
R13, 001 upwards	2	0.4
Total	533	100

Source: Buhlungu (1997: 18)

Table 5.7 How many years do you think you will be working for the union?

Years to stay in union	Number of officials	Percentage
1–2 years	153	27.9
2–5 years	194	35.3
5–10 years	86	15.7
10 years and more	116	21.1
Total	549	100

Source: Buhlungu (1997: 30)

Table 5.8 Length of service of union officials, 1997

Year employed by union	Number of officials	Percentage
1973–77	2	0.4
1978–82	8	1.4
1983–87	59	10.8
1988–92	166	30.3
1993–96	313	57.1
Total	548	100

Source: Buhlungu (1997: 21)

to Buhlungu (1997), means that there was a process of 'generational transformation' taking place among trade union officials.

The above structural changes relate to individual unions. But COSATU has also consciously engaged in a process of organizational restructuring in order to 'co-ordinate and reinforce the collective bargaining strategies of the affiliates' in the context of the 'likelihood that collective bargaining will come under increasing pressure from employers under the guise of international competitiveness and "globalisation"' (COSATU, 1997: 192). These changes implied the setting up of new decision-making bodies and stronger implementation structures.

A new body, the Central Committee, was set up so as to enable the Federation to speed up policy decision-making. As the second highest decision-making structure, this body meets annually to consider policy matters. The first Central Committee meeting took place in June 1998. Apart from these annual meetings, a Central Executive Committee (CEC) was set up to meet twice a year with the national office bearers to consider policy matters.

The National Executive Committee, which in the past met only six times per year, was made smaller, and now meets once a month. This body considers operational and administrative issues and is responsible for driving the negotiations strategy of the federation. Also, instead of once every four years, the National Congress now meets once every three years.

Hence, not only globalization, but a phenomenal growth in trade union size, has impacted on the structures of trade unions, specifically unions affiliated to COSATU. This, coupled with an involvement of trade unions in more and more centralized structures, such as NEDLAC and bargaining councils, has led to shifts in union traditions based on worker control. Although members generally still elect shop stewards, indications are that there is a generational shift taking place, not only among membership, but also among full-time union officials. As a federation, COSATU has responded to the demands of centralized structures for a more involved approach from the Federation by implementing additional structures that meet on a more regular basis. It has also moved towards a more central role for the Federation in coordinating affiliates. In the future, COSATU may organizationally begin to show more similarities with the older trade unions of Western Europe and North America. However, the traditions of unions as social movements may persist, or be revitalized, in the context of campaigns to defend the gains made in the 1980s and 1990s – as has been evident in the level of popular support for COSATU's current campaigns against unemployment.[4]

Conclusion

Historically, the South African case is an example of how workers can use their collective power and alliances with other organizations to win campaigns against inhumane social structures. This campaign was based on durable shop floor structures, organized through shop stewards committees. Membership of the post-1973 trade unions rocketed, not only because trade unions were able to address real problems of their members in their places of work, but also because unions formed part of a broader social movement of civil society alliances. Trade unions were also assisted by unions from abroad – especially those organizing workers in the same trans-national corporations. After 1990, many of these gains were established as rights under a new democratic dispensation.

However, the labour movement did not achieve its broader goal of transforming society economically. Instead, many of the gains are coming under pressure as a result of neoliberal globalization. Indeed, a different level of engagement is required to address the negative social consequences of globalization. But a global agenda cannot be forged without a strong local base of shop-floor organization, based on independent unionism. Global campaigns will be closely tied to localized struggles – the social movement character of unionism in South Africa is at risk in light of shifts towards bureaucratization.

Currently, the concept of 'global social movement unionism' in the South African context remains largely rhetorical and symbolical. There are considerable tensions between trade unions from the 'North' and from the 'South' on issues such as social clauses in trade agreements. The hangover of Cold War labour politics also remains, even though there are indications of possible discussions about a merger between the WFTU and the ICFTU. However, new ideas are slowly transformed into practice, and these emerging practices, in the context of rapid neoliberal globalization can potentially revitalize the labour movement as a significant anti-hegemonic force.

The engagement of labour in campaigns on the global and regional stages also impacts on institutions (see Table 5.9). On a global level, the formal affiliation of the three major South African trade union federations to the ICFTU adds the confederation level to how labour is organized. As NEDLAC has opened up space to impact on national policy, an increased involvement of unionists in global fora such as the ILO and efforts to lobby around labour interests in WTO structures open up further space for involvement in shaping the nature of globalization in some of the institutions where the rules of the game are made (or, at least, influenced). In the Southern African context, the process of regionalization in SADC emphasizes trans-national dynamics – on the labour front, SATUCC can potentially play a significant role in the region. However, as trade unions have capacity constraints to engage in policy-making on a national level, so these constraints will also impact

Table 5.9 Actors in organized industrial relations interest articulation in the globalizing economy, South Africa

Level	Government and governance	Labour	Business
Global	ILO, WTO	ICFTU, WCL, ITSs	
Regional	SADC	OATUU, SATUCC	
National	South African National government, NEDLAC	COSATU, FEDUSA, NACTU, Unions	BSA, NAFCOC, SACOB, AHI
Sub-national regional and industrial	Provincial government, Bargaining Councils	Unions and union regional structures	SEIFSA, AMEO, Chamber of Mines, etc.
Local	Local government	Unions and union branches	Local Chambers of Commerce

on the nature and significance of global campaigns. The ability to mobilize members around global campaigns therefore depends on the ability of unions to use different campaigns on different levels, ranging from the local to the global.

But there is the very real danger that the labour movement in South Africa may become bureaucratized, and will represent workers with relatively stable jobs in the public sector and a declining manufacturing industry. Indeed, as Franco Barchiesi (2000: 8) points out, only 42.6 per cent of the economically active population in Gauteng is employed in full-time occupations. If this trend towards the informalization of work continues, the capacity of trade unions to organize around a traditional workplace identity may diminish, *à la* Castells.

Nevertheless, the strength of social movement unionism is precisely that it does not assume a dichotomy between a class identity and other identities. The struggle for industrial citizenship has been embedded in a broader struggle for political citizenship in South Africa – hence, the movement has not so much been about 'what we do' as opposed to 'who we believe we are', as formulated in the context of Northern industrialized societies, and the bureaucratic model of trade unionism. In taking up broader issues, such as unemployment and the right to social citizenship, as opposed to a narrowly defined political citizenship, the labour movement remains a major actor in civil society. The challenge is for social movement unionism to become a global one, where labour militants and labour unions play an active role alongside and in coordination with the 'new' social movements. 'What we do' remains a key source of identity – and the power of that identity, as has been shown in the struggle against apartheid, lies in its embeddedness.

Notes

1　This chapter is based on research commissioned by the International Institute for Labour Studies, ILO entitled: 'Towards Global Social Movement Unionism? Trade Union Responses to Globalization in South Africa'. The responsibility for opinions expressed in this chapter lies solely with its author (see Bezuidenhout, 2000).

2　This discussion is based on various reports from newspapers such as *Business Day*, *Business Report* and the *Mail & Guardian*.

3　A particular problem with Castells' chapter that deals with changes in the labour market (Chapter 4, 'The Transformation of Work and Employment: Networkers, Jobless, and Flexitimers' in *The Rise of the Network Society*) is the fact that he relies solely on data for OECD countries.

4　An estimated 4 million South Africans supported the national one-day strike, more than double the COSATU membership.

References

Barchiesi, F. (2000) 'Social Citizenship and the Collapse of the Wage-Income Nexus in Post-Apartheid South Africa', paper presented at the Annual Congress of the South African Sociological Association, University of the Western Cape, 2–5 July, Belville.

Barrett, J. (1993) 'New Strategies to Organize Difficult Sectors', *South African Labour Bulletin* 17(6): 45–50.

Baskin, J. (1996) 'Unions at the Cross-roads: Can They Make the Transition?' *South African Labour Bulletin* 20(1): 8–16.

Bezuidenhout, A. (1999) 'Between a Rock and a Hard Place: Productivity Agreements in Gold Mining', *South African Labour Bulletin* 23(4): 69–74.

Bezuidenhout, A. (2000) *Towards Global Social Movement Unionism? Trade Union Responses to Globalization in South Africa*, Geneva: ILO.

Buhlungu, S. (1994) 'The Big Brain Drain: Union Officials in the 1990s', *South African Labour Bulletin* 18(3): 26–32.

Buhlungu, S. (1997) *Working for the Union: A Profile of Union Officials in COSATU*, Labour Studies Research Report 8, Sociology of Work Unit, University of the Witwatersrand.

Buhlungu, S. (1999a) 'Generational Change in Union Employment: The Organisational Implications of Staff Turnover in COSATU Unions', *Transformation* 39: 47–71.

Buhlungu, S. (1999b) 'Gaining Influence but Losing Power? Labour under Democracy and Globalization in South Africa', paper presented to the Annual Congress of the South African Sociological Association, Saldanha Bay, 6–9 July.

Castells, M. (1996) *The Rise of the Network Society*, Malden, MA: Blackwell.

Castells, M. (1997) *The Power of Identity*, Malden, MA: Blackwell.

Collins, D. (1994) 'Worker Control', *South African Labour Bulletin* 18(3): 33–42.

Congress of South African Trade Unions (COSATU) (1997) *Report of the September Commission of Enquiry into the Future of the Trade Unions*, Johannesburg: COSATU.

Department of Labour (1994–95) *Annual Reports*, Pretoria: Government Printer.

Department of Manpower (1976–93) *Annual Reports*, Pretoria: Government Printer.

Fraser, D. (1991) 'The ICFTU in South Africa: Coming on Strong', *South African Labour Bulletin*, 15(7): 27–31.

Hudson, J. (1991) 'The Practice of Solidarity', *South African Labour Bulletin* 15(7): 40–3.

Hyslop, J. (1999) 'The Imperial Working Class Makes Itself "White": White Labourism in Britain, Australia and South Africa Before the First World War', paper presented to the Annual Congress of the South African Sociological Association, Saldanha Bay, 6–9 July.

International Confederation of Free Trade Unions (ICFTU) (2000) 'The Millennium Review', paper presented to the 17th Congress of the ICFTU, Durban, South Africa, 3–7 April.

Keet, D. (1991) 'ICFTU Conference for African Trade Unionists: International Solidarity or Paternalism?', *South African Labour Bulletin* 16(1): 70–81.

Kenny, B. and Bezuidenhout, A. (1999a) 'Contracting, Complexity and Control: An Overview of the Changing Nature of Subcontracting in the South African Mining Industry', *Journal of the South African Institute of Mining and Metallurgy* 99(4): 185–91.

Kenny, B. and Bezuidenhout, A. (1999b) 'The Language of Flexibility and the Flexibility of Language: Post-Apartheid South African Labour Market Debates', paper presented at the Annual Congress of the Industrial Relations Association of South Africa, 4–5 October, Cape Town.

Kenny, B. and Webster, E. (1999) 'Eroding the Core: Flexibility and the Re-segmentation of the South African Labour Market', *Critical Sociology* 24(3): 216–43.

Kilosang Mayo Uno (KMU) (1993) 'The ICFTU: Tainted with Blood and Bribery', *South African Labour Bulletin* 17(5), 60–5.

Lambert, R. (1992) 'Constructing the New Internationalism: Australian Trade Unions and the Indian Ocean Regional Initiative', *South African Labour Bulletin* 16(5): 66–73.

Lambert, R. (1995) 'COSATU and the Challenge of the Asian Economies', *South African Labour Bulletin* 19(1): 91–2.

Lambert, R. (1998) 'Globalisation: Can Unions Resist?', *South African Labour Bulletin* 22(6): 72–7.

Marie, B. (1992) 'COSATU Faces Crisis: "Quick Fix" Methods and Organisational Contradictions', *South African Labour Bulletin* 16(5): 20–6.

Mather, C. (1991) 'Solidarity in a Changing World', *South African Labour Bulletin* 15(7): 13–15.

Meecham, R. *et al.* (1993) 'COSATU, the ICFTU, and Dictatorships in Asia', *South African Labour Bulletin* 17(3): 76–81.

Moody, K. (1997) *Workers in a Lean World: Unions in the International Economy*, London: Verso.

Munck, R. (1988) *The New International Labour Studies: An Introduction*, London: Zed Books.

Munck, R. (1999) 'Labour Dilemmas and Labour Futures', in R. Munck and P. Waterman, *Labour Worldwide in the Era of Globalization: Alternative Union Models in the New World Order*, London: Macmillan.

Naidoo, J. (1991) 'More that Unites than Divides' *South African Labour Bulletin* 15(7): 16–21.

Naidoo, R. (ed.) (1999) *Unions in Transition: Cosatu into the New Millennium*, Johannesburg: Nadeli.

Ngcukana, C. (1991) 'Rooting out Dependency', *South African Labour Bulletin* 15(7): 22–6.

Regini, M. (ed.) (1992) *The Future of Labour Movements*, London: Sage/ISA.

Seidman, G. (1994) *Manufacturing Militance: Workers' Movements in Brazil and South Africa*, Berkeley, CA: University of California Press.

Silver, B.J. and Arrighi, G. (2001) 'Workers North and South', in L. Papitch and C. Leys (eds) *Working Classes: Global Realities, Socialist Register*, Toronto: Monthly Review Press.

Simons, J. and Simons, R. (1983) *Class and Colour in South Africa*, London: International Defence Aid.

Southall, R. (1995) *Imperialism or Solidarity? International Labour and South African Trade Unions*, Cape Town: UCT Press.

Southall, R. (1996) *International Labour and South African Trade Unions*, Labour Studies Research Report 7, Sociology of Work Unit, University of the Witwatersrand.

Standing, G. (1997) 'Globalization, Labour Flexibility and Insecurity: The Era of Market Regulation', *European Journal of Industrial Relations*, 3(1): 7–37.

Stevis, D. (1998) 'International Labor Organizations, 1864–1997: The Weight of History and the Challenges of the Present', *Journal of World-Systems Research*, 4(1): 52–75.

Taylor, R. (1998) *Trade Unions and Trans-national Industrial Relations*, Geneva: International Institute for Labour Studies.

Von Holdt, K. (1993a) 'The New World Economy – Challenge by Labour', *South African Labour Bulletin* 17(5): 72–9.

Von Holdt, K. (1993b) 'A New Labour Internationalism?', *South African Labour Bulletin*, 17(2): 76–9.

Von Holdt, K. and Zikalala, S. (1993) 'The ICFTU in South Africa', *South African Labour Bulletin*, 17(1): 67–71.

Waterman, P. (1993) 'The ICFTU in SA: Admissions, Revelations, Silences', *South African Labour Bulletin* 17(3): 82–4.

Waterman, P. (1999) 'The Brave New World of Manuel Castells: What on Earth (or in the Ether) is Going On?', *Development and Change* 30: 357–80.

Webster, E. (1985) *Cast in a Racial Mould: Labour Process and Trade Unionism in the Foundries*, Johannesburg: Ravan.

Wood, G. (1999) 'Shopfloor Democracy in the Congress of South African Trade Unions in the late 1990s', paper presented to the Annual Congress of the South African Sociological Association, Saldanha Bay.

6 Globalization, economic institutions and workplace change

The economic reform processes in China

John Hassard, Jonathan Morris, Jackie Sheehan and Yuxin Xiao

Privatization and the state-owned enterprise

China has won praise for its gradualist, pragmatic reform path since 1978, particularly in comparison with the countries of Eastern Europe and the former Soviet Union (EEFSU) (Child, 1994; Nolan, 1995). But successful though it has been to date, the reform programme has now come to the point where all the relatively easy and less controversial steps have already been taken, and what remains to be tackled are much more difficult and politically sensitive issues such as employment restructuring, ownership and property rights issues, and the relationships between state-owned enterprises (SOEs) and central and local government. The very nature of the SOE in pre-1978 China means that this stage of reform is inextricably bound up with other wide-ranging reforms such as the abolition of subsidized housing and the effort to set up an urban welfare state in China under local government auspices. It is also occurring at a time of great economic difficulty throughout the region. Some of the steel corporations in this study are finding themselves having to compete for domestic business with Japanese and Russian firms as these seek new markets to replace those lost in South-East Asia because of the financial crisis and economic downturn there, at the same time as they themselves are having to look for new export markets for the same reason. The resulting price competition has reduced profit margins which were often not generous to begin with (Interview 2, 1998).

Aside from these unexpected external factors, problems of ideology and politics are still hindering further progress in state-enterprise reform. Change has generally gone furthest in those areas which are purely internal to the corporation, although even here the influence of existing power structures remains strong in many respects. Externally, despite twenty years of reforms in Chinese industry designed to promote greater enterprise-level autonomy, China's large SOEs are still subject to direct and indirect intervention by an array of state agencies, national and local, and are still constrained by the ideological and political principles and sensitivities of the ruling Chinese Communist Party (CCP) in their efforts to reform and restructure. While they are not to be 'let go', like their small and medium-sized counterparts (many of which have already been sold off, merged, or declared bankrupt), they are subject to conflicting demands and pressures, by no means all of which are pushing them in the direction of 'corporatizing' or marketizing reform. A case in point, and one to which we will return below, is one of the key measures of the latest reform phase, the downsizing of large SOEs' workforces by up to 50 per cent. Large-scale lay-offs have been taking place since 1997, but many of the large corporations involved are constrained by their obligation to support the government's overriding priority of social and political stability and avoid causing further unrest over rising unemployment over the next few years. Thus while the general thrust of China's industrial reforms has been to transform SOEs from old-style 'societies in miniature' (*xiao shehui*) into firms whose sole purpose is efficient production for profit, they have yet to escape completely their previous role as providers of social goods such as full employment.

This chapter is based on an ongoing series of field visits to ten large SOEs in China, most of them in the steel industry. Since the early 1990s these SOEs have been implementing the Modern Enterprise System (MES) and Group Company System (GCS) reform programmes. One of the primary aims of these programmes is to reduce government interference in the running of these large SOEs (Interview 5, 1996) and to encourage them to behave in a more entrepreneurial fashion, enabling them to become internationally competitive firms structured along the same lines as Western corporations, with Boards of Directors accountable to shareholders rather than being subject to the political authority of the CCP. In this way it is intended to make these large corporations subject to a greater degree of market discipline while avoiding the still very politically sensitive step of privatizing any of the 'commanding heights' of Chinese heavy industry.

But although the top leadership is keen to stress that this is not a programme of privatization for the largest SOEs, nevertheless the MES and GCS reforms are very much concerned with questions of ownership and property rights, suggesting, as Steinfeld has pointed out, that Chinese reformers have at least 'internalized the logic' of Eastern European-style privatization strategies (1998: 34), even if they do not openly advocate such a strategy for China. Moreover, some aspects of the wide-ranging reforms currently taking place within state-owned industry in China, such as the selling-off of enterprise housing to workers and the sale of shares to individual investors, bring the programme closer to at least partial privatization than the central government seems willing to admit. There is markedly less reluctance to use the taboo term among SOE managers and academic analysts within China, and some of the former are in fact becoming increasingly frustrated by their inability to forge ahead with, for example, Stock Exchange listings in the face of government unwillingness to grant the necessary approvals (Interview 2, 1998).

On top of these tensions between state-owned corporations and central government institutions, the SOEs in our sample also have to contend with important conflicts of interest between themselves and the local state. Some of these relate to the major shifts in the external institutional environment which are taking place at the same time, such as welfare and fiscal reform and the development of a functioning labour market in China, many of which have direct implications for the relationship between SOEs and local government. The transfer of welfare services from SOEs to local government is proceeding slowly or not at all in many areas, with both SOE management and local authorities having good reason for their reluctance to press ahead with this reform; more will be said about this later. In addition, SOE managers can still find themselves pressured by local government to take over smaller, failing enterprises in the same area and bear responsibility for their wage and pension obligations (Interview 5, 1996; Interview 2, 1998), in order to avoid the unrest among the workers of these smaller firms which bankruptcy would be likely to cause.

The perspective of the large SOE is a useful one from which to observe the multiplicity of state actors at the local level in China and the ways in which various state institutions influence or intervene in the economic reform process. Steinfeld has drawn attention to the opportunities for rent-seeking behaviour by agencies having to seek new roles for themselves in the transition away from central planning, opportunities afforded by the absence of the basic institutions of governance required for a functioning market economy in China, concluding that the right sort of central state intervention to protect SOEs from local institutional predators might still be very necessary at this stage of the reforms (Steinfeld, 1998: 253). This idea, that what large SOEs sometimes require at this stage is not more autonomy from the state but more intervention, has come up in discussions with some of our informants who have found themselves at a serious disadvantage when trying to compete with smaller, locally-based firms in which the local state has a vested interest (Interview 1, 1998). Steinfeld's proposal of a 'constraints-based' approach to SOE reform to replace the prevalent autonomy or 'rights-based' approach is thus supported to some extent by our findings, and it is to a summary of our case study findings to date that we now turn, looking at the areas of workforce downsizing and, first, internal corporate restructuring and reform of enterprise–state relations. These are areas in which the difficulties of responding to the conflicting signals and priorities of the central and local state are evident, and are also areas which demonstrate how politics still exerts a powerful influence over what large SOEs can and cannot do by way of reform in China.

Corporate restructuring in the state sector

Traditionally all state enterprises in China, even relatively small ones, aimed for total vertical integration. Since the early 1990s, though, in the interests of specialization, efficiency, product diversification, and clarification of company functions, the steel-making SOEs in our sample have been engaged in separating off all component parts which are involved in their core line of production (i.e. iron and steel) from others which may be engaged in completely unrelated lines of business, working towards the model of a parent holding company with a range of more or less autonomous subsidiary companies. The core iron and steel subsidiaries are to maintain a fairly close relationship with the parent company, although still enjoying some degree of management autonomy, while the other sub-companies, including social service companies, will have a much higher degree of autonomy from the parent company. The formation of sub-companies serves a number of related purposes. The sub-companies are intended to spread responsibility for results throughout the group, to provide more opportunities for gaining access to capital, especially overseas, and to absorb surplus labour from the core iron and steel businesses. Dividend income from sub-companies (or profit quotas) can be used by the parent company to help cover social welfare costs where these have not been transferred to local government; in addition, since the relationships within the group are now to be governed by market principles, sub-companies will be expected to pay for the provision of social services by the parent company.

All sub-companies will eventually be formed into shareholding or limited liability companies which will be responsible for their own profit and loss, and which will be able to attract outside investment, borrow from banks, and enter into joint ventures with foreign companies in their own right; this ability to attract much-needed outside investment is a primary reason for their formation. A distinction is made between shareholding companies, which are destined for an early stock market listing and whose shares can be bought by anyone, including individuals, and limited liability companies, whose shares can only be bought by institutional investors. These 'public-oriented legal persons' (Keun Lee, 1996) might be state-owned banks or insurance companies, other SOEs, or state trade unions. In some cases 'triangular' debt owed to government bureaux, state-run banks and suppliers has been converted into shares to aid corporations so indebted as to be virtually insolvent in Western terms. Creditors have accepted these arrangements as there seemed little likelihood of recovering any of their money unless some sort of debt write-off was undertaken to enable the corporation to continue in business (Interview 3, 1996; Interview 1, 1998). Some core iron- and steel-making sub-companies are to remain exclusively funded by the parent company, and at present the parent company almost always retains a controlling stake of at least 51 per cent, and often much more, in its sub-companies. In the latest round of interviews, however, we found examples of parent-company stakes of less than 51 per cent in one of our case study corporations, while individual shareholdings could total as much as 20 per cent (Interview 2, 1998).

Sub-companies are responsible for their own profit and loss (although the latter responsibility is sometimes phased in over a period of several years, with a sliding subsidy from the parent company to offset losses which is gradually reduced to nothing). The parent company is only responsible for the money which it has invested in the sub-company, although, as mentioned above, some sub-companies at this stage of the reform are still exclusively funded by the group corporation. In principle, sub-companies can decide on their own staffing levels and appoint their own managers (apart from the top one or two posts) without the approval of the parent company. In practice, however, they are expected to consult with the parent company over any large reductions in their workforce. Sub-companies are allowed to recruit new staff from outside the group, but clearly there is also pressure on them to take up the slack where redundant workers in other parts of the group are in need of new posts (Interview 2, 1996). More will be said about the question of surplus labour in SOEs later.

The degree of control which sub-companies have over their production targets varies depending on whether the group company is their main customer or whether they sell most of their production outside the group (Interviews 1 and 2, 1996). In general they are free to look for markets anywhere, but where they provide a key input to group steel production (such as an iron-ore mining sub-company), the group's orders must be met before production can be sold outside to the highest bidder. Inputs can in theory be bought in from any competitive supplier, but in practice many of our informants observed that it was common for sub-companies to choose to work mainly within existing group relationships whether seeking markets or materials. The parent company was still admitted to have considerable influence over most sub-companies whatever the regulations on corporate structure and governance might say on paper (Interviews 1 and 3, 1996). The parent company must be informed of all sub-company investment decisions, and must give permission for any investment above a certain amount; at one steel corporation for which we have figures, the investment ceiling for sub-companies is RMB 30 million (about £2.25 million).

Superficially at least, MES enterprises in China do now more closely resemble typical Western corporate structures. The steel corporations in our sample now generally have a Board of Directors chosen by shareholders which selects the general manager. But for large, state-owned steel-makers, in most cases the sole shareholder is still the state, which means that in practice candidates for the Board are recommended and appointed by the government, i.e. the CCP, just as top enterprise managers always were before the reforms. It was admitted in two of the corporations we visited that changes in corporate structure were still more form than substance to date, with the ideal of shareholder control falling prey to continued direct government interference. The reportedly high level of government interference in the appointment of Boards of Directors thus has so far negated one of the main declared purposes of the MES programme, the separation of government and management functions. There are no indications that this problem will be resolved in the near future.

Similar problems have arisen with attempts to alter the distribution of power within the enterprise. Before the reforms, power mainly rested with the so-called 'old three committees', the party branch, management, and the official trade union. Under the MES, these are to be replaced by the 'new three committees': the Board of Directors, the Board of Supervisors, and the Shareholders' Congress. If it were carried out as intended, this reform would directly attack the vested interests of many in the old structure, notably the Party and the official trade union, generating resistance. Under the MES, the Board of Directors ought to be the highest level of decision-making, but this was always the role of the Party in the past, and the Party is proving reluctant to give up its power. Many enterprises, including some in the steel industry, have therefore fudged the issue by appointing the branch Party chairperson as chair of the Board of Directors as well, so that the same person can give orders wearing either 'hat'. Similarly, existing managers have been transformed into a new 'Board of Directors' by a stroke of the pen, and Party and union organizations have also found a place on the Board of Supervisors, allowing power to remain in essentially the same hands within the enterprise but under different titles. The question of how to break up the old vested interests in state-owned industry has been described to us as a 'forbidden area' of reform, since it touches on the question of the role of the CCP in a mixed economy and the proper limits of its power.

Discussion of questions of ownership and property-rights reform in large SOEs is still hedged about with political restrictions, despite being a major component of the MES and GCS reform programmes. At the firm level, many state-sector managers are prepared to discuss quite openly the extent to which their subsidiary companies, welfare services, company housing, etc. have been or will be privatized, but the word is still seldom heard in the speeches of the top party leadership, except in assertions that privatization is not an option for China's largest state-owned corporations in the foreseeable future. Despite the announcement by President Jiang Zemin at last year's 15th CCP Congress that all but about 500 of the largest and most strategically significant SOEs would henceforth have to make their own way in the market, and would face merger, bankruptcy or closure if they could not make a profit, any degree of privatization of elements of the largest state-owned corporations remains extremely controversial even as it begins to happen on the ground.

Thus, some of the group corporations in our sample are finding that they have successfully carried out their internal corporate restructuring to establish viable sub-companies with their own 'legal-person' status, only to face difficulty in getting permission for the listings which would bring in vital new funds for investment. Where listings (on the Hong Kong, Shanghai and Shenzhen exchanges) have taken place, they have often been of sub-companies which cannot be identified as part of the parent corporation from their names. One of our case studies has taken a different tack, gaining permission for a listing of just two of its more than a dozen core iron-and-steel sub-companies, but under such a general company title that any and all of the other elements of its steel-making operations could be added to the listing in future without the need for a fresh application for approval to list (Interview 2, 1998). In part this course is intended to avoid too ambitious a listing at a time of great volatility in the region's stock markets, but in the main it is a product of central-government reluctance to countenance creeping privatization in some of its most strategically and ideologically significant corporations.

So far we have looked mainly at areas where our informants report continued, and often unwelcome, central government intervention in their operations. Conversely, though, as mentioned earlier, rather than wanting greater freedom from central state intervention in all cases, some SOE managers have frankly expressed to us their company's need for more central intervention, to redress the disadvantages they can face in dealings with local government institutions. Far from operating on a level playing-field, as was one of the intentions of the MES and related fiscal reforms, SOEs in China are still subject to varying treatment from central and local authorities according to their particular status and history, as well as being affected by regional policy variations (Solinger, 1996; Goodman, 1997). The crucial role of local government can be seen in the very selection of SOEs as reform pilots. One corporation in our sample was co-opted as a GCS pilot enterprise against its own preferences (Interview 5, 1996), and several have been compelled by local government to absorb into the group smaller, loss-making companies which would otherwise have gone bankrupt, throwing their employees out of work (Interview 5, 1996; Interview 2, 1998).

The finances of these autonomous sub-companies are kept separate from those of the parent company, so only limited financial help will be forthcoming from the parent if the sub-companies continue to make losses. Therefore little benefit is gained from this shifting around of unprofitable enterprises by anyone except local government, which divests itself of the responsibility for the small enterprises' losses and has wage payments guaranteed by the group corporation (late payment or non-payment of wages and pensions being a major cause of labour unrest in China in the 1990s (Sheehan 1996, 1998)). Local government also tends, for obvious reasons, to favour those enterprises under its control over those which come directly under the authority of a central government department or bureau, leading the latter to complain that they need more 'government interference', not less, as long as they are not competing on equal terms in a well-established and properly regulated market economy, but instead find themselves in a situation where locally-based firms are favoured whenever contracts are awarded by a local government which has a financial stake in these firms' success. (Interview 1 1998).

Surplus labour in SOEs and political stability

In May 1997 the State Commission for Economic Restructuring (SCER) predicted that 15–20 million surplus workers in the state sector would lose their jobs by 2000, and in turn estimated the total number of surplus workers in SOEs at 54 million, close to half of the total workforce (*South China Morning Post*, 7 May 1997). The proportion of surplus labour in SOE workforces varies across enterprises and is affected by factors such as enterprise size, industrial sector, and geographical location. Our case study enterprises initially planned to reduce their core workforces by between 15 and 50 per cent during the period of the Ninth Five-Year Plan (1996–2000) (Interviews 2, 3 and 4, 1996), although at least one has since extended the deadline to 2003 (Interview 1, 1998). This level of surplus employees is in line with the findings of other surveys of the same sort of large SOE (Kuehl and Sziraczki, 1995: 75). Clearly the numbers involved are substantial, and the problem of how to deal with such a high level of overmanning is one which still largely falls to SOEs themselves to solve (Lin and Sziraczki, 1995: 28), with only limited help from local and national government.

The corporations concerned need to make these cuts in the workforce to reduce their costs and improve their productivity in order to compete both nationally and internationally. It is no exaggeration to say that the continued success of the present reform programme depends on the reductions going ahead, yet at the same time, the single overriding priority of the central government is still the maintenance of social and political stability in China (and of course the maintenance of its own power), and this is already being threatened by state workers' reaction to downsizing and the threat of redundancy. SOE managers are fully aware of the tremendous responsibility they bear in this area, and they have prepared as best they can to achieve the very large-scale redundancies required while keeping serious unrest and resistance to a minimum. The watchword for this part of the reforms is 'making a channel before the water comes'; in other words, have acceptable destinations ready before workers lose their existing jobs.

China still cannot really be said to have a functioning labour market to date (Child, 1994: 162; Warner, 1995: 161), despite the increased flexibility which both enterprises and individuals have gained in an era of widespread contract employment and some enterprise autonomy over the recruitment of employees. Some large SOEs have been replacing contract workers at the end of their contracted period of employment with otherwise redundant permanent workers from within the group (Interview 2, 1996), but given the relatively small proportion of such contract employees in the state workforce as a whole (Warner, 1995: 161), this is not a viable method in itself of making the large cuts in core employment which are planned. Aside from this minority of less securely employed workers, none of our case study corporations has yet been prepared to force out any employee who was not willing to go. Instead they have sought to develop internal labour markets which will offer retraining and re-allocation within the group to workers, or will help them to find alternative employment or self-employment outside the group. Workers are being shifted out of overmanned core production units and into new sub-companies set up for the purpose of absorbing surplus labour (Kuehl and Sziraczki, 1995: 66; Hassard and Sheehan, 1997: 92–3; Interviews 1 and 3, 1997). Many large state-owned corporations now typically contain within them sub-companies running such businesses as shops, hotels, restaurants and travel agencies, as well as social service companies and companies engaged in any kind of manufacturing or service provision where profits can be made. Considerable numbers of workers are involved in these shifts: in one of the large state-owned steel companies studied by the authors, the number of employees transferred out of core iron- and steel-producing units into sub-companies now exceeds the number remaining in iron and steel production by 40 per cent (Interview 4, 1996).

Some large SOEs have set up labour pools for surplus employees where they can undergo re-training for vacant posts elsewhere within the group (Interview 1, 1996). Surplus workers may remain in the group labour-pool for up to two years, but ultimately their employment can be terminated by the corporation if no suitable post is found for them within that time (Hassard and Sheehan, 1997: 93). Alternatively, they may retain their employment status within the enterprise once the two-year period in the labour pool has passed, but instead of continuing to receive their basic salary, they are only paid the monthly amount calculated by the local government as the minimum necessary to cover basic living expenses (Interview 3, 1996). This is an example of the proliferation of different forms of employment status within the firm through which unambiguous dismissal of surplus workers is being avoided. One of our case studies has an alternative system whereby redundant employees are transferred to an in-house 'job centre' which provides retraining and job information. The company will be responsible for three years' basic living expenses for these staff and they will be offered two alternative posts within the firm, but if they turn both of these posts down, the company will have no further responsibility for them (Interview 2, 1998). Again, compulsory termination of employment is implicit in this scheme, although it has not yet happened to any employee.

In many large SOEs a range of employment forms has thus been developed which includes not only permanent waged employment, retraining and redeployment within the firm, voluntary severance, and early retirement, but also stages in between. At one of the large steel plants visited by the authors, surplus workers' options include 'retirement within the company', in which they remain in post with no annual increases in pay; alternatively, they may remain in post without pay but retaining their status as an employee of the unit. This retention of a formal link with the work unit has security benefits for the workers concerned, allowing them, for example, to remain in unit-owned housing at low rents while obtaining work elsewhere or becoming self-employed. The alternative to retaining such a link is known as the 'two don't look fors' (*liang bu zhao*), meaning that the worker will not look for any further help from the unit, and the unit has no further call on its former employee. The various forms of employment status now in existence in the state sector account in part for the discrepancy between China's official urban unemployment rate (which still stands at around 3.5 per cent), and the much higher figures routinely given by academic analysts and even the official trade unions in China, which include the large numbers of workers who have retained some sort of formal relationship, paid or unpaid, with their work unit but are not actually going to work. Estimates for the proportion out of work based on this definition range from 8 to 15 per cent, with even higher local rates cited in parts of the northeast which have concentrations of large and loss-making SOEs.

Besides creating vacancies elsewhere within the enterprise for surplus workers and restricting entry from outside the group, large SOEs are also attempting to increase the number of workers exiting from the group (Kuehl and Sziraczki, 1995: 68). One major method of doing this is to encourage and facilitate early retirement (Interview 2, 1996, Interview 2, 1998). In some cases employees taking advantage of early retirement schemes can receive a lump sum investment from the group company in order to help them start up their own business. To make voluntary severance for workers of any age more attractive to those wishing to change jobs or go into business on their own, the requirement on these employees to pay back the costs of their training if they leave the corporation has been removed (Interview 3, 1996). Inevitably, companies have found that it is not necessarily the right employees, from the enterprise's point of view, who volunteer for this sort of scheme, and some have had to introduce various incentives to ensure the retention of key technical personnel in particular (Interview 3, 1996). To help absorb the increasing numbers of redundant SOE employees, some cities have reserved certain new jobs or self-employment permits, or even entire lines of work, for them. In Beijing certain occupations, including accountants, secretaries, bus conductors, and sales clerks, have been reserved for permanent city residents rather than rural migrants in an attempt to vacate tens of thousands of posts for laid-off urbanites (*South China Morning Post*, 1 May 1997). The municipal government has also reserved 20,000 taxi licences for laid-off workers, asking bankrupt SOEs in the capital to submit lists of recommended workers for this scheme. Beijing's programme in turn is modelled on that of Shanghai, which has pioneered efforts to help surplus workers from SOEs go into business on their own by easing registration procedures and offering tax holidays to new small businesses (*South China Morning Post*, 7 May 1997). This type of programme, however, conflicts with the new market ethos which dictates that the established working class must now compete with migrants from the countryside for the available work, and there is thus conflict among policy-makers about how far the old state-sector workforce can or should be protected from the rigours of the market.

Although the role of government in determining SOEs' levels of employment has been reduced under the reforms (Hay *et al.*, 1994: 130–1), local governments and labour bureaux do still have some influence or authority in some respects (Lin and Sziraczki, 1995: 17), and some managers in large SOEs continue to complain of government interference in areas where they have autonomy on paper. Large SOEs are still sometimes compelled to employ workers (often those laid off by other enterprises) whom they do not need or want, or loss-making enterprises are merged with more successful ones against the latter's will in order to safeguard jobs in the struggling firm (Kuehl and Sziraczki, 1995: 65; Interview 4, 1996). Some enterprises seem better able than others to fend off unwanted impositions of this kind by local government, either because of variations in policy between different cities or regions, or because of the particular circumstances of the enterprise concerned and its past relationship with local authorities (Interviews 5 and 6, 1996; Solinger, 1996). Since 1995 the Labour Law has, however, shifted some of the responsibility for helping the unemployed to find work onto local government institutions rather than leaving enterprises to bear the whole burden (Interview 3, 1996). The national government in 1997 also introduced a period of one to three years' compulsory training for all new entrants to the labour force, a measure intended to ease employment pressures.

Labour unrest and the threat to stability and reform

The caution exhibited to date by management in large SOEs when dealing with workforce reductions is understandable. The prospect of labour unrest fuelled by discontent over job losses and other aspects of China's economic reforms is a real one, and in fact such unrest is already beginning to occur, although it is much more common among the ex-employees of small and medium SOEs than those of the large corporations with which this research is mainly concerned. Lacking the resources to 'make the channel before the water comes', smaller SOEs tend instead to make abrupt announcements regarding merger or bankruptcy which are received by their workers with anger and resentment, and which not infrequently result in street protests and factory sit-ins (Sheehan, 1998). Incipient unrest is not confined to the employees of small SOEs, however. Core, permanently employed state-sector workers were traditionally regarded as the least restive segment of the Chinese working class under CCP rule, but by the end of the 1980s this had changed. State workers were in the vanguard of the 1989 democracy movement as a newly aggrieved group suffering significant relative deprivation under the reforms and angry in particular about high levels of official corruption and inflation (Walder and Gong, 1993; Sheehan, 1998), and there is every likelihood of further protest from them as the long-perceived threat to their vital interests posed by economic reform finally materializes.

Managers in these large state-owned corporations have thus put considerable effort into justifying the planned reductions and persuading workers to accept them. First, they stress the new opportunities available to some workers in the new reform environment. This is more than propaganda: the chance to change jobs, and in particular to set up in business independently, is genuinely welcomed by some state employees. Success stories of former SOE workers making their fortunes are widely publicized in an attempt to overcome workers' fears of losing the security of permanent state employment, with some success (Interviews 2 and 4, 1996). It is plain to all involved, however, that not everyone who leaves state employment is going to do better elsewhere (Warner, 1995: 162). The managers' task then is to convince employees that some have to leave the enterprise if any are to prosper, as in the new 'market socialist' environment, enterprises cannot continue to carry present levels of surplus labour indefinitely while attempting to restructure themselves the better to compete in national and world markets (Interviews 1, 2 and 4, 1996). This approach seemed initially to have been relatively successful, if not in whipping up real enthusiasm for downsizing among state employees, then at least in engendering a mood of resigned acceptance of the end of the 'iron rice bowl' for some (Interviews 2 and 4, 1996; Warner, 1995: 132).

However, in the past twelve months unrest has become so widespread, if still mainly local and sporadic, that it has become one of the major concerns of the top leadership and threatens to cause a significant slowing in the implementation of many reform programmes, such as the housing reform planned to take place by the middle of 1998 (*South China Morning Post*, 2 July 1998). In internal discussions, laid-off workers have been identified as the third most serious threat to political stability in the People's Republic, after separatists in the Muslim northwest and the Tibetan independence movement, with the resort by workers to the organization of independent unions a particular cause for concern (*South China Morning Post*, 1 July 1998). Local governments are coming under even greater pressure from the centre to provide alternative employment or retraining and emergency living allowances to unemployed workers in order to stave off more widespread unrest, and have been particularly warned not to divert government money intended for these purposes to other uses (*South China Morning Post*, 20, 24 June 1998). Local governments are even authorized to make extra payments to workers in areas or at enterprises with a particular record of unrest, setting a dangerous precedent of rewarding those who make the most trouble (Sheehan, 1996: 555; *South China Morning Post*, 17 June 1998). Large state-owned corporations are thus more aware than ever that, at least until a reasonably complete, functioning alternative welfare system is in place, they will not in fact be able to expect society to absorb the large proportion of surplus labour within their workforces.

Most of our case study corporations are still only at the stage of holding preliminary discussions with local government about divesting themselves of their welfare responsibilities. If the transition from enterprise-based to local authority welfare proves a successful one in the only case study city where this has been attempted to date, this might encourage other local governments to work more actively in this direction. But at present, many of the firms in this study are quite pessimistic about the prospects of freeing themselves of this historical burden, both because of the simple inability of society to cope with such a transfer in this period of regional economic crisis, and also because of resistance from their own staff, who fear a reduction in the quality of their schools, for example, if these are taken over by hard-pressed local authorities who already have 'their own' schools to fund and look after (Interviews 2 and 4, 1998). A number of our case study corporations contain within them some of the best schools in their area, nationally recognized for their quality, and thus it is understandable that despite their awareness of the economic burden which running such services constitutes on a modern industrial corporation, employees are still reluctant to see their firms abandon what has often been very successful social provision. Since the very beginning of the reform era in China, the 'economic and social conglomerate' nature of the SOE, providing cradle-to-grave welfare for its employees, has been seen as a major obstacle to improving efficiency and profitability, particularly for smaller SOEs, but also for the largest (Sheehan, 1998: 160). Yet on its own terms, work-unit-based welfare has often been very successful. Besides the evident satisfaction of SOE staff mentioned above, SOE management has also regarded high-quality social service provision as a 'badge of management success' and a means of attracting and retaining workers with scarce skills, and will also lose assets into which it has put considerable investment over the years when service provision is passed to local government (Hannan, 1998: 59–60).

Conclusion

Faced with the scale of such difficulties as the surplus labour problem, it is easy to become perhaps over-pessimistic about the prospects for reform. Given China's record to date of gradual, pragmatic transition away from a planned economy, in contrast to the 'big bang' approach of many EEFSU countries, the recent signs of slowing of reform in response to rising labour unrest may actually be encouraging ones, as they show that the national leadership has recognized the scale and seriousness of the problems reform has engendered and is now proceeding more cautiously. It is also true to say that China since the early 1980s, after its post-Cultural Revolution peak of youth unemployment which coincided with the early 1980s' recession, has had a very good record in job creation, particularly in the non-state sector. However, the unusually high growth rates which have enabled this job creation to take place have been slowing for several years and are likely to be further reduced by the regional economic crisis (and also by 1998's natural disasters in the provinces worst affected). In addition, the number of redundant workers who will have to leave the state sector in the next few years is unprecedentedly high.

The SOEs in our sample are faced with a frustrating dilemma. Above all, if they are to be able to complete their restructuring and technical transformation in the next few years, they need to make very large reductions in their core workforces in order to lower costs and raise productivity. There are substantial markets within China presently filled by imports which could be tapped by these large corporations if the investment were available to enable them to restructure their production accordingly (Interview 2, 1998). Yet the requirements of further state-enterprise reform are now in sharp conflict with the government's top priority of political and social stability and the avoidance of an obvious change in the ownership status of the largest state-owned corporations, and the SOEs in our sample are presently unable to do much more except reform internally as far as they are able while waiting for further change in the policy environment which would enable them to take the next steps. If at present some large SOEs do not appear to be responding in the desired way to reform by becoming less reliant on the state and more entrepreneurial, concentrating solely on improving productivity and return on investment, this is less the result of any strong attachment to the old system of central planning, lack of responsibility for profit and loss, and bottomless government subsidies, than it is a rational attempt to respond to conflicting pressures and signals from a variety of state agencies with different interests in the firm. Moreover, many of the pressures bearing on SOEs at this difficult point in the transition away from central planning are specifically political, the problem of down-sizing and political stability being a notable case in point.

Acknowledgements

The research for this article was funded by a grant from the Economic and Social Research Council. The authors would like to thank Professor Chen Zhicheng of the Institute of Management Science, University of Science and Technology, Beijing, for his invaluable assistance in arranging the Chinese field visits for this project.

Appendix

Interview 1 1995 was conducted on 30 August 1995 with a senior academic expert on management and fiscal science based in Beijing.

Interview 2 1995 was conducted on 1 September 1995 with a senior specialist in economic management at a leading Chinese Communist Party academic institution.

Interview 3 1995 was conducted on 4 September 1995 with an economic specialist working in the Metallurgical Industry Ministry in Beijing.

Interview 4 1995 was conducted on 4 September 1995 with a senior member of staff specializing in research and development at a large steel corporation in Beijing.

Interview 5 1995 was conducted with several senior managers from a non-steel state-owned corporation near Beijing.

Interview 1 1996 was conducted on 6 August 1996 with two group-level directors at a large steel corporation in eastern China.

Interview 2 1996 was conducted on 7 August 1996 with two group-level managers responsible for Human Resource Management and the plant CCP Party branch respectively at the same eastern China steel corporation.

Interview 3 1996 was conducted on 9 August 1996 with an engineering specialist and former group director of a long-established steel corporation in west-central China.

Interview 4 1996 was conducted on 14 August 1996 with a group-level manager previously responsible for enterprise restructuring and now working in economic research and development, and another senior member of the economic research and development institute of a large steel corporation in central China.

Interview 5 1996 was conducted on 15 August 1996 with a senior academic management specialist from a University of Metallurgical Science and Technology in central China.

Interview 6 1996 was conducted on 19 August 1996 with senior group-level managers from a large steel corporation on China's eastern seaboard.

Interview 1 1997 was conducted on 15 August 1997 with the chief engineer and manager of a large steel corporation in Beijing.

Interview 2 1997 was conducted on 25 August with senior group-level managers from a large steel corporation in southwest China.

Interview 3 1997 was conducted on 27 August with several group-level managers from a large steel corporation in south China.

Interview 1 1998 was conducted with several top managers of the steelworks visited for Interview 3 1996.

Interview 2 1998 was conducted with two senior managers from the steelworks visited for Interview 4 1996.

Interview 3 1998 was conducted with a group of top-level managers from the steelworks visited for Interview 6 1996.

Interview 4 1998 was conducted with two senior managers from the steelworks visited for Interview 2 1997.

References

Child, J. (1994) *Management in China During the Age of Reform*, Cambridge: Cambridge University Press.

Goodman, D.S.G. (ed.) (1997) *China's Provinces in Reform*, London: Routledge.

Hannan, K. (1998) *Industrial Change in China: Economic Restructuring and Conflicting Interests*, London: Routledge.

Hassard, J. and Sheehan, J. (1997) 'Enterprise Reform and the Role of the State: The Case of the Capital Iron and Steel Works, Beijing', in A. Bugra and B. Usdiken (eds) *State, Market and Organizational Form*, Berlin: Walter de Gruyter.

Hay, D.A., Morris, D.J., Liu, G. and Shujie Yao (1994) *Economic Reform and State-owned Enterprises in China 1979–1987*, Oxford: Clarendon Press.

Kuehl, J. and Sziraczki, G. (1995) 'Employment Restructuring at Micro-level: Results of the Dalian Pilot Enterprise Survey', in Lin Lean Lim and G. Sziraczki (eds) *Employment*

Challenges and Policy Responses: Chinese and International Perspectives, Beijing: International Labour Office, Area Office Beijing.

Lee, Keun (1996) 'An assessment of the state sector reform in China: Viability of "Legal Person Socialism"', *Journal of the Asia Pacific Economy* 1(1): 105-21.

Lin Lean Lim and Sziraczki, G. (1995) 'Introduction', in Lin Lean Lim and G. Sziraczki (eds) *Employment Challenges and Policy Responses: Chinese and International Perspectives*, Beijing: International Labour Office, Area Office Beijing.

Nolan, P. (1995) *China's Rise, Russia's Fall: Politics, Economics and Planning in the Transition from Stalinism*, London: Macmillan.

Sheehan, J. (1996) 'Is There Another Tian'anmen Uprising in the Offing?', *Jane's Intelligence Review* 8(12): 554–6.

Sheehan, J. (1998) *Chinese Workers: A New History*, London: Routledge.

Solinger, D.J. (1996) 'Despite Decentralization: Disadvantages, Dependence and Ongoing Central Power in the Inland: The Case of Wuhan', *China Quarterly* 145: 1–34.

South China Morning Post, dates in text; Internet edition used unless otherwise stated.

Steinfeld, E.S. (1998) *Forging Reform in China: The Fate of State-owned Industry*, Cambridge: Cambridge University Press.

Walder, A. and Gong Xiaoxia (1993) 'Workers in the Tian'anmen Protests: The Politics of the Beijing Workers' Autonomous Federation', *Australian Journal of Chinese Affairs* 29 (January 1993), 1–29.

Warner, M. (1995) *The Management of Human Resources in Chinese Industry*, London: Macmillan.

7 Globalization and employment in Latin America

Some issues and challenges

Regina M.A.A. Galhardi

Introduction

In the last few years Latin American economies have undergone a remarkable transformation in their economic policies. Nations that sneered at the market system and pursued protectionist policies have suddenly embraced structural reforms aimed at deregulating business practices and becoming integrated with the rest of the world. Macroeconomic policies have taken a radical turn in the past decade, which has boosted economic growth in the region from 2.7 per cent in the latter half of the 1980s to 3.5 per cent between 1990 and 1997, reduced the inflation rate to below 30 per cent in nearly every country, and opened up new opportunities for private investment in the most diverse economic activities. However, despite macroeconomic stabilization and structural reforms, employment problems have persisted in Latin America. During the 1990s, employment has grown at a slower pace than in the second half of the 1980s, unemployment rates have not declined in a sustained manner, informal sector activity has increased and employment in non-tradable goods has escalated. In many countries, wages have stagnated and the rate of job creation has seen a slowdown. Where earnings have risen, enormous wage gaps have opened up between skilled and unskilled workers. These achievements have disappointed and confounded economists and policy-makers, who predicted that the macroeconomic reforms and gross domestic product (GDP) growth of the 1990s would lower unemployment and help to raise the wages of low-skilled workers.

In order to understand this apparent labour paradox we will highlight, first, some common features of the labour market in Latin America during the 1990s. Second, we will try to relate the observed changes in the composition of the demand for labour to the economic reforms being carried out in the region during the last decade and, in particular, to trade liberalization. Changes in trade patterns may have induced firms to introduce technological changes more rapidly, thus exacerbating the reduction in the demand for unskilled labour. There is indeed a growing feeling among many government officials that the continent's high unemployment rate partly results from unfair trade practices. Third, we will try to see how the openness of those economies has affected the structure of output and skills in general and the manufacturing sector in particular.

Employment trends in the 1990s

The labour market in Latin America provides a very heterogeneous picture, owing to the differences of economic development, demographic structures, labour institutions and economic fluctuations of the various economies. Despite this heterogeneity, certain features common to most countries have been perceived.

Job creation has slowed

Employment in Latin America has grown at an average rate of only 2.8 per cent per year during the 1990s, which is 0.5 points slower than in the latter half of the 1980s. Most countries have been affected by this reduced job growth rate, particularly Argentina, Uruguay and Bolivia. Mexico, Paraguay and Peru have seen increases, though at a very modest level (Lora and Marquez, 1998).

Unemployment rates increased as well as inequality

During the past decade, the average unemployment rate in the region has persistently remained around 10 per cent. Although the open unemployment rate remained at about 6 per cent until 1993, it increased in the late 1990s, reaching 7.7 per cent in 1996 and up to 8 per cent in 1998. Moreover, the evolution of unemployment varied also among different population groups. Youth unemployment rates for those aged 15–24 are approximately twice as high as adult rates in most countries and, in some countries, worryingly high, as in Chile, Peru and Panama. Youth unemployment seemed to be a particularly serious problem during the 1990s in Argentina (37.4 per cent), Colombia (37.0 per cent), and Panama (29.5 per cent) (ILO, 1999).

Informal employment has increased and public employment rates have fallen

The job market in Latin America has acquired an increasingly informal character in the 1990s. The proportion of the labour force occupied in the informal sector has increased at a rate of 1 percentage point per year since 1990. The informal employment rate increased from an average of 51.8 per cent in 1990 to 59.0 per cent in 1998. Thus, in this brief period, the percentage of those self-employed, working in small enterprises of no more than five to ten workers, or in domestic work positions and/or people employed in unregistered jobs that offer no benefits or security rose nearly 8 per cent. Therefore, more than half of all workers in Latin America are currently associated with little protection and social security. According to calculations by the ILO/Lima (1999), on average, 85 out of every 100 new jobs created in the region between 1990 and 1998 were concentrated in the informal sector, which accounts for 59 per cent of total non-agricultural employment in the region.

On the other hand, the participation of workers in the formal sector employed in large private enterprises declined from 32.7 per cent in 1990 to 28.4 per cent in

Table 7.1 Latin America: structure of non-agricultural employment, 1990–96 (%)

Countries/years	Informal sector				Formal sector		
	Total	Self-employed workers[a]	Domestic service	Small businesses[b]	Total	Public sector	Large private enterprises
Latin America							
1990	51.6	24.7	6.7	20.2	48.4	15.3	33.0
1996	57.4	27.2	7.1	23.1	42.6	13.0	29.6
Argentina							
1990	47.5	24.7	7.9	14.9	52.5	19.3	33.2
1996	53.6	27.1	7.8	18.7	46.4	13.2	33.2
Bolivia							
1990	56.9	37.7	6.4	12.8	43.1	16.5	26.6
1996	63.1	37.7	5.5	19.9	36.9	11.1	25.9
Brazil							
1990	52.0	21.0	7.7	23.3	48.0	11.0	36.9
1996	59.3	23.8	9.5	26.0	40.7	9.6	31.1
Chile							
1990	49.9	23.6	8.1	18.3	50.1	7.0	43.0
1996	50.9	22.7	6.8	21.4	49.1	7.6	41.5
Colombia							
1990	55.2	23.5	5.4	26.3	44.8	9.6	35.2
1996	57.2	25.9	3.8	27.5	42.8	8.3	34.5
Costa Rica							
1990	42.3	18.1	5.8	18.4	57.7	22.0	35.7
1996	47.2	17.4	5.2	24.6	52.6	17.2	35.4
Ecuador							
1990	51.2	32.5	5.6	13.0	48.8	17.6	31.2
1996	52.9	31.8	5.9	15.2	47.2	13.9	33.3
Honduras							
1990	54.1	36.3	6.9	10.8	45.9	14.9	31.0
1996	56.3	36.5	6.0	13.8	43.6	11.3	32.3
Mexico							
1990	55.5	30.4	5.6	19.5	44.6	25.0	19.6
1996	60.2	32.5	5.4	22.3	39.8	22.0	17.8
Panama							
1990	40.5	20.4	7.2	12.8	59.5	32.0	27.5
1996	41.6	20.7	7.0	13.9	58.3	23.0	35.2
Paraguay							
1990	61.4	21.2	10.7	29.4	38.6	12.2	26.4
1996	67.9	26.9	10.0	31.0	31.1	13.1	19.0
Peru[c]							
1990	51.8	35.3	5.1	11.4	48.2	11.6	36.7
1996	57.9	37.4	4.2	16.3	42.1	8.2	33.9
Uruguay[d]							
1990	36.3	19.3	6.0	11.0	63.7	20.1	43.6
1996	37.9	21.3	6.3	10.3	62.1	17.0	45.1

Venezuela							
1990	38.8	22.1	4.1	12.6	61.2	22.3	38.9
1996	47.7	28.1	2.4	17.2	52.3	19.1	33.2

Source: ILO, based on Household Surveys and other official sources.

ᵃ Includes self-employed workers (except administrative, professional and technical workers) and family-business workers.
ᵇ Corresponds to establishments with less than 10 workers.
ᶜ Corresponds to Metropolitan Lima.
ᵈ Corresponds to Montevideo

1996. The percentage of those working in the public sector fell from 15.5 per cent to 12.9 per cent during the same period (in the 14 countries for which information was available). These figures show that the formal employment rate decreased from an average of 48.4 per cent in 1990 to 41.3 percent in 1998 (Table 7.1).

In Latin America, the growth of informal jobs, most of which are in low-productivity, poorly paid activities, has tended to drive down average labour productivity. The average productivity of the informal sector declined even in countries where output per worker rose. Thus, productivity gains in the modern sector have been largely counterbalanced by the expansion of the informal sector. This explains the current slow growth of average labour productivity, though the regional figures conceal substantial differences between countries and sectors.

As identified by ECLAC (1997), the productivity gains that have been achieved occurred in the modern manufacturing sector, export agriculture, large-scale mining firms, the energy sector, the telecommunications industry and financial services, and tend to be concentrated both across and within sectors. This has, of course, exacerbated productivity gaps between informal and formal activities and stressed the degree of economic concentration in the production structure. The sharp productivity differentials between the bulk of the small and medium-sized enterprises destined to the domestic market and the front runner in each sector are reflected in wide wage differentials and sharp lag in pay levels for low-skill jobs.

Wages have recovered but wage differentials have increased

In most Latin American countries, the performance of real wages has been more favourable to workers in the 1990s than in the latter half of the 1980s. On the average, real wages throughout the region have tended to increase from their lowest point reached in 1991. In some countries, however, real wages have not exceeded the levels achieved in the early 1980s (ILO, official country data).

In those countries where wages have registered the greatest increases during the 1990s, wage differentials between professional and administrative employees (skilled workers) as compared with factory workers and manual labourers (unskilled workers) have increased substantially. The wage gaps have seen the greatest increase in Peru, Colombia and Mexico. In these three countries, the real wages of skilled workers have increased during the 1990s at an annual rate at least three points above those of unskilled workers. The gap has increased more than 30 per cent in Peru, 20 per cent in Colombia, and nearly 25 per cent in Mexico. On the contrary, where wage gaps have been reduced in the 1990s, this has occurred in smaller proportions as illustrated by 5 per cent in Costa Rica (Lora and Marquez, 1998).

A similar phenomenon of wage gap expansion has been observed in other regions of the world. However, Latin America stands out in international comparisons, in both the magnitude and the recent trends in the wage gaps. Using as a basis of comparison the (relative) gap in wages in the industrialized countries Lora and Marquez (1998) found that wage differentials have tended to increase[1] since the late 1980s. Comparing the wage differentials between office workers and manual labourers in four Asian countries, e.g., the Republic of Korea, Hong Kong, Singapore and Taiwan, they found that gaps are twice as large in Latin America. Although real wages have again moved upward in most cases, some countries such as Ecuador, El Salvador and Venezuela have had significant drops. Wages in those countries also fell in the latter half of the 1980s, so that the decline for them has been even sharper.

Employment rates have risen in the non-tradable goods sectors

During the 1990s, all the additional jobs created in Latin America have been in non-tradable goods sectors, largely construction and services. Participation in these types of jobs rose from 58.4 per cent in 1990 to 63 per cent five years later in most of the countries (Lora and Marquez, 1998, p. 10). On average, all the additional jobs created during the 1990s in Latin America have been in the non-tradable goods sectors. The only exception seems to be Brazil. However, a more in-depth analysis of the Brazilian employment structure showed that employment in services fell between 1989 and 1992 because of the recession. After that period, there was a recovery in employment of 10 per cent. The share of services in total employment increased from 45 per cent in 1989 to 50 per cent in 1996.

The increase in the share of the services sector took place as the same time as industrial employment was falling quite sharply. The share of manufacturing in total employment fell from 24 per cent to 18 per cent between 1989 and 1996. It is quite clear that also in Brazil workers have been transferred from the manufacturing sector, mainly non-agricultural tradable, to the non-tradable sectors (Amadeo and Neri, 1998). The growth of employment in the modern sector of the economy has therefore come to depend essentially on the expansion of employment in construction and services, and this has not been rapid enough to offset the decreases registered in employment in manufacturing and the public sector.

The demand for skilled labour has increased

In the 1990s, the demand for labour has not expanded proportionately for all types of work, but has shown a bias toward more skilled workers. Changes in the composition of employment between skilled and unskilled labour necessarily reflect the changes in the relative supply of skilled workers, which has increased throughout the region owing to the expansion in education as exemplified for some countries in Table 7.2. As documented by Duryea and Szekely (1998), highly skilled workers are enjoying rising relative wages because the growth in the supply of highly skilled individuals has been extremely slow relative to the increasing demand for these kinds of employees. Assuming an elasticity of substitution between the two types of workers of 1.5, Lora and Oliveira (1998) concluded that relative demand for skilled workers has increased annually at rates between 2.3 per cent as in Costa Rica and 7.4 per cent as in Mexico, and nearly 5.0 per cent in Bolivia and Venezuela and about 3.0 per cent in Argentina (Table 7.2). Therefore, in some countries, the relative demand for skilled workers has risen even more rapidly than supply which explains why, although these individuals are increasingly plentiful in relative terms, they receive proportionately higher wages as in Mexico and Bolivia.

In short, the composition of the demand for labour in Latin America has changed during the past decade and has been characterized by the growing participation of the services sector, the decline in public employment, the increasing importance of the informal sector and, at the same time, a preference for workers who have higher skill levels. This is a very interesting result because, if, on the one hand, the demand for labour in the services sector can be associated with a higher relative demand for skilled labour, the relative decline in public employment might have diminished the bias toward skilled labour on the other.

However, the shift towards a service economy provides only a partial explanation for the bias toward skilled labour. As many studies have suggested, the incorporation of new technologies via investment in machinery and equipment seems to have great influence in shifting labour demand toward workers who have higher skill levels. Technological change may have magnified the bias toward skilled labour. This effect has been particularly expected in the countries that have opened their economies to foreign trade, not only because of the increase in the stock of imported machinery, but also because of improved access to inputs and increased competitive pressure. This discussion suggests that, in the presence of technological changes, relative demand for skilled labour would rise in the tradable sector.

In the next section, we will try to see whether increased openness has promoted the observed changes in the composition of the labour demand in Latin America by looking at its effects in the manufacturing sector during the last years.

Table 7.2 Relative demand growth for skilled vs unskilled labour

Country/years	Relative supply growth (annual) (%)	Relative wages growth (annual) (%)	Implicit relative demand growth (annual) (%)
Argentina (1980–96)	3.7	−1.7	3.3
Bolivia (1986–95)	3.9	1.8	4.7
Costa Rica (1981–95)	3.1	−0.8	2.3
Mexico (1984–94)	5.1	4.5	7.4
Venezuela (1981–95)	6.8	−0.6	5.1

Source: Lora and Oliveira (1998)

The impact of trade liberalization

According to the conventional view of North–South trade, the industrial North exports high-quality goods to the developing 'South', which exports primary or lower-technology goods to the North. Therefore, trade liberalization in a developing economy should be associated with an increase in the relative demand for unskilled labour and narrowing of wage differentials. However, recent evidence shows that the returns to labour and the skill premium both increase in developing countries after trade liberalization, despite the low skill content of their exports. Moreover, as we have seen before, although wage behaviour has been more favourable to workers in the 1990s than in the latter half of the 1980s in most Latin American countries, the wage gaps between skilled and less-skilled workers have grown wider, and are currently the largest in the world.

Recent evidence from cross-sectional household data for Argentina, Chile, Costa Rica, Colombia, Mexico, and Uruguay shows that liberalization was accompanied by rising relative wages and demand for skilled workers (Robbins, 1996a, 1996b). Table 7.3 summarizes the results of these studies for eight periods in which efforts were made to increase openness by lowering tariffs, easing quantitative import restrictions, or devaluating the currency.

In Chile, apart from the period 1984–92, in which there was very little if any net increase in openness despite a large devaluation, skill differentials in wages (by level of education) widened. The widening occurred principally from the mid-1970s to the early 1980s, i.e. almost immediately trade liberalization took place in 1975. Robbins (1994, 1995) found that although the skill composition of imports exceeded that of exports, skilled labour did not suffer a relative drop in earnings after trade

Table 7.3 Effects of increased openness in six Latin American countries

Country	Years	Changes in trade regime	Skill differentials in wages	Relative demand for skill (time series)
Argentina (BA)	1976–82	barrier reduction with appreciation	widened	rising
	1989–93[2]		narrowed	falling
Chile (Santiago)	1974–79	barrier reduction with devaluation	widened	rising
	1984–92[3]	devaluation	fluctuated	rising
Colombia (7 cities)	1985–94	devaluation to 1989, barrier reduction in 1990–92	widened	rising
Costa Rica	1985–93	barrier reduction and devaluation	widened	rising
Uruguay (Montevideo)	1990–95	barrier reduction	widened	rising
Mexico	1985–93	barrier reduction	widened	rising

liberalization. The returns to skilled labour increased more than conventional trade theory would predict and more than changes in labour supply would predict. According to Robbins, the most likely explanation for the observed changes was the importation of capital that was complementary to skilled labour. Evidence from Colombia shows a similar situation. Using household data for Bogota for the period 1976–89, Robbins (1996a) examined the response of wage differentials to the large rise in exports after the 1984 devaluation. He found that wage inequality increased and attributed this to changes in the composition of the demand for labour towards skilled workers that were induced by trade. In Argentina, with the exception of the period 1989–93, when there was very little increase in openness because the reduction of barriers was offset by appreciation of the exchange rate, skill differentials in wages have widened. In Mexico, the wage gap between non-production and production workers in manufacturing widened after the mid-1980s in parallel with radical liberalization of the trade regime (Feenstra and Hanson, 1995; Revenga and Montenegro, 1995). Robbins (1996b) corroborates this finding for wage differentials by the level of education over the period 1987–93 and shows that the driving force was a shift in relative demand for labour. Hanson and Harrison (1995) assessed the extent to which the increase in the skilled–unskilled wage gap in Mexico was associated with the opening of the Mexican economy. They found that greater integration into the world economy did play a role in explaining the observed increase in wage inequality, but the mechanism was not exclusively through lower tariff or quotas. They argued that, at the plant level, export orientation and the foreign investment share are important determinants of wage inequality. In sum, the Mexican case suggests that the rising wage gap is also associated with changes internal to industries and even internal to plants, such as technological change, that cannot be explained by standard trade theory. Recent additional work carried out by Wood (1997) also found that the relative demand for skilled labour rose in Argentina, Chile, Colombia, Costa Rica, and Uruguay during the periods in which openness did increase. In Peru, similar results were obtained. The increased demand for skilled labour was followed by an increase in the wage of these workers, and, hence, to an increase in the wage differential *vis-à-vis* unskilled workers after trade liberalization, i.e. during the period 1990–94. Saavedra (1996) says that this increase in wage inequality in Peru has been clearly the result of an increase in the relative price of non-tradables, which contributed to the expansion of their production using modern and high-skill intensive technologies. It is not clear, however, how much of this can be attributed to external trade. He also mentioned other factors that may have contributed to widening the wage gap such as the declining importance of trade unions.

The observed increasing differential between wages of skilled and unskilled labour is puzzling in the sense that it contradicts the conventional wisdom that increased openness reduces wages inequalities in developing countries. In a recent article, Pissarides (1997) explains this apparent puzzle by arguing that trade increases technology transfers from industrial to developing countries and that the transfer technology is biased in favour of skilled labour. According to him, developing economies advance by learning from the technology transfer from advanced industrial economies. When a developing economy liberalizes trade, it experiences more transfer technology than before. Learning about the new technology and putting it to use in the South increase the demand for skilled labour, whose wages rise over and above any rise accruing to all kinds of labour from more production. However, as the South learns the new technology, the pace of transfer slows, and the benefits to labour that remain are derived entirely from the production technology. If the transferred production technology is skill-biased, the relative demand for skilled labour causes the relative advantage of skilled over unskilled labour. Therefore, the relative demand for skilled labour increases during the transition following liberalization, and the gains enjoyed by skilled labour become longer lasting when the transferred technology is skill-biased.

This explanation is consistent with the hypothesis of complementarity between trade and skills, i.e. the Skill-Enhancing Trade (SET) hypothesis which considers that trade liberalization, and the exchange-rate devaluations that frequently accompany it, increase trade flows, and, hence, would raise relative wages in LDCs (less developed countries) by inducing technological change and rapid adaptation of modern skill-intensive technologies from the North that are biased towards skilled labour. In short, if greater trade accelerates technology diffusion from North to South, then trade can be skill-enhancing. It is well known that real devaluations typically raise the current account surplus permitting higher levels of machinery imports. Moreover, heightened competition from trade liberalization leads to pressures to modernize via importing state-of-the-art machinery.[4] As stated by Robbins:

> Trade liberalization, if bundled with exchange rate devaluation, will improve the latent current account, thus permitting higher levels of machinery imports, which raise capital-output ratios in the non-tradable and import-competing sectors. Lower tariffs on imported goods may eliminate most of the skill intensive ISI sector. However, while exports may be unskilled-intensive, the imports of machinery and the bundled skill-intensive technology may raise the overall skill-intensity of demand for labour, and hence relative wages.
>
> (1996: 36)

In LDCs emerging from importing-substitution-industrialization (ISI) strategies that limited adoption of foreign technologies, trade liberalization will lead to an initial large jump to more modern and skill-intensive technologies. The liberalized LDC will continue on a skill-intensive biased trend only in the case where technological change is skill-biased.[5] Unfortunately, this is not always the case. Lack of industrial skills, supplier industries and technology infrastructure, passive or non-selective approach to attracting foreign direct investment (FDI) and weakness in physical infrastructure are some of the factors, which have deterred the transfer, and/or adoption of advanced technology by LDCs (Wignaraja, 1998).

In view of the above, transfer of advanced technology is certainly one of the channels through which skill upgrading can occur in LDCs and can explain why both labour returns and wage inequality can increase after changes in trade openness. Indeed, some recent literature identifies technology transfer as the most likely reason for the increase in wage inequality. In the case of Chile and Colombia, for instance, Robbins (1994 and 1996c, respectively) found that trade liberalization is associated with large increases in machinery imports, and that the stock of imported machinery is closely associated with relative demand shift, and hence rising relative wages. Hanson and Harrison (1995) examined plant-level data in Mexico after trade liberalization, i.e. from 1984–90. They found that wage inequality increased during this period, despite the relatively low skill content of Mexico's exports. They concluded that the most likely cause of rise in wage inequalities was the importation of skill-biased technology from abroad. In a recent evaluation of the widening of wage differentials in several developing countries, Wood (1995) concluded that the transfer of technology is one of the two plausible explanations for the widening.[6] Tan and Batra (1995) also using firm-level data in Colombia, Mexico and Taiwan (China) found that firms engaged in technology-advancing activities paid all their workers a premium over and above the wages paid by other firms but that the premium paid to skilled workers far exceeded that paid to unskilled workers.[7]

Sectoral impacts by selected countries

The effects of trade liberalization on the demand for labour in LDCs have, however, to be analysed at the sectoral level as observed by the evidence raised in a recent project on changes on the occupational and skill structure in the manufacturing sector in developing countries (Galhardi, 1997). In these countries, changes in occupations and skills in manufacturing are expected to occur in branches or industries subject to intense international competition, either because there is a large penetration of imports, thus greater pressures to compete with foreign producers in the domestic market, or because a large proportion of output is exported, hence having to compete with international producers abroad. This and other studies undertaken by the ILO[8] on the effects of trade liberalization on employment and income, have concluded that with trade openness, the importing sector increases its related demand for qualified labour, while the export sector augments its related use of less qualified workers. Moreover, the correlation between the demand for workers by level of qualifications and the related wages are, in general, negative. The gap in wages among workers with distinct levels of qualifications, contrary to the traditional view, does not close with market openness. The better-qualified workers and managers are the ones who reap the most benefits (Galhardi, 1998a).

In Chile, for instance, Meller and Tokman (1996), using enterprise survey, found that the wage differential of skilled to unskilled workers during the period post liberalization (post-1974) is much bigger in the export sectors[9] than in the importing-competing sectors[10] (ICSs). In relation to the evolution of the occupational composition during the period 1970–92, it can be observed in Table 7.4 that, at the aggregate level, the ratio of skilled to unskilled workers in the export sectors was the same as in the import-competing sectors during the 1970s. In the 1980s, however,

Table 7.4 Ratio of average employment and wage of skilled worker to that of unskilled worker and annual growth rates: manufacturing in Chile, 1970–92

Occupational composition	Years	Employment			Wages		
		All	Export	ICS	All	Export	ICS
Skilled/	1970	0.26	0.25	0.25	2.81	2.72	3.00
unskilled	1980	0.37	0.29	0.38	3.08	3.29	3.12
	1984	0.36	0.29	0.38	3.54	3.74	3.52
	1992	0.36	0.25	0.40	3.05	3.31	2.93
Annual growth rate (%)							
Skilled	1970–80	1.1	3.4	1.6	9.1	9.2	8.8
	1980–84	−5.2	−12.4	−12.8	3.0	7.1	2.3
	1984–92	8.5	13.0	13.9	0.4	−0.9	0.0
	1970–92	2.5	3.6	3.0	4.8	5.0	4.4
Unskilled	1970–80	−2.5	1.7	−2.5	8.2	7.1	8.4
	1980–84	−4.9	−12.3	−12.6	−0.5	3.7	−0.7
	1984–92	8.7	15.4	13.0	2.3	0.6	2.3
	1970–92	1.0	3.7	0.8	4.4	4.1	4.5
Ratio of skilled worker/unskilled worker to total manufacturing							
Skilled/	1970–80	43.2	17.2	51.8	9.5	21.2	4.0
unskilled	1980–84	−1.6	−0.8	−1.0	15.1	13.6	13.0
	1984–92	−1.1	−15.1	6.2	−14.0	−11.5	−16.8
	1970–92	39.5	−1.3	59.7	8.3	21.8	−2.2

Source: Meller and Tokman (1996)

the ratio was relatively lower in the former than in the ICSs and, in 1992, 40 per cent of the employed persons by the ICSs were skilled workers and only 25 per cent in the export sectors. Since the liberalization of trade in 1975, the ICSs have been using relatively more skilled workers than the export sectors. During the second period of openness (1984–92), the same trend is observed, i.e. the ratio skilled/unskilled labour diminishes for the exports sectors and increases for the ICSs.

The number of skilled workers employed by the export sector increased 3.6 per cent annually and that of unskilled workers by 3.7 per cent during the whole period. In the ICSs, an increase in the number of skilled workers of 3.0 per cent was observed and only of 0.8 per cent for the unskilled. This leads to an increase of 60 per cent in the intensity of use of skilled workers by this sector. As a whole, there was an increase of 43 per cent in the ratio of skilled/unskilled workers employed in manufacturing between 1970 and 1980 and a small reduction of 1.1 and 1.6 per cent during the next two periods respectively. During the period 1970–92, there was an increase of the use of skilled labour in relation to unskilled of 39.5 per cent.

In terms of the distributional effects of trade in the labour market, Table 7.4 shows also that the wage differential between skilled and unskilled workers was almost the same in both sectors at the beginning of the 1970s. During 1984–92, the wage differential tended to decline, but this reduction was more accentuated in the

ICSs. The wage differential decreased about 12 per cent in the export sector and 17 per cent in the ICSs. These losses were due to a reduction in the real wage of skilled workers in the export sector of minus 0.9 per cent and to an increase of only 0.6 per cent in the real wage of unskilled workers in the export. Similarly, there was an increase of 2.3 per cent in the real wage of unskilled workers and no change in the real wage of skilled workers in the ICS sectors that may justify the decrease in the wage differential of about 17.0 per cent during the late 1980s and early 1990s.

Considering the whole manufacturing sector, the study shows that there was an increase of 9.5 per cent in the wage ratio of skilled to unskilled workers between 1970 and 1980; a higher increase of 15 per cent, during 1980–84 and a reduction of 12 per cent during 1984–92. During the whole period (1970–92) there was an increase in the wage differential between skilled and unskilled workers of 8.3 per cent.

Summing up, these results indicate that in the Chilean case, the first commercial openness in the 1970s generated a significant increase in the wage ratio of skilled to unskilled workers. This may have stimulated the labour force to increase its qualification. The bigger relative increase of skilled labour and the export expansion in the 1980s tended to reduce the wage differentials. Nevertheless, the wage gap in the 1990s is still bigger than it was in the early 1970s. Moreover, during the post-liberalization period, the wage differential between skilled and unskilled workers in the export sectors was clearly superior to that observed in the ICSs. However, the share of skilled workers in the ICSs was bigger than in the export sectors.

In the case of Brazil, the impacts of trade liberalization and stabilization[11] on the manufacturing sector have recently been analysed by Amadeo and Neri (1998). Important changes in the trade pattern of the manufacturing sector have taken place since the beginning of trade liberalization in 1990, with import and export coefficients changing quite significantly. The sectoral composition of imports and exports seems to have changed with a reduction in the comparative advantage of sectors intensive in technology, e.g. machinery and electrical and communications equipment, and increase in the comparative advantage of sectors intensive in natural resources such as wood, cellulose, metallurgy and iron and steel industry. Therefore, it can be said that trade liberalization has induced changes in the comparative advantage from human capital-intensive sectors (import-competing sectors) to unskilled and natural resource intensive sectors (export sectors). The opening of the economy has had direct impact on employment since employment fell more in the capital and human capital-intensive sectors (–28.3 per cent) than in the unskilled labour and natural resource-intensive sectors (–19.4 per cent) between 1990 and 1996.

In general, the skill profile in the manufacturing sector has improved in relation to the skill profile for the overall employed population between 1989 and 1996. There was a decrease in the proportion of workers with zero years of schooling and between zero and 4 years of schooling in the manufacturing sector as a whole. As a result, the overall manufacturing skill profile improved during the period 1989–96. The proportion of workers with more than eight years of schooling has improved in relation to the average skill profile of employed workers in the human capital sectors. This may be interpreted as evidence that the demand for skills/education is greater than average in these sectors. The skill profile of natural resource sectors has also improved in the same categories but less than the average skill profile of the total employed population. *Ceteris paribus*, this may be an indication that the demand for skilled/more educated workers in this sector has been weak. The same conclusion can be applied in the unskilled labour sectors.

Therefore, the decrease in the share of employment in the capital and human capital intensive sectors could have led to a deterioration of the overall skill content of manufacturing employment had the intra-sectoral contents remained constant. In fact, however, the intra-sectoral content not only improved but also improved sufficiently to more than compensate the impact of changes at the inter-sectoral level. That is, there was an improvement in the overall skill content of the employed population in the manufacturing sector in spite of the change in the structure of employment in favour of the unskilled labour and the natural resources intensive sector. Moreover, as a result of the incipient trade liberalization process, it is precisely the latter that are expanding export performance. Import coefficients increased specially in the human capital-intensive sectors whereas export coefficients increased in the unskilled and natural intensive sectors.

International trade can affect the overall skill composition by shifting demand for labour between industries. Nevertheless, it should be noted that the intra-sectoral skill content of labour has improved above the average in manufacturing to more than compensate for the (negative) impact at the inter-sectoral level. Considering that changes in the intra-sectoral skill profile of labour result from changes in technology and the organization of work which have an direct impact on the educational content of the labour force, these results seem to support the view that biased technological change plays an important role in explaining changes in the skill profile of manufacturing employment. These observations, however, do not preclude the role played by increased foreign competition on within-industry skill upgrading.

In Mexico, a recent study has shown that after trade liberalization, i.e. during the period 1987–93, employment growth was observed in traditional, low-tech, domestically oriented sectors (food, textiles, leather and wood products) while the growth of employment in the sectors more exposed to international competition, e.g., chemicals, metal products and machinery, was lagging behind. In view of the evidence, it is possible to conclude that the creation of new manufacturing jobs in Mexico was taking place in the domestically oriented sectors with low technological requirements (Alarcon and Zepeda, 1997).

There was also an increase in the relative importance of skilled workers as the proportion of 'production' workers declined during this period of intense structural adjustment and liberalization. As the figures[12] in Table 7.5 show, production workers constitute the largest share of total employment. In 1987–89, they accounted for 68.3 per cent of the total employment. Over 60 per cent were direct production workers (55.8 per cent blue collar workers[13] and 6.6 per cent machine operators) and 5.9 per cent were production supervisors. Executives, professionals, technicians and heads of administrative departments[14] each accounted for two to 2.7 per cent of the labour force. The remaining 14 per cent include different administrative occupations.

Table 7.5 Structure of employment in manufacturing by occupation

Occupation	1987–89 (A)		1991–93 (B)		A/B
	No. of workers	Percentage share	No. of workers	Percentage share	Percentage change
Manufacturing	2,326,260	100.00	2,799,666	100.00	20.35
Non-production	418,425	17.99	501,662	17.92	19.89
managers	63,719	2.74	68,225	2.44	7.07
professionals	46,471	2.00	69,987	2.50	50.60
technicians	56,495	2.43	85,086	3.04	50.61
head of departartment	251,740	10.82	278,364	9.94	10.58
Production	1,588,679	68.29	1,879,863	67.15	18.33
supervisors	136,857	5.88	181,649	6.49	32.73
workers	1,297,468	55.77	1,402,596	50.10	8.10
machine operators	154,354	6.64	295,618	10.56	91.52
Others	319,156	13.72	418,141	14.94	31.01

Source: National Urban Employment Survey (ENEU) (several issues), Mexico

However, it should be noted that the share of production workers has decreased from 68.3 per cent in 1987–89 to 67.1 per cent in 1991–93. Within the production worker's category, it is clear that the proportion of 'workers' declined faster whereas that of 'supervisors'/high-skilled production workers actually increased. Thus, if the division between production workers and other employees was taken as an indicator of the skill composition of the labour force, it could be possible to argue that the relative importance of unskilled labour has decreased during the period of liberalization and structural reforms. This trend appears to be consistent with the significant increase in the share of 'professionals' and 'technicians' within the non-production worker's category.

These employment trends suggest, as in the case of Brazil, the existence of two paradoxes with respect to the skill composition of the labour force in manufacturing: (i) a tendency towards skill upgrading as the proportion of unskilled/production workers declined over time; and (ii) a shift in the sectoral composition of employment as reflected by the growing importance of traditional or natural resources-intensive sectors in a process that may be taken as an indication of the de-skilling of the labour force.

As in Brazil, there was also in Mexico an improvement in the overall skill content of the employed population in the manufacturing sector in spite of the change in the structure of employment in favour of the low-skilled traditional group. A clear improvement in the level of education[15] of workers in manufacturing, in particular in the export and import-competing sectors, was observed (Table 7.6). Workers in the production of metal products achieved the highest level of education while the lowest is found in leather products. The proportion of workers with nine or more years of schooling are clearly the highest in tradable[16] sectors than in those oriented to the domestic market. In 1987–89 a very small proportion of workers in

Table 7.6 Proportion of workers with different educational levels in total employment by sector

Sectors	1987–91			1989–93		
	Basic	Medium	High	Basic	Medium	High
Manufacturing	2.48	8.97	1.04	1.61	9.59	1.27
Domestics	2.23	7.38	0.78	1.54	8.25	0.96
food	2.11	7.37	0.84	1.39	8.37	1.14
textiles	2.45	8.99	0.61	1.41	7.44	0.62
apparel	3.94	8.68	0.47	2.83	11.02	0.82
leather	1.05	3.82	0.32	0.77	3.95	0.27
wood	1.78	8.03	1.28	1.32	8.74	1.27
Tradable	2.74	10.64	1.31	1.67	11.06	1.62
chemicals	2.21	10.00	0.91	1.65	10.94	1.53
metal	2.51	12.21	1.57	1.51	12.43	1.74
machinery	3.06	10.86	1.52	1.69	11.01	1.66

Source: adapted from Alarcon and Zepeda (1997)

manufacturing held a basic or higher degree, 2.48 per cent and 1.04 per cent respectively. Between 1987–89 and 1991–93 the proportion of workers with basic education declined in all manufacturing sectors, while the proportion of workers with medium and high education accelerated, particularly among tradable sectors. This is evidence that there was an increased demand for skills in these sectors.

Differences across sectors are accentuated at the medium and high levels of education. Tradable sectors have a more uniform demand for workers with medium and higher levels of education whereas the skill requirements of domestically oriented sectors are lower and more heterogeneous across sectors. The proportion of workers holding technical degrees and involved in training courses at the firm level were also clearly larger in the exporting, high tech industries. Training activities increased faster in 1991–93 than in 1993–95, which may be interpreted as a response of firms to increasing competitive pressures imposed by the earlier phase of trade liberalization.

The evidence has shown clearly that sectors exposed to international competition, i.e. both ICSs and exporting sectors, had a higher demand for better qualified workers. These changes in the skill composition of the labour force underline the skill enhancing effect of more outward orientation of manufacturing sectors.

In Peru, Saavedra (1996) found that the manufacturing employment dropped from 19.2 per cent in 1985 to 16.8 per cent in 1991, but presented a slight recovery after the reforms and reached 17.6 per cent in 1994. By analysing the figures on employment by export and import-competing sectors, the author observed that employment has declined relatively less in the textiles, basic metals and chemicals sectors, i.e., the export sectors. However, it should be noted that, with exception of textiles, the other sectors are all natural-resource-based sectors what may provide an indication about the skill level.

In Argentina, the adjustment programme that began in 1991 has led to increased demand for skilled workers, and increasing dispersion of wage differentials by skill categories. Wages for professionals have risen more than for white-collar workers and in turn more than for less-skilled workers, whose real wages have stagnated.

Conclusion

Despite the higher economic growth rates that most Latin American countries have enjoyed in recent years, the regional's performance has been disappointing from a social perspective during the 1990s. Stabilization and structural reforms have led currencies to appreciate in real terms while reducing the cost of using capital. This has had a major impact on the labour market. It is clear that the rate of new-job creation has slowed to an average of 2.8 per cent per year, about half a percentage point below the rate in the 1980s. And unemployment has actually risen, from a regional average of 6 per cent in the 1980s to around 8 per cent in the 1990s.[17] Moreover, the informal employment rate has also been rising. Between 1990 and 1996, the percentage of people who were self-employed, were domestic workers or were employed in enterprises with 5–10 workers rose from 51.6 per cent to 57.4 per cent. And while real wages have risen slightly in most Latin American countries since 1990, they have risen much more rapidly for high-skilled workers than for low-skilled ones. In addition, the construction and services sectors have shown greater job-creating power than the sectors most exposed to international trade, i.e. agriculture and industry. Furthermore, the demand for employment has shifted toward skilled labour, thereby widening wage gaps among workers.

These developments have disappointed and confounded economists, who had predicted that the macroeconomic reforms and GDP growth of the last decade would lower unemployment and help to bring up the wages of low-skill workers. Among the economic reforms that have characterized the development of the countries in the region during the last decades, the opening up of trade had an important impact on labour-related transformations in these economies, insofar as it contributed to the changes in the composition of the demand for labour and the relative pay scales between skilled and unskilled workers. Openness has particularly affected the structure of output and skills, in particular in the manufacturing sector.

However, as the evidence reviewed above indicates, the effects of changes in trade patterns on labour demand in selected Latin American countries contradict the prediction that the abundant factor, i.e. unskilled labour, would benefit from trade liberalization. The 'opening up' of the region's economies, has not had the effect of raising demand for and relative remuneration of unskilled labour. According to this wisdom, it is to be expected that the openness would raise relative remuneration of the factors that are abundant in a given country and reduce it for those that are scarce. In Latin America, such a development would have entailed changes in relative wages in the direction opposite to what has been observed. It is not the purpose of this chapter to explain the predictive failure of this theory. Whatever the explanation, the existing studies for Latin America acknowledge in their findings that changes in trade patterns influenced employment and labour remuneration, not via the feared displacements of workers brought about by higher imports, nor through the changes in relative remuneration forecast by conventional theories of international trade but via their effect on investment in physical capital, technology and relative demand for skilled labour.

Where there may be adverse short-term effects for the uneducated and unskilled, incentives should be put in place for the acquisition of schooling and skills for young people, coupled with more comprehensive and effective job training programmes for adults, and also the prospects for growth in the economy at large. The prospects for faster growth and higher wages depend on many factors, especially the Latin American countries' ability to increase exports. Rapid growth with rising real wages will require both higher export growth and an increase in the value-added content of the region's exports. Achieving this upgraded export growth is the region's fundamental challenge.

Abundant evidence suggests that countries with an open economy grow faster than those that restrict international trade. Countries that are active in international trade and export high-value-added goods, i.e., goods whose production requires relatively high volumes of capital, sophisticated technologies, and skilled labour, have high real wages. Countries that export basic goods, on the other hand, have lower real wages. It is therefore possible to increase a country's real wages by changing its export role.[18] However, successful integration of the Latin American economies into the world economy relies ultimately on more qualified and productive human resources, who can provide the complementary skills to proceed to increasingly more sophisticated, high-value industrial niches (Galhardi, 1998b).

Almost a decade after the initiation of market-oriented reforms, most Latin American countries continue to export mostly natural resource-based products with low value added. From a long-term perspective and assuming that the growth of the world market will continue to be biased towards technologically advanced sectors, this trade pattern can be a threat to the competitive insertion of the Latin American countries into the global market. A key challenge for Latin America policy-makers is, then, how to increase net exports of higher-value-added products without imposing trade barriers or distorting the market system. This is of fundamental importance to macroeconomic, microeconomic and sectoral policies as well as to policies aimed at building a social consensus among the various actors in respect to the main direction that the development process should take.

Notes

1 These trends reflect the education gap in Latin America. The average number of years of education of the work force in Latin America has increased in the 1990s at a rate of 0.9 per cent per year and currently averages 5.3 years. This rate of increase falls substantially short of the figures recorded in the 1960s (averaging 1.6 per cent), and is well below the rates commonly encountered in the fast-developing economies. The sluggish growth of education has meant that Latin America's labour force currently has two years less education than one would expect on the basis of global standards and on the basis of the region's development levels, and four years' less education than the countries of East Asia.

2   In Argentina in 1989–93, there was little if any net increase in openness, because the reduction of barriers was offset by appreciation of the exchange rate.

3   In Chile also it seems unlikely that openness increased during 1984–92, despite large devaluation, because by that time almost no quantitative restrictions were placed on imports.

4   The pressures to be more competitive are not only driving firms to buy more capital goods, they are increasing demand for skilled labour and enhancing incentive schemes.

5   A related hypothesis is that TL frees capital flows that will move from the low interest rate, capital-rich North to the high interest, capital-poor South. Even without bundled technology, this would lead to higher capital-output ratios. Because of complementarity between capital and skill, this would raise relative demand for skill.

6   The other one is the increase in the supply of low-technology goods in world markets because of the expansion of Chinese exports (Wood, 1995).

7   Although the direct contribution of exports was less important than that of R&D and worker training, they claim that TL increased the R&D activities of firms and, then, the demand for skilled labour.

8   E. Amadeo and M. Neri, (1998) *Opening, Stabilization and the Sectoral and Skill Structures of Manufacturing Employment in Brazil*, Employment and Training Working Papers No. 11, ILO, Geneva. L. Low (1998) *Jobs, Technology and Skill Requirements in a Globalized Economy: Country Study on Singapore*, Employment and Training Working Papers No. 13, ILO, Geneva. Cheon B-You (1998) *The Changes in the Employment, Occupation and Skill Structure of the Korean Manufacturing in View of Increased Exposure to International Markets: 1970–90*, Employment and Training Working Papers No. 39, ILO, Geneva. R. Galhardi (1998) *The Impact of Trade and Technology on the Skill Profile in Brazil and the Republic of Korea*, Employment and Training Working Papers No. 40, ILO, Geneva.

9   Export sectors comprise the following industrial sectors: Wood and wood products, paper and paper products, industrial chemicals, non-metallic mineral products, and basic non-ferrous metal industry.

10 ICSs include food, beverage and tobacco industry, refined petroleum products, publishing, printing and reproduction, leather, leather products and footwear, textiles and textile manufactures, iron and steel industry, rubber products, glass production and glass products, fabricated metal products.

11 Trade liberalization started in the late 1980s and early 1990s but its most dramatic effects show up in 1994 when the stabilization plan was launched with important impacts both on international trade (due to the appreciation of the currency) and aggregate demand (due to the increase in the access to credit).

12 The figures are based on information provided by the National Urban Employment Survey (ENEU). This survey reports workers classified in eighteen different occupations organized into seven groups: professionals, technicians, executives, heads of administrative departments, workers, machine operators, and others.

13 'Workers' means direct production workers. 'Machine operators' are workers operating fixed machinery and equipment. The 'others' category includes a mix of all other occupations: workers in education, artists, entertainment and sports personnel, sales personnel, workers in retail and wholesale trade, workers with non-fixed establishments, workers in personal services, domestic workers, operators of mobile machinery and transportation, police and army, agricultural and related workers, non-specified.

14 'Professionals' were defined as those workers that have college education or who hold a university degree. 'Technicians' are usually employed as assistants to professionals but also include specialized personnel. 'Executives' include directors, managers and owners of private enterprises. 'Heads of departments' are chairpersons in administrative departments within the firm or supervisors in administrative tasks.

15 Workers with basic education are represented in Table 7.6 by the proportion of workers with six or more years of school attendance. The proportion of workers with

medium education corresponds to those with nine or more years of school attendance. Finally, workers with twelve or more years of school attendance were included in the group of high education.

16 Tradable are those manufacturing sectors whose ratio of imports and exports to the value of gross product was larger than the average for manufacturing. They include both exporting sectors and ICSs. Remaining sectors were classified as domestics because they are clearly oriented to the domestic market with a relatively low level of exposure to internal competition (Alarcon and Zepeda, 1997).

17 This apparent paradox was recently investigated by Lora and Oliveira (1998). They concluded that economic cycles explain the fluctuations of employment and unemployment rate (around their structural levels), while price stabilizations and structural reforms have affected the composition of labour demand and relative wages.

18 The integration options for developing countries depend to a significant degree on the kind of export roles they assume in the global economy. According to this perspective, industrial development and integration are enhanced as countries move or evolve through particular combinations of export-processing assembly; component-supply subcontracting; original equipment manufacturing; and original brand name manufacturing.

References

Alarcon, D. and Zepeda, E. (1997) *Jobs, Technology and Skill Requirements in a Globalized Economy: The Case of Mexico*, report prepared for the Employment and Labour Market Policies Branch/ILO, Geneva: ILO.

Amadeo, E. and Neri, M. (1998) *Opening, Stabilization and the Sectoral and Skill Structures of Manufacturing Employment in Brazil*, Employment and Training Working Papers no. 11, Geneva: ILO.

Cheon, B-You (1998) *The Changes in the Employment, Occupation and Skill Structure of the Korean Manufacturing in View of Increased Exposure to International Markets: 1970–90*, Employment and Training Working Papers No. 39, Geneva: ILO.

Duryea, S and Szekely, M. (1998) *Labour Markets in Latin America: A Supply-Side Story*, Office of the Chief Economist, Working Paper no. 374, Washington, DC: Inter-American Development Bank, March.

ECLA (1997) *The Equity Gap: Latin America, the Caribbean and the Social Summit*, Santiago, Chile: *United Nations*.

Feenstra, R. and Hanson, G. (1995) 'Foreign Investment, Outsourcing, and Relative Wages', in R. Feenstra, G. Grossman and D. Irwin (eds) *Political Economy of Trade Policy: Essays in Honour of Jagdish Bhagwati*, Cambridge, MA: MIT Press.

Galhardi, R. (1997) *Jobs, Technology and Skill Requirements in a Globalized Economy: A First Approach Towards an Overview of Four Country Case Studies*, mimeo, ILO/POLEMP, December, Geneva.

Galhardi, R. (1998a) *The Impact of Trade and Technology on the Skill Profile in Brazil and the Republic of Korea* Employment and Training Working Papers no. 40, Geneva: ILO.

Galhardi, R. (1998b) 'Changing Occupational Structures and Human Resources Development: Implications for Developing Countries' Regional and Global Integration', *Science and Public Policy* 25(1), February: 55–64.

Gereffi, G. (1995) 'Global Commodity Chains and Third World Development', paper prepared for Forum Meeting Regionalization and Labour Market Interdependency in East and South-East Asia, Bangkok, 23–26 January.

Hanson, H.G. and Harrison, A. (1995) *Trade, Technology, and Wage Inequality*, NBER Working Paper 5110, Cambridge, MA: NBER.

ILO (1999) *Employing Youth: Promoting Employment-intensive Growth*, Report for the Inter-regional Symposium on Strategies to Combat Youth Unemployment and Marginalization, 13–14 December, Geneva.

ILO/Lima (1999) *Decent Work and Protection for All: Priority of the Americas*, Report of the Director-General, Lima, Peru, August.

Lora, E. and Marquez, G. (1998) 'The Employment Problem in Latin America: Perception and Stylised Facts', Paper prepared at the 1998 IDB/IIC Annual Meeting: The Employment Problem in Latin America: Roots and Remedies, Inter-American Development Bank, Cartagena, March.

Lora, E. and Oliveira, M. (1998) *Macro Policy and Employment Problems in Latin America*, Working Paper no. 372, Office of the Chief Economist, Washington, DC: Inter-American Development Bank.

Low, L. (1998) *Jobs, Technology and Skill Requirements in a Globalized Economy: Country Study on Singapore*, Employment and Training Working Papers no. 13, Geneva: ILO.

Meller, P. and Tokman, A. (1996) 'Chile: Apertura comercial, empleo y salarios', Working Paper no. 38, Regional Office of the ILO, Lima.

Pessino, C. (1995) 'Labour Market Consequences of the Economic Reform in Argentina', in D. Turnham, C. Foy and G. Larrain (eds) *Social Tensions, Job Creation and Economic Policy in Latin America*, Paris: OECD.

Pissarides, C. (1997) 'Learning by Trading and the Returns to Human Capital in Developing Countries', *The World Bank Economic Review* 11(1): 17–32.

Revenga, A. and Montenegro, C. (1995) 'North American Integration and Factor Price Equalization: Is There Evidence of Wage Convergence between Mexico and the United States?', in S. Collins (ed.) *Imports, Exports, and the American Worker*, Washington, DC.

Robbins, D. (1994) 'Relative Wage Structure in Chile, 1957–1992: Changes in the Structure of Demand for Schooling', *Estudios Económicos*, University of Chile, October.

Robbins, D. (1995) 'Should Educational Spending be Redistributed from Higher to Primary Education in LDCs? A Note with Application to Chile', *Revista de Análisis Económico*, ILADES, Chile, June.

Robbins, D. (1996a) 'Will the Colombian Wage Structure Continue to Compress, or Has Trade Liberalization Reversed the Trends? Evidence from Bogotá, 1976–1989', *Colombia: An Opening Economy*, in F. Gunter, J.R. Aronson, C. Cohen, C. Callahan and M. Smith de Barrero (eds) Leigh University Press.

Robbins, D. (1996b) *HOS Hits Facts: Facts Win; Evidence on Trade and Wages in the Developing World*, Development Discussion Paper no. 557, Cambridge, MA: Harvard Institute for International Development, Harvard University, October.

Robbins, D. (1996c) *Stolper-Samuelson (Lost) in the Tropics: Trade Liberalization and Wages in Colombia: 1976–1994*, mimeo, Cambridge, MA: Harvard University, July.

Saavedra, J. (1996) *Peru: Apertura Comercial, Empleo y Salarios*, Working Paper no. 40, Lima: Oficina Regional de la OIT para America Latina y El Caribe, Lima.

Tan, H. and Batra, G. (1995) *Technology and Industry Wage Differentials: Evidence from Three Developing Countries*, Private Sector Development Department, World Bank, Washington, DC: World Bank.

Wignaraja, G. (1998) *Trade Liberalization in Sri Lanka: Exports, Technology and Industrial Policy*, London: Macmillan.

Wood, A. (1995) *Does Trade Reduce Wage Inequalities in Developing Countries?*, Institute for Development Studies, University of Sussex, mimeo.

Wood, A. (1997) 'Openness and Wage Inequality in Developing Countries: The Latin American Challenge to East Asian Conventional Wisdom', *The World Bank Economic Review* 11(1), The International Bank for Reconstruction and Development, Washington, DC: The World Bank.

8 Beyond convergence and divergence – contextualizing the implications of globalization on industrial relations

The cases of Germany and France

Frederic Speidel and Melanie Simms

Introduction

The vast field of research questions dealing with globalization can, broadly speaking, be divided into two interrelated but nevertheless different types of work. One which is preoccupied with the phenomenon itself, in other words proving and respectively disproving the new quality of internationalization, and one which takes intensified globalization for granted as a new reality and therefore concentrates on its consequences on socio-political systems and actors. Whereas the first category of work has dominated social science in the last ten years, the second has attained great importance more recently, notably in the field of comparative political economy. At the forefront of these studies is the question of whether or not economic internationalization leads to institutional convergence. This core question of comparative political economy is experiencing an impressive renaissance in the literature (see for example Crouch and Streeck, 1997; Kitschelt *et al.*, 1999). It also stands at the beginning of our conceptual remarks on the implications of globalization on industrial relations.

The point of departure of our conceptual remarks is the predominantly German debate of whether or not German industrial relations prove capable of preserving institutional distinctiveness in the face of globalization-induced pressure. As a result of the ongoing process of internationalization and the uncertainty of the future state of industrial relations in a globalized economy, the existing positions on this question represent (more or less plausible) hopes and fears rather than grounded evaluations of the current state of industrial relations. Since industrial relations are still in a process of adapting to external pressure, arguing for either development, convergence tendencies towards workplace-oriented industrial relations or stability of specific centralized institutions seems, in our view, rather premature. Instead of relating the current development of different systems of industrial relations to each other by simply looking at converging or diverging tendencies between them, we argue for a transnational comparison which pays particular attention to the changed character of industrial relations in each country across time. The aim of integrating an explicit *diachronic* (longitudinal) perspective is to go beyond a merely 'aesthetic' evaluation of the current shape of industrial relations institutions and to bring forward the dynamic change of the 'inner life' of these institutions.

Following Locke and Thelen (1995), who have significantly contributed to the re-conceptualization of comparative labour politics, we emphasize the necessity of a holistic understanding or, as they call it, 'contextualized comparison'. We attempt to make a first step towards applying the methodological approach advocated by Locke and Thelen (ibid.) in two test cases – the responses of French and German industrial relations to economic globalization with particular reference to the automotive industry. In doing so, we attempt to reinterpret the 'story' of the effects of globalization on industrial relations in these two countries. It is therefore necessary to specify the existing interdependence between globalization and industrial relations and to sensitize the reader to the explanatory weaknesses linked to the exclusive reference to either convergence or divergence of industrial relations in Europe which leads us then to the discussion of an alternative methodological concept.

Globalization and industrial relations – harmonization of national structures?

When analysing the general relationship between economic globalization and industrial relations it would be misleading to refer to the relevance of globalization solely in quantitative terms. Spending too much time on the question of whether the economy is currently more internationalized than it was before 1914 (see, for example, Hirst and Thompson (1996) for a sceptical analysis) might obscure the view of ongoing changes in industrial relations caused by qualitative as well as quantitative aspects of globalization. From an industrial relations perspective, it is common sense today that the controversy over whether globalization is a 'reality or a myth' (Hyman, 1999) is of only minor importance. At least as important as the quantitative dimension of the phenomenon itself is the kind of effect that the *ideology* of globalization has had on national regulatory regimes in recent years – notably through the increasing locational competition it has engendered between advanced industrialized countries.

The bargaining and regulatory procedures of these countries are condemned to functioning as transmission belts that improve or worsen the conditions for attracting foreign direct investment and employment. This has led to a recasting of industrial relations in Europe which is characterized by the tendency toward increasingly market-oriented relations between capital and labour (Altvater and Mahnkopf, 1993). This kind of market-induced competitive restructuring has been additionally favoured by a system of multilevel regulation of industrial relations in Europe which has relied on the principle of supranational co-ordination of national diversity rather than legal and institutional harmonization (Streeck, 1998). Almost inevitably, the principle of co-ordination has been followed by regime competition among national industrial relations where the employers, as the decisive new actors, are capable of achieving comparative advantage by mixing national or sectoral traditions of regulation (path dependency) and regulatory experiments (path changes).

Of vital importance is the fact that in the past the recasting of national industrial relations by regime competition has not necessarily presupposed much actual movement of production across national borders (Streeck, 1998: 436). At least as relevant as *real* transnationalization was in many cases the mere *potential* for firms to leave behind national regulatory systems which, as a credible threat, had become a powerful means to impose their conditions on labour (Dörre, 1996; Streeck, 1998).[1] In accepting the double-edged sword nature of globalization which consists, on the one hand, of the realization of transnational reorganization of production, which has become a regular event in several industries (e.g. automotive, pharmaceuticals), and, on the other hand, its potential feasibility, we perceive globalization in accordance with Dörre *et al.* (1997) as a 'realistic option' that enterprises have. We argue that against the background of high unemployment and increased international competition, the realistic option for enterprises to globalize their activities has considerably destabilized the delicate balance of power between capital and labour by enabling capital to increase the pressure on such factors as wages, social standards, working time and the volume of employment.[2]

The tendency towards a considerable increase of structural power on the side of the employers has led various experts in the field of comparative industrial relations to address the question of whether the potential to internationalize production and firm organization will further undermine existing institutionalized regulation on a national level. It is interesting to note that the recent emphasis on nationally distinctive adjustment paths to pressures for industrial rationalization now increasingly competes with the renaissance of modernist assumptions of the 1950s and 1960s. 'Convergence theory is back again' (Boyer, 1996). Convergence theory may be back again, but in a modified version insofar as international competition rather than technological determinism is considered to foster the alignment of national systems of regulation.

The ongoing dispute between proponents of convergence and divergence in industrial relations can best be illustrated by looking at Germany. Those theorists who argue for convergence in the case of German industrial relations see a universal tendency from centralization to decentralization of wage bargaining which resembles the Japanese version of enterprise unionism (Dore, 1996; Inagami, 1996). The ongoing transformation of German industrial relations is perceived as a gradual devolution from 'a system of class-conscious labour representation to . . . a plain system of labour representation' (Dore, 1996: 172). Workplace-based industrial relations represent, according to this view, the new centre of gravity. Opponents of convergence or 'Japanization' have a more optimistic view on the resilience of German institutions. These authors maintain that the workplace has always been the centre of gravity of German industrial relations and that the German example is the ideal-typical case of centralized industrial relations on top of enterprise-based ones (Streeck, 1996). Further, it is argued that German industrial relations consist of an institutional setting which is resilient enough to adapt to new circumstances (Müller-Jentsch, 1995).

This brief summary of the German controversy reveals the obvious explanatory deficiencies of convergence and divergence as explanatory categories for the comparison. Since both tendencies are simultaneously present within and across industrial relations regimes in Europe (Visser, 1996; Katz and Darbishire, 2000), the plausibility of one or the other of the two tendencies will always depend on the particular details one is willing to include in the picture. In the following, we propose a different perspective on the relationship between economic globalization and industrial relations which attempts to avoid the relative 'subjectivity' linked to the exclusive use of the notions of convergence or divergence. The main point we are making is that a differentiated discussion of the impacts of globalization on industrial relations must overcome the dependence on these categories.

The coexistence of structural divergence and functional convergence

One crucial shortcoming of the debate between convergence theorists and those in favour of divergence is their implicit neglect of the differentiation between *results* and *mechanisms* of mediation. Depending on the assumption authors intend to advocate, the argument will focus either on results or on mechanisms of mediation as the central aspect of analysis. Advocates of convergence would stress increasing national similarities in the responses to pressures for globalization disregarding the kind of institutional mediation by which they are produced. Conversely, advocates of divergence would reply that the mechanisms of mediation are in accordance with their institutional legacy and, thus, can be seen as path-dependent adaptation to external pressures.

The empirical evidence can, in fact, be interpreted from either exclusive perspective. Let us first outline the case of increasingly similar results. Examples of converging responses to the demands for flexibility and competitiveness in industrial relations all over Western Europe can be found at company as well as at national level.

One tendency of international convergence at company level can be seen in the increasing number of agreements dealing with securing employment and production location that have been concluded in several European companies in recent years, notably in the automotive industry (Zagelmeyer, 2000). In one way or another, these agreements are all concerned with securing employment and production locations in exchange for efforts by the labour unions to make working time more flexible. The origins of these new company agreements can be traced back to the Volkswagen agreement of 1993 which as the first and most innovative of its kind linked the temporary reduction of weekly working hours to wage concessions (Hancké, 2000). This type of convergence coincides with the 'revival of neo-corporatism' (Ferner and Hyman, 1998) on national level which has led to the conclusion and implementation of several 'new social pacts' in Western Europe. The shared commonality between these new social pacts lies in their aim to improve national competitiveness through the establishment of a national mode of 'competitive corporatism' (Rhodes, 1997) which, in the case of industrial relations, imposes the framework for moderate collective bargaining results inferior to the level of productivity (Schulten, 1998).

Against the argument of convergence, however, it can be replied that the panoply of existing company agreements as well as the different variants of national social pacts reflect persisting national diversity. Not surprisingly, in the case of securing employment and production location through company agreements, works councils are the relevant actors in German industry whereas trade unions are the relevant actors in most other countries. Also, in the case of neo-corporatism on a national level there is an obvious diversity among the new social pacts. Most visible are the differences regarding initial timing and intent. The only real congruency between, for example, the resurgence of corporatism in the late 1980s in Ireland and the Dutch 'Agreement of Wassenaar' in 1982 is the tripartite agreement on wage moderation.

Sitting uncomfortably within contributions which emphasize increasingly similar results is the underlying assumption that convergence towards best institutional practice is the natural outcome of rationally behaving economic agents trying to design optimal co-ordination mechanisms. More convincing on first examination is the argument that different mechanisms of mediation reflect the 'stickiness' of specific institutional arrangements which cannot be transformed or even abolished simply by rational choice. Theorists in favour of this position assume that there are different ways of responding to common competitive pressures. In their eyes, different national systems of mediation operate as 'functionally equivalent' institutions capable of achieving the same results through different mechanisms (see, for example, Boyer, 1996). Those who argue in even starker contrast to the convergence perspective go a step further by demonstrating the competitive virtue of the institutional means. In this case institutional specificities are held responsible for providing crucial comparative advantages (see, for example, Soskice, 1997).

Despite empirical evidence of diversity and the obvious plausibility of the argument for the capability of industrialized countries to solve the same economic challenge through very different institutional arrangements, we do not intend to close the case in favour of persisting divergence by simply referring to institutional differences. We doubt whether paying more attention to nationally differing mechanisms of mediation, rather than to increasingly similar results, proves appropriate for a critical understanding of the current state of industrial relations in Europe.

To put it another (more provocative) way, isn't the functional change of industrial relations toward 'competitive corporatism' more noteworthy than persisting institutional divergence? Furthermore, doesn't the current *functional dynamic* in industrial relations indicate increasing similarities far more than *institutional stasis* indicates substantial differences?

From a radically functionalist perspective, one could maintain that against the background of essentially identical results (e.g. greater flexibility in return for safer employment), institutional variations are of nothing more than merely aesthetic interest and therefore one could always argue that 'divergence in form is accompanied by convergence in substance' (Hansen *et al.*, 1997: 364). Although far from being a functionalist, Streeck underlines this point by admitting that what is changing far more radically than the nationally divergent structures in European industrial relations are their functions (1998: 438). From a more general politico-economic perspective, Strange expressed her scepticism towards a comparison focusing solely on institutional aspects with a well-known metaphor:

> My quarrel with most comparativists is that they seem to me not to see the wood for the trees, to overlook the common problems while concentrating on the individual differences . . . Concentrating on the differences instead of the similarities immediately obscures the wider character of the wood.
>
> (1997: 184)

Streeck (1998) and Strange (1997) remind us of two important things: first of the crucial difference between the notion of *functional equivalence* and the reality of *functional convergence* in industrial relations and, second, that the latter must not be underestimated. Streeck reminds us that emphasizing the notion of functional equivalence can obscure a precise evaluation of the current development in industrial relations outlined above. From a critical point of view, one could argue that the notion of functional equivalence suggests nothing more than the primacy of a universally valid function which in the name of competitive restructuring must be fulfilled at any price. But at the same time, however, the extent to which industrial relations concerned with competitive restructuring give up 'work rules that place a ceiling on employee effort' (Streeck, 1998: 439) or previous regulatory standards (e.g. solidaristic wages) tends to be neglected by those contributions which are preoccupied with the identification of functionally equivalent institutions across different countries.

Our conclusion, therefore, is that substantial findings about the implications of globalization on industrial relations can only be gained by explicitly considering functional change in industrial relations over the years. Once aware of functional change, the crucial comparative question which then has to be tackled is whether the pan-European tendency of functional convergence towards increasingly market-oriented industrial relations has the same significance for each country, sector and/or company.[3]

In order to establish this, it is not sufficient simply to concentrate on current developments. A conventional matched comparison of different countries or sectors gives us an impression of the various adjustment processes of industrial relations but tells us little about how significant these have been for each country. A deeper understanding of each particular adjustment process under the impact of globalization can *only* be provided if a synchronic (snapshot) and a diachronic (longitudinal) perspective are combined into a 'contextualized comparison' (Locke and Thelen, 1995).

Making sense of functional convergence: the necessity of contextualizing

The goal of a contextualized comparison is to render possible an in-depth comparison of 'apples with oranges' i.e. of substantially different phenomena from country to country (Locke and Thelen, 1995.) In our case, these phenomena are the different processes of competitive restructuring of industrial relations. The first step, therefore, is to look more closely at intervening socio-economic variables in order to identify the very different 'starting points' (ibid.) in the different countries. Relevant socio-economic variables for a better understanding of the increasing competitive restructuring of industrial relations are macro-political factors such as the degree of openness of the economy and nationally specific strategies of competition (cost-based or product differentiation strategies).

The awareness of nationally different socio-economic starting points is, in our case, crucial for tackling the question of whether functional convergence toward more market-oriented industrial relations in Western Europe is mainly taking place under the current influence of globalization or whether events in the past might have provoked the process of restructuring far more significantly.

Taking into consideration broader socio-economic conditions, however, is only the precondition of the contextualized comparison. In addition, contextualizing means bringing in an analytical perspective that combines a traditional institutionalist approach with a political constructionist one. The latter represents an enrichment for an in-depth comparison as it overcomes the traditional institutionalist approach by paying particular attention to the 'identities' of the actors concerned. Identity, as it is discussed by Locke and Thelen, refers to particular attitudes the actors have towards change due to their specific identity formation in the past and their ideological background. The identity of the industrial actors has to be taken seriously in the eyes of these authors insofar as the range of possible responses to external pressures is usually interpreted in light of past experiences, existing problem-solving techniques and common cognitive focal points.[4]

By equally considering the identities of the actors as well as their institutional embeddedness, the contextualized comparison enables a cross-national analysis of 'analytically parallel (even if formally diverse) phenomena for comparison' (Locke and Thelen, 1995: 344). By identifying analytical parallels between different countries it becomes possible to show why the same external influence does not necessarily provoke the same conflicts in different national contexts. The interesting aspect about contextualized comparison if applied to our question is that it makes clear that the effect of the independent variable 'globalization' depends also on intervening *non-institutional aspects* and not solely on the *institutional setting* of our dependent variable 'industrial relations'.

In other words, the methodological concept of a contextualized comparison suggests two relevant preliminary findings without necessarily having to refer to empirical details of the current situation. First, the apparently independent variable globalization does not 'possess' the same independence everywhere, i.e. does not *a priori* have the same destructive potential and, second, one cannot derive the mediation capacity of collective industrial actors purely from the institutional setting in which they are embedded.

While these conclusions are of methodological importance, it is necessary to introduce empirical data to illustrate the use of contextualized comparison. We use the cases of the German and French automotive industries to demonstrate the way in which such a contextualization can lead us to a radical reinterpretation of existing empirical evidence.

Contextualizing the implications of globalization on industrial relations: the cases of Germany and France

Different starting points: globalization and economic restructuring

From a contextualizing perspective, globalization appears to 'mean' something different for French and German industrial relations. The different meaning of globalization has to do with country-specific socio-economic preconditions which have triggered an asynchronic development of the French and German economy over the past twenty years. Due to very different socio-economic starting points in France and Germany, crucial 'critical junctures' at which the industry of both countries engaged the restructuring of its production regime took place at different times. In France, the crisis at the beginning of the 1980s represented the starting point for decisive reforms of production policies and industrial relations, whereas in Germany the more recent upheaval of 1992/93 has been fundamental in ensuring that the German economy has been exposed to the pressures of the global economy.

The French crisis of 1982/3 can be seen as 'home-made' (Hancké, 1999) insofar as it was the result of insisting too long on *dirigiste* policies or, as Boyer (1997) calls it, on a mode of 'Fordist-type growth'. Until the beginning of the 1980s France represented the classic example of a state-led political economy which was characterized by a highly interventionist industrial policy, a high proportion of nationalized industries, diplomatic pressure in support of exports and a system of national planning (Hall, 1986). The quasi-protectionism of some large French industries enforced an industrial policy which ignored the *Zeitgeist* of an increasing international interdependence at the beginning of the 1980s. At a time when in advanced industrial countries the virtue of specialized goods that compete in quality markets became clear (Piore and Sabel, 1984), French planners still assumed that future growth would come from high volumes of mass-produced commodities competing on price terms. Further, no particular attention was paid to the development of comparative advantage as it was assumed that France could compete in most sectors (Hall, 1986: 211).

The disastrous consequences of industrial and economic misconceptions led to the well-documented 'U-turn' in French macro-economic policy. The retreat from redistributive Keynesianism to the introduction of 'competitive disinflation' can be seen as the retreat away from typical aspects of French interventionism towards market-oriented policies which resembled some of the more German aspects of macro-economic *laissez-faire* (Boltho, 1996: 97). International competitiveness became a decisive parameter in economic policy (Röttger, 1997). By the mid-1980s the French government had adopted a more market-oriented approach with the clear intention of helping corporate actors to compete more successfully in domestic and international markets.

One important legislative step in this direction was the introduction of a series of labour laws, known collectively as the Auroux laws. The Auroux laws were the attempt to modernize French industrial relations by reconciling the German example of social partnership with the employers' increasing desire for firm-level flexibility. The concept of the legislation was that social relationships should rely on regular collective bargaining, conflicts should be regulated only by trade unions and employers without the intervention of the state and the strengthening of works councils and the introduction of *groupes d'expression*[5] should render the firm more democratic.

The shift in the 1980s from 'active interventionism to gradual disengagement' (Smith, 1998) provided French industry with a strong financial and competitive impetus. Through the radical change of their internal organization, enterprises formerly described as 'lame ducks' became among the most profitable enterprises in the OECD in the 1990s. The retreat of the government from quasi-protection of 'national champions' was no handicap for international competitiveness. On the contrary, with the intention of reducing the 'time to market' from the mid-1980s onwards, French enterprises caught up with internationalization and by 1990 came third with regard to outward FDI behind the USA and Japan (Taddéi and Coriat, 1993).

An outstanding example of the French 'metamorphosis' (Jacquemin, 1993) is provided by the car industry. Both Renault and Peugeot overcame near bankruptcy through a thorough restructuring of their production policy which enabled them to continue to compete in high quality markets. Key components of the adjustment process in both enterprises were a large reduction in jobs, a human resources strategy based upon the replacement of the old, unskilled workforce by younger workers with a good education, and co-operative union–management relations. Not surprisingly, the new profit strategy on which Renault and Peugeot had embarked – which consisted of combining the production of high quality vehicles as well as different vehicles – made them relatively immune to the tough recession at the beginning of the 1990s.

The restructuring of the German economy developed in contrast to the French one. Whereas French industry struggled in the 1980s to find new ways of becoming competitive again, German industry at that time was not as adversely affected by the second oil crisis because of its inherent strengths. The export-oriented character of the German economy made industry particularly sensitive to the increasing shift of low-skill manufacturing industries to developing countries in the course of the 1970s and 1980s. Instead of trying to compete with low-wage countries, German enterprises engaged in product upgrading to improve their chances in quality markets.

The seemingly counter-productive institutional rigidities of industrial relations in fact played an important role in supporting this strategy. On the one hand, relatively high salaries and strong social protection proved incompatible with a low-wage economy and, on the other, it pushed German firms to be more innovative. Streeck, who saw the clear competitive advantage of the latter, spoke of the transformation of constraints into resources. In his eyes, strong trade unions did not inhibit but helped management to embark on more demanding and, in the long run, more successful strategies (1989: 150).

An impressive example of the correlation between strong industrial relations institutions and a good economic performance is provided by the development of the automotive sector in the 1980s. German industrial relations proved highly appropriate to tackle the flexibilization of production and work organization. The specific interaction of centralized collective bargaining and plant-level codetermination inhibited the shift in industrial relations towards more firm-level concerns with productivity becoming synonymous with a mode of management-dominated decentralization. Specifically, the pragmatic co-operation between management and works councils through the institution of co-determination became crucial for a German-style 'negotiated adjustment' (Thelen, 1991) to industrial change in the 1980s. The model case of powerful productivity coalitions between management and labour which co-operated over, on the one hand, the introduction of new production methods and product strategies and, on the other, protected workers against the negative effects of industrial rationalization was found in the automotive industry. The works councils in particular became the decisive partner in firms' decision-making. Due to their legal status as well as to their fruitful co-operation with IG Metall (the German metalworkers' union) which provided them with relevant information, modernizing the organization of work without them was impossible. Work reorganization in this industry was therefore the result of negotiation and compromise between management and works councils (Kern and Schumann, 1984: 117).

The 'virtuous circle' of strong institutions and high competitiveness ended with the deep recession in the early 1990s and the emergence of new competitors on the world market capable of making the same quality products at lower prices. Rigid cost reductions imposed on German industry by intensified international competition led to the emergence of a modified version of the old production regime which had to address the difficult task of combining cost competitiveness with the legacy of strong industrial relations (Hancké, 1997). In the car industry, which was particularly hit by the recession, catching up with the higher productivity of its competitors necessitated the restructuring of several interrelated areas such as product policy, production structures, plant and shop-floor organization and industrial relations (Schumann, 1997). International competitiveness in this industry could be regained, however, at the price of destabilizing the delicate balance of the old production regime between economic efficiency and social equity – at the expense of the latter.

From these asynchronic restructuring periods, it follows that both of these countries have been confronted with pressures resulting from globalization in opposite ways. In Germany, it can be argued that one crucial *reason for* the restructuring of the economy and major organizations in the 1990s was the pressure of globalization. Conversely, in France pressures for globalization can be seen as the *result of* major economic restructuring after the upheaval of 1982/83. The industrial transformation of the 1980s 'from active interventionism to gradual disengagement' has, in the case of France, resulted in an economy that from the second half of the 1980s onward has opened itself up to the international market.

The opposite role globalization plays in the German and French economy accounts for the different impact of globalization on industrial relations in both countries in the 1990s. In the following sections we will argue that globalization had (and still has) more influence on German than on French industrial relations.

Globalization and industrial relations

In France the traumatic period for industrial relations was the second half of the 1980s – long before globalization became a relevant issue. One reason for this was the structural shortcomings of the Auroux laws. The optimistic assumption that increasing bargaining and increasing union strength would mutually complement each other proved highly inconsistent with the existing weakness of French trade unions. The attempt to encourage trade unions to co-operate with management on the shop floor through participative management stood in clear opposition to the traditional identity of French unions (Martin, 1994). With regard to a trade union identity which has been formed much more around mobilization at a centralized level than around shop-floor commitment, the Auroux laws proved inappropriate to strengthen the position of trade unions at firm level. On the contrary, the reforms became an instrument for large firms to neutralize trade union influence on restructuring policies. They enabled employers to introduce a mode of participative management that integrated workers' skills into the production process without integrating unions in corporate decision-making structures (Hancké, 1999).

As a result, although not simply due to the legislative reform, trade union density fell between 1980 and 1990 from approximately 20 per cent to 10 per cent. (Goetschy and Rozenblatt, 1992). From the second half of the 1980s onwards, labour became almost invisible as a collective actor in the private sector, notably in the auto industry (Smith, 1998). The decrease of labour influence in the private sector also took place at the level of the works council (*comité d'entreprise*) where the union confederations throughout the 1980s lost their majorities. De-unionization at the workplace was not the best way to deal actively with increasing flexibilization and locational competition resulting from competitive pressures in the second half of the 1990s. As most obviously documented by the closure of the Renault plant in Vilvoorde (Belgium), the possibilities for labour to influence the decision process were nil. By the time the Renault workers from all over Europe organized the first 'Euro-strike', the closure had already been decided.

Despite the undeniable impact of globalization pressures on labour in French industry in the 1990s, the French case differs considerably from the German one insofar as the destructive potential of globalization remains limited to single cases rather than affecting the industrial relations system as a whole. This has largely to do with the ambiguous consequences of the profound restructuring of labour relations in the 1980s. The modernization of French workplace organization which followed from the restructuring and provided the key to the economic health of French enterprises could partly compensate for the decreasing influence of trade unions at firm level. The positive side of modernization was that workers became integrated more closely into new production methods. This changed the character of French workplace relations completely. For the first time in French industrial development, change was no longer simply blocked by notoriously suspicious unions but more and more sustained by local productivity coalitions between management and the workforce on the shop floor (Linhart, 1991). This new adjustment process resembled in parts the German type of firm-level negotiation which was crucial for the successful adaptation of German firms to economic challenges in the 1980s (Streeck, 1989). Indeed, French enterprises which had opted for a thorough workplace reorganization could considerably improve their economic performance – Renault, for example, managed to double its productivity between 1984 and 1994 without an increase in capacity (Hancké, 1999: 22).

Globalization in the sense of increasing competition certainly reinforces the upgrading of the enterprise in France and reinforces the pressures on industrial relations for competitive restructuring. The increasing decentralization of collective bargaining in recent years can be seen as an indicator of this (EIRO, 1999). Interviews with union delegates in the automobile industry, however, have shown that globalization itself is not perceived as a new and predominant threat for the trade unions. Rather, it is seen as a side issue within an ongoing process of company restructuring which started in the 1980s. Taking a carefully optimistic view of the current state of industrial relations in France, one might underline the potential for the industrial relations actors that is linked to the increasing 'glorification of the enterprise' (Dufour and Hege, 1997). Why should the international restructuring of French enterprises not encourage a workforce that actively promotes enterprise strategies and thus gradually 'lead[s] to a repositioning of the collective actors within both public and private enterprises, to the advantage of the workforce' (ibid.: 346)?

In stark contrast to France, globalization has in the German context provoked an intense discussion of its impact on industrial relations in particular and the German social model in general. At the heart of this discussion is the debate on the locational conditions of the German economy (the *Standort* debate) which arose in the course of German unification and emerging new competitors on the Eastern borders of the EU. By far the dominant scenario depicted by German commentators was that the relatively skilled and cheap labour available abroad seriously endangers the future of the organized West German economy and may bring to an end the success story of 'Rhenish capitalism' (Albert, 1991). Maintaining competitiveness was only expected if wages and social benefits were reduced and the labour market sufficiently liberalized. Putting to one side any clear evidence for their success, these assumptions have considerably contributed to the 'downward spiral of deregulation' (Ferner and Hyman, 1998) in German industrial relations.

However, the rhetorically exaggerated 'siren song of deregulation' (Allen, 1998) inherent in most political contributions to the *Standort* debate must not hide the real and detrimental effects of globalization resulting from the specific structural character of the German social model. What is crucial is that globalization contradicts the tradition of a highly nationally organized social model whose post-war capital–labour relations implicitly relied on the limited mobility of the factors of production across national borders (Streeck, 1995). By abolishing national boundaries, and thus increasing the mobility of capital and labour, globalization dissolves negotiated co-ordination between them and 'replaces it with general hierarchical dominance of the former over the latter' (ibid.: 23). The realistic option of capital relocating economic activities to countries with lower social standards increases the pressure on German labour, notably in the control of labour costs. Not surprisingly, the competition with low-wage countries threatens German industrial relations as it calls into question the formerly distinctive virtuous relationship between economic performance and strongly institutionalized regulation. Institutional constraints such as legally regulated collective bargaining and codetermination – which in the 1980s represented decisive resources for economic innovation – seemed increasingly to become expensive obstacles to international competitiveness in the 1990s.

It is not surprising, however, that due to their political and historical 'stickiness' these institutional obstacles could not just be abolished. Following the Anglo-American example of de-institutionalization is simply impossible, given the political context of Germany, and has never been a real alternative to the 'high wages, high skill, high quality' model. In fact, what is crucial for the German economy is that radical de-institutionalization was not necessary to regain competitiveness. German firms managed to find ways of keeping the 'high road' economy without encouraging the dismantling of industrial relations institutions (as in Britain) or circumventing them (as in France). A first examination of the recent German adjustment path confirms that the institutional apparatus of the German dual system once again proved resilient enough to adapt to the challenges of the 1990s.

It would be misleading, however, to derive from this typical institutional resiliency (Thelen, 1991; Dufour, 1998) a never-ending, path-dependent success story of German industrial relations. The reconfiguration of institutions and strategies – which are not immediately obvious on first analysis – are far too important simply to close the case in favour of path dependency in German industrial relations. In order to obtain a full picture of the current reconfiguration of German industrial relations one has to look more closely at the dynamic process which is taking place beyond a relatively stable institutional surface.

The current coexistence of stability and change in the German dual system can best be generalized with reference to Thelen and Steinmo (1992) as a variant of institutional dynamic where exogenous changes have produced changes in outcomes 'as old actors adopt new goals within the old institutions' (ibid.: 17). The new goal which is imposed on the industrial relations actors through German unification and intensified international competition can be described as the difficult task of combining competitiveness and the defence of employment. Although the institutional prerequisites of the German dual system are sufficiently flexible, meeting this new imperative further destabilizes the delicate relationship between centralized and decentralized regulation at the expense of the former. New firm-level agreements which specify the protection of employment and production location reverse the old hierarchical logic of sectoral agreements setting the basic conditions for firm-level codetermination. Contrary to the former primacy of trade unions, there is currently the tendency in German industrial relations for works councils to gain significantly greater influence and, as a consequence, specific circumstances at the firm level increasingly set the basic conditions for collective agreements on sectoral level (Kern, 1998). This gradual upgrading of the works council's position carries with it the danger of exacerbating the 'old' German problem of exclusion. Works councils which form productivity coalitions together with management for the sake of protecting the jobs of the currently employed tend to promote a closure of internal labour markets (Hohn, 1988) and thus reinforce the exclusive tendencies inherent in the structure of the German dual system.

More obvious even than the successive widening of the gap between the 'insiders' and 'outsiders' of the labour market is the increased pressure on those who are currently in employment through systematic benchmarking. In a situation where the multitude of international production sites has stimulated locational comparison and competition within individual enterprises, management proves able to exert constant pressure on the working conditions 'at home' by reference to better and cheaper performances in foreign plants. In such cases, works councils have no other choice but to react to management pressure by embarking on disadvantageous trade-offs between the security of employment and the more flexible use of the workforce. The firm-level agreements that are concluded quite often undermine existing sectoral agreements by combining concessions from works councils on working time flexibility, work organization and wages. In the automotive industry works councils have been used to actively co-manage the process of industrial rationalization first by translating 'new production concepts' (Kern and Schumann, 1984) into action and later by co-conceptualizing innovative work policies (Schumann and Gerst, 1996). In this industry particularly, these new agreements have, compared to the past, far more the character of reactive concession bargaining, inhibiting only the worst effects of globalization.

Further, it is important to note that the increased inter-plant competition within and across countries has led to a considerable undermining of German codeter-mination by introducing the 'insider–outsider' problem into the company. The 'new mode of codetermination' (Kern, 1998) covers fewer and different employees than traditional codetermination. First, the price for securing the employment of the core workers is the worsening of the conditions of the unskilled workers who become more and more exposed to 'strategic' redundancy (Bergmann *et al.*, 1998). Second, and less obvious on first examination, is that even the former 'winners' of industrial rationalization, the highly skilled manual workers, tend to be negatively affected by the new agreements. In their function of supporting innovation in the domestic plants, works councils which embark on new forms of codetermination tend to improve the situation of highly qualified engineers at the expense of the interests of those workers formerly protected by codetermination (Kern, 1998: 33).

A revealing insight behind the apparently stable institutional facade of codetermination is provided by Kotthoff (1998). Kotthoff shows that the omnipresent globalization argument has brought about a tacit alliance between the works council and management. The fear of relocation has so much influence that the works councils increasingly perceive the concessions they make as a totally acceptable contribution to improve the competitiveness of the company (ibid.: 95). Their acceptance of the economic rules can even go so far that the original division between their interests and those of management becomes hardly noticeable. Rather than having an antagonistic relationship with management where they defend the interests of the workforce against managerial arbitrariness, works councils tend to play the role of management's junior partner competing against other companies on the world market (ibid.: 87).

Summarizing, it can be said that the 'shock' of globalization for industrial relations has been stronger in Germany than in France. In Germany, globalization pressures have been the decisive catalyst not only for the successive erosion of centralized bargaining but for the reconfiguration of the entire dual system. On the contrary, the current competitive restructuring in French industrial relations results from the continuation of decentralization tendencies which have been building up more gradually since the 1980s, rather than representing a sudden break with the *status quo ante*.

Conclusion

The aim of this chapter has been to demonstrate the strengths of a contextualized comparison when applied to the empirical data. The widespread discussion concerning the implications of globalization on industrial relations means that this is a critically important exercise. We have questioned the usefulness of conventional analyses which, we argue, overplay the importance of convergence or divergence of industrial relations in different countries, resulting in analyses that, at best, lack explanatory potential and, at worst, place inappropriate emphasis on the convergent or divergent tendencies of industrial relations.

The methodological approach of 'contextualized comparison' aims to explain the present by explicitly relating it to the past. In other words, to combine a synchronic analysis with a diachronic one. In this chapter, we have attempted to demonstrate the methodological advantage of the approach developed by Locke and Thelen (1995) and apply it to a comparison of the implications of globalization on French and German industrial relations. Comparing the development of industrial relations not only across countries but also explicitly over time should underline that 'labor movements in different countries confront seemingly similar challenges with varying degrees of intensity and/or at different historical moments' and that 'apparently similar issues possess very different meanings in different national settings, depending especially on differences in starting points and in the impact of various changes on traditional arrangements' (ibid.: 340).

We have attempted to apply Locke and Thelen's approach and have argued that it is necessary to look at processes of institutional dynamic in such a comparison. As such, we have reassessed the existing literature on the relationship between globalization and industrial relations in the two countries. In doing so, we place considerable importance on the different 'starting points' and the different adjustment processes of German and French industrial relations in response to globalization. We argue that the 'meaning' of globalization is different in the two countries and that in adding an historical perspective to the analysis we can establish that the 'shock' of globalization in Germany has been greater than in France. We acknowledge that this may be a somewhat counter-intuitive conclusion and it is important to note that we are not attempting to comment on the relative merits, or otherwise, of the outcomes of this process. We are merely reassessing the adjustment processes that have taken place in the two countries and rejecting an overly deterministic approach to such an analysis.

Thus, the apparently convergent tendencies of, for example, the development of concession bargaining at the level of the enterprise in both the French and German automotive industries, must be interpreted in light of the different 'meanings' of globalization in each country. In order to achieve this contextualized comparison, we must reassess the pressures for globalization and the related socio-political developments in each country. In doing this, we see that the tendency towards decentralized bargaining in France represents far less of a break with the recent past than in Germany where globalization pressures have proved to be the decisive catalyst for such a development. To restate the argument, the opposite role globalization has played in the French and German economy accounts for the different impact of globalization on industrial relations in both countries in the 1990s.

Notes

1 The paradigmatic example for this aspect of globalization is the case of the German radiator manufacturer Viessmann whose management exploited its potential mobility to impose an unpaid weekly overtime of three hours, in return for not relocating its production in the Czech Republic.
2 In a second step of the argument, however, we take distance from a purely structural understanding of power which in our eyes equates the increase of potential mobility too simplistically with the increase of bargaining power on the side of the employers. The other face to globalization which has to be taken very seriously is the increase of *relational power* on the side of the employees due to the 'employers' heightened dependence on stable and predictable relations with labour at the plant level, in the context of tightly coupled production networks and the demands of producing at high quality on a just-in-time basis' (Thelen and Kume, 1999: 478; see also Streeck, 1998).
3 More than ever before it is crucial to take into consideration regulation levels other than the nation–state – above as well as below the nation–state. Locke (1995) quite explicitly raised the awareness of the increasing relevance of 'subnational' systems of industrial relations. MacDuffie (1995) demonstrated the increased relevance of company-specific variations in manufacturing and work organization practices in the international auto industry. His view has recently been confirmed in the field of industrial relations by Katz and Darbishire (2000) who in their analysis of worldwide changes in industrial relations come to the conclusion that persisting international

convergence coexists with variation between unionized and non-unionized sectors of one and the same country – a coexistence which inspired the authors to speak of 'converging divergences'. It should be noted, however, that although indispensable for a comparative in-depth analysis of empirical evidence the precise identification of the regulation level does not prove pivotal for the sake of our argument.

4   Locke and Thelen illustrate this point by showing the different significance of the flexibilization of wages in Sweden and Germany. Whereas wage flexibility undermines Swedish unions who in the past have invested considerable resources into a policy of egalitarian wages, wage flexibility is not resisted so much by German unions due to their identity which is generally less linked to wage policy (1995: 343).

5   Literally 'expression groups'. In other words, discussion forums between managers and employees and their representatives at firm level.

References

Albert, M. (1991) *Capitalisme contre capitalisme*. Paris: Editions du Seuil.

Allen, C.S. (1998) 'Institutions Challenged: German Unification and the "Siren Song of Deregulation"', in L. Turner (ed.): *Fighting for Partnership: Labor and Politics in Unified Germany*, Ithaca: Cornell University Press.

Altvater, E. and Mahnkopf, B. (1993) *Gewerkschaften vor der europäischen Herausforderung – Tarifpolitik nach Mauer und Maastricht*, Münster: Westfälisches Dampfboot.

Bergmann, J., Bürckmann, E. and Dabrowski, H. (1998) *Reform des Flächentarifvertrags? Betriebliche Realitäten, Verhandlungssysteme, gewerkschaftliche Politik*, Hamburg: VSA-Verlag.

Boltho, A. (1996) 'Has France converged on Germany?', in S. Berger and R. Dore (eds) *National Diversity and Global Capitalism*, Ithaca, NY: Cornell University Press.

Boyer, R. (1996) 'The Convergence Hypothesis Revisited: Globalization but still the Century of Nations?', in S. Berger and R. Dore (eds) *National Diversity and Global Capitalism*, Ithaca, NY: Cornell University Press.

Boyer, R. (1997) 'French Statism at the Crossroads', in C. Crouch and W. Streeck (eds) *Political Economy of Modern Capitalism*, London: Francis Pinter.

Crouch, C. and Streeck, W. (1997) 'Introduction: The Future of Capitalist Diversity', in C. Crouch and W. Streeck (eds) *Political Economy of Modern Capitalism*, London: Francis Pinter.

Dore, R. (1996) 'Unions Between Class and Enterprise', *Industrielle Beziehungen* 3(2): 154–72.

Dörre, K. (1996) 'Globalstrategien von Unternehmen – ein Desintegrationsphänomen? Zu den Auswirkungen grenzüberschreitender Unternehmensaktivitäten auf die industriellen Beziehungen', in *SOFI-Mitteilungen*, No. 24, Göttingen, pp. 15–27.

Dörre, K., Anders, R.E. and Speidel, F. (1997) 'Globalisierung als Option. Internationalisierungspfade von Unternehmen, Standortpolitik und industrielle Beziehungen', in *SOFI-Mitteilungen*, 25, Göttingen, pp. 43–70.

Dufour, C. (1998) 'Industrielle Beziehungen – wie modellhaft ist das deutsche Modell?' in B. Cattero (ed.) *Modell Deutschland, Modell Europa – Probleme, Perspektiven*, Opladen: Leske+Budrich.

Dufour, C. and Hege, A. (1997) 'The Transformation of French Industrial Relations: Glorification of the Enterprise and Disaffection on the Streets', *European Journal of Industrial Relations* 3(3): 333–56.

EIRO (1999) http://www.eiro.eurofound.ie/1999/07/features/FR9907198F.html

Ferner, A. and Hyman, R. (1998) 'Towards European Industrial Relations?', in A. Ferner and R. Hyman (eds) *Changing Industrial Relations in Europe*, Oxford: Blackwell Publishers.

Goetschy, J. and Rozenblatt, P. (1992) 'France: The Industrial Relations System at a Turning Point?', in A. Ferner and R. Hyman (eds) *Industrial Relations in the New Europe*, Oxford: Blackwell Publishers.

Hall, P.A. (1986) *Governing the Economy. The Politics of State Intervention in Britain and France*, Oxford: Oxford University Press.

Hancké, B. (1997) 'Vorsprung aber nicht länger (nur) durch Technik. Die schnelle Anpassung der deutschen Automobilindustrie an neue internationale Wettbewerbsbedingungen', in F. Naschold *et al.* (eds) *Ökonomische Leistungsfähigkeit und institutionelle Innovation – Das deutsche Produktions- und Politikregime im globalen Wettbewerb*, WZB-Jahrbuch 1997, Berlin: edition sigma.

Hancké, B. (1998) 'Industrial Restructuring and Industrial Relations in the European Car Industry: Instruments and Strategies for Employment', *WZB-Discussion-Paper*, FS I 98–305.

Hancké, B. (1999) 'Revisiting the French Model: Coordination and restructuring in French Industry in the 1980s'. *WZB-Discussion-Paper*, FS I 99–301.

Hancké, B. (2000) 'European Works Councils and Industrial Restructuring in the European Motor Industry', *European Journal of Industrial Relations* 6(1): 35–59.

Hansen, L.L. *et al.* (1997) 'The Complex Reality of Convergence and Diversification in European Industrial Relations Systems: A Review of the 1996 IREC Conference', *European Journal of Industrial Relations* 3(3): 357–76.

Hirst, P. and Thompson, G. (1996) *Globalization in Question*, Cambridge: Polity.

Hohn, H.-W. (1988) *Von der Einheitsgewerkschaft zum Betriebssyndikalismus – Sozial Schließung im dualen System der Interessenvertretung*, Berlin: edition sigma.

Hyman, R. (1999) 'National Industrial Relations Systems and Transnational Challenges: An Essay in Review', *European Journal of Industrial Relations* 5(1): 89–110.

Inagami, T. (1996) 'The Death of the "Labour Movement" and the "Japanisation' of Industrial Relations', *Industrielle Beziehungen* 3(2): 173–86.

Jacquemin, A. (1993) 'L'industrie française face à ses défis', in B. Coriat and D. Taddéi (eds) *Entreprise France: Made in France 2*, Paris: Librairie Générale Française.

Katz, H.C. and Darbishire, O. (2000) *Converging Divergences: Worldwide Changes in Employment Systems*, Ithaca, NY and London: Cornell University Press.

Kern, H. (1998) 'Mitbestimmung und Innovation', in *Mitbestimmung und neue Unternehmenskulturen*, Berlin: Verlag Bertelsmann Stiftung.

Kern, H. and Schumann, M. (1984) *Das Ende der Arbeitsteilung*, Munich: C.H. Beck.

Kitschelt, H., Lange, P., Marks, G. and Stephens, J.D. (1999) *Continuity and Change in Contemporary Capitalism*, Cambridge: Cambridge University Press.

Kotthoff, H. (1998) 'Mitbestimmung in Zeiten interessenpolitischer Rückschritte – Betriebsräte zwischen Beteiligungsofferten und "gnadenlosem Kostensenkungsdiktat"', *Industrielle Beziehungen* 5(1): 76–100.

Linhart, D. (1991) *Le torticolis de l'autruche – L'éternelle modernisation des entreprises françaises*, Paris: Seuil.

Locke, R.M. (1995) *Remaking the Italian Economy*, Ithaca, NY and London: Cornell University Press.

Locke, R.M. and Thelen, K. (1995) 'Apples and Oranges Revisited: Contextualised Comparisons and the Study of Labor Politics', *Politics and Society* 23(3): September: 337–67.

MacDuffie, J.P. (1995) 'International Trends in Work Organization in the International Auto Industry: National-Level vs. Company-Level Perspectives', in K. Wever and L. Turner (eds) *The Comparative Political Economy of Industrial Relations*, Madison, WI: IRRA.

Martin, D. (1994) *La démocratie industrielle*, Paris: Presse Universitaire Française.

Müller-Jentsch, W. (1995) 'Auf dem Prüfstand: Das deutsche Modell der industriellen Beziehungen', *Industrielle Beziehungen* 2(1): 11–24.

Piore, M.J. and Sabel, C.F. (1984) *The Second Industrial Divide: Possibilities for Prosperity*, New York: Basic Books.

Rhodes, M. (1997) 'Globalisation. Labour Markets and Welfare States: A Future of "Competitive Corporatism"?', *EUI Working Papers*, RSC No. 97/36.

Röttger, B. (1997) *Neoliberale Globalisierung und eurokapitalistische Regulation: Die politische Konstitution des Marktes*, Münster: Westfälisches Dampfboot.

Schulten, T. (1998) 'Tarifpolitik unter den Bedingungen der Europäischen Währungs- union – Überlegungen zum Aufbau eines tarifpolitischen Mehr-Ebenen-Systems am Beispiel der westeuropäischen Metallindustrie', *WSI-Mitteilungen* 7, July, 51: 482–93.

Schumann, M. (1997) Die deutsche Automobilindustrie im Umbruch', *WSI-Mitteilungen* No. 4, April, 50: 217–27.

Schumann, M. and Gerst, D. (1996) ' Innovative Arbeitspolitik – Ein Fallbeispiel. Gruppen- arbeit in der Mercedes-Benz AG', *SOFI-Mitteilungen* No. 24, Göttingen, pp. 35–52.

Smith, R.W. (1998) *The Left's Dirty Job: The Politics of Industrial Restructuring in France and in Spain*, Pittsburgh: Pittsburgh Press.

Soskice, D. (1997) 'Technologiepolitik, Innovation und nationale Institutionengefüge in Deutschland', in F. Naschold, *et al.* (eds) *Ökonomische Leistungsfähigkeit und institutionelle Innovation – Das deutsche Produktions- und Politikregime im globalen Wettbewerb*, WZB-Jahrbuch 1997, Berlin: edition sigma.

Strange, S. (1997) 'The Future Of Global Capitalism; Or, Will Divergence Persist Forever?', in C. Crouch and W. Streeck (eds) *Political Economy of Modern Capitalism*, London: Francis Pinter.

Streeck, W. (1989) 'Successful Adjustment to Turbulent Markets: The Automobile Industry', in P. Katzenstein (ed.) *Toward the Third Republic: Industry and Politics in West Germany*, Ithaca, NY: Cornell University Press.

Streeck, W. (1995) 'German Capitalism: Does it Exist? Can it Survive?', *MPIFG-Discussion Paper 95/5* November.

Streeck, W. (1996) 'Comment on Ronald Dore's *Unions Between Class and Enterprise*' *Industrielle Beziehungen*, 3 (2): 187–96.

Streeck, W. (1998) 'The Internationalisation of Industrial Relations in Europe: Prospects and Problems', *Politics and Society*, 26(4), December: 429–59.

Taddéi, D. and Coriat, B. (1993) *Made in France: L'industrie française dans la compétition mondiale*, Paris: Librairie Générale Française.

Thelen, K.A. (1991) *Union of Parts: Labor Politics in Postwar Germany*. Ithaca, NY: Cornell University Press.

Thelen, K. and Kume, I. (1999) 'The Effects of Globalization on Labor Revisited: Lessons from Germany and Japan', *Politics and Society* 27(4), December: 477–505.

Thelen, K.A., and Steinmo S. (1992) 'Historical Institutionalism in Comparative Politics', in K.A. Thelen, S. Steinmo and F. Longstreth (eds) *Structuring Politics: Historical Institutionalism in Comparative Analysis*, Cambridge: Cambridge University Press.

Visser, J. (1996) 'Traditions and Transitions in Industrial Relations: A European View', in J. Van Ruysseveldt and J. Visser (eds) *Industrial Relations in Europe: Traditions and Transitions*, London: Sage.

Zagelmeyer, S. (2000) 'Brothers in Arms in the European Car Wars: Management-Labour Pacts in the Context of Regime Competition', MPIfG Working Paper 00/2, February 2000
http://www.mpi-fg-koeln.mpg.de/publikation/working_papers/wp00-2/index.html

9 Human resource management responses to global strategy in multinational enterprises

Peter Kidger

Introduction

It is increasingly recognized that we are living and working in a global environment in which almost all firms are competing in international markets. As barriers to the movement of capital and tariff walls have been reduced, firms are responding to consumer demands for the cheapest and the best, irrespective of national origin. As a consequence of new technology and changing communications, the production process is no longer contained within national boundaries but has spread across them. Globalization is impacting on the social, technological, economic and political environment, and is reshaping the lives of people around the world.

A key player in the global economy is the multinational enterprise (or MNE or multinational). The growth of international competition and opportunities for foreign investment have contributed to the growth in the number and size of multinationals so that it now claimed that they dominate the world economy (Dunning, 1993; Kobrin, 1997; Dicken, 1998). The management and organization of MNEs are therefore important aspects of understanding globalization and its impact on the social as well as the economic environment. This chapter is concerned with the management of people in multinational enterprises, and its aim is to examine the implications for human resource management (HRM) of globalization in MNEs. It is based upon a qualitative research project in which information on strategy, structure and management practice was obtained from a sample of multinational firms with operations in the UK. Interest in HRM in multinational firms has been steadily growing over the last decade, but it is still a relatively young field of study. This research was undertaken as a contribution to the development of a systematic and comprehensive knowledge of what is happening in firms that are operating in a global economy

Globalization and the multinational enterprise

For the purposes of this chapter, a multinational enterprise may be understood as a firm which carries out value-adding activities and employs people in more than one country. An MNE can therefore be distinguished from organizations that compete in foreign markets through exporting or forming alliances, without becoming international employers. Multinationals are complex organizations that internalize operations across national boundaries, and have often diversified into a number of different product markets. The larger MNEs have developed complex structures within which are managed the sometimes competing demands of different country units, different business units and different management functions.

Multinationals have to operate in a changing and turbulent world environment. The international economy where fairly discrete geographically defined markets were linked by trade and cross-border investment is said to have changed into a global economy which is characterized by a greater integration of economic activity across boundaries. The extent to which globalization is occurring is a controversial issue, and it seems reasonable to accept the view of Dicken (1998) that while there are globalizing forces at work, there is not yet a fully globalized economy. Some industry sectors are more global than others, and it is useful to distinguish between multidomestic industries, which are characterized by relatively independent national markets, and global industries, in which are found cross-national similarity in customer demands and the use of global supply chains (Porter, 1990). In global industries, the similarity in product demand allows firms to reap scale economies through standardization. Greater standardization in turn facilitates the international integration of operations, and encourages the pursuit of further economies through the centralization of production at fewer locations (De Wit and Meyer, 1998: 722). A global firm therefore employs an integrated world-wide approach to the organization of its activities, in contrast to a multidomestic firm which has fairly autonomous national subsidiaries, usually controlled through financial targets. Since globalizing companies tend to seek global suppliers, they expand or create global industries, and thus become a cause of further globalization.

A counterbalance to the pressure for global convergence is provided by the forces of national diversity. Each country subsidiary of an MNE is affected by its national context, and indeed country characteristics can provide competitive benefits (Porter, 1990). Cultural differences affect markets and the internal running of companies especially in relation to communication and the use of common systems and policies. In some sectors technology has made it possible to give customers more choice about aspects of products, and producers seek a marriage of standardization and difference. MNEs have therefore been urged to balance the global and the local (Ohmae, 1994). Bartlett and Ghosal (1992) suggested that MNEs in complex environments might adopt the 'transnational solution' in which they organize themselves so as to achieve global efficiency, local responsiveness, and world-wide innovation through knowledge sharing and learning. The transnational was originally presented as an idealized organization type, and has been described as elusive and unstable (Edwards *et al.*, 1996), but it provides a useful template against which to assess the structure and processes of globalizing firms.

The choice of a global or multidomestic strategy will be reflected in the structure of an MNE, and a central issue for all multinationals is the balance to strike between integration and differentiation in the relationship between corporate headquarters and local subsidiaries (Kamoche, 1996). An MNE may have a centralized structure in which dependent subsidiaries are controlled through such mechanisms as a top-down strategic plan, parent company nationals in senior management positions and head-office originated systems. In contrast, many established MNEs have operated with a differentiated or polycentric structure in which independent subsidiaries develop and carry out a local mandate, within financial and other performance targets agreed with the centre. In the transnational or globally integrated MNE, the relationship between the centre and subsidiaries is interdependent, with control being exercised through corporate culture and possibly a jointly developed strategic plan. However, in making these distinctions, it should also be noted that within an MNE, there may be different relationships with different subsidiaries, depending on such factors as how long a unit has been established, its location and the nature of the contribution which is made by the unit to the whole organization (Casson *et al.*, 1998; Taggert, 1998).

Human resource management in the multinational enterprise

If firms are adopting a more global strategy and structure, this is likely to have implications for HR practices in MNEs, especially if management accept the conventional wisdom that HR policies and practices should be aligned with organizational strategy (Storey, 1995: 6). In this section it is proposed to look more specifically at the HR processes which may be important to companies that are integrating activities across national borders.

Since one of the triggers of global integration is said to be the competitive environment, a useful starting point for the discussion of HRM in MNEs is the axiom of human resource management that people are an important source of competitive success to the firms that employ them (Pfeffer, 1994; Storey, 1995; Pfeffer, 1998). A theoretical basis for this premise is found in the resource-based view of the firm, from which it is argued that valuable and difficult-to-imitate resource assets provide a firm with sustainable competitive advantage (Wernerfelt, 1984; Barney, 1991; Boxall, 1996). Of the types of assets that may be possessed, tangible assets are only of short-term benefit since they are relatively easy to duplicate. Intangible assets, including patented ideas, brand names and service reputation, are a more important source of advantage, and capabilities are even more important because of the difficulty of imitation. To these firm-specific assets, a multinational firm may add the country-specific resources of all the locations in which it is operating, so that competitive success in a global environment is dependent on firm-specific resources, country-specific resources and strategies for balancing global efficiencies with local responsiveness (Fahy, 1998).

Competitive human resource advantage is the product of human capital advantage and human process advantage (Boxall, 1996). This means that as well as having skilled and knowledgeable people, the MNE must have the processes that will ensure their HR capability is effectively utilized towards organizational ends. In many cases the most important human capital resource is the firm-specific know-how that develops through informal learning and social interaction, since it is that kind of knowledge and organizational process that is difficult to reproduce elsewhere

(Mueller, 1998; Scarbrough, 1998). Organizational learning is an aspect of strategic HRM that can be linked to the emphasis on world-wide learning and innovation in the transnational solution of Bartlett and Ghosal. If there is beneficial know-how in one part of the MNE, whether the parent company or elsewhere, the firm will want to leverage the advantage by imitating it in some, if not all, other centres of operation. An important aspect of globalization in the MNE is establishing effective ways to transfer knowledge across national boundaries, and thus promote organizational learning.

A number of mechanisms exist for this, including international development and training programmes, conferences, networking and visits (Carr, 1994; Haddock and South, 1994; Edwards *et al.*, 1996). Kamoche (1997) suggested that an important source of organizational learning in MNEs is repatriates, if the knowledge acquired through individual assignments can be widely diffused, although the literature on expatriate assignments suggests that this rarely happens. Cross-national learning is also occurring in some multinationals through the use of international project teams, who work on common problems or opportunities, and who, with modern means of communication, do not even have to be based in the same location (Snell *et al.*, 1998). Martin and Beaumont (1998) looked at the use of internal benchmarking in a large multinational, ABB, and concluded that in the right circumstances it could facilitate internal learning and the transfer of best practice. Dixon (2000) has provided case studies of the different approaches to knowledge transfer used by multinationals such as Ford, Lockhead-Martin and BP Amoco.

In centralized MNEs where subsidiaries are seen as being dependent on the parent, the flow of information is predominantly one-way. In the polycentric MNE knowledge accumulates within the independent units, and transfer of the lessons of experience is haphazard. A key feature of the globally integrated or transnational MNE should be that knowledge transfer is encouraged and is multi-directional. Achieving this may require management and organizational development interventions in order to create a geocentric orientation across all parts of the enterprise.

Adler and Ghadar (1990) suggested that as organizations move from a multidomestic to a global strategy, the focus of international HRM shifts from the management of expatriates to the development of an international management corps with shared organizational values, as well as to the promotion of cross-national learning. In the global firm, the best people are sought for key managerial roles irrespective of nationality, and such a policy needs to be supported by integrated processes for identifying and nurturing the competence to manage in different cultural environments. Global firms are therefore seeking to identify the characteristics of effective international managers to aid the selection and development processes (Borg and Harzing, 1995: 187).

The development of an international group could also contribute to establishing the shared values of a corporate culture, which can be seen as a useful integrating mechanism in multinationals, and particularly so in global firms (Paauwe and Dewe, 1995). There are, however, problems with the use of culture as a control mechanism. Empirical studies in this area suggest that it is not as easy to manipulate organizational culture as some of the prescriptive literature has claimed (Ogbonna and Harris, 1998). In addition, the theoretical case for a strong corporate culture in a multinational is weakened by the possibility that too much standardization may be a barrier to innovation. The continuing need to be locally responsive is likely to be assisted by national diversity rather than global uniformity, even if such a thing is possible. It is arguable that multinationals would benefit from being a cultural mosaic rather than a melting pot (Schneider, 1988), in which parent companies are open to learn from their culturally different subsidiaries (Laurent, 1989). Management need to build sufficient commitment to shared values and practices so that there is a cross-national sense of cohesion within the organization, but should also welcome the value of cultural diversity.

International HR policies

In the pursuit of competitive advantage, firms at all levels seek to apply best practice in all aspects of their operations. In a global world, ideas as well as goods are traded, potentially contributing to the development of international norms of what constitutes good management. In the global MNE, it is expected that the integration of operations will be supported by the integration of management practice. However, it has often been assumed that, compared to technological know-how, HR practices are less transferable because of the differences of national culture, employment laws and industrial relations systems. In general, research has found that the tendency in MNEs is for subsidiaries to follow local norms rather than use centralized HR policies (Rosenzwaig and Nohria, 1994; Guest and Hoque, 1996; Monks, 1996). Nevertheless studies of MNEs do show that there is some inter-unit sharing, and the greater integration of operations brought about by globalization might be expected to increase pressures for similarities in HR policies. This might generally be at the level of principle, with scope for national variation in the application of policy (Stroh and Caligiuri, 1998).

One of the current debates in human resource management is whether there is a set of HR practices that are universally promoters of high performance, or whether more stress should be laid on matching HRM to organizational strategy (Boxall, 1996; Brewster, 1999). There is some evidence from studies in the UK and the USA that the 'high commitment' model of HRM is linked to high performance (Wood, 1995; Huselid, 1995; Pfeffer, 1998; West and Patterson, 1998). An area of interest in international HRM is, therefore, how widely the components of the high commitment system are recognized across the world as good practice in HRM. Teagarden and Von Glinow (1997) suggested that while many HR practices are culturally specific, there are what they called HRM design philosophies that can be generalized across cultures. They refer in some detail to the 'control' and the 'development' design philosophies. The latter turns out to be similar to what others have called a commitment system (Walton, 1985; Arthur, 1994; Wood, 1995), and the authors state their belief that 'a firm's ability to develop and diffuse a developmental design philosophy or human resource culture is the essence of best human resource practice in the global economy'. The developmental design is claimed to give MNEs the ability to implement global strategy while being sensitive to host countries and their cultures.

Such a view may under-estimate the importance of industry and national contexts as influences on HR policies (Brewster and Bournois, 1993: 50). The USA and Japan have been seen as having different traditions of people management, while in Europe cultural and other factors have created distinctive national patterns of HRM that have complicated attempts by multinationals to streamline HR practices in response to the single European market (Sparrow and Hiltrop, 1997). Even if a more common approach to HRM emerges in Europe, it is likely to differ from the American model (Thurley, 1990; Sparrow and Hiltrop, 1994: 183–209; Brewster, 1995). While some international convergence of HR practice has been reported (e.g. Mroczkowski and Hanaoka, 1997), it is still appropriate to consider policy development in any firm within its various contexts.

Even within the same country, organizations use different employment systems from one another and for different groups of employees (Purcell, 1996). Contingency theory would justify this, especially if the HR system is aligned with organizational strategy. Statements of 'best practice' are often described at a level of principle, which would still allow for differences in the way the practices are implemented (Becker and Gerhart, 1996).

Taylor *et al.* (1996) developed a model of strategic international human resource management that identified factors that might be determinants of the degree of similarity between the HR systems of MNE parent organizations and subsidiaries. One factor they suggested was whether parent company management was orientated to export its own HR system to foreign subsidiaries, or to adopt local practices in each location, or to aim for an integrative approach using the best ideas from any national source. They suggested that the extent of similarity might vary for different country subsidiaries, and different employee groups, depending on such factors as the cultural and legal closeness of countries and the importance of the contribution of a particular employee group to achieving competitive success. Their views were consistent with other models of parent–subsidiary relations in suggesting that the extent of integration might vary within the firm.

In summary, studies of human resource management in multinational enterprises have been concerned with the transfer of know-how, the development of international managers, the promulgation of an international corporate culture, and the creation of international HR policies. These themes provided the basis for the research project described in this chapter.

A study of international HRM

Although there have been a number of empirical studies of HRM in multinationals, the bank of knowledge of what is happening in the real world is inevitably limited, given that this is a world-wide phenomenon which is subject to a changing environment. It is suggested therefore that there is scope for further investigation of how HRM processes are being shaped in MNEs responding to the pressures of globalization. The research that is reported here was intended to contribute to the development of a fuller picture of international HRM by investigating a number of the key issues that have emerged from previous studies.

The following argument was derived from the literature on the strategy and management of multinationals. As a result of changes to the world economy, multinational enterprises face increasing global competition, which they are meeting by looking for improvements in both efficiency and quality. To be successful, MNEs have to learn to be both globally efficient and locally responsive. A consequence of this will be the creation of complex organizational structures, which combine global integration with devolution to business and country units who are close to the customers. However, really long-term success will go to those firms that are able to sustain advanced capability on a world-wide basis, hence the importance given to innovation and the transfer of know-how within the firm.

Global integration is also likely to require an international approach to manager selection and development, in order to create and sustain global mind-sets, and foster shared responsibility for the success of the whole enterprise. The aim would be the development of international management and a world-wide approach to identifying and securing management capability. This policy may be coupled with the promotion of shared organizational values as one of the means of creating a common sense of identity across national boundaries.

The encouragement of sharing within the organization, the development of international management, and the need for some standardization in the treatment of employees who are part of a more integrated organization is expected to result in the creation of international HR policies in areas which are regarded as important for the achievement of corporate objectives. However, employment policies have to take account of the differences of national context, particularly in relation to societal culture and employment law, so there will inevitably be a global/local balance to be found. This may mean distinguishing between global principle and local practice, or may mean that similarity is more likely in some policy areas than others, or in relation to some groups of staff rather than others.

Globalization, then, is likely to result in a convergence of human resource management both through the development of international policies and the sharing of successful practice in multinational enterprises. Internally this should provide international roles for the HR function in global firms that would not be needed in multidomestic firms.

A set of research questions was developed from this argument to provide a framework for the research study:

1   Are global firms fostering world-wide learning and innovation?
2   Are global firms integrating management development and succession?
3   Are global firms promoting shared organizational values?
4   Are global firms developing international HR policies?
5   Is there evidence of cross-national convergence of HR practice?
6   What role is played by the corporate HR function in global firms?

The research method was a qualitative survey of MNEs with operations in the UK. In a qualitative survey the number and type of cases to be included are not determined by statistical sampling requirements but by what is relevant to the research questions, and will help to understand the process under investigation (Mason, 1996). In this study, the plan was to have a balance between UK, other European, US and Japanese ownership, so as to minimize bias from country of origin. The sample was also varied in size, length of experience as a foreign direct investor, and whether supplying consumer or industrial products. They were, however, all manufacturers from the engineering and chemicals processing industries. Companies were selected from existing contacts and by identifying possible participants from *The Personnel Manager's Yearbook*.

The research adopted a qualitative methodology since this was felt appropriate in an investigation that concerned cross-national relationships, and would need to explore the informal as well as the formal dimensions of organizational life. Semi-structured interviews were used as the main method of data collection in order to ensure that issues related to the research questions were explored in each case, while having the freedom to respond to what might emerge about a potentially diverse and fluid situation. Regular reviewing of the data as it accumulated meant that discussions could be channelled towards particular issues in order to build up a complete picture. In most cases the primary informant was the senior HR/ Personnel executive of the unit visited, or an HR executive with international responsibilities. In a number of instances the main interview was supplemented by conversations with other managers. In addition, written documents on strategy, mission, structure and HR policies were collected wherever possible. Information on the twenty-four multinationals that participated in the survey is provided in Table 9.1.

A possible limitation of the research design was that UK executives of foreign investors might not be aware of policies in their organization in other countries. This would be most likely in multidomestic firms, but was not expected to be a problem in global firms. As with all interviews with company executives about their own areas of responsibility, there was the possibility of bias through a natural tendency of senior managers to present the best image to the outside world. Where the UK executive had a responsibility for HR activities in subsidiaries, there was the possibility that cultural or other problems with policy implementation might be played down. Any lessons drawn from the findings of the research would have to take account of these possible limitations.

In the following sections, the results of the research are discussed. There are first of all some general comments about the impact of globalization on the companies, and this is followed by discussion of the results under headings that reflect the research questions listed above.

The impact of globalization

The sample of companies varied by country of ownership, sector, size and time they had been foreign investors. Yet it was clear that all of them were affected by

Table 9.1 Organizations participating in the survey

Country	Sector	Strategy	UK sales	UK nos	Main informant
1 US	Engineering	Regional	£71 million	770	UK HR Manager
2 US	Process	Regional	£1.1 million	1,000	Europe HR Dir
3 US	Engineering	Multidomestic	£100 million	750	Europe HR Mgr
4 US	Engineering	Global	£1 billion	10,000	UK HR Manager
5 US	Process	Regional	£105 million	670	UK HR Manager
6 US	Process	Regional	£500 million	2,200	Europe HR Manager
7 US	Engineering	Global	£4,300 million	28,000	International HR Mgr
8 UK	Process	Global	£376 million	10,000	International Employment Manager
9 UK	Process	Multidomestic	£1,723 million	10,000	International HR Dir
10 UK	Engineering	Move to global	£2,000 million (worldwide)	32,000 (world-wide)	UK HR Manager
11 UK	Process	Global	£300 million	5000	International HR Mgr
12 UK	Process	Multidomestic	£300 million	2,700	UK HR Director
13 UK	Engineering	Move to global	£800 million	5,800	Division Head HR
14 UK	Process	Move to global	£303 million	4,300	UK Personnel Director
15 Germany	Engineering	Become global	£1.5 billion	10,000	UK HR Manager
16 Switzerland	Process	Global	£804 million	4,000	UK Development Manager
17 France	Process	Global	£300 million	5,500	UK HR Director
18 Sweden	Engineering	Multidomestic	£20 million	230	UK HR Manager
19 Norway	Process	Multidomestic	£30 million	32	UK CEO
20 France	Engineering	Multidomestic	£20 million	340	Division UK HR Mgr
21 Belgium	Process	Multidomestic	£5 billion	38,000	UK Works Manager
22 Japan	Engineering	Regional	£2.5 billion (region)	9,000	Division UK HR Mgr
23 Japan	Engineering	Global	£230 million	1,800	UK HR Director
24 Japan	Engineering	Multidomestic	£12 million	84	UK Finance and Personnel Director

globalization. The majority of the firms that participated in the study saw international growth as vital to their future, and this was being pursued through organic development, acquisition and joint venture. There was a strong perception that competition is stronger and has to be met by better performance. So as well as finding new markets, the companies were looking at how they could be more efficient, improve product quality, and be responsive to customers.

Ten of the companies were long-established multinationals that had moved from a multidomestic to a global strategy, with integration across all activities. Others were moving in that direction but displayed more of a mix of multidomestic and global characteristics. In some cases there was coordination rather than integration, but in all these firms national boundaries were diminishing in importance. Regional centres were also found in some of the companies, with integration at that level rather than world-wide.

A variety of control and coordination mechanisms were in place, including global planning frameworks and corporate culture, in the sense of shared understandings of the business and its objectives. It was possible to identify two globalization types in this sample. One was the centralized global firm, in which authority was retained in the parent office, and exercised through a hierarchy in which parent country nationals occupied the key roles. The second type was the decentralized or federal global firm, in which the structure was a complex matrix through which authority was devolved to business units. Seven of the companies could perhaps be put in the second category, on the basis of their structure, reporting relationships and processes of cross-national decision-making.

Learning and innovation in global firms

Changing technology in both telecommunications and travel has facilitated new approaches to parent management control in MNEs, and developments in IT have introduced new forms of global interaction that can be used to foster organizational learning. Foreign investors often bring new knowledge into a country, and traditionally most of the flow of expertise in MNEs has been from parent to subsidiaries. However, in the transnational ideal, knowledge transfer is multidirectional and directed at sharing innovative capability.

The picture that is presented by the companies in this study is somewhat mixed, reflecting different experiences and expressions of globalization. In nine of the companies knowledge transfer was predominantly from parent to subsidiaries, and sharing between subsidiaries was very limited. By contrast, another seven of the companies, those which in the previous section were categorized as federal, were fostering a much more geocentric learning capability. The remaining nine were moving in the same direction, but their ideas were less developed.

In the global firms, communication between units is needed because of greater integration of activities and of dealings with customers or suppliers. The ease of world travel and development of electronic mail have obviously facilitated this. However, there is also a concern to promulgate best practice, which might be developed anywhere in the organization. Methods that were being used to achieve organizational learning included:

- cross-national meetings of managers;
- corporate seminars and training programmes;
- internal benchmarking and audit;
- access to global databases;

- knowledge facilitators visiting units;
- recognizing units as centres of excellence for particular processes or products;
- cross-national project teams.

Informants from companies that until recently had had a multidomestic strategy were aware that when subsidiaries were independent there was variability of standards and the tendency to hoard rather than share resources. One reason for arranging cross-national management meetings and international training courses was to create a different culture, one in which people see themselves as part of a larger whole to which they are willing to contribute. This is probably an important aspect of building a learning organization since a great deal of knowledge transfer is likely to be through informal channels. It was interesting to find that, in some of the subsidiaries, managers from the UK were networking with colleagues elsewhere even when there was little corporate encouragement of this.

The recognition of 'centres of excellence' is one way of both building and utilizing innovative knowledge, and means that capability that develops in a particular country can be nurtured and made available as a corporate resource. There was, however, a contrast in the study firms between those that centralized know-how and then diffused it to operating units, and those that encouraged units to network and share directly with one another. It is the latter who are nearer the transnational ideal.

While these different methods of knowledge transfer are obviously necessary, it could be argued that what is of most importance to the development of world-wide learning is to develop the right climate. What separated the 'advanced' from the 'beginners' among the group of companies in the research was the pervasiveness of a learning culture that came through in some of the interviews. The leading companies in this aspect of transnationalism were those where there was a clear encouragement to learn from others, and the breaking down of the idea that the parent organization was the sole source of expertise.

Two things seemed to be driving this concept. The main one was the need for greater efficiency in the face of competitive pressures. Identifying and promoting good practice so that all units come up to the standard of the best is one way of achieving this that also leads to consistency between country units producing the same products for the same or similar customers. However, there was also a socio-cultural dimension to these developments. The concept of cultural diversity seems to have made its mark, and several contributors spoke of moving away from a past practice of trying to impose parent company norms on subsidiaries. The policy of encouraging staff to learn from elsewhere supports the climate of geocentrism that many of the companies are trying to foster.

International management development

Management capability may be as important as technological capability in achieving competitive success. The findings of the research confirm that firms following a global strategy take an international view of management succession.

Succession is coordinated so that information flows from subsidiaries, and the businesses and countries are involved in decisions on appointments. A common device is a committee that plans and manages the appointment and development of senior management, and may also find ways of giving international experience to more junior staff with potential. Cultural awareness and other international issues are built into management training programmes. The aims are twofold: first, to widen the pool from which appointments are made. Second, to give managers and potential managers international experience, which global companies believe to be essential for those in senior positions. As a result of the international approach, more third country national appointments are made, which in time can mean foreign nationals on the top parent executive group. In some of the MNEs in the study, the coordination of appointments was at a European level as well as globally.

The global companies usually designate an international management group, who are regarded as a corporate resource and whose role assignment and remuneration are determined in the corporate head office. A common evaluation scheme, such as the Hay Guide Chart, may be used to provide for some parity of reward. Setting up this group does not necessarily mean that large numbers of them will be on foreign assignments at any one time. The cost of foreign assignments is a factor to consider against the benefit they bring. Several participants in the research commented on this, and were obviously giving thought to the most effective way of developing an international culture. Based on some of their comments, a good practice model might contain the following elements.

- provision of international experience to professional staff early in their career rather than waiting until they move into the top echelon;
- organization of international management training events that bring people from different cultures together, and also incorporation of 'international' material into training programmes run in businesses and countries;
- designation of the level at which managers are treated as part of a corporate resource whose career is managed centrally;
- establishment of a representative international group to oversee international appointments;
- careful and selective use of foreign assignments for senior managers;
- promotion of networking rather than assignments as a way of developing cultural awareness and experience of contributing to international issues.

Organizational culture in the multinationals

One aim of potentially transnational MNEs is the creation of a sense of common identity and purpose across the whole organization, since in this MNE form managers from subsidiaries have to cooperate with one another with an eye to the objectives of the whole firm and not just their particular unit. A common organizational culture may provide the necessary linking mechanism that gives the people in different countries a sense of oneness with each other.

Organizational culture is often equated with shared values and beliefs, and so participants were asked whether their organization had core values that were intended to be understood and accepted on a world-wide basis. Twenty of the companies reported having a mission statement, although interestingly several of these did not respond to a request for a copy. Six of those twenty indicated that the mission statements were of little or no influence. The statements that were available nearly all consisted of fairly general commitments to customers, employees and the community that seemed almost interchangeable between companies. Although in many cases the value statements were widely promulgated and discussed through induction courses, their usefulness was uncertain. There were only two firms where the informants were enthusiastic about the importance of the shared values and beliefs of a corporate culture.

Organizational culture turns out to be something that managers think they can distinguish but find difficult to describe. There is not a common language for discussing culture, and so descriptions in the interviews focused on different things. These included product quality, management style, commitment to employees, closeness to customers, and office layout. Individual informants tended to select something that represented the company's culture to them, but if others had been asked, different answers might have been forthcoming. In that sense, organizational culture is contained in the patterns of meaning that the social actors ascribe to processes and events. A statement of corporate values may contribute to some sense of common purpose, but is often regarded as mainly symbolic. To many UK managers in foreign subsidiaries, value statements emanating from the parent are too general to be of importance in management decision-making. A manager in one of the American subsidiaries, for example, commented that the value statement meant little to the shop floor, but went on to say that employees could relate to the more specific objectives for performance improvement which they had been involved in developing.

Shared understandings in a society develop through shared experience and discourse. If anything like a common culture is to develop in a multinational, it is likely to be facilitated by extensive communication between people, and that is something that is developing in the globalizing companies. Participants referred to the objective of becoming more international, which they generally saw as about mind-sets. There were sometimes the twin aims of thinking globally, and thinking about the whole organization rather than the local unit. The ways in which this was being achieved might be summarized as understanding differences and sharing solutions to common problems. While mission statements may have some value, it would seem that organizational culture is being built primarily by networking and developing common processes.

The changing world of travel and communication is obviously facilitating coordination and has made dialogue between company members in different parts of the world easier. It is therefore not surprising that regular meetings of general and functional management groups should have become an integrating mechanism in many multinationals. Face-to-face contacts at management meetings or through visits are combined with electronic communication through the internal global networks. Networking supports the movement towards international approaches to marketing, purchasing, manufacturing standards and product development. The globalizing companies are concerned to achieve high performance through the application of best practice or world class standards. What also seems to be recognized is that this cannot be imposed, and that parent companies have to be wary of managerial imperialism. So although some companies have explicit statements of values, and utilize top-down planning systems, good practice comes about through dialogue and persuasion. While this is the aim, it is difficult to know whether the outcome will actually be ethnocentric, promoting ways of working that come from the parent company, or whether multinational groups of managers can develop something that is genuinely geocentric.

International policies and practices in HRM

A focus on learning and knowledge transfer in global companies is likely to lead to sharing of 'best practice' in all functional areas, including HRM, with the intent of improving organizational performance. In most of the companies in the study, HR/Personnel executives are meeting together in the same way that other functional and business managers from different countries are meeting, and are discussing best practice in areas of HRM. Even where this does not happen, there may be regular communication between executives in the head office and subsidiaries. The opportunity is there to introduce successful practice from elsewhere, but it was not clear how much this was happening. There were apparent differences in attitude among the Personnel executives participating in the study. Some of them believed they could learn from what was happening elsewhere, and expected that over time there would be more international convergence of HRM practice. Others were a lot more cautious about the value of cross-national sharing. The more positive views were found in companies that were doing more to promote international sharing, and individuals might change their views as their own organizations become more experienced at international cooperation. On the other hand, the varying attitudes of UK managers are also a reminder that some people are more ethnocentric than others, and this may affect how successfully they can learn from other cultures.

Companies in the study were sometimes selective in the areas of shared know-how, and so might, for example, be promoting common approaches to work organization, but not to employment processes, particularly where the latter are seen as more culturally bound. However, if success in an increasingly competitive environment means creating an organizational culture that values innovation and constant improvement to all aspects of work, the logic of this is to encourage the sharing of experience even in areas where it may at first seem less promising.

As well as encouraging the sharing of information about successful HR practice, global firms are developing HRM policies in support of a global strategy. Global integration of activities and the recognition of the need to develop a global orientation are supported both by the encouragement of cross-unit communication and by establishing global policies or policy guidelines. When informants were asked what determined if there should be an international policy for some HRM issue, the most common answer was business need. This was usually to support globalization, or performance improvement. Thus, international policy related to such areas as training, appraisal, performance management, competencies, and communication. In a few cases corporate principles or values prompted international policies, for example, in regard to equal opportunity.

As a generalization, policies were laid down as principles or guidelines, so that practice might vary. A policy guideline could, for example, be that all employees have a regular performance appraisal to identify development needs, or that a system for identifying training needs be established, or that special contributions by individuals or teams are recognized. Even so, there were some accounts from informants of difficulties with international initiatives, and the ownership of policies may be a relevant factor. For some issues an acceptable approach might be that a principle is established by corporate head office, or through discussion at an international managers' meeting, which is then implemented locally in a variety of different ways. However, there may be other policy matters for which a more bottom-up approach to development would be preferable. One way of doing this is to set up a cross-national team to prepare recommendations, so that the policy guidance is not seen as a head office imposition.

Resistance to central HR policies may also be a reflection of national ethnocentrism. As the units in an MNE move from an independent to an interdependent relationship, it may take time for country managers to develop the appropriate geocentric attitudes. The HR director of the UK subsidiary of a Japanese MNE remarked that he could always head off suggestions from parent country managers by referring to the law and possible tribunal appearances, and no doubt national managers everywhere use similar defensive tactics to counter initiatives that they do not welcome. In the interviews it was often possible to detect a slight sense of 'them and us' when talking about other units. With managers from the UK companies this was with reference to subsidiaries; with managers from subsidiaries it was with reference to head office. Policy development is a social and political process, and head office executives need to recognize this when considering the development of international policies.

In eight of the research companies there were virtually no international HRM policies, apart from parent company policies on expatriate assignments and top management rewards. However, in some of these, policy changes in the UK subsidiary were subject to head office approval, and in others communication within the HR function or the influence of expatriate managers meant that there were policy similarities. In other words, deciding if there are international policies is not always straightforward. If account is taken of the history of the companies, the research findings confirmed that where an MNE followed a multidomestic strategy, there were few if any international HR policies other than those to control parent company assignments. However, in every case where an MNE had made a strategic decision to globalize, there were international HR policies or guidelines. Generally, these were more developed in the companies were there was a more globally integrated structure. The overall picture from the study is that global companies do develop international HR policies that apply across the organization, where such policies are perceived as supportive of business strategy.

There does, however, seem to be a fine line between a dependent and an interdependent approach. Globalization may lead to more centralization, with managers in subsidiaries feeling no sense of ownership for what are perceived as corporate initiatives. Cultural differences on attitude to hierarchy may also affect the willingness of people to contribute to the development of common policies. This is an issue that needs to be recognized, and possibly countered by such devices as bringing cultural differences to the surface, holding meetings in different countries, rotating meeting leadership, or making a point of recognizing ideas from subsidiaries. The aim should be to exploit the benefits of cultural diversity and bring a plurality of perceptions to bear on any problem.

International norms of best practice in HRM

Informants were asked which of a range of human resource policies were in operation in the UK, and which of them were also found in other country units. The purpose was to judge if there was any convergence of policy that was independent of corporate policy guidelines. Nearly every UK informant knew something of policies elsewhere, which is perhaps a reflection of the greater sharing of information that is going on within multinationals. A tentative conclusion from the interviews, including comments that were made about discussions in Personnel function meetings, is that there is some agreement on what constitutes good practice in HRM among the HR/Personnel executives of MNEs in the sectors represented in the study. It is still common for companies to differentiate between professional and shop floor staff, and there was slightly more commonality in the management of management level employees.

There has been disagreement among HR scholars as to whether a high commitment system of HRM will contribute to better performance in all organizations, or mainly in those that are following a quality differentiation strategy (Becker and Gerhart, 1996; Guest, 1997). None of the organizations covered by this research had an exclusively cost leadership strategy, and in several instances companies were trying to position themselves in niche markets where they could compete on quality. However, cost was still important, and was a driving force behind global restructuring. It is not surprising then, that HR policy developments reflected needs both to improve performance and to reduce labour costs. There was more cross-national consensus about the former than the latter. Thus, an emphasis on training was universal, and there was general agreement on communicating with employees, consulting to gain consent for change, involvement in process improvements and appraisal. The principle that workers should share the benefits of performance improvement seemed widely accepted, although there were the expected differences of view on linking individual performance to pay. There were differences in the organization of work, with some companies, particularly in the processing industries, using multitask teams while others retained a more traditional assembly line. On the whole, job design differences between companies did not seem to reflect country of origin, although some of the UK units reported that they had been able to make more progress in negotiating changes with unions than their colleagues elsewhere.

There was a general perception that good human resource management anywhere is about building employee commitment to the achievement of organizational goals. Overall, in the cases studied, the main factors that influenced commonality of HR practice were associated with development and performance management.

While there was some uniformity in what was being done to improve individual performance, there seemed to be more differences between country units in the measures being taken to reduce labour costs, and several informants contrasted the UK and other European countries. This is what would be expected in the light of the different legal and industrial relations frameworks. The UK environment has allowed firms to pursue leanness, and the study companies have been downsizing, delayering and re-engineering processes. Their counterparts in France, Germany and other EU countries have had similar objectives, but were reported as having more difficulty in achieving them.

One conclusion that could be drawn from the research is that the EU is having a small but definite impact on MNEs. In some cases the EU has been the main trigger for establishing European coordination in the MNE. European Works Councils (EWC) now exist in most of the study companies, and the European Commission is driving forward its social programme. European HR/Personnel executives are in contact before EWC meetings, and are discussing EU employment initiatives at their meetings. It will be interesting to see what impact there is at the micro level from the attempts of European managers in MNEs to work together.

An international role for personnel

In the research study it was found that as firms globalize, they integrate senior management appointments, encourage cross-national sharing of experience and develop international HR policies on issues that support corporate objectives. This in turn places new demands on the HR function within businesses and at corporate head office. The narrow view that international HRM concerned expatriate assignments has to be replaced by a broader conceptualization of what the HR/Personnel function should deliver to support the move to a global strategy.

In the global companies, one clear HR responsibility is the development of international management. The aim of this is to ensure the senior managers of the future can give leadership in a cross-national environment, but it is often also intended to change the culture by building an international mind-set that permeates all levels of the organization. The responsibility embraces a number of activities such as defining competencies, setting up development programmes and managing succession. It includes establishing international standards for the management of expatriate assignments to ensure some consistency of treatment. It may mean establishing a cross-nationally acceptable appraisal system that provides information on performance and potential. Leadership in any organization is a crucial contributor to success, which is perhaps why management development is recognized as an important responsibility for the international HR function.

Coupled with this has been the development of international HR policies where these seem appropriate to support corporate or business division objectives. The resource-based view of the firm suggests that HR policies and systems can be a source of competitive advantage if they contribute to building and releasing human capability. In the global company, the HR function is seeking best practice and ensuring that in each national location the most appropriate policies are implemented, whether they reflect local or international norms.

The HR function should also be in a position to spearhead the development of a world-wide learning organization, although in the study it was only in three of the companies that this came through as a direct objective of the function. If nothing else, the HR function can act as a role model through its own processes of interchanging information and comparing experience. As HR executives learn to do this in relation to their own activities, they are in a better position to coach others to do the same thing.

The starting point for the HR executives participating in the study was nearly always the needs of the business. It is evident that the concept that HRM should be aligned with corporate and business strategy has become virtually a basic assumption of HR practitioners. In thinking about their own contribution to the organization, senior HR executives need to identify where and how they can add value through their own activities and their support of line colleagues.

Conclusion

This chapter has discussed findings from an investigation into human resource management in multinational enterprises, looking particularly at the impact of globalization on HRM. The results show that in global firms there is, as expected, encouragement of world-wide learning, an international approach to management development and more cross-national integration of practice. Global firms are trying to create a sense of belonging to the international organization, not just to its local manifestation. Communication technology facilitates networking with colleagues around the world, with whom problems and solutions can be shared. HRM has often been seen as the area of management where national differences are greatest, but this is not preventing the HR specialists from developing cross-national principles that are applied in different countries.

However, as in any large organization, there are issues of power and subtleties of relationships. There are different forms of globalization, and a distinction can be made between those firms where the corporate management has a centralized approach and those firms where the operation of the structure is more federal. In the latter, it can be suggested that communication and learning are prime processes that are being used to build a sense of world-wide cohesion. If there is the openness to allowing ways of working and solving problems to emerge from cross-national networking, this may result in the development of shared understandings that will have more validity than some corporate mission statements.

This poses some interesting challenges for the HR function in contributing to building a firm in which culturally diverse people collaborate together to achieve agreed goals. As the formal processes that are being used in global firms become clearer, the attention of future research might centre on the informal, to understand better how cross-national relationships are working in those organizations that aspire to the transnational ideal.

References

Adler, N. and Ghadar, F. (1990) 'Strategic Human Resource Management: A Global Perspective', in R. Pieper (ed.) *Human Resource Management: An International Comparison*, Berlin: De Gruyter.

Arthur, J.B. (1994) 'Effects of Human Resource Systems on Manufacturing Performance and Turnover', *Academy of Management Journal* 37: 670–87.

Barney, J. (1991) 'Firm Resources and Sustained Competitive Advantage', *Journal of Management* 17(1): 99–120.

Bartlett, C.A. and Ghoshal, S. (1992) *Managing Across Borders*, London: Century Business.

Becker, B. and Gerhart, B. (1996) 'The Impact of Human Resource Management on Organisational Performance: Progress and Prospects', *Academy of Management Journal* 39(4): 779.

Borg, M. and Harzing, A. (1995) 'Composing an International Staff', in A. Harzing and J. Van Ruysseveldt (eds) *International Human Resource Management*, London: Sage.

Boxall, P. (1996) 'The Strategic HRM Debate and the Resource-based View of the Firm', *Human Resource Management Journal* 6(3): 59–75.

Brewster, C. (1995) 'Towards a European Model of HRM', *Journal of International Business Studies* 26(1): 1–21.

Brewster, C. (1999) 'Strategic Human Resource Management: The Value of Different Paradigms', in R.S. Schuler and S.E. Jackson (eds) *Strategic Human Resource Management*, Oxford: Blackwell.

Brewster, C. and Bournois, F. (1993) 'A European Perspective on Human Resource Management', in A. Hegewisch and C. Brewster (eds) *European Developments in Human Resource Management*, London: Kogan Page.

Carr, R. (1994) 'The Development of a Global Human Resource Management Approach in ZENECA Pharmaceuticals', in D. Torrington (ed) *International Human Resource Management*, Hemel Hempstead: Prentice-Hall.

Casson, M., Loveridge, R. and Singh, S. (1998) 'Human Resource Management in the Multinational Enterprise: Styles, Modes, Institutions and Ideologies', in G. Hooley, R. Loveridge and D. Wilson (eds) *Internationalization: Process, Context and Markets*, London: Macmillan.

De Wit, B. and Meyer, R. (1998) *Strategy: Process, Content, Context*, 2nd edn, London: International Thomson Business Press.

Dicken, P. (1998) *Global Shift*, 3rd edn, London: Paul Chapman Publishing.

Dixon, N. (2000) 'The Insight Track', *People Management*, 17 February: 34–9.

Dunning, J.H. (1993) *Multinational Enterprises and the Global Economy*, Wokingham: Addison-Wesley.

Edwards, P., Ferner, A. and Sisson, K. (1996) 'The Conditions for International Human Resource Management: Two Case Studies', *The International Journal of Human Resource Management* 7(1): 20–40.

Fahy, J. (1998) 'The Role of Resources in Global Competition', in G. Hooley, R. Loveridge and D. Wilson (eds) *Internationalization: Process, Context and Markets*, London: Macmillan.

Guest, D.E. (1997) 'Human Resource Management and Performance: A Review and Research Agenda', *The International Journal of Human Resource Management* 8(3): 263–76.

Guest, D.E. and Hoque, K. (1996) 'National Ownership and HR Practices in UK Greenfield Sites', *Human Resource Management Journal* 6(4): 50–74.

Haddock, C. and South, B. (1994) 'How Shell's Organisation and HR Practices Help it to be Both Global and Local', in D. Torrington (eds) *International Human Resource Management*, Hemel Hempstead: Prentice-Hall.

Huselid, M. (1995) 'The Impact of Human Resource Management Practices on Turnover, Productivity, and Corporate Financial Performance', *Academy of Management Journal* 38: 635–72.

Kamoche, K. (1996) 'The Integration-differentiation Puzzle: A Resource-capability Perspective in International Human Resource Management', *The International Journal of Human Resource Management* 7(1): 230–44.

Kamoche, K. (1997) 'Knowledge Creation and Learning in International HRM', *The International Journal of Human Resource Management* 8(3): 213–25.

Kobrin, S.J. (1997) 'The Architecture of Globalisation: State Sovereignty in a Networked Global Economy', in J.H. Dunning (ed.) *Governments, Globalisation and International Business*, Oxford: Oxford University Press.

Laurent, A. (1989) 'A Cultural View of Organisational Change', in P. Evans, Y. Doz and A. Laurent (eds) *Human Resource Management in International Firms*, London: Macmillan.

Martin, G. and Beaumont, P. (1998) 'Diffusing "Best Practice" in Multinational Firms: Prospects, Practice and Contestation', *The International Journal of Human Resource Management*, 9(4): 671–95.

Mason, J. (1996) *Qualitative Researching*, London: Sage.

Monks, K. (1996) 'Global or Local? HRM in the Multinational Company: The Irish Experience', *The International Journal of Human Resource Management*, 7(3): 721–35.

Mroczkowski, T. and Hanaoka, M. (1997) 'Effective Rightsizing Strategies in Japan and America: Is There a Convergence of Employment Practices?', *Academy of Management Executive* 11(2): 57–67.

Mueller, F. (1998) 'Human Resources as Strategic Assets: An Evolutionary Resource-based Theory', in C. Mabey, G. Salaman and J. Storey (eds) *Strategic Human Resource Management*, London: Sage.

Ogbonna, E. and Harris, L.C. (1998) 'Managing Organisational Change: Compliance or Genuine Change?', *British Journal of Management* 9(4): 273–88.

Ohmae, K. (1994) *The Borderless World*, London: HarperCollins.

Paauwe, J. and Dewe, P. (1995) 'Human Resource Management in Multinational Corporations: Theories and Models', in A. Harzing and J. Van Ruysseveldt (eds) *International Human Resource Management*, London: Sage.

Pfeffer, J. (1994) *Competitive Advantage Through People*, Boston: Harvard Business School Press.

Pfeffer, J. (1998) *The Human Equation*, Boston: Harvard University Press.

Porter, M.E. (1990) *The Competitive Advantage of Nations*, Basingstoke: Macmillan.

Purcell, J. (1996) 'Human Resource Bundles Of Best Practice: A Utopian Cul-de-sac?', paper presented at ESRC Seminar Series on the Contribution of HR Strategy to Business Performance, 1 February.

Rosenzweig, P. and Nohria, N. (1994) 'Influences on Human Resource Management Practices in Multinational Corporations', *Journal of International Business Studies* 25(2): 229.

Scarbrough, H. (1998) 'Path(ological) Dependency? Core Competencies from an Organisational Perspective', *British Journal of Management* 9(3): 219–32.

Schneider, S.C. (1988) 'National vs Corporate Culture: Implications for Human Resource Management', *Human Resource Management* 27(2): 231–46.

Snell, S.A., Snow, C.C., Davison, S.C. and Hambrick, D.C. (1998) 'Designing and Supporting Transnational Teams: The Human Resource Agenda', *Human Resource Management* 37(2): 147–58.

Sparrow, P.R. and Hiltrop, J. (1994) *European Human Resource Management in Transition*, Hemel Hempstead: Prentice Hall.

Sparrow, P.R. and Hiltrop, J. (1997) 'Redefining The Field of Human Resource Management: A Battle between National Mindsets and Forces of Business Transition?', *Human Resource Management* 36(2): 201–19.

Storey, J. (1995) 'Human Resource Management: Still Marching on or Marching Out?', in J. Storey (ed.) *Human Resource Management: A Critical Review*, London: Routledge.

Stroh, L.K. and Caliguiri, P.M. (1998) 'Strategic Human Resources: a New Source for Competitive Advantage in the Global Arena', *The International Journal of Human Resource Management* 9(1): 1–17.

Taggert, J.H. (1998) 'Configuration and Coordination at Subsidiary Level: Foreign Manufacturing Affiliates in the UK', *British Journal of Management* 9(4): 327–39.

Taylor, S., Beechler, S. and Napier, N. (1996) 'Towards an Integrative Model Of Strategic International Human Resource Management', *Academy of Management Review* 21(4): 959–85.

Teagarden, M.B. and Von Glinow, M.A. (1997) 'Human Resource Management In Cross-Cultural Contexts: Emic Practices Versus Etic Philosophies', *Management International Review* 37(Special Issue): 7–21.

Thurley, K. (1990) 'Towards a European Approach to Personnel Management', *Personnel Management* 22(9): 54–7.

Walton, R.E. (1985) 'From Control to Commitment in the Workplace', *Harvard Business Review* 64(2): 77–84.

Wernerfelt, B. (1984) 'A Resource-based View of the Firm', *Strategic Management Journal* 5: 171–80.

West, M. and Patterson, M. (1998) 'Profitable Personnel', *People Management* 8 January: 28–30.

Wood, S. (1995) 'The Four Pillars of HRM: Are They Connected?', *Human Resource Management Journal* 5(5): 49–59.

10 Globalization, employment relations and 'reverse diffusion' in multinational companies

Tony Edwards

Introduction

Over the last three decades an extensive literature has emerged concerned with the diffusion of employment practices in multinational companies (MNCs). The level of interest in this issue reflects the growing size and scope of MNCs: they are seen as 'the primary shaper of the contemporary global economy' (Dicken, 1998: 177). MNCs are becoming increasingly influential in patterns of international trade, accounting for around two-thirds of world exports of goods and services, while foreign direct investment has consistently grown much faster than output. In employment terms estimates suggest that MNCs directly employ around one in five workers in developed economies, with this proportion rising to two in five once those working in suppliers of MNCs are taken into account (Ruigrok and van Tulder, 1995).

The literature tells us much of interest about the nature of employment practices in the foreign subsidiaries of MNCs. For instance, a series of studies in the 1970s and early 1980s showed US MNCs to employ practices characteristic of the US system of employment relations. For instance, in the UK American MNCs were pioneers of the practice of productivity bargaining and displayed a preference for formalized agreements and procedures over 'custom and practice'. Similarly, numerous recent studies have demonstrated that Japanese MNCs have brought with them many of the practices characteristic of the Japanese economy, such as lean production (see Ferner, 1997 for a review of the literature). However, where the literature is less useful is in developing an understanding of the employment practices in the domestic workplaces of MNCs (Edwards, 1998a). Two-thirds of the total number of people who work for MNCs do so in domestic workplaces but very few studies have set out to investigate the implications of the internationalization strategies of MNCs for these workers. Does this omission matter?

It might be argued that it does not. In a response to some of the claims about MNCs becoming stateless players which are detached from their country of origin (e.g. Ohmae, 1990; Reich, 1990), several writers have shown that they are in fact still firmly embedded in and shaped by their national base. Hirst and Thompson (1996), for example, used survey data to examine the geographical distribution of the assets, sales and employees of MNCs, demonstrating a strong concentration of all three in the country in which the multinational originated. Moreover, MNCs typically turn to their home base when raising finance, conducting research and development and recruiting senior managers. Thus, far from being global or stateless, MNCs should be seen as 'national firms with international operations' (Hu, 1992). The implication is that, since MNCs are still strongly influenced by the country of origin, employment relations in the domestic plants will not diverge significantly from nationally established structures and practices and, hence, there is little point in studying them.

On the other hand, however, there are good reasons for believing that the internationalization strategies of MNCs will indeed have important consequences for domestic workers. Much of the literature on MNCs in the field of strategic management and international HRM is concerned with how MNCs can adopt 'best practices' from anywhere within the organization and subsequently diffuse these to plants in other countries (e.g. Bartlett and Ghoshal, 1998; Gupta and Govindarajan, 1991). In this way domestic plants can operate practices that originated abroad. The prevalence of such a 'transnational' or 'geocentric' orientation is likely to grow as MNCs gradually increase the extent to which they are geographically distributed.

This chapter investigates the process that has been termed 'reverse diffusion' (Edwards, 1998a): the direction of diffusion is reverse in the sense that it is from foreign subsidiaries to the home base, the opposite direction to that of the more commonly studied form which is termed 'forward' diffusion. It is argued that reverse diffusion (RD) has the potential to lead to significant changes in the nature of employment relations in the domestic workplaces of MNCs. Specifically, the chapter examines two issues. First, it considers the way in which structural characteristics of MNCs, such as their international structure and the extent to which they are globally spread, shape both the incidence of RD and the mechanisms and channels of influence through which RD takes place. In other words, it examines the influences on RD which are internal to MNCs. Second, it investigates the nature of MNCs' competitive environment in shaping the practices that are diffused. Thus it also considers the way that factors external to MNCs shape the substance of RD.

The chapter is organized as follows. The next section considers competing theoretical approaches to explaining the diffusion of employment practices across borders. Following this, data from four mini case studies are presented and used to assess the extent of RD in these four MNCs. Then the impact of structural characteristics of these MNCs on the incidence and process of RD is investigated, and the role of the external environment on the substance of RD is examined. The key findings and their implications are spelt out in the conclusion.

Theoretical approaches to diffusion in MNCs

In the literature in MNCs, as Edwards, P. *et al.* (1993: 7) note, 'much effort has been devoted to devising typologies to distinguish different kinds of MNC. Usually, some notion of "strategic contingencies" relating to market and environment is seen as the basis of differentiation'. Porter (1986), for example, argued that a firm's internal structure depends on the nature of competition in the industry: MNCs in sectors in which competition takes place at the international level structure themselves along 'global' lines with international divisions as the primary axis of internal organization, whereas those in sectors characterized by competition being primarily at the national level tend towards 'multi-domestic' structures whereby national subsidiaries are accorded primary importance. Such an approach is 'structural' in that it explains managerial actions with reference to the structural characteristics of the organization and its environment.

In the field of employment relations in MNCs, the structural approach has been deployed to identify the circumstances which make management in MNCs favourably disposed, or at least not hostile, to the emergence of transnational management–union consultative arrangements (Marginson, 1992). These are most likely to exist, Marginson argues, in MNCs which have a single management structure at European level, which have grown through the establishment of greenfield operations rather than through merger or acquisition and which have commonalities in their operations across countries. Hamill's (1984: 30) work on the degree to which decision-making in MNCs on IR issues is centralized also stresses structural factors. Hamill presented a theoretical explanation of why firms differed in this respect which was derived 'by reference to the wider environmental factors which define the basic operating characteristics of MNCs such as size; date and method of establishment in the UK; the degree of inter-subsidiary production integration; profitability; and so on'.

The structural approach suggests that the potential for diffusion in general and RD in particular is greater where certain environmental and organizational factors are present: in other words, certain structural factors promote the incidence of diffusion. The primary criticism of the structural approach, however, is that it is deterministic in implying that outcomes, in this case managerial approaches to employment relations in MNCs, follow unproblematically from environmental and organizational factors, thereby downplaying the scope for choice that managers possess. As Child (1972: 16) argued, the 'many available contributions to a theory of organisational structure do not incorporate the direct source of variation in formal structural arrangements, namely the strategic decisions of those who have the power of structural initiation – the dominant coalition'. The political approach to diffusion is based on this line of analysis: it views organizations as comprised of different groups of actors whose interests and priorities will often diverge from those of other groups. Consequently, the extent and nature of diffusion are the result of the conscious political decisions of organizational actors.

An illustration of the political approach is Broad's (1994) case study of a Japanese MNC operating in the UK in which the introduction of Japanese-style high involvement management (HIM) practices into the plant was characterized as a 'contested process' between Japanese expatriates and UK managers. The latter group were unenthusiastic about the initiative, seemingly more concerned with the 'traditional obsession' of prerogative and secrecy associated with UK management. In order to block the diffusion the group had formed an informal network which secured information from the shopfloor through rumours and gossip, keeping this from the expatriates. The failure to fully implement HIM should be understood, Broad argued, more as the result of conflicting priorities between different groups of actors than any notion of external environmental contingencies. Another illustration of the political approach demonstrates the way in which managers at the HQ attempt to create an imperative at plant level to introduce new practices which the HQ favours. Mueller and Purcell (1992) document the systematic comparisons of the plants of automotive MNCs according to their costs, quality and productivity, arguing that these 'coercive comparisons' are used to break down resistance to diffusion at plant level.

The political approach, therefore, reveals the importance of analysing the choices which groups of organizational actors exercise and the ways in which they use whatever sources of power they possess in order to pursue their objectives. However, using this argument to ignore the role of structural factors altogether would be a mistake since the choices that organizational actors take are not made in a vacuum but rather are strongly influenced by characteristics of the environment and the organization of which they are a part. As Whittington (1993: 28) puts it, managerial decisions are 'rooted deeply in densely interwoven social systems'. In a similar vein, DiMaggio and Powell (1983: 149) argue that firms are subject to strong 'isomorphic pulls' which force 'one unit in a population to resemble other units that face the same set of environmental conditions'.

Rather than adopting either the structural or the political approach, it is preferable to see diffusion as the result of the interaction of structural and political factors. Moreover, as has been argued elsewhere (Edwards *et al.*, 1999), the relationship between structural and political factors can be characterized as 'bi-directional': that is, political processes within MNCs are shaped in part by the nature of the structural context, while this structural context is in turn influenced by political activity. The role of product markets in diffusion illustrates this bi-directional relationship. Where consumer tastes are very similar in different countries, the HQ of a MNC is less reliant on local expertise in serving a national market and, consequently, the power of managers at this level is high in relation to those at plant level, giving them some scope for forcing through the diffusion of practices which are met with scepticism by managers at plant level. In contrast, where national markets are distinct from one another, the role of plant managers as key inter-mediaries between the MNC and the local market affords them more scope to resist central pressure to introduce practices they see as problematic. In this way, the extent to which markets are standardized, a structural factor, influences the relation-ship between managers at different levels, a key aspect of the political processes within MNCs. The nature of product markets also demonstrates the way in which political processes can shape structural factors. The size and financial clout of many large MNCs give them the ability to devote large amounts of resources to marketing and advertising, thereby influencing consumer tastes. In this way MNCs possess a degree of power in their product markets, enabling them to shape the extent to which competition is standardized across borders. Thus the actions of powerful MNCs, themselves the result of political activity of course, shape the nature of product markets, a structural factor.

How, then, does this discussion inform analysis of reverse diffusion? Primarily, it points to the need to investigate the internal processes within MNCs. In particular, how do structural factors shape the incidence of RD? And how do these structural factors influence the processes through which RD occurs? The discussion also highlights the need to analyse the impact of firms' external environment and the way it shapes the substance of RD. To what extent do competitive forces and 'dominant' forms of production within an industry influence what goes on within MNCs? These issues are considered here in the analysis of data drawn from four mini case studies. The background details to these MNCs and the extent of evidence of RD is set out in the following section.

The evidence of RD in four MNCs

All four MNCs were medium-sized, UK-owned firms operating in the manufacturing sector. Fieldwork consisted of in-depth semi-structured interviews with respondents at multiple levels. In every case, interviews were conducted at plant and HQ levels and where appropriate at divisional level too. A subsequent step in two of the companies was to carry out interviews at US plants. These data were supplemented by analysis of company documents and press reports. The data were assessed to ascertain the existence of reverse diffusion in the four MNCs. Two requirements were necessary for the conclusion to be drawn that there was evidence of RD: first, the channels and mechanisms through which diffusion occurred could be identified; and, second, a practice could be identified in the UK plants which had originated in a specific overseas plant and had been diffused within the company.

In two of the MNCs there was no evidence of RD. The first company, PowerCo, employed around 40,000 people and was structured around two business areas, both of which related to different areas of the engineering sector. Foreign activities accounted for a small but growing proportion of total employment (around 20 per cent), with much of this being in North America. The personnel department in the business area studied was attempting to achieve greater commonalities in personnel policy across its sites, designing guidelines on employment practice for all of its plants. However, these guidelines were formed from UK influences:

> We say World Class but there is still an element of looking UK-based rather than a much wider footing. I think the reason is the differences from country to country – we tend to discount these rather than saying can we learn from them.
>
> (HQ respondent)

The second multinational, Pack&Print, employed around 30,000 people in five business areas within the manufacturing sector. Around 60 per cent of the group's employees were located outside the UK, spread widely across the world: the company had a presence in North America, Western Europe, Asia and increasingly Eastern Europe. In keeping with PowerCo, management at the HQ were trying to generate greater coherence across their sites in different countries through the development of stronger international structures and greater integration. However, this process was at an initial stage and had not got to the point of creating strong international structures which had facilitated reverse diffusion:

> We are moving from being a mini-BTR – a holding company – to being something much more integrated and looks like a 3M. Under a BTR you really don't need the bits to talk to each other; if you want to be a 3M you've got to have a lot of cohesiveness, so we're heading down that road. . . . But we're in the early days of that transition.
>
> (HQ respondent)

In neither of these two MNCs, therefore, was there any evidence that practices which had developed in foreign subsidiaries had been diffused to the domestic plants. One concern about this conclusion might be that RD went undetected in these firms. This is possible, though unlikely since exhaustive questioning with multiple respondents at HQ and plant level produced no evidence that practices had been diffused from overseas to domestic plants.

In the other two MNCs, in contrast, there was clear evidence of RD. The first of these, ChemCo, employed about 20,000 people in three business areas, all of which were involved in manufacturing chemical or plastic goods. Just over half of the workforce are employed abroad, spread widely across the world. In recent years the company has sought to sell off operations which do not form a core part of any of the three business areas and, following this, the HQ had become more proactive in monitoring and guiding employment practice at plant level:

> It is my perception that part of the debate about the role of the centre was what can be the role of the HR function and what flavour should there be, if any, of something common to ChemCo world-wide. It was in that setting that the idea of focusing on two or three very basic things that people can buy into regardless of where they come from.
>
> (HQ respondent)

> There are some things about ChemCo – you'd probably call them the values or the behaviour of the business – which are set corporately. So we've got an underlying approach to people and people management that's pretty well common across the business and we interpret that against the needs of the local business.
>
> (UK plant respondent)

A part of this greater coordination was the reverse diffusion of practices, which was detectable in two areas. First, there was a clear North American influence on management's approach to training and development in the UK operations. The HQ had been impressed by the approach of the American operations in this area and as a result a US manager was brought over to the UK to run the training department, bringing with him many of the practices he had developed in the USA.

The second area in which there was evidence of RD was employee involvement. The HR managers from sites in different countries held regular meetings to discuss matters of common concern. One issue was how the company could appear to be listening and responding to employees' views: the practice that was decided upon was an employee opinion survey, which had been developed in the US operations, with management at plant level expected to respond to the output. This practice was not only diffused to the British plants but also to the other overseas plants.

Engineering Products, the final MNC, was structured around three business areas in which just over 30,000 people worked. The biggest of these business areas was automotive components, which accounted for two-thirds of employees and was spread across Europe and North America, developing to the point where operations were highly integrated with the divisional HQ playing a very influential role over plants. It was clear that the HQ at this level had made a concerted attempt to tap the foreign subsidiaries for best practice and, consequently, developments in the foreign subsidiaries were exerting a very strong influence on employment practice in the domestic plants of the automotive division:

> If we go back to the early 1990s the lessons in manufacturing were being learned from our operations in France. They were the benchmark. Since then other operations have provided initiatives which have been shared around. Probably now Spain is being visited as much as anywhere else because there are some good lessons to be learned there.
>
> (HQ respondent)

Three particular initiatives were detected which had originated in the foreign plants and been diffused across the division. First, the US operations were piloting a system of core competencies for engineers. This initiative had identified the basic competencies that were generic to the automotive division world-wide and were to be applied in the other plants. The progress of this development was discussed at international meetings of personnel managers who were expected to implement a similar practice in their plants. The new practice was set to bring important consequences for all engineers in the division, standardizing their training and making them more mobile between plants. Second, one of the French plants had developed a way of breaking up a large factory into a series of small production units which enjoyed a degree of autonomy but were responsible to the 'internal customer' at the next stage in the production process. The aim was to develop a much stronger focus among all workers with the success of their unit and to develop a culture within a unit that they were both a supplier and a customer for others within the factory. This practice was diffused to other plants through one of the managers responsible for it being sent as an internal consultant. Third, a form of cellular assembly, developed in one of the Spanish plants, involving an assembly line being reorganized from a linear into a U-shaped form, had been diffused. This practice had profound implications for operators, requiring them to work in teams within the cells and to move from job to job within these teams. Furthermore, under the cell structure fewer operators were needed for the same output, meaning that numbers employed were falling. Diffusion of this practice to other plants occurred through engineers from the Spanish plant being seconded to implement the new practice in the company's other plants.

This section has demonstrated that RD was found in two of the four MNCs. In one of these companies, Engineering Products, RD was a key influence on employment practice, testifying to its potential significance. In the other two MNCs, however, there was no evidence of RD. The next section attempts to explain why RD is found in some MNCs and not others through examining the structural factors which promote its incidence and the way in which these structural factors influence, and are influenced by, political processes within the MNCs.

Internal factors promoting reverse diffusion

How can we explain why RD is found in two of the MNCs but not in the other two? What are the structural factors which promote its incidence? And how do these shape political activity within MNCs? In this section, five such factors are identified and the way in which these promote RD and shape the processes through which it occurs are investigated.

The first of these factors is the nature of international business structures. Porter (1986) distinguished between MNCs in which territorial units, normally national subsidiaries, are the primary axis of internal organization and those in which international business divisions, which link similar operations in different countries, are dominant. In practice, many MNCs adopt elements of both types, forming a matrix structure in which plants report both to their national HQ as well as to the divisional HQ: indeed, all four of the case studies possessed a matrix structure. What differed, though, was the strength of the national and divisional elements to the matrix. In PowerCo national structures were more influential than the divisional ones, with plant managers' primary lines of reporting being to those at the national HQ and the contact with other plants mainly being with those in the same country. This was broadly true of Pack&Print, too (though the divisional structures were gradually assuming more weight). In contrast, in ChemCo and particularly in Engineering Products, the divisional element was stronger. In the latter case this had resulted in the HR function at the divisional HQ exerting an influence over more and more areas of employment practice, such as work organization, training, employee involvement and management development, and had also resulted in plant managers being in regular contact with their counterparts in other countries. This factor was central in promoting reverse diffusion. The strength of the divisional structure also shaped the process of RD, primarily through generating stronger ties between managers from different countries engaged in similar operations. The automotive components division was a first-tier supplier to the large car manufacturers and increasingly these customers were moving towards dealing with the same suppliers in different countries. The serving of the same customers provided a common interest between plant managers within the division, leading to an identification with the division and a willingness to work together through, for example, sharing best practice. The divisional HQ had actively encouraged such collaboration through the creation of mechanisms such as training courses and international conferences and, further, had sought to encourage the movement of managers across sites on expatriate assignments.[1] In contrast, in Pack&Print the divisional element of the international structure was much weaker and, accordingly, the pressures for plant managers in different countries to collaborate were also weaker. Mechanisms bringing together personnel specialists in Pack&Print, such as meetings, conferences and committees, solely operated at the national level.

The nature of international business structures is strongly linked to the second structural factor promoting RD, namely the extent to which production is integrated across borders. In both PowerCo and Pack&Print the plants primarily served customers in their own national market, resulting in significant differences in the nature of the products and also in the processes and practices used in production. Consequently, production was not highly standardized across sites, nor was there much in the way of intra-enterprise trade. In the two MNCs in which RD was found, however, production was much more integrated. One of ChemCo's products was paint for ships. The ship owners required ChemCo to supply and administer the paint at a range of different ports so the firm had to produce paint to identical standards in its plants in different countries and had sought to standardize work organization as a result. This customer pressure to integrate production was even stronger at Engineering Products where the two biggest customers, Ford and GM, sought identical components to their operations in different countries. The pressures towards greater integration not only acted to promote reverse diffusion but also strongly shaped the process through which it occurred. As described above, serving the same customers internationally provided a common interest for greater collaboration within the divisional structure. Moreover, the placing of orders centrally by the division's main customers strongly shaped the power relations between HQ and plants. Specifically, the HQ was now in a position to determine which plants received orders and did so according to the performance of plants in terms of costs and quality, meaning that plants were systematically compared in a process referred to above as 'coercive comparisons'. In one sense this internal competition for orders created a tension with the impetus to collaborate: why should plants which are in competition share innovations and new practices with one another? At Engineering Products, the divisional HQ had partially overcome this tension by rewarding plants with investment and orders not only for favourable performance but also for the contribution of new practices to the rest of the group. In this way, internal competition, which was made possible by greater production integration, underpinned the softer mechanisms for encouraging diffusion, such as training and conferences.

A third factor which promotes RD is 'maturity'. Both of the MNCs in which RD was found were mature in the sense that they had operated internationally for over twenty years. In both cases it was clear that the process of international integration in general and the move towards engaging in reverse diffusion in particular were lengthy processes. PowerCo, on the other hand, had relatively recently begun expanding internationally and had made some sizeable acquisitions in North America only two years prior to the fieldwork being conducted. The way in which the maturity of the multinational promotes RD reflects the political processes at work. Where management at HQ decide to seek greater integration, they face the task of convincing plant managers to participate in the process. This may not be unproblematic: evidence suggests that managers at local level often guard their autonomy jealously and, hence, may resist attempts at standardization, using their expertise in the local environment to do so (Broad, 1994; Edwards, P. *et al.*, 1993). Even where the HQ is able to convince, or coerce, local management into participating in integrating production, the design and setting up of mechanisms capable of diffusing practices across borders will also take considerable time.[2] Moreover, the implementation of new practices diffused across the multinational may also be a slow process since local management may have to negotiate their introduction with workforce representatives. The lengthy process through which MNCs engage in diffusion reflects the complexities in changing the orientation of a multinational, something Perlmutter (1969) referred to as 'the tortuous evolution of the MNC'. Maturity alone, however, is not enough to promote RD but, rather, is contingent upon other factors. An MNC which is globally structured and highly integrated is most likely to be engaging in RD where these conditions have existed for some time, so that it is the maturity of these conditions rather than the company itself which promotes RD. This was well illustrated by the case of Pack&Print in which the MNC had operated overseas for decades but the strategy of integrating activities was new and had not resulted in the diffusion of practices.

A fourth structural factor which promotes RD is growth through acquisition. This factor was evident in facilitating RD at ChemCo. The North American plants, which had produced practices in the areas of training and employee involvement that were diffused to the UK, had been established through acquisition, demonstrating how this maximizes the firm's exposure to practices characteristic of different national systems. Thus firms that expand in this way 'acquire' new practices as they do so and have scope to diffuse these to their domestic plants. Growth through acquisition, however, is sometimes associated with political tensions. The act of acquisition can create resentment among actors in the acquired firm, particularly if this is the result of a hostile take-over (Lindgren and Spangberg, 1981). Thus many MNCs are wary of introducing significant organizational change in the immediate aftermath of acquisition and, consequently, absorbing and integrating the acquired firm and its practices into the rest of the group are likely to be a lengthy process. While growth through acquisition promotes reverse diffusion, the data also showed how RD can flow from greenfield sites: the US plants of Engineering Products, which produced the practice of competence-based training for engineers, had been established through organic growth. Greenfield sites inevitably demonstrate some features of the national system in which they operate, with this tendency increasing over time (Wilkinson and Ackers, 1995). Therefore, there is also scope for RD from greenfield sites, especially mature ones, though the scope is greater from acquired sites.

The fifth factor which promotes RD is a high degree of global spread. As was mentioned above, MNCs are disproportionately located in and influenced by their home national business system. Clearly, in MNCs which are very highly concentrated in their country of origin, the scope for RD is low, whereas MNCs which are more highly globally spread have greater scope for observing a range of different practices and diffusing those they view favourably across their organization. The data illustrate this: global spread was high in both ChemCo and Engineering Products, with around 50 per cent of employees based overseas in both cases. Moreover, in the automotive components section of Engineering Products, the area in which RD was clearly evident, global spread is even higher, with more than 80 per cent of the workforce located abroad. A contrast with PowerCo is instructive since in this company only 20 per cent of employees work outside the home country, thereby constraining the scope for internal initiatives to be generated abroad. Moreover, the extent of global spread shapes the influence of different managerial groups. In MNCs which are highly concentrated in the country of origin key strategic activities tend to also remain at home, resulting in the home country plants performing key functions. On the other hand, in MNCs which are highly globally spread, the likelihood of functions such as R&D, training and even the HQ itself being located overseas is greater, a process referred to as 'internationalisation of the second degree' (Forsgren *et al.*, 1992). Sites which perform such functions are likely to hold an influential position within the company, giving them an important role in the process of diffusion. Accordingly, Ferner and Varul's (2000) evidence demonstrates how the more internationalized German MNCs have granted influential roles to some foreign subsidiaries. In particular, many of the UK and US plants in the UK and the USA have been accorded a key role in providing flexible corporate control mechanisms that the rest of the group can learn from. As a result, the Anglo-Saxon subsidiaries have taken on the role of 'vanguards', being used by the centre to lever change across the company.

This section has established five factors which promote reverse diffusion and in each case has shown how these shape the internal dynamics of diffusion. These are: (a) a global structure; (b) a high degree of production integration; (c) maturity; (d) growth through acquisition; and (e) a high degree of global spread. In the next section we turn to consider the relationship between MNCs and the environment in which they are embedded, examining how this shapes the substance of diffusion.

Reverse diffusion and the external environment

The external environment presents two key influences on the nature of practices that form the substance of RD. The first of these is that RD may be constrained by the lack of 'openness' of a national business system to a different management style and its associated practices (Whitley, 1992: 277). Constraints on the diffusion of new structures and practices in the home business systems arise in part out of the legal framework for employment. Elements of this framework close off totally or partially the scope for introducing new practices, one illustration of which are provisions for employee representation. MNCs in Germany, for instance, are to some extent constrained in the extent to which they can alter the nature of representative structures by the statutory provisions governing representation and bargaining. The strength of labour market institutions also constrains the introduction of new practices. The influence of Spanish trade unions over the operation of teamworking has demonstrated that they are able to minimize its impact on the pre-existing pattern of employment relations (Ortiz, 1998), implying that practices that are reverse diffused will be adapted to fit the home country business system. The culture of the home business system also constrains the ability of an MNC to implement new practices. Practices diffused from other business systems may be modified by management prior to being implemented so as to suit the expectations of actors at plant level, or they may be reinterpreted by these actors and consequently operate differently in their new setting (Ferner and Varul, 2000). Powerful MNCs may, of course, be able to avoid or minimize these legal, institutional and cultural constraints, but they do present genuine limitations on the scope MNCs possess to engage in RD.

The reverse diffusion of cellular assembly within Engineering Products illustrates the way that national systems of employment relations influence the operation and impact of a diffused practice. In the UK plants the introduction of the practice was negotiated with the union, and the union representatives successfully obtained guarantees concerning job security. Thus management achieved agreement to greater functional flexibility in return for a policy of no compulsory redundancies. The US plants, in contrast, were non-union and the introduction of cellular assembly was imposed rather than negotiated. Consequently, there was less emphasis on assurances of job security than in the UK plants and the workforce was reduced partly through enforced lay-offs.

The extent to which the home business system is 'open' is not just determined by these constraints, however, but also by the skills and expertise of the workforce. Some practices are dependent on workers possessing a high level of skills or on a supportive infrastructure for the provision of new skills. Some Japanese MNCs in Brazil, for instance, have been able to diffuse only partial versions of the Total Quality Control systems favoured by the HQ because of the limited skills of the local workforce (Humphrey, 1995), while some German MNCs have been unable to introduce German-style vocational training into their UK plants because of the low level of skills of employees when recruited and because of the absence of a multi-employer system of training (Dickmann, 1999, cited in Ferner and Varul, 2000). In this way, strong institutions can facilitate the introduction of new practices and, consequently, deregulated host countries such as the UK are not always more receptive or 'open' to new practices than more strongly regulated ones.

The external environment not only presents some constraints to reverse diffusion but also creates pressures to engage in the diffusion of practices from other national business systems. The way in which MNCs attempt to take advantage of the elements of the different business systems in which they operate, both the home country and various host countries, is strongly shaped by the relative strength of particular countries within the international economy. Strong economic performance in one country creates pressure for the diffusion to other countries of elements of the model of economic organization concerned. Smith and Meiksins (1995: 255–6), for example, argue that the hierarchy of economies within the international capitalist system gives rise to 'dominance effects': at any one time, they argue, countries 'in dominant positions have frequently evolved methods of organising production or the division of labour which have invited emulation and interest'. For reverse diffusion, MNCs with foreign subsidiaries in a strongly performing country are able to exploit the advantage of having experience of particular practices in order to diffuse them to their domestic operations. Moreover, the forces of competition between multinationals with such opportunities may exert pressure on firms to do so.

There is a parallel in the discussion of dominance effects with the argument of DiMaggio and Powell (1983) concerning isomorphism: isomorphic pulls, they argue, act as forces for organizations to become more similar to one another. In a context of a competitive market, on the one hand, and ambiguity and uncertainty, on the other, 'mimetic processes' lead organizations to model themselves on other organizations, particularly those which are perceived to be successful. They do so partly because of the benefits in terms of enhanced efficiency, but they also have a ritual aspect: 'innovations' are adopted in order to enhance an organization's 'legitimacy'. Thus in relation to the reverse diffusion of practices in MNCs, management may be able to enhance, first, the efficiency of the firm by adopting in the domestic operations practices developed in other business systems and, second, its legitimacy in the eyes of key groups external to the multinational, particularly its customers.

The effects of the need for enhanced efficiency and legitimacy were in evidence in the reverse diffusion of practices in Engineering Products. Those managers interviewed were convinced that the practices that were diffused from foreign subsidiaries to the domestic plants had increased efficiency. The introduction of U-shaped cells, for instance, had freed up space on the shop-floor, had increased through-put times and had led to a reduction in the numbers of employees required to produce a given level of output. This practice and the break-up of a factory into a series of small production units each serving an internal customer, are of course not initiatives particular to Engineering Products. Rather, they are common developments in manufacturing world-wide and, to some extent, we can see them as reflecting the influence of the dominance in recent years of 'lean production' with which these initiatives are consistent. It is also clear that the motivation for managers in Engineering Products to implement these practices was to do with creating a positive impression with their customers. One of the firm's principal customers was a Japanese automotive manufacturer which was anxious to ensure that its suppliers were adopting what it perceived to be 'best practice'. Thus the diffusion of practices associated with lean production can be seen as an attempt to derive legitimacy with the firm's customers.

Conclusion

This chapter has investigated the phenomenon of reverse diffusion. It has been argued that diffusion within MNCs occurs through the interaction of structural factors and political processes. This perspective has been used to examine the particular case of reverse diffusion, demonstrating the way in which structural factors which promote RD also shape the processes through which it takes place. Moreover, it has been argued that the way in which reverse diffusion occurs is shaped by the external environment in which MNCs are embedded.[3]

What are the implications of the process of globalization for this analysis? Primarily, we might expect RD to become more prevalent as the process of globalization proceeds because this process has been accompanied by a growth in the structural factors which promote RD. The increasingly homogenized nature of product markets across countries has led many MNCs to structure themselves around international business divisions and to seek greater integration of their international operations. Moreover, a key part of globalization has been the way in which MNCs have increased the extent to which they are globally spread. The process of globalization is also likely to alter the relative influence of different groups of organizational actors in a way that affects the process of RD. The greater standardization of product markets makes the HQ less dependent on local plants, increasing the extent to which the HQ can exert a strong influence over employment practice across the firm. Globalization has also altered the power of domestic plants in relation to foreign plants: the influence of the former declines as MNCs gradually become more widely geographically distributed and accord key strategic roles to plants outside the home country. The process of globalization and the phenomenon of reverse diffusion are, therefore, strongly linked.

Notes

1   Accordingly, Marginson *et al.* (1995) have shown that a global structure is strongly associated with the existence of a world-wide personnel policy committee, with regular international meetings of personnel managers and with senior managers moving between sites on international assignments.
2   Analysis of survey data supports this: world-wide personnel policy committees and regular international meetings of personnel managers are rare in MNCs which have operated internationally for a short time (Edwards, P. *et al.*, 1996).
3   This chapter has tried to build on earlier work of the author into reverse diffusion (Edwards, 1998b; Edwards, 2000).

References

Bartlett, C. and Ghoshal, S. (1998) *Managing Across Borders: The Transnational Solution*, London: Random House.

Broad, G. (1994) 'The Managerial Limits to Japanisation: A Manufacturing Case Study', *Human Resource Management Journal* 4(3): 52–69.

Child, J. (1972) 'Organisational Structure, Environment and Performance: The Role of Strategic Choice', *Sociology* 6(1): 1–22.

Dicken, P. (1998) *Global Shift: Transforming the World Economy*, London: Paul Chapman.

Dickmann, M. (1999) 'Balancing Global, Parent and Local Influences: International Human Resource Management of German Multinational Companies', unpublished PhD thesis, London: Birkbeck College.

DiMaggio, P. and Powell, W. (1983) 'The Iron Cage Revisited: Institutional Isomorphism and Collective Rationality in Organizational Fields', *American Sociological Review* 147–160.

Edwards, P., Armstrong, P., Marginson, P. and Purcell, J. (1996) 'Towards the Transnational Company? The Global Structure and Organisation of Multinational Firms', in D. Gallie and K. Purcell (eds) *Corporate Restructuring and Labour Markets*, London: Routledge.

Edwards, P., Ferner, A. and Sisson, K. (1993) 'People and the Process of Management in the Multinational Company: A Review and Some Illustrations', *Warwick Papers in Industrial Relations*, no. 43, Coventry: IRRU.

Edwards, T. (1998a) 'Multinational Companies and the Diffusion of Employment Practices: A Survey of the Literature', *Warwick Papers in Industrial Relations*, no. 61, Coventry: IRRU.

Edwards, T. (1998b) 'Multinationals, Employment Practices and the Process of Diffusion', *International Journal of Human Resource Management* 9(4): 696–709.

Edwards, T., Rees, C. and Coller, X. (1999) 'Structure, Politics and the Diffusion of Employment Practices in Multinationals', *European Journal of Industrial Relations* 5(3): 286–306.

Edwards, T. (2000) 'Multinationals, International Integration and Employment Practice in Domestic Plants', *Industrial Relations Journal* 31(2): 115–29.

Ferner, A. (1997) 'Country of Origin Effects and HRM in Multinational Companies', *Human Resource Management Journal* 7(1): 19–37.

Ferner, A. and Varul, M. (2000) '"Vanguard" Subsidiaries and the Diffusion of New Practices: A Case Study of German Multinationals', *British Journal of Industrial Relations* 38(1): 115–40.

Forsgren, M., Holm, U. and Johansen, J. (1992) 'Internationalisation of the Second Degree: The Emergence of European-Based Centres in Swedish Firms', in S. Young and J. Hamill (eds) *Europe and the Multinationals: Issues and Responses for the 1990s*, Aldershot: Edward Elgar.

Gupta, A. and Govindarajan, V. (1991) 'Knowledge Flows and the Structure of Control within Multinational Corporations', *Academy of Management Review*, 16(4): 768–92.

Hamill, J. (1984) 'Labour Relations Decision Making within Multinational Corporations', *Industrial Relations Journal* 15(1): 30–4.

Hirst, P. and Thompson, G. (1996) *Globalization in Question*, Cambridge: Polity.

Hu, Y. (1992) 'Global or Stateless Corporations are National Firms with International Operations', *California Management Review* 34(2): 107–26.

Humphrey, J. (1995) 'The Adoption of Japanese Management Techniques in Brazilian Industry', *Journal of Management Studies* 32(6): 767–88.

Lindgren, U. and Spangberg, K. (1981) 'Management of the Post-Acquisition Process in Diversified MNCs', in L. Otterbeck (ed.) *The Management of Headquarters-Subsidiary Relationships in Multinational Corporations*, Aldershot: Gower.

Marginson, P. (1992) 'European Integration and Transnational Management-Union Relations in the Enterprise', *British Journal of Industrial Relations* 30(4): 529–46.

Marginson, P., Armstrong, P., Edwards, P. and Purcell, J. (1995) 'Managing Labour in the Global Corporation: A Survey-based Analysis of Multinationals Operating in the UK', *International Journal of Human Resource Management* 6(3): 702–19.

Mueller, F. and Purcell, J. (1992) 'The Europeanisation of Manufacturing and the Decentralisation of Bargaining: Multinational Management Strategies in the European Automobile Industry', *International Journal of Human Resource Management* 3(1): 15–34.

Ohmae, K. (1990) *The Borderless World*, London: HarperCollins.

Ortiz, L. (1998) 'Union Response to Teamwork: The Case of Opel Spain', *Industrial Relations Journal* 29(1): 42–57.

Perlmutter, H. (1969) 'The Tortuous Evolution of the Multinational Firm', *Columbia Journal of World Business*, Jan.–Feb., 9–18.

Porter, M. (1986) *Competition in Global Industries*, Boston: Harvard Business School Press.

Reich, R. (1990) 'Who Is Us?', *Harvard Business Review*, Jan.–Feb., 53–64.

Ruigrok, W. and van Tulder, R. (1995) *The Logic of International Restructuring*, London: Routledge.

Smith, C. and Meiksins, P. (1995) 'System, Society and Dominance Effects in Cross-National Organizational Analysis', *Work, Employment and Society* 9(2): 241–67.

Whitley, R. (1992) *European Business Systems: Firms and Markets in their National Contexts*, London: Sage.

Whittington, R. (1993) *What is Strategy – and Does it Matter?* London: Routledge.

Wilkinson, A. and Ackers, P. (1995) 'When Two Cultures Meet: Industrial Relations at Japanco', *International Journal of Human Resource Management* 6(4): 849–71.

11 Globalization and Diversity Management

Empirical evidence from Australia

Santina Bertone and Mary Leahy

Introduction

One of the managerial challenges of trading in a globalized marketplace is the need to service an increasingly sophisticated, differentiated and competitive market. We are told that customers have become more educated, affluent and discerning in their choices. This has led, in turn, to demands that companies tailor their products and services more closely to customer needs and tastes (Karpin, 1995: 17). Since globalization has opened up competition across all sectors of an economy, no enterprise, whether large or small, appears to be exempt from such pressures (ibid.: 16). This is true whether companies trade domestically or internationally.

Customization and niche marketing rely heavily on an intimate understanding of customer needs and the marshalling of a range of 'soft' people skills such as cultural knowledge, empathy and interpersonal communication. Managers are increasingly exhorted to identify and nurture such skills among employees, and develop their own people management skills (ibid.: 25). Cross-cultural communication and diversity management skills are an important part of this skill set. They are particularly relevant in the context of mass movements of peoples across the globe and the emergence of diverse labour markets. Diversity within the domestic and international contexts would seem to demand the effective harnessing of diverse human resources.

But does this really occur? Has globalization led to a greater valuing of workers of diverse backgrounds and attributes, as some had hoped (Cope and Kalantzis, 1997)? Are companies trying to reflect the diversity of the marketplace in their organizations? Have the traditional elites who run organizations been prepared to make way for people of diverse gender, race, culture and background? Or is 'cultural cloning' more prevalent as authority in organizations is devolved and more responsibility is placed on individual employees (ibid.: 107)?

This chapter reports on two research projects conducted in Australia, which has been exposed to rapid globalization of its economy over the past seventeen years and has a high level of cultural diversity within its population. The research follows a decade of federal government policy in the area of diversity management, in the context of wide-ranging microeconomic reforms implemented by both the Labor government of the early 1980s to mid-1990s, and the Liberal-National Coalition government elected in 1996.

The first research project sought to measure the take-up rate of diversity management policies across a large slice of business and industry, and gauge the attitudes of senior managers to the notion of harnessing the productive capacity of people from non-English-speaking backgrounds (NESBs). The second project was based on detailed case studies in two multinational corporations – a major Australian-owned financial services group and a US-based energy company – deemed to have advanced diversity management policies in place. The latter study sought to investigate the factors that promote and inhibit the implementation of effective diversity management and to measure the business benefits flowing from this. In the process, the studies delved into equity and social justice issues that are often marginalized in the public discussion of diversity management in Australia, particularly in relation to the employment of an ethnically diverse workforce.

The studies provide a useful insight into the motives and priorities of Australian business leaders in this area, the shortcomings of government policy and the powerful influence of social factors in shaping employment outcomes at the workplace. While the business benefits of valuing and using a diverse workforce are supported by the research findings, it is clear that only a minority of business leaders are aware of them and prepared to make diversity a priority management issue. Moreover, the economic pressures created by rapid globalization have undermined the value of equity and social justice arguments which might have been used, highlighting the primacy of 'bottom-line' considerations.

Unless the bottom-line benefits to management can be demonstrated unequivocally, most managers are not interested in the issue of diversity. Yet, paradoxically, as the case studies show, even where economic objectives are achieved, the effective implementation of diversity policy may be hampered and potentially sabotaged by ongoing issues of equity and justice in the workplace. The case study research suggests that not all players in the globalized workplace are motivated by economic factors. It also confirms the Marxist doctrine that the economic interests of employers and individuals can and inevitably, do, clash. But in a world economy where the commitment and creativity of individual employees may be the key to business success, some accommodation of interests may well be necessary. This points to the need for corporations to address both the diverse social and economic factors in employment, including issues of equity and social justice.

The following sections provide a brief overview of the Australian economy and labour market, followed by a discussion of the characteristics of diversity management policy in Australia, particularly with respect to race and ethnicity. The impetus behind the two research projects and methodological issues are discussed. The findings of the research projects, including debates concerning the definitions of diversity and diversity management are then presented and analysed. The chapter concludes with a discussion of the implications of our research for the understanding of human resource management within a globalized economy, and possible directions for future public policy.

The Australian economy and society

Australia is one of the richest countries in the Asia-Pacific region, but in common with other OECD countries has experienced low economic growth rates since the early 1970s (Karpin, 1995: 54). Its prosperity has traditionally been funded by primary exports such as minerals and agricultural products, mainly exported to Europe and North America. However this has changed, as export markets have shifted and competition has intensified.

Until the early 1980s, the Australian manufacturing industry was protected by high tariffs and primarily focused on the domestic market (ibid.: 56). With a population of close to 20 million, the market for local manufactures is relatively small and increasingly difficult to sustain in the face of competition from imports, particularly from Asia.

By the early 1980s a sense of crisis had gripped Australian policy-makers, as the country endured the puzzling but common dilemma of double digit inflation and unemployment figures. The incoming Labor government in 1983 resolved, in partnership with the Australian trade union movement through the Prices and Incomes Accord, to simultaneously tackle both problems and promote economic growth through consensus-based interventionist measures and restrained incomes growth (Wilson *et al.*, 2000: 13).

Soon after gaining office, however, the Labor government floated the Australian dollar and deregulated the banking and finance industry, thus exposing the economy quite abruptly to global market forces. A programme of general deregulation and tariff reduction followed, associated with increasing calls for labour market flexibility and greater attention to productivity issues in wage setting (ibid.). The centralized wage fixing system, which had been underpinned historically by tariff protection, gave way to more decentralized and fragmented forms of bargaining (Bertone, 1996: 75). Unemployment declined slowly over the late 1980s (down to about 6 per cent), only to increase dramatically again (to 10 per cent) in the recession of 1991–92. More recently, unemployment has declined again to 6.3 per cent (ABS, 2000).

By the mid-1990s Australia was on the way to becoming one of the most open economies in the world, with tariff and other barriers to incoming trade and investment being virtually negligible (Karpin, 1995: 55). At the same time, an increasing proportion of Australian merchandise exports were going to Asia and significantly more direct investment by Australian companies was occurring in that region (ibid.: 56). A rise in both service exports and elaborately transformed manufactures took place, although a large current account deficit (about 5 per cent of GDP) continues to be a problem (Genoff and Green, 1998).

Demographically, Australia is the product of one of the largest immigration programmes in the world. Immigration has been a continuing feature of Australian modern history since the arrival of the first British fleet in 1788, and the great majority of Australians are either immigrants or the descendants of immigrants (Castles *et al.*, 1998: 1). But it has only been since the post-World War II period that significant numbers of non-English-speaking background (NESB) people have been encouraged to immigrate.

Today, the Australian population comprises 2 per cent Aboriginal and Torres Strait Islander people, 23 per cent who were either born in a non-English-speaking country or have at least one parent from such a country and 75 per cent from Anglo-Celtic backgrounds (including first-generation English-speaking background immigrants) (Race Discrimination Commissioner, 1998: 9; ABS, 1996). Similarly, about 14 per cent of the Australian labour force are people who were born in a non-English-speaking country, and altogether 15 per cent of Australians speak a language other than English at home (ABS, 1996). About 21 per cent of Australia's 800,000 small businesses are owned or operated by people of NESBs and international visitors whose first language is not English exceed 3 million per year (Race Discrimination Commissioner, 1998: 9).

The lived reality of these figures has posed a major challenge to Australia's historical self-image as a largely British-based society. It has also impacted on the labour utilization and human resource management strategies of a number of industries where NESB immigrants have congregated. Several researchers have shown that mass non-British immigration was largely fuelled by the need to build population, boost consumption, and importantly, staff the factories and undertake a range of less desirable blue-collar jobs shunned by Anglo-Celtic Australians (Collins, 1992). The result was that some sectors of industry, such as manufacturing, construction and infrastructure, designed their employment and business strategies around large-scale employment of immigrants.

Others have argued that Australia's official policy of multiculturalism, which recognizes and promotes a plurality of cultural, religious and ethnic identities under the umbrella of an overarching Australian citizenship, masks the reality of Anglo-Celtic domination of our social and economic life, with other groups relegated to the periphery (Collins, 1992; Stratton, 1998). According to most social and economic indicators, people of English-speaking backgrounds, including immigrants from English-speaking countries, are both advantaged and more powerful than other groups (see, for example, Foster *et al.*, 1991). They enjoy higher average incomes and lifestyles and are less likely to suffer unemployment than NESB people, who are over-represented among the unemployed relative to their share of the labour force (O'Loughlin and Watson, 1997; ABS, 2000).

Most Australian institutions, such as the parliaments, trade unions, corporations, the judiciary, arts and cultural bodies and the public services continue to be dominated by Anglo-Celtic people (Bertone and Griffin, 1992; Bertone *et al.*, 1998). Also the vast majority of Australian national icons, popular culture and media are dominated by Anglo-Celtic symbols, performers and works (Bertone *et al.*, 2000; Jakubowisz, 2000).

It is in this context that we examine the diversity management policies of Australian business and the adequacy or effectiveness of government policy in this area.

Productive diversity in Australia

'Productive diversity' or 'managing diversity' are concepts which have been variously defined. However framed, they usually call for the development of conscious strategies to deal with human differences in society, whether these lie in organizations, markets or other institutions. Such differences may be innate (such as age or gender), structural (such as social class) or acquired (such as lifestyle or dress). 'Productive diversity' is an Australian government policy that has focused more particularly on race and ethnicity and the way these issues are addressed within employment. It advocates the more productive use of diversity in this sense, such as the systemic use of second languages in the workplace and tapping of cultural knowledge and networks to assist business interactions within a globalized marketplace.

However, the term is evolving and broadening, as more research is undertaken into diversity strategies. In 1998, when managers from a range of industries were asked what they thought of productive diversity, many were unfamiliar with the term while some spoke of 'managing diversity' or 'valuing diversity', terms derived from North American literature and experience (Bertone *et al.*, 1998: 67). But all agreed on two fundamental points: if diversity management were to be adopted by senior management, there must be a strong case that it would improve the 'bottom line' (or profitability) in organizations, and there was a need to develop case study material to help managers implement it in an informed and coherent manner. Most managers also supported a broad definition of diversity which encompassed all manner of human differences, including race and ethnicity (ibid.: 2).

A review of the literature in 1998 showed that most work on this subject had been published in the USA and to a lesser extent, Australia, with the terms 'managing diversity' and 'productive diversity' often used interchangeably in this country. As suggested, no single definition of either concept exists. The discussion of such terms ranges from narrow, business-oriented visions to considerably broader, more idealistic conceptions of the role that productive/managing diversity can play in the economy and society.

In Australia, it is necessary to distinguish between productive diversity as defined by academics, community activists and consultants, on the one hand, and government agencies and policy-makers, on the other. While the scope of the concept varies amongst the first group, it is almost always narrowly conceived by the latter. So, in the literature we find roughly five definitions:

1   The traditional equal opportunity definition, which deals with differences in gender, racioethnicity and age (Overell, 1996). Equal opportunity is generally concerned with eradicating discrimination and raising the profile and outcomes of disadvantaged groups, such as women and the disabled.

2   Broader definitions which recognize a range of human differences, such as physical ability, personal attributes and habits and sexual orientation, not all of which are associated with disadvantage (cf. Woods and Sciarini, 1995; Wallace *et al.*, 1996).

3   Definitions based on the broadest possible concept of diversity, incorporating hierarchical levels, functions and backgrounds (Cox, 1993). This definition does not particularly highlight issues of disadvantage.

4   The notion that a culture of valuing diversity has the capacity to create a pluralistic social order, resulting in organizational cohesion and international harmony (Cope and Kalantzis, 1997).

5   Business-oriented definitions, which view managing diversity as driven by business needs (Dawkins *et al.*, 1995; Hay, 1996; Overell, 1996).

(extracted from Bertone *et al.*, 1998: 22–3)

Productive diversity policy as adopted by the Australian government in the late 1980s is most closely aligned with the business-oriented definition in 5 and even more narrowly focused on one specific kind of diversity, namely the diversity associated with the presence of large numbers of NESB people, many of whom have maintained their own subcultures, identities, social networks and languages. The term has recently evolved towards a broader definition of diversity, but given its home in the federal immigration bureaucracy (multicultural affairs branch), the emphasis continues to be on ethnicity and linguistic differences, with productive diversity viewed primarily as a tool for improving business outcomes in a globalized economy.

It should be noted that diversity management is a term that is also increasingly being used to refer to equal employment opportunity programmes for women, people with disabilities, homosexual and transgender individuals, but in this case the history of the term is very different. Legislation to prevent and outlaw gender discrimination has been present in some or all jurisdictions within Australia since 1962, with the most recent federal legislation, Equal Employment Opportunity for Women, enacted last year. Programmes to promote equal employment opportunity for women have been mandated by legislation for larger employers (having 100+ employees) for over a decade and overseen by different government agencies (Equal Employment Opportunity for Women Agency, Office of the Status of Women, Work and Family Unit) from the one responsible for multicultural policy and productive diversity. The use of 'diversity' in terms referring to programmes for women, etc. therefore carries a very different historical legacy from those relating to NESB people.

The history and genesis of the term 'productive diversity' partly explain this emphasis. As shown in the previous section, Australia in the 1980s was a country gripped by economic angst over low growth and declining markets for our traditional, primary exports. Globalization had become a harsh reality in the early 1980s and affected all facets of industry, including the emerging services sector. With large numbers of business and skilled migrants arriving in Australia, many of them Asian, productive diversity was conceived as a policy to harness these diverse skills in the project of opening new markets for Australian companies in Asia. It was not primarily aimed at eliminating discrimination or promoting equity in employment (issues addressed in earlier equal opportunity and racial discrimination legislation at state and federal level) but at improving business performance.

As the 1998 report of our research explained, the key to productive diversity is twofold:

1   The emphasis on economic outcomes resulting from the successful manage-
     ment of a multicultural workforce
2   The removal of barriers and the development of strategies to ensure that all
     employees can contribute the full range of their skills and knowledge, whether
     formal or informal.

(Bertone *et al.*, 1998: 6–9)

We found three broad applications of this concept in Australia:

1 *Making use of ethnic differences within a workforce to understand, reflect and respond to the different needs of a multicultural domestic market.* This is the idea that a workforce should reflect, to a significant degree, the diversity of the client base, enabling businesses to develop products/services which cater to the different needs of the local market. As we have previously observed, a high degree of international competition or exposure within this market renders this a globalized market. Examples include: the use of multicultural marketing strategies aimed at promoting products/services to a linguistic niche market, e.g. Chinese Australians; or the development of ethno-specific government services, utilizing interpreters and the linguistic or cultural knowledge of employees to communicate with a diverse range of users.

2 *Making use of language, knowledge and cultural skills within a workforce to develop and expand export markets.* This is the most well-known application of productive diversity as promulgated in Australia, and involves tapping the wide range of formal and informal skills held by ethnic communities here, such as overseas business networks, languages, cultural knowledge and knowledge of overseas business norms that can assist Australian businesses to develop, maintain and expand export markets.

Examples include: sending a multicultural export team to Vietnam which includes Vietnamese Australians who are fluent in the Vietnamese language and can understand and interpret the requirements of the overseas buyers. Or establishing export development teams in Australia comprising employees from the ethnic backgrounds of prospective buyers to discuss, conceptualize and develop products/services that meet the needs and tastes of overseas clients. Concrete applications of this approach span the whole range of product and service development, from making saucepans with two handles for the Asian market, to the development of culturally appropriate airline menus, to more effective marketing of Australia as a tourist destination to overseas clients, such as Germans and Americans (Cope and Kalantzis, 1997; Bertone *et al.*, 1998).

3 *Breaking down ethnic barriers and prejudices within the workforce to enable more harmonious work relations, increased productivity, flexibility and innovation.* This is probably the least well understood application of productive diversity, where the grey line between social justice initiatives, such as equal opportunity and anti-discrimination legislation, and the business goals of productive diversity, cloud the recognition of ways that effective diversity management can promote both equity and efficiency in the workplace. The debate about this version of productive diversity becomes enmeshed in claims that equal opportunity is a luxury that Australian businesses cannot afford, given the intense global competition faced in most product markets.

In reality, it would seem that Australian businesses can ill afford to overlook the reservoir of talent held by marginalized groups who, together with other groups, may hold the key to improved product innovation, quality and employee commitment. However, some research suggests that the reservoir can only be tapped if businesses become more open, democratic and responsive to different points of view, rather than imposing a unitarist corporate ideology which fails to resonate with the values of most of their employees (Cope and Kalantzis, 1997). At the same time, Australian businesses are bound to comply with federal and state anti-discrimination laws which prohibit direct and indirect discrimination on a range of grounds, including race and ethnicity (Race Discrimination Commissioner, 1998).

Examples of this application of productive diversity include: developing a strong equal employment opportunity (EEO) policy in the workplace, which ensures genuine opportunity for the recruitment, retention and development of people from all races and ethnic groups; the provision of cross-cultural training programmes to increase awareness and understanding of other cultures, both within the workforce and the product market; the recognition of overseas gained skills and qualifications, through the collection of data on the full range of employees' skills, and efforts to develop employees' access to suitable career paths; or the development of cross-cultural work teams, tapping the different perspectives and problem-solving skills of people from around the world, through open communication channels and input by employees into workplace decision-making (Bertone *et al.*, 1998: 8–9).

The research projects – Diversity and Dollars and Business Benefits of Productive Diversity

The empirical data for this chapter came from two funded research projects conducted through the Workplace Studies Centre, Victoria University, in Melbourne, Australia. The first project, later published as *Diversity and Dollars: Productive Diversity in Australian Business and Industry*, was awarded to the Centre in late 1997, with data collection occurring in the first half of 1998. The major funding body was the Department of Immigration and Multicultural Affairs (DIMA), the federal agency responsible for immigration and multicultural policy and the provision of settlement programmes for new immigrants to Australia. In recent years, DIMA has also funded research into issues related to immigration and multiculturalism. DIMA's research grant was provided through a host organization, the Committee for Economic Development Australia (CEDA), a national, independent research and education body which includes membership from large and medium-sized businesses, educational institutions and government agencies. CEDA administered the research grant and provided significant in-kind support to the project, such as access to its membership list, office facilities, a project reference group and editorial/publication support leading to an approved CEDA publication, Information Paper No. 58, which was widely publicized and distributed throughout the business and academic communities.

The project terms of reference had been discussed and agreed by the chief researcher (lead author of this chapter) and the auspicing bodies prior to project commencement. These centred largely on the two project aims, which were: (a) to determine the extent to which Australian businesses in six target industries had applied productive diversity principles, as promulgated by the federal government: (b) to understand the effects which productive diversity was reported to have had on business policy and operations, particularly in the human resource management area.

The terms of reference stipulated the collection of both quantitative (survey based) and qualitative (interviews, focus groups) data and set clear timeframes for completion of the study. Beyond these rather brief (one page) terms of reference, the academics conducting the research were free to exercise full professional judgement with respect to sample development, questionnaire design, focus group selection, literature search, data analysis, interpretation and writing up. It was agreed at the beginning of the study that the Workplace Studies Centre would provide impartial, independent research and the involvement of CEDA as a mediating body underscored this arrangement, particularly given CEDA's independent charter and the fact that its chief executive was formerly a senior university academic and keen to ensure the integrity of the research. The steering group, comprising high level representatives of major business organizations and senior DIMA bureaucrats, met several times during the course of the study to offer guidance and assistance to the study, but in no sense directed or shaped its conclusions. The chief investigator of the project was Santina Bertone, assisted by research associates Alexis Esposto and Rod Turner.

The second project evolved out of the first. The Diversity and Dollars research had shown there was a dearth of detailed information about the processes of diversity management within Australian organizations. Managers who participated in each of the focus groups were unanimous in expressing their concern about the complexity of the concept and the need for detailed, practical guidance on how to implement it in their organizations. They also emphasized that if it was to be done, senior managers would need to be convinced it would bring major business benefits to the organization. Those managers who had read widely on the subject bemoaned the lack of Australian cases and texts. Most literature in this area originates in North America, where the social, legal and economic framework for diversity management is very different from Australia. While federal and state governments in Australia had published a range of promotional brochures on productive diversity, research participants were either not aware of them or felt they were not sufficiently concrete and specific for their needs.

The recommendations in the Diversity and Dollars report to DIMA and CEDA reflected these concerns. Among thirteen recommendations to government and business, we recommended the funding of case studies within organizations and collaboration with higher education institutions to ensure this literature was incorporated into management education courses. The department subsequently accepted these recommendations, establishing the Productive Diversity Partnerships Program and funding eight university studies to provide detailed intelligence on productive diversity for inclusion into university curricula. A research contract was awarded to Santina Bertone through the Workplace Studies Centre, to conduct case studies in organizations which had an advanced diversity management policy. Mary Leahy provided research support to the study. Reflecting DIMA's particular interest in exploring the business case, the project was titled Business Benefits of Productive Diversity. Other organizations joined in a partnership arrangement to help fund these case studies: Victoria University, the Australian Multicultural Foundation, Mobil Oil Australia and a major financial services group (FSG).

The aims of this second project were twofold: (a) to establish clearly the factors which both promote and inhibit effective diversity management in an organization, with particular reference to the management of ethnic differences, and paying attention to processes, attitudes, values and perceptions at the organizational level; and (b) to measure more specifically, where relevant, the business benefits of productive diversity. In so doing, the researchers took the view that both the positives and negatives should be thoroughly explored. Our aim was not to 'prove' the utility of productive diversity (although evidence collected to date did point in this direction), but rather to explore, dissect and investigate it in greater detail than had previously been the case. As such, we aimed to go beyond the glossy promotional literature on this area, as Prasad *et al.* (1997) and others have critiqued, and go to the heart of the experience of diversity in organizations. To do this, we needed to spend time speaking to different groups and stakeholders within the workplace, and investigate both official and unofficial policies through documents, participant observation, and so on.

The funding arrangements for this study were different from the first. While DIMA continued to be the lead agency, the other organizations also provided significant cash or in-kind contributions. In the case of Mobil and the FSG, this included access to their organizations to conduct the case studies. A simple exchange of letters underpinned the funding from the Australian Multicultural Foundation (AMF) and Victoria University, which were both interested in supporting curriculum development in this area. The AMF is an independent community-based organization originally set up by the Australian Bicentennial Authority to promote commitment to Australia as a multicultural society and spread awareness of cultural diversity within Australia as well as tolerance and understanding between all cultural groups. The Foundation is currently funded by a trust account administered by a tripartite community board and initiates projects and activities within the multicultural field. Victoria University is the researchers' employing institution. Its main interest in funding this research was to promote industry–research collaborations, increase the university's research effort and obtain research findings that could be incorporated into its management course offerings and strategic policy development.

In the case of the other three organizations – DIMA, Mobil Oil Australia and the FSG (which prefers, for commercial reasons, to remain unnamed) – formal contractual arrangements were entered into separately between Victoria University as the research institution and the three funding bodies. These contracts were analogous in content. They stipulated the aims and hypotheses of the research, the broad methodology proposed by the Workplace Studies Centre in its original submission to DIMA, the agreed timelines and 'deliverables', in the form of a contract report and presentation of a conference paper at DIMA's 21st Century Business: Delivering the Diversity Dividend conference, to be held in Melbourne in November 2000. Importantly, they gave intellectual ownership of all research and curriculum material arising from the project to Victoria University, and confirmed the project as an independent academic exercise. In the case of the two business organizations, the contracts also stipulated that wherever possible, if anonymity in the case studies was desired, the researchers would take all necessary steps to write the findings in a manner that would avoid identification of the case study organization. This proved important for the FSG, which is a global player in the international financial market place and for which the issue of diversity management offers major competitive opportunities and challenges. They were particularly keen to ensure that their identity was safeguarded. Mobil, on the other hand, had a fairly relaxed attitude towards public disclosure of their case study findings.

The two case study organizations were selected in late 1999 and studied in the first half of 2000. Mobil Oil Australia is a multinational American-owned petrochemical company which had recently merged with Exxon; the FSG is a major financial services group operating globally and in Australia. At time of writing the case studies had been completed and preliminary results presented at the DIMA conference and another, academic conference. It is hoped to attract further funding to undertake case studies in other organizations and industries in 2001 and beyond.

Outline of methodologies and issues/limitations

As previously outlined, the Diversity and Dollars research was particularly interested in gauging the extent and incidence of the take-up of productive diversity policies across Australian businesses. This was important for two major reasons: considerable efforts had been made by the Office of Multicultural Affairs and later, the Multicultural Affairs branch of DIMA, to promote this concept as a key strategy to capitalize on Australia's ethnic diversity and tap overseas export markets. It was also seen as an important microeconomic reform policy for promoting greater business efficiency and competitiveness in a global market place. This may partly have influenced the choice of industries which the study focused on.

Essentially, the research involved three major data collection methods:

1   A comprehensive literature review.
2   The conduct of five focus group discussions with a total of thirty-four middle and senior managers between March and June 1998. These were drawn from six industries: passenger motor vehicles (PMV) and automotive parts; energy – coal, oil and gas; communications and information technology (IT); tourism, recreation and leisure; health care and biotechnology; and property and financial services. All these are major industries in Australia which face significant international competition; in at least half of these, government strategies to 'open up' the economy to international forces for example, via privatization and tariff reduction have been a key factor.

3   The third prong of the study was the conduct of a national mail survey of human resource managers and chief executives across a structured stratified sample of 2,000 businesses within these industries. The survey was undertaken throughout May and June 1998.

The focus groups provided the richest and most illuminating insights into managers' perceptions and views on this topic. Most participants were human resource managers, a few were chief executives and others were managers of multicultural marketing. Each group discussion followed a standard set of questions put by the study leader, with sessions lasting between 75 and 90 minutes. Group numbers varied between five and ten, and three groups were made up of participants from a single industry. Four in-depth face-to-face interviews were later held with participants whose organizations seemed well advanced in adopting diversity management principles, and the results of these presented in the report as cameo 'case studies'. The focus group discussions dealt with the following topics:

- initial reaction to the concept of productive diversity;
- personal thoughts on the concept;
- perceived managerial reactions to the concept within their organizations;
- benefits and disadvantages of a multicultural workforce;
- extent to which the employing organizations valued and utilized the skills of a multicultural workforce;
- experiences of productive diversity and benefits observed;
- factors that prevented an organization from utilizing productive diversity;
- arguments and strategies for implementing productive diversity measures in the workplace.

All participants were assured that their individual contributions to the discussions would not be attributed in the report, and the identity of their businesses would be kept confidential. All focus group discussions were tape recorded and transcribed, and later summarized for inclusion in the published report. Key findings in relation to all focus group questions were summarized and coded, noting the source and level of support for such responses. A more holistic analysis of these findings was then made for individual focus groups by considering the comments as a whole, noting the tone and thematic direction of the discussions as well as the content.

There are a number of advantages in using focus groups for research purposes. They enable a large amount of detailed and descriptive data to be collected from people in a relatively short time, saving costs and time. They are interactive, which arguably promotes a greater engagement with the issues by participants than more individual data collection instruments such as, for example, interviews and survey questionnaires. This can often lead to more sophisticated analysis and discussion by participants than might otherwise be the case. Focus groups also offer immediate availability and analysis of the data for researchers. For participants, they can offer a learning experience which is more satisfying than filling out a survey form or participating in a one-to-one interview.

However, there are disadvantages. The lead times for organizing focus groups, particularly for those involving high profile, busy people (as this study did) can be considerable. Each of our focus groups took anywhere between four and six weeks to organize. The difficulties of gaining participation by senior managers, who are daily faced with conflicting demands on their times, are high. The social nature of focus groups may militate against the expression of individual opinions. Although the facilitator emphasized there was no requirement to reach consensus, encouraging all participants to have a say, some individuals dominated the discussions. The danger of individuals having their views influenced by others is an issue. There may also be a reluctance to divulge sensitive or potentially damaging organizational information in front of others from the same industry or across industries. Given the focus of our research on one policy issue – productive diversity – it is likely that managers self-selected themselves for participation because of a prior interest in or knowledge of the issue. Others with no knowledge or sympathy for this policy may have absented themselves.

However, this self-selection effect is also present with other research techniques. Despite the limitations, the researchers believe the focus group method was appropriate for this study, given the topic of the research and the complexity of the issues. It proved especially useful given the variability in the level of knowledge that participants brought to the sessions (although all participants were supplied with a three-page background paper on productive diversity before the discussions). Those who knew less about the topic were able to learn from other participants and in turn, articulate their observations from this basis. Despite the potential concerns about confidentiality, reluctance to divulge business practices and so on, participants proved remarkably forthcoming and outspoken in their observations and criticisms of current corporate practice. Overall, the data generated by the five focus groups were rich, detailed and complex, offering insights that assisted in our interpretation and understanding of the survey data, which was subsequently collected on this topic.

The survey collected broad statistical data on the spread and incidence of diversity management policies across the industries, the importance placed on such policies and the reported strategies used. It consisted of thirty-nine structured questions with structured response categories. These categories included yes/no/not sure answers, rating answers in order of importance and choosing the most appropriate statement. There was also space provided on the questionnaire for open, unstructured comments. Some attitudinal questions were also included to gauge managers' philosophical stance on a range of diversity and equal opportunity principles. These were based on a number of statements to which managers responded according to a five-point Likert scale. The questionnaire was confidential and divided into five sections. It collected information in the following areas:

- organizational information (such as size, industry, number of employees, and so on);
- philosophical issues concerning diversity management;
- policy and practice within the organization;

- benefits and problems perceived with diversity management;
- further organizational information (more detailed questions such as percentage of women and NESB migrants on boards of directors, and so on).

The survey results were based on 320 returns from 1,814 usable questionnaires, a response rate of 18 per cent.

The majority of survey respondents were senior managers working in private sector businesses, with slightly more than one-quarter in public sector or non-profit businesses. Most were large employers in Australian terms (employing more than 100 persons) and more than three-fifths were Australian owned. More than half reported that NESB people comprised less than 20 per cent of the organization's workforce. However, more than a third of respondents worked in organizations where at least 20 per cent of the workforce was NESB. The survey data were analysed using SPSSX (statistical package for the social sciences) software.

To construct the survey sample, information about the total population of businesses in Australia and number of businesses within the six industries was obtained from the Australian Bureau of Statistics (ABS) Business Register. The sample was constructed to reflect three size bands within this population and include both public and private sector businesses. Mailing lists of businesses were drawn from a number of industry data bases which were randomly sampled. All questionnaires were mailed out in May 1998 and marked to the attention of the Chief Executive or Human Resource Manager. They were accompanied by a pre-addressed, reply-paid envelope.

The main limitations of this method was the relatively low response rate (although response rates of 20–30 per cent are common for mail-out surveys) and the skewing of the sample towards larger businesses, despite the care taken to structure the mail survey to broadly reflect the population. It seemed larger businesses were more willing or had greater resources to complete such a questionnaire. Alternatively, they may have had more familiarity with the diversity management concept than smaller businesses. The problem with small sample size is that the responses received cannot be assumed to represent the broader population, most of whom chose not to answer. Furthermore, structured questionnaire formats only allow simplified information to be collected which cannot be further interrogated or investigated. Nevertheless, such information provides a useful overview of the policies and activities of those businesses which responded to the survey. The combination of both survey-based data and qualitative data collection techniques used in this study (focus groups, interviews) allows more detailed and interpretive findings to be reached than one method alone. Finally, while the 320 survey businesses may not be broadly representative of the population, they are nevertheless a very sizeable group from which a range of valuable information can be gathered.

Turning to the design of the Business Benefits of Productive Diversity study, this centred on the selection of suitable organizations and the application of qualitative research techniques. Selection of the organizations was based on a number of criteria including the presence of a formal diversity management policy or strategies, the designation of a position within the organization (such as a diversity or human resource manager) having responsibility for this policy and evidence that diversity was valued within the organization. As such, we looked for organizations which had made some progress in this area and had a set of experiences that could be investigated and analysed. As case studies, the organizations could not be considered representative of the population of organizations in any way, but would hopefully be able to provide significant insights into how diversity management was experienced and the kinds of results which could be obtained.

Our search involved approaching a number of organizations either known or recommended to the researchers as having diversity management policies in place. Altogether nine businesses, most of them large, national organizations, were formally approached to participate in the study. Large organizations were approached initially because of circumstantial evidence (for example, from the 1998 survey) that they were more likely to be interested and active in this area. However, it is intended that later case studies will cover smaller and medium-sized enterprises.

The case studies themselves consisted of a mixture of face-to-face interviews, focus groups, participant observation, literature review and analysis of a range of corporate documents. At the FSG, fifteen face-to-face interviews were conducted with a range of senior and middle managers, including diversity managers, human resource managers and those involved in diversity initiatives, such as multicultural marketing, together with some lower level employees and managers who were not involved with diversity initiatives. An employee focus group was also held. Corporate documents examined included policy papers, employee statistics, the annual report, website information and enterprise bargaining agreement, customer needs analyses, corporate research reports, publicity materials, newsletters and so on. At Mobil, the researchers conducted nine face-to-face interviews and two employee focus groups, and analysed a similar range of corporate documents. The interviews included senior managers, human resource managers and diversity managers, as well as members of diversity committees and others not directly involved in such initiatives. The employee focus groups were drawn from blue- and white-collar areas of the organization.

These data were analysed by key themes and questions asked, based on transcripts of the interviews from tape recordings. The transcripts were also summarized, and key findings tabulated and compared under the major question headings and certain illustrative quotations from the interviews noted.

One of the strengths of this approach to the research was the capacity to collect data from multiple layers of the organizations that were detailed, insightful and historically informed. A diverse range of people had the opportunity to explain how they saw diversity management within the organization and its impact on them and others, and this could be contrasted with a reading of 'official' company documents and policies. However, a major limitation was the small number of people interviewed (this was necessitated both by project deadlines and delays in organizing interviews because managers were busy and schedules tight) and the inability to collect broader, survey-based data from the employees within these organizations. There were also problems in accessing data regarding the measurement of business benefits, primarily because no organization collected this kind of information in any rigorous way. Indeed, one organization, the FSG, explained that it would not seek to collect such data, as it did not wish, for reasons of equity and morale, to target its multicultural marketing personnel by measuring their performance differently from other marketing personnel.

Given the paucity of case study evidence in Australia regarding productive diversity, we were pleased to have made this initial foray and reaped such rich and complex data. This is seen as a good start to further research efforts of this nature.

The Diversity and Dollars findings

Our focus groups with senior managers showed that productive diversity, as promulgated by the federal government, was not well understood by all participants, although it was generally well regarded once it was explained. However, participants stressed that their own support for the concept did not necessarily reflect the prevailing attitudes and practices of many middle and senior managers. While a significant minority worked in organizations where productive diversity programmes were underway, these were relatively recent (introduced over the past five years) and not spread uniformly across the organization (Bertone *et al.*, 1998: 2).

Participants consistently emphasized the need to show that productive diversity contributes to measurable and positive outcomes for the enterprise before senior managers would commit to it. In cases where this had been demonstrated, it was evident that executive level commitment had been instrumental in reaping gains. The emphasis on the 'bottom line' was most apparent in the energy, communications and IT, finance and PMV industries, whereas quality and responsiveness of service appeared to be more important in the tourism and health care industries. In health care, saving unnecessary costs, improving access to essential services and making better use of taxpayers' money were key objectives (ibid.).

Several participants sought to widen the definition of productive diversity beyond ethnicity and race to cover all human diversity in the workforce. Their argument was that all differences are relevant to doing business in society, both locally and globally, that the workforce should reflect such differences and the contribution of all groups should be acknowledged and harnessed (ibid.). They believed that productive diversity would only work when implemented along with a genuine commitment to diversity of views and genuinely participative management (ibid.).

Numerous examples of successful productive diversity from participants' own experiences were provided, yet most stated it was low or non-existent on the management agenda, and many reported a 'backlash' or resistance to it from entrenched interest groups in the workplace, referred to as 'the old boys' club' (ibid.). Successful examples spanned all three manifestations of productive diversity described in the previous section, and included: the development of cross-cultural international troubleshooting teams in the energy industry, saving millions of dollars; the provision of multilingual services to NESB customers in the banking industry, leading to increased market share; the use of NESB employees' cultural knowledge in designing advertising campaigns for the tourist industry, leading to increased visitor numbers; the establishment of export development teams assisted by

NESB Australians in telecommunications, increasing export performance; and the involvement of NESB people in management (energy industry), leading to an improved public image and more harmonious work relations (ibid.).

Managers also articulated a range of perceived benefits associated with productive diversity, including greater capacity for innovation and creativity; improved quality and responsiveness; reduced costs; increased market share; enhanced public image; reduced disputation and litigation; respect and tolerance for different peoples; the opening up and expansion of export markets; and increased customer satisfaction and opportunities for personal learning (ibid.: 3).

The survey, on the other hand, showed particularly strong support, almost unanimous in some cases, for values which underpin a productive diversity approach, such as equal employment opportunities (EEO) and valuing human differences within a workforce. Despite this, just over two-fifths of businesses reported having a policy to support productive diversity, and only a tenth had a written policy. In most cases, the policy commitment to diversity management was part of EEO policy (which, as we have earlier noted, is mandatory for large businesses), suggesting that the distinction between EEO and productive diversity was not well understood or articulated. In those firms which had no productive diversity policy, the most commonly cited reasons were that the business had too few NESB employees, followed by 'never thought about it' and 'not a high priority'. As with the focus groups, establishing a clear link between productive diversity and the bottom line was the most popular strategy for promoting the concept (ibid.).

Of the businesses which had a productive diversity policy, the majority provided for the removal of discriminatory barriers to NESB people's employment, recognition of overseas skills and knowledge, targeted use of such skills and knowledge, use of languages other than English (LOTEs) at work and comprehensive skill audits (Table 11.1).

Only one-quarter of respondents reported that their organization collected statistics on employees' countries of birth or language abilities, however, raising doubts as to how these strategies might be implemented in a coherent and informed way (ibid.). Echoing the views of focus group participants, productive diversity was ranked lowest out of a range of management policy issues, such as new technology, occupational health and safety and employee relations. Very few of those who were active in this area (3 per cent of businesses) reported gaining no benefits from productive diversity, while high proportions reported such benefits as improved EEO outcomes (53 per cent), a more productive workforce (44 per cent), higher employee morale (42 per cent), improved public image (37 per cent) and more satisfied customers (36 per cent) (ibid.: 4). Conversely, 47 per cent of such respondents perceived there were 'no problems' with productive diversity, and relatively low proportions nominated problems such as 'increased expectations by employees' (24 per cent), confusion and misunderstanding (18 per cent) and resistance from managers (13 per cent) (ibid.: 84).

We concluded at the time that a substantial minority of businesses in the six industries had implemented productive diversity strategies, and that many which

Table 11.1 Strategies provided in the managing diversity policies of businesses

Response	Number	(%)
Remove barriers to employment/promotion of NESB people	94	73.4
Recognition of overseas skills and qualifications	74	57.8
Targeted use of employees' overseas knowledge/experience	52	40.6
Skill audits of all skills/qualifications held by employees	52	40.6
Use of languages other than English at work	49	38.3
Cross-cultural training programs	46	35.9
Collection of statistics on languages other than English spoken by employees	35	27.3
Collection of statistics on employees' country of birth	32	25.0
Cross-cultural teams	32	25.0
Multicultural marketing strategies	29	22.7
Multicultural export strategies	11	8.6
Other	10	7.8
Payment of language availability allowances	6	4.7
None of the above	2	1.6

Note: Percentages do not total 100 due to respondents choosing more than one response N = 128

Table 11.2 Benefits businesses gained from implementing managing diversity

Response	Number	(%)
Improved EEO outcomes	64	53.3
More productive workforce	53	44.2
Higher employment morale	50	41.7
Improved public image	45	37.5
More satisfied customers	43	35.8
More creative problem solving	35	29.2
Lower employee turnover	28	23.3
Less absenteeism	17	14.2
Increased sales	15	12.5
Greater market share	13	10.8
Increased exports	11	9.2
Other	7	5.8
Not relevant	5	4.2
None of the above	4	3.3

Note: N = 120

had commenced on this path had reaped the benefits (Table 11.2). However, there appeared to be insufficient awareness of the potential gains to be made, particularly in the area of multicultural marketing, both in Australia and overseas. There was also a blurring of the lines between EEO and productive diversity, although this is advocated by many writers, who would like to see diversity management firmly anchored to equity and social justice. Notwithstanding this, we called for a demonstrated link between dollars and diversity to be underlined in future strategies.

Given the findings of the focus groups and the survey, we concluded that without such a link, it was likely that productive diversity would continue to rank low on management agendas.

Delving into the organizational reality – Business Benefits of Productive Diversity

According to recent US literature (cf. Prasad *et al.*, 1997) it can be a long and difficult road for managers who set out to build an inclusive organizational culture that accepts racial, ethnic and other human differences. This is because the dominant paradigm in most organizations is not particularly open to diversity. In Australia, for example, most executive boards are dominated almost exclusively by males of English-speaking backgrounds (Karpin, 1995; Bertone *et al.*, 1998: 73). The ranks of senior managers below that are also very thinly populated by women and members of ethnic minorities. Studies have shown that most people in authority prefer to keep within their 'comfort zones' and so recruit and work with people like themselves (Watson, 1997). This does not always prevent the recruitment of NESB people and others who are needed to perform certain work which the dominant group does not find attractive or appropriate. In fact, some managers may positively discriminate by designating certain jobs to members of certain groups (Brosnan, 1996). But it can mean that wider employment and career opportunities for members of minority groups are lacking. These observations are relevant to an examination of our case study evidence.

Both case study organizations are large successful companies with operations extending throughout Europe and Asia; Mobil also has extensive operations in America. Both are major employers in Australia, with approximately 17,000 employees at the FSG and 2000 in Mobil. Each company has a long-standing and well-articulated diversity policy. In the FSG's case, moves in this direction began thirteen years ago, with considerable expansion of the policy programme about three years ago. At Mobil, the diversity issue has been actively considered since the early 1990s, with most formal policy activity occurring since 1995.

However, the two companies could not be more different in the way they manage diversity. At the FSG, ethnic diversity is targeted through a national multicultural marketing strategy aimed at local niche markets, such as Australians of Asian or Middle Eastern descent. It uses the bilingual and bicultural skills of staff to sell financial products in Australia to businesspeople from these ethnic communities. The programme is separate from other diversity policies of the FSG, such as equal employment opportunity, work/life programmes and employment for disabled people.

At Mobil, a national programme called Diversity and Inclusion is directed specifically towards employees rather than customers. It promotes diverse work teams, encourages open communication and aims to raise commitment and productivity by making all employees feel included. All human differences are encompassed in the programme, which is highly integrated with human resource and operational policies.

In terms of globalization, it was clear that both organizations' policy development had been greatly influenced by competitive pressures arising from internationalization of the domestic and overseas markets. In the FSG's case, the deregulation of the banking sector in the early 1980s had intensified competition in the product market as overseas groups set up operations in Australia and domestic FSGs competed more fiercely for customer patronage. According to the history provided by senior managers, the FSG began to address the issue of ethnic niche marketing in 1987, after the General Manager became convinced there were niche markets here which the organization was missing. Niche marketing was seen as an important strategy for shoring up and/or expanding the FSG's market share. The policy was clearly about bottom-line issues rather than addressing ethnic disadvantage or equity issues. As one informant noted:

> It's just money and business sense and not able to neglect what is probably a fairly considerable segment of business for particular ethnic groups . . . I think it is heavily motivated towards bottom line . . . But at the same time I mean they were very strong in saying that they want to be perceived in the community to be a good corporate citizen.

Another commented:

> part of the business case for diversity is that if we can leverage off differences that our employees bring, then we're going to be better able to service our customer base. Our customer base aren't all white Caucasians and males so why should our employees be the same? Obviously [we are] in a global market, our customer base and our customer needs are changing and so we need to keep pace with that.

At Mobil, interviewees spoke of the recognition from the late 1980s in the US parent company that diversity was to become a global business imperative. To some extent this was driven by equal opportunity legislation in the USA, but it was also recognized that the traditional pool of white male recruits had shrunk markedly. As one interviewee commented:

> In the US . . . if Mobil was to hire white males, it would only have recruited from 20 per cent of college graduates. This doesn't reflect the community, and brains aren't handed out on the basis of colour or gender.

Mobil also came to recognize the importance of retaining staff in which the company had invested considerable training and investment. Another key factor motivating the company was the poor business performance of the Australian affiliate in the late 1980s and demands from the US parent company that the Australian operations improve their performance, including a refusal to commit funds to capital upgrades until that occurred. Diversity and Inclusion was one plank in the parent company's demands for change. It was underscored by the appointment of a Singaporean

Manager from the USA, PC Tan, who seemed universally admired by inter-viewees and was said to personify, in his open and inclusive managerial style, the principles of Diversity and Inclusion. Tan worked for the Australian organisation for three years, building support for the policy within the company's board and management.

This history shows that international competition and the influence of the multinational parent company were important elements in Mobil Australia's adoption of diversity policy. Diversity and Inclusion was seen as a means of increasing the company's competitiveness, by ensuring the recruitment and utilization of the best skills available.

One Mobil interviewee summed it up succinctly:

> We are not out to win awards. It's all about business drivers for doing it [Diversity and Inclusion]. If there is no business focus senior management won't do it. The business imperatives are about the pool of talent, labour turnover, training costs, retention and about extracting that discretionary effort that makes your business get ahead of the competition.

Our research suggests that the diversity programmes in these two companies had common strengths: a belief that diversity management would lead to major business benefits; the commitment of senior management; appointment of high level champions to coordinate policy; the investment of significant resources in the diversity policy; a long-term perspective on the gains to be made; the pro-vision of targeted research by the company; and the dissemination of success stories which helped spread the diversity (and in Mobil's case, Inclusion) message through the organization. In both cases, diversity management is built into key results areas (that is management performance indicators), but it is also recog-nized that diversity alone is not sufficient to achieve results – it must be linked to key competencies such as financial management and communication with customers.

It is particularly worth highlighting the long-term horizons of these policies and indications in both cases that major cultural change was far from complete. Also noteworthy was the importance of change leaders or champions who were authorized to drive the change programme over a number of years. In both organizations, the change leaders were members of senior management and had a personal commitment to the diversity policy. In Mobil Australia, they were supported by a national Diversity Inclusion Council made up of staff representatives across the organization. At the FSG, change leaders had been appointed in most states to lead and coordinate the multicultural marketing programme.

Their role was far from easy, but it appears to have been pivotal to the success of the policy. At the FSG, the change leaders had a number of organizational and attitudinal hurdles to jump. One of them had been criticized in the past as 'just killing time' in his role, and as a consequence, had 'had to work hard to justify his position'. The role 'always has to be backed up by results' if it was to be accepted. An interviewee commented:

> They [the two multicultural marketing managers] have been pushing diversity management for a number of years, but getting it across to HR is another issue . . . General managers may agree, but they have to get it across to HR.

These observations support recent claims in the literature (cf. Prasad *et al.*, 1997) that diversity management, by challenging existing practices, values and power relations within an organization, can engender conflict and require many years of sustained policy work before it can be said to be truly entrenched. At Mobil, a seven-point scale had been used to gauge the organization's standing on Diversity and Inclusion. It was generally believed that the organization had attained a ranking of 3 or 4 (middle of the scale) since its adoption five years ago. This represented a state defined as 'Awareness – We have some diversity and inclusion issues and it means we're not getting the best from our people (3)' and 'Intuition – Maybe effective diversity and inclusion management can help us get better business results (4)'. Managing diversity was regarded as harder than many other management policies to implement. As one FSG interviewee put it:

> At the end of the day, we're asking a group of senior men, if you set a target of 30 per cent then you're saying that 30 per cent . . . need to make room for some others and I think it's also the system has served them very well, why would they want to give it up?

Another commented:

> It's more difficult to implement . . . less tangible, less clear-cut than other changes. Changing culture is less measurable, it's less easy to appreciate how effective you've been and see the fruits of your labour. Some people can talk the talk but not believe what they say.

While both policies had led to successful programmes in the case study organizations, there were gaps and problems within each of them. At the FSG, concern was expressed that Asian managers risked being typecast or trapped in niche marketing roles. Issues of racism and heavier workloads were reported, with Asian women managers being vulnerable to both ethnic and gender stereotyping. Some of the comments here were illuminating:

> When they hear my accent, they assume I am a teller, not a manager.

> [For a woman] . . . there are a lot of obstacles, you need to be so tough and focused . . . the [FSG] expects you to work very long hours . . . females need to have much better results, 25–30 per cent more than males, and for an Asian it's even harder.

> There's a high expectation of people of ethnic backgrounds . . . that they should bring in a lot of business. Whereas if they are from an Anglo-Saxon background and don't bring business no-one seems to question it.

At the FSG, the multicultural marketing policy is selective in targeting business people from certain ethnic communities and therefore benefits relatively affluent immigrant Australians. This supports the contentions of those such as Burton (1992) and Hall (1995) that diversity management will not benefit disadvantaged people unless it is clearly linked to equity and justice policies. The diversity policy has a relatively low profile in the FSG and is not well integrated with so called 'mainstream' (dominant) operations and policies. So, for example, there is little mention in equal opportunity policies and manuals of the particular issues faced by NESB Australians, such as direct and indirect discrimination on the basis of accent, appearance, dress and behaviour. This is surprising, given the FSG's determination to differentiate its service to key customers according to language and ethnicity.

In contrast, at Mobil, the high profile Diversity and Inclusion policy has permeated most parts of the organization, but issues such as race and ethnicity have been relegated to the same level as dress styles and leisure interests. The focus on differences among individuals tends to obscure the often systematic ways in which society discriminates against some groups, such as ethnic minorities. This is in line with the views of such writers as Moore (1999) and Prasad *et al.* (1997) who have cautioned against the 'blancmange' effect of dealing with all human differences together as if they all had the same issues and problems. Diversity at Mobil also appears to be a lesser focus than Inclusion, which is primarily about participative management, and the policy is currently under review as a result of the merger with Exxon.

Notwithstanding these problems, both cases demonstrate major business benefits for the companies involved. The FSG has experienced significant lending growth in its target niche markets, as Asian Australian managers had grown their portfolios and won a disproportionate share of internal banking awards. We estimated that approximately 1.6 per cent of managers in Victoria were specifically recruited to service the Asian Australian market, yet this group picked up between a quarter and a half of the internal FSG awards from 1997 to 1999. How had they been so successful? As one award winner put it:

> I have been told to identify Asian needs, they like to see an Asian-speaking manager, they will tell me more perhaps because I am an Asian, and that helps me to understand their business better.

As a consequence, the multicultural marketing programme has been expanded to encompass more target communities in different states.

Mobil reported major gains in a number of business units, such as the drivers and lubes areas, and through its work/life policies. Ailing businesses, such as the Altona refinery in Victoria, had been 'turned around', and the company had saved hundreds of thousands of dollars by retaining highly skilled female staff. However, it is not clear how much of this can be credited to the Diversity or Inclusion aspect of the policy.

Debates in the literature

The previous section has largely covered the key findings of our two research projects into productive diversity. In this section, we examine some of the theoretical and practical debates in the existing literature on managing diversity and relate our findings to these broad debates. We conclude the section by attempting to answer the major questions posed at the outset, chief of them being: has globalization led to a greater valuing of workers of diverse backgrounds and attributes?

As indicated previously, the term 'productive diversity' is strongly suggestive of the business case and as such is considered by many working in the field as too limited. Through our research on both research projects, we also found the term does not have wide currency (Bertone *et al.*, 1998; Smith, 1998; Bertone and Leahy, 2000: 1). Terms such as 'managing diversity', 'valuing diversity' and 'workplace diversity' seem to be preferred by a range of managers, while 'managing diversity' is the term favoured in the USA. If 'productive diversity' is to be used, the consensus seems to be that it be broadly defined, the advantage of a broad definition being that it provides space for the acknowledgement of multiple group membership and complex identities. A broad definition accommodates intersections of race, ethnicity, gender, education, class, ability, location, etc. and helps ensure that identity does not assume a uniformity of interests and issues.

Such complex constructions of identity are a common theme of cultural studies and postcolonial theory. Bhabba describes the political necessity of moving away from 'the singularities of "class" or "gender" as primary conceptual and organisational categories'. He considers how identity, both singular and plural is formed 'in-between' or in excess of, the sums of parts of difference' such as race, class, gender, etc. (Bhabba, 1994: 1–2). However, it is pertinent to note that 'developing . . . [a] broader view [of diversity] may simply serve to focus and action orientation off some issues that are specifically of concern to a particular type of diversity' (Moore, 1999: 210). Indeed, the adoption of generalized language can be seen as a deliberate managerial tactic to avoid action or deflect attention from difficult management issues (ibid.).

This is the crux of the debate between feminists and others regarding the use of diversity terminology to replace terms like equal employment opportunity and equity and social justice. In addition, literature from the United States and Australia has begun to question the efficacy of managing diversity and other similar policies to deal with 'the more serious dimension of difference in organisations' (Prasad *et al.*, 1997: 3). Prasad *et al.* argue the need to focus on what they describe as the common dilemmas of diversity, in particular: 'The backlash against any commitment to multiculturalism, the continuing anger and disappointment of women and minorities, and the systematic resistance within organizations against difference' (ibid.). They note that the concept of workplace diversity has become extremely popular in the mass media and, more recently, in human resource and organizational behaviour textbooks. In these sources diversity is invariably described in terms of one of a number of positive metaphors: the melting pot, the patchwork quilt, the multicultural mosaic and the rainbow (ibid.: 4). Noting the history of discrimination in the United States, they state that at one level the celebration of diversity in literature is to be applauded. However:

> There are persistent signs that the management of diversity is a Herculean task requiring much more than managerial enthusiasm, optimism and good intentions. Managing diversity at the workplace presents as many dilemmas as triumphs, and is constantly fraught with innumerable tensions, conflicts and contradictions.
>
> (ibid.: 5)

Another strong criticism of managing diversity from Australia is that it fails to reflect differences in power and has a tendency to equate fundamental differences such as race and ethnicity with less significant differences such as sporting interests (Burton, 1992 in Hall, 1995):

> Managing diversity is a powerful rhetorical strategy; it hides structural inequality which become invisible when the problem is individualised and broadly dispersed in this way to cover all differences . . . This strategy serves to conceal power relations and resultant forms of discrimination which are embedded in social and organisational structural arrangements.
>
> (ibid.: 24)

This criticism is relevant to the findings of the Mobil case study, where diversity was broadly defined to include all human attributes and behaviours, such as lifestyle, dress and sporting interests, as well as more structural characteristics such as race and gender. While there was no evidence that senior management had consciously obfuscated the power relations inherent in these various differences, the lack of significant movement on issues such as gender, ethnicity and race (in terms of ethnic minority and female representation in senior management, for example) did suggest that the more difficult to tackle issues were being overlooked in preference to the finer differences of social behaviour and culture.

Hall, another Australian writer, is critical that managing diversity focuses on 'managing individuals rather than members of groups'. She argues that where discrimination based on group membership is pervasive, it would be more efficient to develop a programme-based response, rather than deal with individual cases (1995: 22). Burton adds that, to be effective, managing diversity programmes need to be implemented in conjunction with or as extensions of equal opportunity programmes (Burton, 1992 in Hall, 1995: 23). If not, it is likely the only beneficiaries will be professional women and migrants from non 'alien', English-speaking backgrounds (ibid.).

These observations are particularly relevant to the findings of our case study research on the FSG, where the lack of integration between equal employment opportunity policy on the one hand, and the multicultural marketing programme on the other, had led to certain groups in the organization and marketplace benefiting (in this case, highly qualified or affluent Asians of Chinese and Vietnamese origins) but not other groups, such as indigenous people and those from Africa. Senior managers at the FSG pointed out that multicultural marketing strategies for those other ethnic groups were being studied at the time, however, it was clear that they would only be supported if there was a sufficiently strong business case.

The benefits of multicultural marketing were considerable: for the Asian employees they centred on their recruitment into highly paid ethno-specific managerial roles where they could exercise their second language skills and earn awards and recognition. For the customers, it was the opportunity to receive sophisticated financial services in their own languages from people who understood their cultural needs and mores. However, even those who belonged to this group of beneficiaries found themselves contending with equity issues, such as the propensity of the organization to label or 'pigeonhole' Asian managers, so that other employment/career opportunities were potentially closed to them or more difficult to access than for other, non-Asian managers.

This seems to support the criticisms of the feminist writers who argue that the business case alone is not sufficient to produce equitable outcomes for members of traditionally disadvantaged groups, and to that extent, managing diversity programmes that rely on the business case will have limited benefits.

The findings of both case studies also support the contentions of those such as Prasad *et al.* (1997) that managing diversity can be a Herculean task that takes more than just good will and optimism. At both case study organizations, the diversity management policies had been in place and actively implemented for many years – thirteen, in the case of the FSG, and at least five years at Mobil. Each organization had appointed champions or change leaders to facilitate cultural change towards diversity in the organization and taken a long-term view of what could be achieved. At the FSG, some of the change leaders had taken some criticism for their role and were reportedly having to justify their existence on an ongoing basis, despite some of the obvious achievements of the multicultural marketing programme. Neither organization felt that it had yet progressed to an advanced stage of policy development, and interviewees in both organizations readily conceded that much attitudinal change was needed before there was widespread adherence within the organization to the principles of productive diversity or managing diversity. Despite the commitment of executive management, there was still a long way to go to change employees and managers' attitudes generally towards the value of diversity.

Conversely, Greenslade (1991) argues that, as diversity management is not a deficit model it goes one step further than equal employment opportunity. It is argued that the focus of diversity management is on changing organizational culture, so that difference is accepted, rather than merely attempting to increase the representation of diverse groups in what is essentially an assimilationist model.

One very powerful demographic factor in favour of diversity management is the likelihood that women, people from diverse ethnic backgrounds, and older workers will soon constitute a larger, if not the major part, of the workforce. This was certainly a major factor in the thinking at the Mobil case study, where a number of interviewees mentioned the importance of recruiting the most talented people to the company, regardless of their personal attributes. However, unless it is expected that people adapt to the prevailing mono-culture, a more diverse workforce will require a different type of management that is prepared to widen its recruitment pool significantly and ensure that diverse employees receive the conditions necessary to perform to their best. Business case perspectives can also recognize that managing diversity may make employees feel valued and included and therefore more productive; can improve customer service if the employees and management of the organization reflect the general population, and can result in better understanding of local and global markets. However, the evidence from the FSG study suggests that the business case does not always acknowledge these considerations, particularly issues of how valued and included employees feel (and thus how committed they are to the organization and likely to stay with it). The argument is that if employees perceive the organization will treat employees fairly and equitably, they are likely to be more motivated and committed. Second, organizations obtain leverage from perceptions that they are good corporate citizens and may improve their market share. The business case did not seem to prevent a situation where ethno-specific managers at the FSG were labelled as different and possibly less valued as a result for being different. This suggests the need for a strong equal employment opportunity and social justice framework to be integrated with the business case.

Burton (1991) argues that workplace heterogeneity helps avoid the problems of 'group think' and cloning, which in turn increases productivity and reduces costs. Likewise, Moore finds there is ample evidence that 'diverse groups with the skills and support systems to integrate effectively, are likely to be significantly more effective than non diverse or homogeneous groups in the same activities' (McLeod and Lobe, 1992; Maznevski, 1994 in Moore, 1999). However, poorly integrated heterogeneous groups can be as damaging as overly integrated homogeneous groups (Stephenson and Lewin, 1996). Studies in diversity initiatives in North America have shown a strong correlation between good diversity practices and profits (Hayles and Mendez, 1997, in Smith, 1998). There is also evidence of the cost of not accommodating a diverse workforce. One particularly tangible measure is the cost of replacing disaffected staff. Studies have calculated the cost of turnover as anywhere between 95 to 250 per cent of the employee's salary (Robinson and Dechant, 1997, in Smith, 1998).

In Australia, as we have noted, white Anglo-Celtic people dominate most institutions, and white Anglo-Celtic males in particular manage the Australian workforce (Karpin, 1995; Smith, 1998; Sinclair, 1998). Recently, we have seen a withdrawal of support for multiculturalism by the federal government, 'demonstrated by a subtle change of rhetoric, some fear, with an accompanying change in public policy' (Kalowski, 1999: 36). The policy remains but is undermined by an emphasis on the 'mainstream' or the majority culture. In a powerful critique on multiculturalism in Australia, Hage argues that those who support and those who oppose multicultural migration are linked by a shared assumption that they have ownership and control of the nation and as such are in a position to welcome or reject newcomers. He describes this as the White Nation fantasy, the fantasy of a nation for and governed by White people (Hage, 1998: 19). Hage uses the concept 'White' rather than Anglo or Anglo-Celt, arguing that Whiteness is an aspiration, which up to a point can be accumulated or acquired. He remarks that there are many non-Anglos who also embrace the 'White Nation fantasy'. The key distinction he draws is not between people from non-English-speaking backgrounds and Anglos, or between Europeans and non-Europeans but between 'those who are Third World-looking and those who are not' (ibid.).

The national media attention given to the One Nation party, a right-wing party opposed to immigration, multiculturalism and indigenous programmes is further evidence of the recent decline in left-liberal values and the notion that national values of fairness and equality are out of style (Rothwell, 1999: 29). Such 'debates' may have contributed to the situation observed by researchers that the issue of race has become an 'undiscussable' in corporate circles (Da Gama Pinto *et al.*, 2000: 29).

To conclude this section, we would say the answer to our overriding question in this chapter is answered ambiguously. Both our research projects provide strong indications that globalization is forcing more organizations to reassess their fitness to trade in a global market, and they are attempting to upgrade the diversity of their human resources to meet these challenges. However, in Australia, this has happened very slowly and only by a minority of organizations to any significant extent. Moreover, from the evidence of our two case study organizations, although it is obviously limited to those cases, it appears that even organizations that have progressed some distance with diversity management are experiencing attitudinal and structural barriers which hamper the full valuing of a broad spectrum of workers of diverse backgrounds and attributes. Some of the detailed reasoning behind this is provided in our conclusion.

Conclusion

This chapter has explored the literature and discussed the findings of Australian research on diversity management, with particular reference to ethnic differences within a workforce. We found that globalization has been a major force driving companies in Australia to reconsider the way they approach and utilize the culturally diverse labour pool available to them. However, only a minority of companies appear so far to have made the connection between globalization of product markets, diversity in the customer base and diversity of human resources needed to service that market. Just as few appear to have recognized that discriminatory human resource practices can impede an organization's capacity to compete effectively in the globalized market place, whether that is a domestic or overseas market.

Our research found that a significant minority of companies in Australia are drawing these connections and many report profiting from this approach in various ways, such as by securing greater employee commitment, market share and customer satisfaction. However, diversity management is in its infancy in Australia, and even long-standing diversity issues such as gender discrimination remain to be tackled satisfactorily, despite decades of proactive legislation. Policies to address racial and ethnic discrimination and make the most effective use of ethnic diversity, such as by offering wider employment opportunities to minorities, appear even less well developed. This is in spite of the fact that more than a quarter of the Australian population derives from non-British stock, the efforts of federal and state governments for more than a decade to promote diversity management policies and the adoption of multicultural policy in Australia since the 1970s.

The case study research in particular supports the contentions of those writers, such as Prasad *et al.* (1997), Hall (1995) and Burton (1992) that diversity management is not an easy path for managers to tread. Entrenched interest groups, such as senior managers and other groups within the workplace, will generally fight to retain their privileged position, even where the evidence demonstrates that diversity management will help the organization survive and prosper in a globalized economy. This was particularly evident in the financial services study, where in spite of the superlative performance of ethno-specific (Chinese and Vietnamese Australian) managers, there were widespread indications of 'pigeonholing' or typecasting of such people, leading to blocked career paths. Indeed, the multicultural marketing policy in this FSG had the potentially negative consequence of inverting the intent of multicultural marketing, so that the possession of second language skills (Mandarin, Cantonese, Vietnamese) had become a liability when recruitment to non-multicultural marketing jobs was considered.

While the interview data cannot be conclusive on this, there were a number of suggestions that people with a second language would only be considered if there was an ethno-specific role for them to perform. Other jobs would not, presumably, be open to them on the basis of general merit. This was partly because they would have been difficult to replace as multicultural marketing managers, but also, it appears, because their suitability for 'mainstream' (non-ethno-specific) jobs was questioned. Such views were held in spite of the fact that most multicultural marketing managers had successfully serviced the Anglo-Celtic dominant market together with their ethno-specific clientele. Clearly, this would undermine the equity principles embedded in relevant racial discrimination legislation, and represent a cruel parody of the case for multicultural marketing. The same principle might well apply to other niche marketing programmes where they were applied, for example, banking services geared to women or the disabled.

These findings suggest that social factors at work, such as ethnic and racial stereotyping and various forms of indirect discrimination, are particularly difficult to shift. Rational arguments based on market imperatives alone are probably insufficient to tackle such issues successfully, and as several writers contend, there are limits to the diversity management model, which emphasizes efficiency issues to the exclusion of social justice and equity principles. Their advocacy of the need to combine diversity management with equal opportunity in the workplace programmes seems to be supported by our case studies.

The Mobil study seems to illustrate the criticism of several writers (Moore, 1999; Burton, 1992) that treating all human differences under the umbrella of diversity management also has its limitations. The most important is the tendency to focus on individual rather than group differences and overlook the significant power imbalances facing certain groups. We found that, where all differences are included, such as dress style, leisure pursuits, schools attended as well as gender, age, and so on, some major and confronting differences such as race, tend to be overlooked. This reflects the findings of other researchers such as Da Gama Pinto *et al.* (2000) that the issue of race has become, for reasons related to national ideology and controversy, an 'undiscussable' in Australian corporate life.

The case study data also show that basing diversity management primarily on the business case tends to exclude less privileged and powerful groups in the market and the workforce, whose contribution may not be seen to improve the 'bottom line'. In the FSG, more recently arrived immigrant groups such as Somalians and Ethopians, together with indigenous Australians, were not targeted by the multicultural marketing policy as they were not regarded as affluent or having developed sufficient business acumen. This meant such groups were not targeted for recruitment into business banking roles within the FSG. As such, the ongoing under-representation of such groups in senior staffing levels within Australian organizations was likely to be perpetuated.

In summary, the economic imperatives associated with globalization appear to have led to contradictory outcomes with respect to the management of diverse human resources. On one hand, it has highlighted the challenges of operating in a culturally diverse marketplace where cultural knowledge, customs and ways of doing business, together with linguistic preferences, can be crucial in gaining a competitive edge against rivals. Such challenges tend in principle to point to the need to recruit widely from the available pool of talent, irrespective of gender, age, race or ethnicity, and develop and utilize such talent in the most effective manner. Some companies have met these challenges and are gaining a competitive edge by doing so. However, the empirical research and the literature show that changing the way that organizations manage their cultural capital is neither straightforward or unproblematic. Where human values, preferences and tastes are concerned, either managers are prepared to behave irrationally, with extreme conservatism, or opt to protect their own privileged position at the cost of overall organizational performance. Diversity management, it seems, is a limited paradigm unless such inherent conflicts of interest and power issues are addressed in a systematic way.

References

Adler, N.J. (1997) *International Dimensions of Organisational Behaviour*, Cincinnati, Ohio: South Western Publishing.

Australian Bureau of Statistics (ABS) (1996) *Census of Population and Housing*, Canberra: ABAS.

Australian Bureau of Statistics (ABS) (2000) *Labour Force Australia*, 6203.0, July, Canberra: ABAS.

Bertone, S. (1996) 'Migrants, Industry Policy and Decentralisation: From the Accord to the Workplace Relations Act 1996', *International Employment Relations Review* 2 (2), December: 75–89.

Bertone, S., Esposto, A. and Turner, R. (1998) *Diversity and Dollars: Productive Diversity in Australian Business and Industry*, CEDA Information Paper no. 58, Melbourne: CEDA.

Bertone, S. and Griffin, G. (1992) *Immigrant Workers and Trade Unions*, Canberra: AGPS.

Bertone, S. and Leahy, M. (2000) *Business Benefits of Productive Diversity – Case Studies*, report to Department of Immigration and Multicultural Affairs, Canberra, Australia, September.

Bertone, S., Keating, C. and Mullaly, J. (2000) *The Taxi Driver, the Cook and the Greengrocer: the Representation of NESB People in Film, Television and Theatre*, Sydney: Australia Council.

Bhabba, H.K. (1994) *The Location of Culture*, London and New York: Routledge.

Brosnan, P. (1996) 'Labour Markets and Social Deprivation', *Labour and Industry* 7(2), December: 3–31.

Burton, C. (1991) *The Promise and the Price: The Struggle for Equal Opportunity in Women's Employment*, Allen & Unwin, Sydney.

Burton, C. (1992) *Managing Difference and Diversity – The Changing Role of Human Resource Management in the 90s*, International Women's Day Seminar Series, Canberra: Public Services Commission, 6 March.

Castles, S., Foster, W., Iredale, R. and Withers, G. (1998) *Immigration and Australia: Myths and Realities*, St. Leonards, NSW: Allen & Unwin.

Collins, J. (1992) *Migrant Hands in a Distant Land*, Sydney: Pluto Press.

Cope, B. and Kalantzis, M. (1997) *Productive Diversity: A New Australian Model for Work and Management*, Annandale, NSW: Pluto Press.

Cox, T. Jr. (1993) *Cultural Diversity in Organisations*, San Francisco: Barrett-Koehler Publishers Inc.

Da Gama Pinto, C., D'Netto, B. and Smith, D. (2000) *Theoretical and Practical Issues in Diversity Management: From Tolerance to Inclusion*, report to Department of Immigration and Multicultural Affairs, Australia, July.

Dawkins, P., Kemp, S. and Cabalu, H. (1995) *Trade and Investment with East Asia in Selected Service Industries*, Institute of Research into International Competitiveness, Canberra: AGPS.

Foster, L., Marshall, A. and Williams, L. (1991) *Discrimination against Immigrant Workers in Australia*, Canberra: AGPS.

Galagan, P. (1993) 'Leading Diversity', *Training and Development Journal*, 47(4): 38–43.

Genoff, R. and Green, R. (1998) *Manufacturing Prosperity: Ideas for Industry, Technology and Employment*, Annandale, NSW: Federation Press.

Greenslade, M. (1991) 'Managing Diversity: Lessons from the United States', *Personnel Management*, December: 28–33.

Hage, G. (1998) *White Nation: Fantasies of White Supremacy in a Multicultural Society*, Annandale, NSW: Pluto Press.

Hall, P. (1995) *Affirmative Action and Managing Diversity*, Affirmative Action Agency Monograph No. 8, Canberra: AGPS.

Harrison, E.F. (1995) *The Managerial Decision Making Process*, 4th edn, Boston: Houghton Mifflin.

Hay, I. (1996) *Managing Cultural Diversity: Opportunities for Enhancing the Competitive Advantage of Australian Business*, Canberra: AGPS.

Hayles, R. and Mendez, R.A. (1997) *The Diversity Directive: Why Some Initiatives Fail and what to Do About it*, Madison and Chicago: Irwin Professional Publishing.

Jakubowicz, A. (2000) 'Accent-uate the Positive: Implications and Possibilities Raised by "The Taxi Driver, the Cook and the Greengrocer", Issues and Strategies in Ethnic Minority Participation in Theatre, Film and TV', report to Australia Council, Sydney.

Kalowski, J. (1999) 'Australia in Context: The Cross-cultural Imperative', in HREOC, *Cultural Dimensions: Approaches to Diversity Training in Australia*, Sydney: Race Discrimination Commissioner.

Karpin, D. (1995) *Enterprising Nation: Renewing Australia's Managers to Meet the Challenges of the*

Asia-Pacific Century, Report of the Industry Task Force on Leadership and Management Skills, Canberra: Commonwealth of Australia.

Kramer, R. (1997) 'Managing Diversity', in E.M. Davis and V. Pratt, *Making the Link: Affirmative Action and Industrial Relations*, Sydney: Affirmative Action Agency and Labour Management Studies Foundation, Graduate School of Management, Macquarie University.

Loden, M. and Rosener, J.B. (1991) *Workforce America! Managing Employee Diversity as a Vital Resource*, Homewood, Ill: Business One Irwin.

McLeod, P.L. and Lobe, S.A. (1992) 'The Effects of Ethnic Diversity on Idea Generation in Small Groups', *Academy of Management, Best Papers Proceedings*: 227–31.

Maznevski, M.I. (1994) 'Understanding our Differences: Performance in Decision Making Groups with Diverse Members', *Human Relations* 47(5), May: 531–53.

Moore, S. (1999) 'Understanding and Managing Diversity among Groups at Work: Key Issues for Organizational Training and Development', *Journal of European Industrial Training*, 23, (4/5): 208–17.

O'Loughlin, T. and Watson, I. (1997) *Loyalty is a One Way Street: NESB Immigrants and Long-Term Unemployment*, University of Sydney, Sydney: ACIRRT.

Overell, S. (1996) 'IPD says Diversity is Next Step for Equality', *People Management*, December: 12–13.

Prasad, P., Mills, A.J., Elmes, M., Prasad, A. (1997) *Managing the Organisational Melting Pot: Dilemmas of Workplace Diversity*, Thousand Oaks and London: Sage.

Race Discrimination Commissioner (1998) *Diversity Makes Good Business Sense: Training Package for Managing Cultural Diversity in the Workplace*, Sydney: Human Rights and Equal Opportunity Commission.

Riach, P.A. and Rich, J. (1991) 'Testing for Discrimination in the Labour Market', *Cambridge Journal of Economics*, 15: 239–56.

Robinson, G. and Dechant, K. (1997) 'Building a Business Case for Diversity', *Academy of Management Executive*, 11(3): 21–32.

Rothwell, N. (1999) 'Everyday Hero', *The Weekend Australian*, 5–6 June: 29,

Sinclair, A. (1998) *Doing Leadership Differently: Gender, Power and Sexuality in a Changing Business Culture*, Carlton: Melbourne University Press.

Smith, D. (1998) 'The Business Case for Diversity', *Monash Mount Eliza Business Review*, November: 72–81.

Stephenson, K. and Lewin, D. (1996) 'Managing Workforce Diversity: Macro and Micro Level HR Implications of Network Analysis', *International Journal of Manpower* 17(4/5): 168–96.

Stratton, J. (1998) *Race Daze: Australia in Identity Crisis*, Sydney: Pluto Press.

Thomas, R.R. Jr. (1991) *Beyond Race and Gender: Unleashing the Power of Your Total Workforce*, New York: Amacom.

Watson, I. (1997) *Opening the Glass Door: Overseas-Born Managers in Australia*, Canberra: AGPS.

Wallace, P., Ermer, C. and Motshabi, D. (1996) 'Managing Diversity: A Senior Age Discrimination', *Equal Opportunities International* 14(6/7): 61–8.

Wilson, K., Bradford, J. and Fitzpatrick, M. (2000) *Australia in Accord: An evaluation of the Prices and Incomes Accord in the Hawke-Keating Years*, Melbourne: South Pacific Publishing,

Woods, R. and Sciarini, M. (1995) 'Diversity Programs in Chain Restaurants', *Cornell Hotel and Restaurant Administration Quarterly* June, 36(3): 18–23.

12 Globalization, global human resource management, and distance learning

A study of the effectiveness of a global learning partnership

Marcie LePine, George Milkovich, Ningyu Tang, Larry Godfrey and Rob Gearhart

Introduction

The increasing use of multimedia distance learning (MDL) technology for training delivery has been well documented (Bassi and Van Buren, 1999). As organizations and educational institutions become more global, a distinct advantage of MDL technology is that it enables trainers to deliver training programs simultaneously to a number of different sites worldwide. Proponents of MDL technology note that this practice reduces the cost of trainers and training facilities (Rand, 1996) and allows for the delivery of training programs to individuals at sites that might not otherwise receive these programs.

Although there are several advantages to using MDL technology for training purposes, there are also disadvantages. For example, MDL technology may inhibit the interaction between students and the instructor and among students and may decrease overall participation within a classroom environment (Rand, 1996). When these problems negatively impact the learning of students, the result is ineffective or less effective training programs. Few empirical studies have been conducted that rigorously examine the relationship between the global/local classroom environments and perceptions of course effectiveness (Frost and Fukami, 1997). Given the increasing use of MDL technology both in organizations and university classrooms, it is important to better understand how to more effectively use MDL technologies. Thus, the purpose of our study is to examine the relationship between the MDL learning environment and participants' perceptions of course effectiveness in a global HRM course that combines global with local in-class environments and virtual-global and local out-of-class team experiences. We begin by describing the MDL global course in greater detail. Next we discuss our operationalization of effectiveness, identify the components of the learning environment that are of interest, and provide the hypotheses for the study. Finally, we test the hypotheses and discuss our findings and limitations.

Description of the global HRM MDL course

The global HRM course was created at Cornell University's ILR School, in partnership with Shanghai Jiao Tong University (China), University of Ljubljana (Slovenia), and Universidad Metropolitana (Venezuela). The ninety-five participants from four continents included graduate students at the four universities and corporate managers from ten companies worldwide (students and managers will be referred to as participants throughout the remainder of the chapter).

Every other week, participants came together electronically for live discussion sessions at the four sites (USA, Venezuela, China and Slovenia) using synchronous (ISDN) video teleconferencing. During these synchronous sessions the global instructor (George Milkovich) lectured and led discussions among participants world-wide across the four sites; participants responded to issues raised by other participants and delivered presentations to the global classroom. Guest lecturers discussed how their organizations were responding to globalization pressures, and participants formed global (multi-site) teams to analyse cases. On the intervening weeks, classes met locally in each of the different sites. These local sessions were facilitated by local instructors (the global and local instructor was the same person for the US group) and conducted in a combined lecture-based/discussion group delivery style that allowed for exchanges between instructor and participants. The local instructors had all been trained at Cornell's ILR School. Ningyu Tang (Shanghai) spent the previous six months attending Cornell HR classes and working with the global instructor. Professor Nada Zupan received her MS degree from Cornell, and she and Milkovich had previously team-taught at courses at the MBA program at Ljubljana University. Alejandro Fernandez also earned a graduate degree at Cornell and worked with the Cornell faculty in Venezuela. Consequently, the instructional team had previously worked together and developed similar techniques.

In addition to the in-class instruction, participants were involved in out-of-class team learning experiences. Every participant was a member of two teams: one team was comprised of participants from across the four sites (virtual-global team) and the other team was comprised of participants within one's own site (local team). Team activities included discussions and interactions related to case projects, readings, and lectures. Cases and projects included e-HR; Developing Global Competencies and Mindsets; Taking Stock Options Global; and Attracting and Retaining Critical Talent. These projects were part of the assignments of the course; participants developed a final report and shared conclusions via the Internet, class websites, and live teleconferencing sessions. The virtual-global teams collaborated on-line with a blend of technologies (chat rooms, email, faxes, conference calls); local team members collaborated face to face.

The design of the course enabled us to examine the relationship between components of the global and local learning environments (in-class and out-of-class learning) and perceptions of effectiveness. The factors that are hypothesized to relate to effectiveness include instructor–participant communication, participant–participant team cooperation, others' perceptions of MDL technology, and connectedness perceptions.

Development of hypotheses

In this study, we focused on factors we hypothesized to be related to the effectiveness of an MDL-delivered course. First, we define effectiveness reactions. Second, we offer support for the hypothesized relationships between selected components of the global and local learning environments and effectiveness reactions.

Effectiveness reactions

Researchers have recently noted that participants' reactions to training are important when measuring training effectiveness (Alliger *et al.*, 1997). According to Alliger *et al.* there are two broad categories of effectiveness reactions: affective reactions and utility reactions. Affective reactions measure an individual's liking of a training program; utility reactions measure an individual's assessment of the usefulness of the training. Of the two forms of reaction measures, Alliger *et al.* found that utility reactions correlated more highly with learning and with the transfer of gained knowledge to on-the-job performance than did affective reactions. Moreover, utility reactions correlated more highly with transfer than did measures of immediate and retained learning.

Although previous researchers have identified two forms of reactions: affective and utility, we suggest that it is important to also examine *learning* reactions (perceptions of learning as a result of participating in a course) and *behavior* reactions (perceptions of future use of the material learned in a course).[1] The three latter forms of reactions (utility, learning, and behavior) correspond to three of Kirkpatrick's (1959a, 1959b, 1960a, 1960b) training criteria: results, learning, and behavior, respectively; with the fourth, affective reactions, corresponding to the way in which reactions have been traditionally discussed (Kirkpatrick, 1959a). We hypothesize that individuals' assessments of (or reactions to), liking, learning, future behavior, and results, represent distinct reaction criteria that are equally important to investigate. Furthermore, we hypothesize that specific components of the learning environment (e.g., virtual-global team cooperation) will be related to the form of reaction criteria that most corresponds with the type of learning taking place (e.g., virtual-global team learning reaction). These hypotheses are provided in detail in the following section.

Relationship between the global and local learning environments and effectiveness reactions

One of the primary propositions of adult learning theory is that adult learners' experiences play a role in their acquisition of knowledge (Knowles, 1984). To the extent that training methods tap into these experiences, more effective adult learning experiences result. Ways in which training methods enhance the experiential learning of adults is through active involvement in classroom discussions and engaging peer group activities (ibid.). We begin by discussing factors that contribute to participants' active involvement in classroom discussions, then factors that contribute to effective peer group interactions, followed by factors that contribute to overall training environment perceptions.

Active involvement in classroom discussions

One of the most effective ways to convey course material is through face-to-face discussions that provide for a dialogue between instructor and students (Daft and Lengel, 1986; Lauzon, 1992). This instructor-as-facilitator approach enables the instructor to rely on a variety of cues (body language, tone of voice) to communicate course material, to personalize the material to fit students' needs, to provide immediate feedback, and to facilitate discussions among students. The approach enables students to become active participants in the exchange of information (Daft and Lengel, 1986). According to Armstrong-Stassen *et al.* (1998) when adult learners perceive themselves to be active participants in the classroom experience, they perceive learning to be more effective.

Although active participation has been utilized in traditional classroom settings for years, only recently has there been a movement towards integrating active participation into DL and MDL classrooms (Lauzon, 1992; Rand, 1996; Alavi *et al.*, 1997). One factor that enhances active participation in both traditional and MDL classrooms is the opportunity for students to communicate with the instructor. Although efforts can be made to increase the communication between instructor and students during MDL sessions, MDL technology presents communication challenges different from those found in traditional classroom environments (e.g., communication flows effected by participants' level of comfort with the camera). Given the importance of communication to promote active participation, and the inherent communication challenges in the MDL classroom, we hypothesize the following:

> H1: The Opportunity to Communicate with the Global Instructor/Local Instructor will be positively related to effectiveness reactions. More specifically, the greater the opportunity to communicate with the global/local instructor, the more positive the general affective, the general learning, the behavior, and the results (value in years and dollars) reactions.

> H2: The Opportunity to Communicate with the Local Instructor will be rated more highly than the Opportunity to Communicate with the Global Instructor.

Peer group interactions

When individuals work together in teams, the members of the team share ideas, opinions, judgements, and experiences. Through this form of information sharing, a process that facilitates the building of a common understanding is evoked (i.e., team members learn from each other; Daft and Lengel, 1986).

In the context of this course, team members may enhance learning by examining the similarities and differences of their HRM experiences and perspectives. Local team members can provide local HRM insights and HRM examples; virtual-global team members can provide insight and examples from their country of origin (Alavi *et al.*, 1997; Knoll and Jarvenpaa, 1995). To the degree that participants work cooperatively together, local and virtual-global team learning experiences will be perceived as more effective.

The communication barriers discussed in the previous section are also relevant for local and virtual-global team cooperation. The local teams have the opportunity to meet, discuss, and resolve issues face to face with culturally homogeneous members; thus barriers to communication are at a minimum. However, the virtual-global teams must cooperate via non face-to-face mechanisms (e.g., chat rooms, emails, and faxes) with members from a variety of cultural backgrounds. Given the use of technology as the communication medium and the greater likelihood that barriers to communication will arise (i.e., the high heterogeneity of these groups across several dimensions such as languages, cultures, etc. will result in greater communication difficulties), cooperation is likely to be impeded. These and the above considerations lead to the following hypotheses:

> H3: The cooperation of the virtual-global team/local team will be positively related to perceived effectiveness reactions. More specifically, the better the cooperation among virtual-global team members, the more positive the perceived virtual-global team learning. The better the cooperation among local team members, the more positive the perceived local team learning.

> H4: The cooperation of the local team will be rated more highly than the cooperation of the virtual-global team.

Overall environmental perceptions

The social influence model of technology suggests that attitudes of others toward technology affect one's own attitudes (Fulk *et al.*, 1990). In the classroom context, this suggests that the perceived attitudes of instructors and classmates toward the usefulness of technology in the classroom will affect the attitudes of participants (ibid.). Previous research supports this assertion (Webster and Hackley, 1997). Thus, if instructors and classmates are perceived to evaluate technology as useful for learning purposes, similar attitudes will exist among the participants. Although we suggest that this relationship will be strongest for the general affective reaction, we hypothesize that these perceptions will also relate to other effectiveness reactions. Specifically, we hypothesize:

> H5: Perceived instructors'/participants' perceptions of MDL will be related to perceived effectiveness reactions. More specifically the more positive the perceived instructors' attitudes, the more positive the general affective, the learning, the behavior, and the results (years of value and dollars) reactions; the more positive the perceived participants' attitudes, the more positive the general affective, the learning, the behavior, virtual-global and local team learning, and the results (years of value and dollars) reactions.

Little research has been conducted on connectedness perceptions of participants (Cavanaugh *et al.*, 2000). We define connectedness perceptions as the psychological distance that participants perceive between the environment they are currently in (e.g., traditionally a remote site) and the environment in which the instructor is present (e.g., traditionally the origination site). As previously noted, adult learning theory proposes that adult learners prefer active learning experiences. One might expect that if participants view themselves as connected to one learning environment, they may view themselves as a more active participant in that learning environment and thus, evaluate the learning experience more positively. We hypothesize:

> H6: Connectedness perceptions will be related to perceived effectiveness reactions, such that the greater the perceived connectedness the more positive the general affective, the learning, the behavior, virtual-global team learning, and the results (years of value and dollars) reactions.

The pattern of expected significant relationships between the components of the learning environment and the effectiveness reactions is provided in Table 12.1. The literature does not provide us with information regarding which of the MDL learning environment components are most highly related (explain the most amount of variance) in each of our effectiveness reaction measures. Given that this information will facilitate the development of specific recommendations for the design of MDL courses, we examine these relationships purely in an exploratory manner. (Currently the literature suggests that utility reactions are related to learning and behavior more highly than affective reactions are related to learning and behavior. No research has been conducted on learning and behavior reactions.)

> Research Question: Which of the learning environment components explain the most amount of variance in each of the effectiveness reaction measures?

Methods

Participants and procedure

The participants were from different cultural backgrounds, with differing English proficiency, and ages (Table 12.2). In addition, the 'percentage who are from the location country' indicates that the US sample was the most culturally diverse as only 59 per cent of the participants were originally from the United States. Further examination indicates that of the participants in the US location, ten participants were originally from the USA, one participant each was from China, the Czech Republic, and Taiwan, and two participants each were from Argentina and India.

The participant groups did not differ on those items for which the course was designed to instruct them: prior experiences with MDL technology courses ('Number of classes taken using MDL') and prior experience with the course material ('I understand how HR systems differ around the world'). Moreover, the

Table 12.1 Hypothesized and actual relationships

	General affective reaction	General learning reaction	Behavior reaction	Virtual-global team learning reaction	Local team learning reaction	Results reaction (value in years)	Results reaction (value in $s)
Opportunity to Communicate with Global Instructor	+ (+)	+ (+)	+ (0)	0 (+)	0 (0)	+ (0)	+ (0)
Opportunity to Communicate with Local Instructor	+ (+)	+ (+)	+ (0)	0 (0)	0 (0)	+ (0)	+ (+)
Cooperation of Virtual global team	0 (0)	0 (0)	0 (0)	+ (+)	0 (0)	0 (0)	0 (0)
Cooperation of Local team	0 (0)	0 (+)	0 (0)	0 (0)	+ (+)	0 (0)	0 (0)
Instructor Perceptions of MDL	+ (+)	+ (+)	+ (+)	+ (+)	0 (+)	+ (0)	+ (+)
Classmates Perceptions of MDL	+ (+)	+ (+)	+ (0)	+ (+)	+ (+)	+ (0)	+ (+)
Connectedness Perception	+ (+)	+ (+)	+ (0)	+ (+)	0 (0)	+ (0)	+ (0)

Notes: + indicates that a significant positive relationship was predicted; 0 indicates that a relationship was not predicted; actual significant relationships, according to correlation coefficients (up to .1 level of significance), are provided in parentheses.

Table 12.2 Means by country, overall means and standard deviations, and differences by country for participant characteristics

	Overall mean	Standard deviation	Country means				F
			USA	Venezuela	Slovenia	China	
Number of classes previously taken that used Distance learning technology[f]	0.89	2.87	0.29	2.53	0.17	0.39	2.74*
Number of classes previously taken that used multimedia based distance learning technology[f]	0.50	1.63	0.06	0.94	0.17	0.72	1.11
Computer expertise (1 = do not use; 5 = expert)[f]	3.41	0.77	3.71	3.06	3.42	3.47	3.32*
I understand how HR systems differ around the world (1 = strongly disagree; 7 = agree)	5.33	1.22	5.24	5.41	5.17	5.47	0.20
Percentage who have worked in a multicultural team prior to this class	46.03%	0.50	64.71%a	64.71%b	41.67%	11.76%a,b	5.06**
For those who have worked in a multicultural team – number of years worked in multicultural teams	2.02	4.08	4.06a	3.00	0.40	0.18a	3.89**
Percentage who have lived in a country other than his/her home country	49.21%	0.50	52.94%a,b	94.12%a,c,d	50.00%c,e	0.00%b,d,e	18.21**
For those who have lived in a different country – number of years lived in a different country	1.86	3.32	2.26	4.50a,b	0.20a	0.00b	8.88**
Percentage who are originally from the 'location' country	na	na	58.82%	94.12%	100%	94.12%	na
Years of experience in business	6.60	8.72	7.09a	13.76a,b,c	0.67b	1.80c	10.07**
Percentage students	64.06%	.48	76.47%a	0%abc	100%b	88.89%c	40.93**
Percentage male[f]	54.69%	0.50	47.06%	41.18%	91.67%	50.00%	3.04*
Age	28.87	8.57	29.27a,b	38.19b,c,d	24.67c	23.06a,d	19.15**
English proficiency (1 = not at all proficient; 7 = very proficient)[f]	6.14	0.86	6.61a	6.41b	5.83	5.63a,b	6.10**

Notes: a-e Similar lettered means are significantly different from each other according to Tukey honest significant difference (HSD) for unequal N:
f None of the individuals means were significant at ≤.05 according to Tukey HSD for unequal N.
na = not applicable
t $p < .1$; * $p < .05$; ** $p < .01$

mean values indicate that on average the participants had previously taken less than one course that used MDL technology and they were only slightly sure that they understood how HR systems differ around the world.

Measures

Effectiveness reactions

General Effectiveness Reaction was measured with three items; one item was adapted from Webster and Hackley (1997) (sample item: 'I would like to take other MDL courses in the future'; 1 = strongly disagree to 7 = strongly agree; alpha = .84). *Behavior Reaction* was measured with four items; one item was adapted from Webster and Hackley (1997) (sample item: 'I believe that I will be able to use the WHRM course content in the future'; 1 = strongly disagree to 7 = strongly agree; alpha = .73). *General Learning Reaction* was measured with one item ('I learned more in this course than I do in traditional courses due to the use of MDL technology'; 1 = strongly disagree to 7 = strongly agree). *Team Learning Reaction (Virtual-Global and Local)* was measured with two items for each adapted from Alavi (1994) (sample item: 'The virtual group contributed to learning'; correlations: virtual = .71**; local = .54**). *Results Reactions (Value in Years and Utility in US $)* was measured with one item each ('What I have learned in the course will have ___ years effect on my future performance'; 'The dollar value that I will be able to create for my organization after taking this course is estimated to be around ___').

To determine the dimensionality of the reaction effectiveness measures we conducted an exploratory factor analysis. Results are provided in Table 12.3. These results suggest that five factors emerged that explained 79.99 per cent of the variance. As a result of cross-loading, two items were dropped from the analyses: Behavior Reaction 1 and 2. The correlation between the remaining Behavior Reaction items (3 and 4) was .84 ($p < .01$). We decided to keep the General Affective Reaction items and the General Learning Reaction item as separate constructs. All other items were combined into mean constructs with the number of items and alpha reliabilities/correlations as noted above (e.g., Virtual-Global Team Learning items were combined to form the construct Virtual-Global Team Learning Reaction, etc.).

Learning environment

Opportunity to Communicate with Global/Local Instructor was measured with one item for each ('I had sufficient opportunity to communicate with the global (local) session instructor.'). *Cooperation of Virtual-Global/Local Team* was measured with one item for each ('My virtual-global (local) team was cooperative.').

Instructors'/Classmates' Perceptions of MDL was measured with two items for each adapted from Webster and Hackley (1997) (sample item, 'Compared to traditional classroom learning, how useful do you think your global session instructor considers MDL?' correlations: instructors = .62**; participants = .48**).

Table 12.3 Results of exploratory factor analysis[a]

Reaction items	General affective/Learning reaction factor	Virtual-Global Team learning reaction factor	Behavior reaction ractor	Local team learning reaction factor	Results reaction factor
			Factor loadings		
General Reaction 1: I would like to take other multimedia based distance learning courses in the future.	0.87				
General Reaction 2: I would recommend this type of course to someone else.	0.84				
General Reaction 3: Multimedia based distance learning is ___ effective than traditional classroom learning.	0.81				
Behavior Reaction 1: This course allowed me to make valuable connections that will benefit me in my future.		0.63	0.34		0.57
Behavior Reaction 2: This course will allow me to perform better in the future.	0.56		0.45		0.48
Behavior Reaction 3: I believe that I will be able to use the technology (internet, videoconference, etc.) in the future.			0.84		
Behavior Reaction 4: I believe that I will be able to use the course content (WHRM) in the future.			0.87		
Learning Reaction 1: I learned more in this course than I do in traditional classes due to the use of multimedia based technology.	0.73			0.40	
Virtual-Global Team Learning Reaction 1: The virtual group work contributed to course quality.		0.89			
Virtual-Global Team Learning Reaction 2: The virtual group work contributed to learning.		0.87			
Local Team Learning Reaction 1: The local group work contributed to course quality.				0.85	
Local Team Learning Reaction 2: The local group work contributed to learning.				0.86	
Results Reaction 1: I think that what I have learned in this course will have about ___ years effect on my future performance.					0.86
Results Reaction 2: The dollar value that I will be able to create for my organization (a future organization I will work for) after taking this course is estimated to be around ___.					0.56

Note: [a] Factor loadings .30 and higher are included in the table; factor loadings lower than .30 were omitted.

Connectedness Perception was measured with two items ('I felt personally involved in the seminar during the global sessions' and 'It felt as though the other participants were all in the same classroom during the global sessions;' correlation = .39**).

Location Control: previous research indicates the need to control for the site of origin (Webster and Hackley, 1997). Given our unique sample, and the significant differences across samples we chose to control for location. The omitted location was Venezuela.

Analyses

We first examined whether significant country differences existed for the variables of interest in this study. To examine whether differences exist, analysis of variance (ANOVA) techniques were used. We first examined whether location explained a significant amount of variance in the study variables through the use of One-Way ANOVAS. Finally, we conducted Tukey honest significant difference (HSD) tests to determine the nature of any differences by location.

To formally test the study hypotheses we conducted correlational analyses, t-tests (differences between means), and ordinary least squares (OLS) regression analyses. Correlational analyses were used to test Hypotheses 1, 3, 5–6. T-tests were used to test Hypotheses 2 and 4. OLS regression analyses were used to examine the Research Question.

Results

Descriptive statistics including means, standard deviations, and country differences are reported in Table 12.4. It was not unexpected that the US participants would rate the Opportunity to Communicate with the Global Instructor significantly higher than two of the other groups as the global instructor was present only at the US location (the origination site). The other results for which there were statistically significant differences across different locations indicated that the Slovenia group was typically the group that was different from the other three groups. That is, the Slovenia group rated Classmates' Perceptions of MDL as significantly lower than participants at other locations; their General Affective Reaction was significantly lower than that of the participants from China; and Local Team Learning Reaction was significantly lower than that of the participants from the US.

Correlations between MDL learning environment and learning outcomes

Hypothesis 1 stated that the greater the opportunity to communicate with the global/local instructor, the more positive the general affective, the general learning, the behavior, and the results (value in years and dollars) reactions. Congruent with Hypothesis 1, Opportunity to Communicate with the Global Instructor was significantly positively related to General Affective Reaction ($r = .33$; $p < .05$) and General Learning Reaction ($r = .36$; $p < .05$); Opportunity to Ccommunicate with

Table 12.4 Means by country, overall means and standard deviations, and differences by country for the study variables of interest

				Country means			
	Overall mean	Standard deviation	USA	Venezuela	Slovenia	China	F
Opportunity to Communicate with Global Instructor	4.12	1.86	5.56[a,b]	3.33[a]	4.00	3.13[b]	6.94**
Opportunity to Communicate with Local Instructor[f]	5.40	1.50	6.19	4.67	4.83	5.47	3.12*
Cooperation of Virtual-Global Team	4.06	1.63	3.63	4.56	4.08	4.20	0.69
Cooperation of Local Team[f]	6.00	1.03	6.44	6.33	5.75	5.53	2.81*
Connectedness Perception[f]	4.63	1.12	4.19	5.33	4.17	5.07	4.08**
Instructor Perceptions of MDL[f]	5.19	1.16	5.88	5.22	4.25	5.20	5.69**
Classmates Perceptions of MDL	4.94	1.10	5.30[a]	5.44[b]	3.92[a,b,c]	5.13[c]	6.26**
General Affective Reaction	5.15	1.04	5.27	5.33	4.42[a]	5.51[a]	3.08**
General Learning Reaction	4.42	1.26	4.63	4.44	3.92	4.60	0.88
Behavior Reaction	6.21	0.69	6.31	6.44	5.88	6.23	1.40
Virtual-Global Team Learning Reaction	4.68	1.18	4.71	5.22	4.00	4.83	2.05
Local Team Learning Reaction	5.85	0.81	6.40[a]	5.89	5.17[a]	5.83	6.92**
Results Reaction (Value in Years)	3.37	2.32	3.57	2.17	3.13	4.10	1.41
Results Reaction (Value in $s)	3.26	1.81	4.15	2.63	2.64	3.27	1.93

Notes: [a–c] Similar lettered means are significantly different from each other according to Tukey honest significant difference (HSD) for unequal N.
[f] None of the individuals means were significant at ≤ .05 according to Tukey HSD for unequal N.
t p < .1; * p < .05; ** p < .01

the Local Instructor was significantly positively related to General Affective Reaction ($r = .53$; $p < .01$), Results Reaction of Value in U.S. Dollars ($r = .35$; $p < .05$), and marginally significantly positively related to General Learning Reaction ($r = .26$; $p < .10$).

Contrary to the hypothesis, Opportunity to Communicate with the Global Instructor was not significantly related to Behavior or Results Reactions; Opportunity to Communicate with the Local Instructor was not significantly related to Behavior or Results Reaction of Value in Years.

According to Hypothesis 3, the better the cooperation among virtual-global team members, the more positive the perceived virtual-global team learning; the better the cooperation among local team members, the more positive the perceived local team learning. Congruent with the hypothesis, Cooperation of the Virtual-Global Team was significantly positively related to Virtual-Global Team Learning Reaction ($r = .52$; $p < .01$); Cooperation of the Local Team was significantly positively related to Local Team Learning Reaction ($r = .34$; $p < .05$). In addition, Cooperation of the Local Team was significantly positively related to General Learning Reaction ($r = .32$; $p < .05$).

In partial support of Hypothesis 5 (the more positive the perceived instructors' attitudes, the more positive the general affective, the learning, the behavior, and the results (years of value and dollars) reactions; the more positive the perceived participants' attitudes the more positive the general affective, the learning, the behavior, virtual and local team learning, and the results (years of value and dollars) reactions), Instructors' Perceptions of MDL were significantly positively related to General Affective Reaction ($r = .47$: $p < .01$), General Learning Reaction ($r = .45$; $p < .01$), and marginally significantly positively related to Behavior Reaction ($r = .25$; $p < .10$) and Result Reaction in Dollar Value ($r = .29$; $p < .10$). Also in support of the hypothesis, Participants' Perceptions of MDL was significantly positively related to General Affective Reaction ($r = .53$: $p < .01$), General Learning Reaction ($r = .42$; $p < .01$), Behavior Reaction ($r = .35$; $p < .05$), Virtual-Global Team Learning Reaction ($r = .36$; $p < .05$), Local Team Learning Reaction ($r = .45$; $p < .05$), and marginally related to Result Reaction in Dollar Value ($r = .25$; $p < .10$).

Contrary to Hypothesis 5, Instructors' and Participants' Perceptions of MDL were not related to Value in Years. Although not predicted, Instructors' Perceptions of MDL were significantly positively related to Local Team Learning Reaction.

Congruent with Hypothesis 6, Connectedness Perception was significantly positively related to General Affective Reaction ($r = .50$; $p < .01$), General Learning Reactions ($r = .44$; $p < .01$), and Virtual-Global Team Learning Reaction ($r = .39$; $p < .01$). Contrary to the hypothesis, Connectedness Perception was not significantly related to Behavior Reactions or Results (Value in Years and Value in Dollars). See Table 12.5 for details of correlation coefficients among all study variables.

Table 12.5 Correlation coefficients among all study variables

	1	2	3	4	5	6	7	8	9	10	11	12	13	14	15	16	17	18
1 Opportunity to Communicate with Global Instructor	—																	
2 Opportunity to Communicate with Local Instructor	39**	—																
3 Cooperation of Virtual-Global Team	25t	19	—															
4 Cooperation of Local Team	18	22	34*	—														
5 Connectedness Perception	10	05	34*	16	—													
6 Instructor Perceptions of MDL	29t	24	12	24	10	—												
7 Classmates Perceptions of MDL	13	16	23	31*	26t	56**	—											
8 General Affective Reaction	33*	53**	22	14	50**	47**	53**	—										
9 General Learning Reaction	36*	26t	12	32*	44**	45**	42**	67**	—									
10 Behavior Reaction	-11	19	-12	22	19	25t	35*	40**	19	—								
11 Virtual-Global Team Learning Reaction	25t	22	52**	13	39**	20	36*	28t	11	21	—							
12 Local Team Learning Reaction	04	18	01	34*	22	50**	45**	33*	44**	37*	30*	—						
13 Results Reaction (Value in Years)	00	-05	03	04	12	05	06	25t	32*	-01	-26t	03	—					
14 Results Reaction (Value in $s)	08	35*	00	21	08	29t	25t	36*	29	27t	02	25t	37**	—				
15 United States	45**	31*	-19	30*	-35*	34*	21	10	16	16	04	46**	04	27t	—			
16 Slovenia	-07	-17	01	-12	-24	-62**	-58**	-52**	-38**	-36*	-34*	-54**	-04	-15	-33*	—		
17 China	-28t	00	07	-31*	32*	10	18	31*	17	05	14	02	20	06	-42**	-40	—	
18 Venezuela	-09	-17	12	17	28t	18	19	08	03	15	16	05	-25t	-21	-27t	-25t	-32*	—

Note: t $p < .1$; * $p < .05$; ** $p < .01$

T-test results

In support of Hypothesis 2, Opportunity to Communicate with the Local Instructor was rated significantly higher than Opportunity to Communicate with the Global Instructor (t(51) = 4.91, p < .01).

In support of Hypothesis 4, Local Team Cooperation was rated significantly higher than Virtual-Global Team Cooperation (t(51) = 8.37, p < .01).

Regression results

As noted in the Research Question, it is unclear which of the learning environment components would explain the most variance in each of the effectiveness measures. To answer this question, we conducted a series of regression analyses. Table 12.6 presents the results of these regression analyses. The results reveal that Opportunity to Communicate with the Local Instructor, Classmates' Perceptions of MDL and Connectedness Perception explained the most variance in General Affective Reaction; Connectedness Perception explained the most variance in General Learning Reaction; and Cooperation of the Virtual-Global Team explained the most variance in Virtual-Global Team Learning Reaction. The remaining regression analyses are more difficult to interpret owing to the lack of statistically significant findings (Behavior Reaction, the Result Reactions) or potential suppressor effects (Local Team Learning Reaction).

Discussion

The purpose of this study was to examine the MDL learning environment components that relate to the effectiveness of an MDL-delivered global HRM course. Generally, we hypothesized that the factors that relate to the effectiveness of an MDL-delivered course that combines global and local environments include (1) instructor–participant communication; (2) participant–participant group cooperation; (3) others' perceptions of MDL technology; and (4) connectedness perceptions. The results suggest that several of the hypotheses were supported or partially supported.

The opportunity to communicate with the global instructor was significantly or marginally significantly positively related to general affective reaction, general learning reaction, and virtual-global team learning reaction; the opportunity to communicate with the local instructor was significantly or marginally significantly positively related to general affective reaction, general learning reaction, and results reaction (value in dollars). Table 12.5 also indicates that the opportunity to communicate with the global/local instructor was positively related to the USA (site of origin). These findings suggest differences in the opportunity to communicate with instructors, in general, for participants at the site of origin vs. those at remote sites. While it is expected that the participants at the site of origin would have greater opportunities to communicate with the global instructor (the global instructor was physically present at this site), it is unclear why differences exist between the site of

Table 12.6 OLS regression of the reactions on the learning environment and location dummy variables

	General affective reaction	General learning reaction	Behavior reaction	Virtual-global team learning reaction	Local team learning reaction	Results reaction (value in years)	Results reaction (value in $s)
Opportunity to Communicate with Global Instructor	.24	.29	-.26	.04	-.42**	-.04	-.33
Opportunity to Communicate with Local Instructor	.34**	-.05	.30t	.14	.00	-.21	.29t
Cooperation of Virtual-Global Team	-.09	-.21	-.28t	.50**	.01	-.04	.02
Cooperation of Local Team	-.06	.19	.19	-.17	.08	.10	-.05
Instructor Perceptions of MDL	.05	.20	.07	-.19	.35*	.18	.12
Classmates' Perceptions of MDL	.35*	.19	.30t	.16	.03	.00	.11
Connectedness Perception	.31*	.35*	.16	.16	.35*	.25	.24
United States	-.19	.03	-.07	.00	.64**	.53t	.61*
Slovenia	-.09	.14	-.04	-.33	.02	.44t	.33
China	.07	.23	-.08	-.10	.07	.50*	.21
R^2	.58**	.39*	.34t	.46**	.55**	.17	.28
F	5.44	2.47	1.96	3.08	4.44	.77	1.32

Note: Standardized Beta are shown; t $p < .1$; * $p < .05$; ** $p < .01$

origin and remote sites with respect to local instructor communication. Additional research is needed to understand the instructor–participant communication barriers in both the global (non-origin) and local (non-origin) learning environments.

The results of the t-test suggest that the opportunity to communicate with the local instructor was rated significantly higher than the opportunity to communicate with the global instructor. Given the relationship between communication and effectiveness, this finding suggests that additional research needs to be conducted to help us understand how the barriers to distance communication can be eliminated. We caution that distance learning classes without local classroom interaction may be more seriously impacted by global instructor–participant communication barriers (i.e., there is no local instructor to compensate for the communication loss).

Cooperation of the virtual-global team was significantly positively related to virtual-global team learning reaction; cooperation of the local team was significantly positively related to local team learning reaction in addition to general learning reaction. The USA was significantly positively related to cooperation of the local team and China was significantly negatively related to cooperation of the local team. These findings suggest clear differences in the perceived cooperation of team members across countries. One explanation for this finding may be that US participants had more experience working in teams. Moreover, it is likely that several of the US participants had previously worked together in team projects for other courses. The participants' team-based familiarity may have enabled the group to work more cooperatively. Future research will need to address virtual/local team issues and the role of team-member familiarity.

The results of the t-test suggest that, in general, the local teams were rated as more cooperative. Additional research needs to be conducted to examine whether these differences resulted from technology and/or cultural barriers.

Instructors' perceptions of MDL were significantly or marginally positively related to general affective reaction, general learning reaction, behavior reaction, local team learning reaction, and results reaction (value in dollars). Classmates' perceptions of MDL were significantly or marginally positively related to general affective reaction, general learning reaction, behavior reaction, virtual and local team learning reaction, and results reaction (value in dollars). The USA was significantly positively related to instructors' perceptions of MDL and Slovenia was significantly negatively related to instructors' and classmates' perceptions of MDL. Once again, these results suggest that differences existed across sites and these differences are important to explore.

Connectedness perceptions were significantly positively related to general affective reaction, general learning reaction, and virtual-global team learning reaction. The USA was significantly negatively related to connectedness perceptions; China and Venezuela were significantly or marginally positively related to connectedness perceptions. These findings suggest that connectedness perception is important. The negative finding for the USA and positive for remote sites may indicate a fishbowl effect for the US participants. It may have seemed to the US team that the camera was 'on' them a disproportionate amount of the time given that the global instructor presented from that site. This may have created a fishbowl effect that led to the reduction of connectedness from the other sites. Future research will need to examine these issues.

Overall, the regression equation suggests that connectedness perception was the learning environment factor of primary significance, holding all other factors constant. Future research should further explore this construct.

The general lack of significance for the results reactions suggests that (a) perceptions of the learning environment are not related to results reactions, or (b) results reactions were not adequately measured. We suggest that the lack of significance is due to a combination of both. It is likely that components of the learning environment are less related to utility reactions (perceptions of future *on-the job* usefulness) as they provide perceptions that are further removed from the learning environment than the other forms of reactions (perceptions of general learning and use). In addition, we recognize that efforts to develop construct valid MDL utility reaction measures are needed.

Limitations

There are several limitations to be noted. First, only selected components of the MDL learning environment were investigated. It is very possible that other components of the environment that were not measured in this study may also be of importance. For example, significant efforts were not made to ensure that the local classroom activities/interactions were completely consistent across all sites. Controlling for location in the analyses alleviated any statistical problems as a result of these differences, but potentially masked additional understanding of the location specific issues. Future research in this area needs to provide a balanced investigation of the activities/interactions within both global and local environments.

The use of a selected sample is a second limitation. All participants volunteered to participate in the global human resource management course. Thus, our sample may include individuals with more positive attitudes toward MDL courses or toward working with individuals from around the world. However, if this is the case, we would be less likely to find the effects we found (range restriction).

A third limitation is the use of single and two indicator items for several of the variables for which there is currently unknown validity and reliability (e.g., Connectedness Perceptions, Communication/Cooperation, Value in Years, and Utility in US $). Future research should focus on the development and refinement of the constructs that are specific to MDL learning environments.

In summary, this study has helped us to understand the design factors that are important in an MDL-delivered course: the opportunity to communicate with the global and local instructors, the cooperation of the virtual and local teams, positive MDL perceptions of instructors and classmates, and most importantly, a sense of connectedness. Practically, these findings suggest that planned classroom activities and instructor teaching styles that facilitate the interaction among and between participants and instructors should be part of any MDL course design. However, this is only a beginning. It is our hope that researchers continue to investigate the questions that this research evoked, so that we might gain a richer understanding of the factors that relate to effective MDL training programs.

Note

1   We distinguish behavior reactions from utility reactions in that behavior reactions focus on the perception of the *use* of what was learned; utility reactions focus on the perception of the *usefulness* of what was learned.

References

Alavi, M. (1994) 'Computer-mediated Collaborative Learning: An Empirical Evaluation', *MIS Quarterly* 18, 159–74.

Alavi, M., Yoo, Y. and Vogel, D.R. (1997) 'Using Information Technology to Add Value to Management Education', *Academy of Management Journal* 40, 1310–33.

Alliger, G.M., Tannenbaum, S.I., Bennett, Jr. W., Traver, H. and Shotland, A. (1997) 'A Meta-analysis of the Relations among Training Criteria', *Personnel Psychology* 50, 341–58.

Armstrong-Stassen, M., Landstrom, M. and Lumpkin, R. (1998) 'Students' Reactions to the Introduction of Videoconferencing for Classroom Instruction', *The Information Society* 14, 153–64.

Bassi, L.J. and Van Buren, M.E. (1999) '1999 ASTD State of the Industry Report', *Training and Development* 17–18.

Cavanaugh, M.A., Milkovich, G.T. and Tang, J. (2000) 'The Effective Use of Multimedia Distance Learning Technology: The Role of Technology Self-Efficacy, Attitudes, Reliability, Use and Distance in a Global Multimedia Distance Learning Classroom', in *A New Time for Distance Learning: New Media, New Students, New Content*, symposium conducted at the Academy of Management Conference, Toronto, Canada, August.

Daft, R.L. and Lengel, R.J. (1986) Organizational Information Requirements, Media Richness and Structural Design, *Management Science* 32, 554–71.

Fulk, J., Schmitz, J. and Steinfield, C.W. (1990) 'A Social Influence Model of Technology Use', in J. Fulk and C. Steinfield (eds) *Organizations and Communication Technology*, Newbury Park, CA: Sage, pp. 117–41.

Frost, P.J. and Fukami, C.V. (1997) 'Teaching Effectiveness in the Organizational Sciences: Recognizing and Enhancing the Scholarship of Teaching', *Academy of Management Journal* 40, 1271–81.

Kirkpatrick, D.L. (1959a) 'Techniques for Evaluating Training Programs', *Journal of ASTD* 13, 3–9.

Kirkpatrick, D.L. (1959b) 'Techniques for Evaluating Training Programs: Part 2 – Learning, *Journal of ASTD*, 13, 21–6.

Kirkpatrick, D.L. (1960a) 'Techniques for evaluating training programs: Part 3 – behavior', *Journal of ASTD* 14, 13–18.

Kirkpatrick, D.L. (1960b) 'Techniques for evaluating training programs: Part 4 – results', *Journal of ASTD* 14, 28–32.

Knoll, K. and Jarvenpaa, S. (1995) 'Learning to Work in Distributed Global Teams', in J.F. Nunamaker, Jr. and R.H. Sprague, Jr. (eds) *Proceedings of the Twenty-eighth Annual Hawaii International Conference on System Sciences*, vol. 4. Los Alamitos, CA: IEEE Computer Society Press, pps. 92–101.

Knowles, M. (1984) *The Adult Learner: A Neglected Species*, Houston, TX: Gulf Publishing Company.

Lauzon, A.C. (1992) 'Integrating Computer-based Instruction with Computer Conferencing: An Evaluation of a Model for Designing Online Education', *The American Journal of Distance Education* 6, 32–44.

Rand, A. (1996) 'Technology Transforms Training', *HR Focus*, 73, 11–13.

Stanton, J.M. (1998) 'An Empirical Assessment of Data Collection Using the Internet', *Personnel Psychology*, 51, 709–25.

Webster, J. and Hackley, P. (1997) 'Teaching Effectiveness in Technology-mediated Distance Learning', *Academy of Management Journal*, 40, 1282–309.

13 Responses to globalized production

Restructuring and work reorganization in the clothing industry of high-wage countries

Ian M. Taplin and Jonathan Winterton

Introduction

In a period of increased global competition, dramatic changes in consumer demands, and a reconfiguration of production technologies made possible by micro-processor innovations, firms face heightened market uncertainty and flexibility pressures. This has forced many firms to re-examine their market position and assess the optimal use of their resources in a market place that is increasingly characterized by consumer pull rather than manufacturer push. In the search for sustained competitive advantage, firms are experimenting with new organizational forms that will allow them to outperform the market (Porter, 1993), focusing more closely on their core competencies (Hamal and Prahalad, 1990), and endeavouring to position themselves in markets that permit full utilization of their resources.

In this chapter we assess the outcomes of such changes for the organization of work and employment conditions in the clothing industry of high-wage economies. Clothing manufacture is a major industry in terms of output and employment in many of the OECD countries. In most cases the industry structure is highly competitive and is undergoing restructuring as firms seek ways of responding to heightened global competition. Since much of the clothing production process remains inescapably labour intensive, it has been easily adopted by low wage newly industrialized countries (NICs) who see clothing and textile production as part of export-led national economic growth strategies. Dramatic import penetration of Western markets by such low-cost producers since the 1970s has increased the competitive pressures on higher wage manufacturers in Western societies.

In the face of such pressure and eroding market share, many firms in high wage economies have restructured their production, modifying their traditional focus on low-cost production strategies. And yet the responses to this heightened uncertainty vary considerably. Some firms (and sectors) in some countries have attempted to become niche players, with an emphasis upon high value-added production which can more easily absorb their high wage costs. Others have attempted to improve their links with buyers and find stability in improved value chain networks. Still others have resorted to work intensification as a way to realize productivity gains without sacrificing their low-cost production status. Clearly, each of these strategies has profound repercussions for workers since it can involve a significant reorganization of work and possible changes in skill levels of workers.

This chapter begins with an examination of the pressures that firms in high wage economies face following increased globalized production. We then outline the various responses, and the patterns that emerge, to such changes. We look at country as well as sector differences, relating such differences to both institutional factors as well as market activities. Finally, we assess the implications of such changes for workers, both in broad labour market terms as well as for wages and general employment conditions.

Why clothing?

Clothing manufacture is an important industry throughout the world in terms of the wealth created by garment production and the number of individuals who depend upon the industry for their livelihoods. In general, clothing enterprises, even in the most developed industrialized countries, are small in comparison with other branches of manufacturing, and are very labour intensive. The level of technical innovation potential is limited by the difficulty of automating fabric handling (Hoffman and Rush, 1987). New entrants are attracted to the industry by the low barriers to entry. The workforce has been predominantly female, trade union organization is weak and managerial practices tend to be very traditional.

These characteristics are shared by all clothing industries, but a distinction can also be made between the clothing industries of the high-wage economies and those of the low-wage economies. In the increasingly global economy, clothing manufacturers in the high-wage countries have been facing intensified competition from enterprises in the low-wage economies (Taplin and Winterton, 1997). The low barriers to entry which are characteristic of the industry also operate at the level of nations, so entrepreneurs in newly-industrialized countries are attracted to garment production. Clothing manufacture in the high-wage economies is often regarded as a 'sunset industry', undergoing rapid restructuring in an effort to adjust, with clothing enterprises closing down or at least downsizing, and leaving garment production to the newly industrialized low-wage countries as part of an international division of labour (Dicken, 1992).

To a considerable extent this 'sunset industry' image is accurate, but it fails to capture the complexity of either the changes which are occurring in the global clothing marketplace, or of the restructuring processes taking place within the clothing industries in high-wage economies. For while there are considerable pressures on high-wage manufacturers to shift production overseas, changing market demand conditions provide opportunities for high value-added and time-sensitive production to be performed close to the final market for products. As a consequence many firms in high wage economies are looking for ways to change their competitive strategies and move 'up-market' or retain high value-added activities domestically while relocating low value-added production overseas.

Restructuring and institutional pressures to change

The restructuring undergone by clothing manufacturers in recent decades can be seen against a backdrop of broader changes within manufacturing industries as they faced heightened competition from the 1970s onwards. Particular concern focused upon labour market rigidities. Limited flexibility, heightened variable costs and impediments to technological innovation were all associated with labour market structures that were products of the old oligopolistic systems. Given such concerns, not surprisingly labour market restructuring to increase flexibility became a focal point for public policy. It was reaffirmed in the United States and became a key policy objective of UK governments after 1979.[1] Although particularly associated with the USA and the UK, the influence of labour market deregulation has been global, albeit somewhat less extensive in countries such as Germany and France. In Italy, a large informal sector is well established and provides flexibility as long as firms remain small (fewer than 15–25 workers).

Clearly, the globalization of economic activity has revealed the vulnerability of labour-intensive mass production industries to imports from low-wage economies, since Taylorist production is easily replicated in newly industrialized countries (Dicken, 1992). As a consequence, many firms have attempted to exploit market fragmentation as a way of creating advantages that differentiate them from other firms (Porter, 1993; Oster, 1994). In some cases this has involved more flexible forms of organization, as firms restructure around the production of high-quality, low-volume products for niche markets. The increased responsiveness to market changes is also made possible with flexible microelectronics-based innovations (see, for example, Womack *et al.*, 1990), although the production paradigm is independent of any particular technology.

It has been argued that the new segmented markets have encouraged the growth of small manufacturing enterprises, centred on much smaller specialized production units than their mass production forerunners (Piore and Sabel, 1984). In contrast with the mass production paradigm, in such firms the skills and energies of all workers contribute to the efficient and flexible use of resources. The need for adaptability requires more skilled workers who enjoy more discretion over re-integrated tasks and autonomy in using general-purpose machine tools. However, the empirical evidence to support such a generalized assertion is mixed.[2] In the case of clothing, a rather mixed organizational pattern has emerged, with variations often dependent upon institutional settings rather than as a response to market imperatives. New technology has not always led to the need for more highly skilled workers, and many small firms rely upon work intensification to achieve requisite levels of flexibility and increased productivity.

Globalization and restructuring

Restructuring, as indicated above, refers to firm responses to broad changes in the regulation of economic and institutional activity as well as a reaction to specific threats posed by increased competition. Faced by an often confusing array of opportunities for change, firms typically chart a course which combines innovation and modification of traditional practices as they search for a new 'best practice' strategy. In an era of increased uncertainty, firms appear more constrained and forced to seek optimal organizational design through new input combinations (Streeck, 1987). In other words, critical contingencies are forcing change, but the logic for the new configurations is less clear.

For the clothing industry, fundamental changes in the internationalization of production began in the mid-1960s with the emergence of low-cost products from Asia. These changes produced restructuring responses in high wage economies as firms there struggled to adjust to the new competitive pressures.

The Asian challenge

The growth of clothing manufacturing in Asia (Hong Kong, South Korea, Taiwan, Singapore and China) by the mid-1960s constitutes the first significant production shift. As part of export-led industrialization strategies in these countries, clothing was one of several labour-intensive industries that capitalized upon plentiful supplies of low cost, high quality and well motivated labour. Because domestic markets were small in these developing countries, their strategy focused upon production for export to industrialized countries (Dicken, 1992).

Such a strategy proved remarkably successful and they were able to make significant penetration into Western markets. By virtue of their overall low production costs, firms in these countries (often with the help of institutional support for export programmes) were able to undercut Western manufactured goods' prices. Sectors in the West were disrupted and this early import penetration exposed many of the weaknesses of the large batch, standardized production system that was widespread amongst Western manufacturers.

The bulk of Western clothing manufacture, employing specialized sewing machines on a production line, provided a classic example of Taylorization where division of labour narrowed workers' skills and reduced their autonomy. This was also the main mechanism by which the labour process became 'feminized' in these countries after the turn of the century. It was a fairly rigid system and quality was inspected at the end of production. Piece rate payment was designed to motivate workers and also provided employers with opportunities to re-structure the effort bargain (through manipulation of the standard operating minute upon which payment is based) if they needed to alter their cost structure. However, when confronted initially with import penetration, the only significant responses were lay-offs and demands for political initiatives to regulate imports (Jones, 1984; Silberston, 1993).

Since the 1940s, the principal mechanism for establishing the ground rules for international trade has been the General Agreement on Tariffs and Trade (GATT), and in 1974 GATT established the Multi-Fibre Agreement (MFA). The major role of the MFA has been to 'agree permitted growth rates for the increase of exports from developing countries' (West Midlands Low Pay Unit, 1991: 12). The MFA was seen by most developed countries as a temporary arrangement to allow their own textile and garment industries 'time to restructure in order to better withstand the consequences of a trading system free of quotas' (NEDC, 1990: 4).

Despite the existence of tariffs and quotas, import penetration of Western markets continued. Many Asian producers moved into product areas that were not covered by existing quotas, and the clothing industry in this region continued to expand. South Korea, for example, experienced a sevenfold increase in clothing production between 1973 and 1988 (ILO, 1995).

By the late 1970s, other Asian countries sought to emulate these earlier successes and embarked upon a similar round of export-led industrialization in which clothing manufacturing figured prominently. Countries such as Malaysia, Indonesia and the Philippines were important in this regard. Their growth was also triggered by the shift of some manufacturing to them from countries such as Hong Kong and Singapore where rising wage rates were undermining their position as low cost producers.

Outsourcing and the relocation of production

Clothing manufacture has traditionally relied upon production networks whereby one firm (contractor) might design a garment and purchase the fabric but then send it to another firm (sub-contractor) for manufacturing. Typically a multitude of sub-contractors, most of whom employ few people, work in conjunction with a few design firms. The latter are able to maintain production flexibility and keep their overheads to a minimum by sub-contracting (or outsourcing as it is also called) low value-added tasks to the sub-contractors. The sub-contractors typically accept the work for a certain payment then must find ways to manufacture it according to the specifications of the contractor. Such a system inherently contains mechanisms for shifting production to firms where labour costs are low and/or can be easily manipulated. It is also a central component of low-cost production strategies since firms with high variable costs (particularly those where labour can account for 20–50 per cent of production costs) can shift garment manufacture to those with a lower cost structure.

The reaction by many firms in high wage countries to the continued growth of import penetration was to restructure, both internally and externally. This involved outsourcing production to low cost areas, both domestic and overseas, as well as internal organizational changes designed to improve operational efficiency.

External restructuring led to the relocation of many labour-intensive or low value-added activities to lower-cost production areas in the developing world. This was in many ways the logical extension of sub-contracting but in this case the outsourcing of garment assembly was on a trans-national basis.

Despite the low wages of clothing workers relative to workers in other manufacturing industries in high-wage economies, the differential labour costs between high and low-wage countries remain large because of the labour intensity of garment manufacture (Scheffer, 1994: 112). In fact the magnitude of the labour cost gap (in $ per standard minute) between the high-wage and low-wage economies is so great that even taking other costs into account (such as infrastructure, service and delivery), clothing manufacturing costs in the UK, towards the bottom of the high-wage range, are about 40 per cent higher than the comparable costs in Turkey, towards the top of the low-wage economies, and 200 per cent higher than China, towards the bottom of the low-wage economies. Outsourcing production to low-wage economies therefore offers one possible route for clothing manufacturers in high-wage economies to retain market share while remaining a low-cost competitor (Anson, 1993). Table 13.1 provides an overview of comparative compensation costs in the clothing sector for a selection of high and low wage countries.

The increased dependence on subcontracting arrangements has two primary objectives. First, it is designed to improve cost competitiveness, defending market share against imports when expenditure on clothing is in many cases declining. Second, sub-contracting assists a marketing strategy of focused differentiation by devolving responsibility for quality to the sub-contractors.

In addition to outsourcing to independent contractors overseas, many Western manufacturers have also invested in overseas production sites, as increasingly did the distribution networks whose links with the more powerful retailers consolidated their position in the supply chain. Whether through joint ventures or direct foreign investment, this process has aided the industry's growth overseas in industrializing nations while contributing to its decline in the industrial nations.

Internal restructuring involved attempts to improve the production process through the introduction of new manufacturing systems and technological innovations, as well as refocusing product lines away from standardized goods to those with higher value-added content.

Table 13.1 Hourly compensation costs (wages and social contributions) in US dollars

Country	1990	1993
United States	8.76	9.14
Mexico	0.92	1.08
Germany	7.23	17.22
France	12.52	14.84
Italy	12.50	12.31
United Kingdom	8.02	8.42
Bulgaria	1.25	0.26
Hungary	0.92	1.62
Romania	1.73	0.25
Morocco	0.92	1.06
Tunisia	1.46	1.54
China	0.26	0.25
Hong Kong	3.05	3.85
Indonesia	0.16	0.28
Japan	6.34	10.64
Philippines	0.46	0.53
South Korea	2.46	2.71
Taiwan	3.41	4.61
Malaysia	0.56	0.77

Source: Werner International Inc. (1994)

The introduction of teamwork has been perhaps the most significant innovation in manufacturing systems and the major component of work re-organization. In an attempt to improve the efficiency of production systems and attain greater flexibility, many firms have experimented with teams (generally of eight to fifteen workers), in which the members are cross-trained in different tasks. With team workers paid an hourly wage plus a bonus if they exceed their production quota, teams have frequently been used by firms to lower their supervision costs, since workers are in theory 'self-directed', and build quality into the production process (rather than inspect for it at the end). Teams have also been used to increase output flexibility and reduce inventory; the former mandated by new retailer supply schedules that will be discussed later; the latter another cost-cutting measure.

Although the complete automation of clothing manufacture is very difficult, reasonably low-cost technological innovations in the pre-assembly stage have become more widely available over the past two decades and transformed part of the production process. New technology has mainly been introduced to the following stages: design (computer-aided design software packages) and cutting (laser-driven computerized cutters); the transport of garments between machines and the overall monitoring and control of production operations (computerized production monitoring systems); and *ad hoc* modifications to existing sewing machines (such as button holers) that increase production speed. Make-up or garment assembly has not been appropriate for the extensive application of new technology in clothing for technical reasons and because labour is cheap. Clothing enterprises in the high-wage economies generally enjoy better access to capital and have more scope for exploiting economies of scale where mass markets have persisted, so there is more opportunity to adopt new technologies (OTA, 1987; OECD, 1994).

The rate of adoption of new technologies in clothing manufacture has generally been slow, and innovation is normally concentrated in the larger enterprises (Hoffman and Rush, 1985). Nevertheless, piecemeal technological changes have had a significant impact upon work organization (Barlow and Winterton, 1996). However, it is important to recognize the disincentives that many firms face in innovating technologically, in addition to the practical difficulties in automating garment assembly. The growth of what has become a *de facto* international division of labour has meant that the persistence of low labour costs has often deterred the adoption of new technologies. Furthermore, there is evidence that the low-tech clothing companies are no less profitable than those that have invested in new equipment (Groves and Hamblin, 1989; R. Winterton, 1992).

Finally, product market changes and the growing power of retailers over the past two decades have transformed the industry from one that was manufacturer driven to one that is retailer driven. The decline of formal wear markets has led many companies to close production facilities for suits and to concentrate on retail operations, buying in casual and fashion wear from other manufacturers, both overseas and domestic. More recent market developments have included a revival of formal clothing, but with the emphasis on design, quality and exclusivity. In virtually all clothing sectors there has been a move away from price towards quality and style as a strategy to compete with imports.

There is also a temporal dimension to the market segmentation, as more seasonal changes have been introduced. Part of this impetus comes from retailers who have been searching for ways to lower their costs. By moving to more numerous 'seasons', smaller quantities of more varied goods can be shipped to stores immediately prior to the selling season. These goods are held for a shorter period of time by the retailers, which results in dramatically lower inventory costs. Many retailers have also introduced electronic ordering and product replenishment systems that require greater production flexibility by manufacturers. As a result of these market changes, the size of production runs has steadily declined along with the time available for manufacturers to respond to product demand.

Institutional changes

These different forms of restructuring were set against a background of broader institutional change associated with de-regulation. Particularly in the UK and the USA, de-regulation has acted as a major facilitator of firm restructuring in promoting an increase in small-scale clothing enterprises which compete with imports by replicating the employment conditions of low-wage economies. Adopting strategies of work intensification, many small firms have flourished, often as sub-contractors, by offering low cost, flexible and quality production. Even where there is a relatively high degree of labour market regulation, as in Germany, a section of the garment industry draws upon the secondary labour market, using ethnic minorities, migrant workers and homeworkers (OECD, 1994; ILO, 1996). Much of the growth in small clothing firms, in Germany, France and the UK, is in inner city areas and disproportionately involves ethnic minority workers and entrepreneurs (Hoel, 1982; Mitter, 1986; Phizacklea, 1990; Ram, 1994, 1996). Italy meanwhile has capitalized upon its flourishing SME sector and the networks of contractors that exist within them. Here, state regulations encourage the growth of small firms by providing an infrastructures of specialist services that sustain their activities. In the USA, the attraction of California, Texas and New York for the location of garment manufacture is similarly related to the opportunities for wage depression (Taplin, 1995).

Relocation and increased market segmentation

Since the early 1990s, continued globalization of production has been facilitated by further changes in trade specifications, most notably EU arrangements for trade with Central Europe and North Africa and the passage of NAFTA in the Americas. In terms of products, further consolidation among retailers and their resulting increased buying power have led to increased product market segmentation. High-wage manufacturers have also embarked more earnestly upon demand-expanding and quality-enhancing strategies for domestic production, abandoning in many cases their cost reduction strategies (ILO, 1996: 20). Here they have refocused attention on design and image for the higher fashion market, often combining this up-market move with innovations in quick response and materials handling.

Progressive liberalization of trade

It was anticipated in 1992 that by the end of a ten-year transition period the complex system of controls then in force with the MFA would be dismantled (Anson, 1992: 16). In January 1993 slight changes were made to conform to the 'single market' and Community quotas replaced individual country quotas. Textiles and clothing were reintegrated into GATT following discussion at the Uruguay Round of negotiations and this will result in both a faster growth of the size of import quotas and the removal of a large proportion of the quotas already in existence. The MFA had been renewed and extended several times, but following the expiry of the last MFA at the end of 1993, the 1994 GATT agreement included provision to phase out the textiles and clothing import controls soon after the end of the millennium (Jones, 1994; Khanna, 1994).

The removal of the MFA and the further globalization of clothing markets (OECD, 1994) have acted as an impulse for further production change, causing an acceleration of the restructuring of garment manufacture in high wage economies. While the precise impact of such restructuring is difficult to assess because of differences between particular product areas, it has been estimated for instance that UK-based clothing production and employment will decrease by around 30 per cent (Jones, 1996) and the high-wage economies overall may lose as much as 50 per cent of indigenous production. According to a recent European Community report, the severity of the loss of jobs in clothing following import penetration has been further exacerbated by a drop in consumption and the general economic recession that hit counties in this region during the early 1990s.

In response to the cost problem, many European firms have relocated production to Central Europe. This follows a trend, started in 1980s by firms in the Netherlands and Germany that were looking for a combination of low cost and close proximity for production. Somewhat different to international outsourcing that was mentioned earlier, this process involves EU firms exporting garment parts for assembly in another country, then re-importing them as finished garments. Known as outward processing trade (OPT), this 'de-localization' of production exists within legal frameworks that specify import duties only on the value-added in the 'assembly' country (Scheffer, 1994). Poland, Hungary, Romania, and the Czech and Slovak Republics are the sites of much production of this nature. Since each of these countries had an established clothing industry, following market reforms in the 1980s and privatization, much of their production has been shifted to meet this new export need. In addition to their low labour costs and skilled work force, these countries have the added attraction of geographic proximity to Western European markets. This permits the fast shipment of goods that is now required by many retailers. Table 13.2 provides a summary of this relocation of production for the biggest European clothing countries.

In a similar vein, Tunisia and Morocco have become the site of OPT to Western Europe. In addition to their low production costs, political stability, and quality labour, they have also been able to exploit their preferential trade relations, particularly with France. Geographic proximity to Europe, and the resultant

Table 13.2 Shares of firms' turnover derived from own production and
sub-contracting, extra-EC and intro-EC, 1983–92 (% of turnover)

	1983	1992
Germany		
Sub-contracting extra-EC	29	44
Production extra-EC	8	12
Sub-contracting EC	3	12
Production EC	59	32
France		
Sub-contracting extra-EC	13	31
Production extra-EC	1	23
Sub-contracting EC	12	13
Production EC	74	33
Italy		
Sub-contracting extra-EC	2	13
Production extra-EC	–	8
Sub-contracting EC	57	50
Production EC	41	28
UK		
Sub-contracting extra-EC	3	15
Production extra-EC	–	8
Sub-contracting EC	11	9
Production EC	86	72

Source: Scheffer (1994)

shipment time factor, also give this region a competitive edge over lower cost Asian production and encouraged European firms to increasingly source production there now that speed as well as cost are important factors.

In the Americas, the implementation of NAFTA further increased production relocation trends to lower-cost peripheral regions (principally Mexico). Earlier trade agreements encouraged a form of OPT between the USA and Mexico plus several Caribbean countries. Along the Mexico/US border, many Mexican firms have, since the late 1960s, engaged in export assembly for the United States. This trend continues – note the 42 per cent increase in the number of these companies between 1989 and 1993. However, there has also been significant growth of clothing manufacture in other regions of Mexico following the passage of NAFTA, and in recent years some Mexican firms have begun to move into higher quality/cost production niches and still remain cost competitive with US markets.

While Mexico has been the major beneficiary of the agreement, especially in terms of jobs and export earnings, the United States and Canada have both experienced a reduction of the workforce following the relocation of production overseas.

Continued retailer concentration and market segmentation

During the past two decades there has been extensive financial restructuring of enterprises in response to the globalization and fragmentation of product markets, and as a result of government initiatives such as privatization and measures to promote employee share ownership. The capital restructuring which has taken place in clothing industries in recent decades has involved a continued concentration of ownership at the retail end and new capital formation, especially involving SMEs, in garment production (Kurt Salmon Associates, 1993). This process has been inextricably linked with the firm restructuring associated with horizontal market segmentation. In turn, this has been accompanied by vertical segmentation of production, with small establishments sub-contracting a limited range of operations in the overall production cycle (Anson, 1993). Vertical segmentation of production in the USA and the UK, for example, has been characterized by major manufacturers or retailers retaining control over design and quality, with garment assembly being sub-contracted to smaller 'cut, make and trim' (CMT) firms.

Forced to diversify their products to meet the greater variability of demand by increasingly powerful retailers, as well as keeping their costs low, high wage manufacturers have continued with their own cost-cutting strategies and pursued further work re-organization. Part of the problem lies in the fact that manufacturers are caught between retailers, who as buyers of their products are demanding more and more flexibility of them, and textile companies that prefer to supply large quantities of standardized fabric. In contrast with earlier vertical integration, in recent years the supply chain has become disintegrated. The textiles and retail sectors, representing the upstream and downstream linkages with clothing manufacture, have, however, continued to become more concentrated (Taplin and Ordovensky, 1995). As a consequence, clothing manufacturers interface with more powerful monopolies and monopsonies, increasing the pressure for greater efficiencies to maintain shrinking profit margins. Textile companies are large, often capital-intensive operations that continue to prefer the economies of scale associated with standardization.

In order to meet this increased buyer–supplier pressure, many manufacturers have further reduced in-plant production and increased their reliance upon outsourcing, in this case to geographically proximate sites that facilitate the implementation of quick response. The sub-contractors are generally small firms, but there is also evidence of an increased use of homeworkers (ILO, 1996). The latter, in turn, are a product of institutional changes, particularly de-regulated labour markets.

The work re-organization has focused upon achieving greater output flexibility and generally this has involved further usage of teamworking (for the USA, see Berg *et al.*, 1996). Changes in work organization, however, are for the most part, independent of any significant technological change, and while there is empirical evidence of improvements in job satisfaction, upskilling has been less important than work intensification in many instances (Bailey, 1993).

Restructuring and employment

The increased pace of globalization of production after the 1960s led to a substantial redistribution of clothing employment, principally from higher-wage to low-wage countries. Cyclical fluctuations in demand, changes in buyer–supplier relationships, technological innovations and revisions to the regulation of trade, all contributed to a general trend of restructuring in high-wage economies. Throughout this time the general trend has been a shift in clothing employment from the higher wage to the lower wage countries.

In the period 1976 to 1990, the four major European clothing manufacturers (Germany, France, the UK, and Italy) recorded a fall in the number of employees of, respectively, 38.1 per cent, 40.9 per cent, 30.9 per cent, and 41.2 per cent (ILO, 1995: 26). In the United States employment fell by 27 per cent, from 1,332,000 in 1978 to 977,000 in 1993. It was during this time period that the relocation of production from high to low wage countries took hold.

Table 13.3 provides an outline of employment decline in clothing compared to manufacturing as a whole in the main European clothing manufacturer countries plus the United States. Japan is also included, although it did not lose employment in clothing during that time period. However, it has registered employment losses in clothing since then, with a 2.7 per cent decline between 1991 and 1993. On the other hand, it did witness a 16.2 per cent decline in textile employment during the 1980–90 period which is not too dissimilar from textile employment trends in the other listed countries.

Table 13.4 meanwhile lists a selection of countries that made clothing manufacture a cornerstone of their industrialization programme. Employment gains for some of the earlier mentioned industrializing countries (such as Taiwan, Singapore and Hong Kong) had already peaked by the mid-1980s, and in many of

Table 13.3 Percentage change in employment in manufacturing and clothing, industrial countries

Country	Classification	1980–90
France	manufacturing	−14.7
	clothing	−37.9
Germany (Federal Republic of)	manufacturing	−1.5
	clothing	−37.2
Italy	manufacturing	−17.3
	clothing	−9.5
Spain	manufacturing	−20.0
	clothing	−16.6
United Kingdom	manufacturing	−25.8
	clothing	−23.1
United States	manufacturing	−8.9
	clothing	−29.8
Japan	manufacturing	9.4
	clothing	14.6

Source: ILO (1996) from *Industrial Statistics Yearbook*

Table 13.4 Percentage changes in employment for industrializing countries

Country	Classification	1980–90
South Korea	manufacturing	46.8
	clothing	24.3
Malaysia	manufacturing	66.4
	clothing	192.2
Philippines	manufacturing	−0.1
	clothing	74.4
China	manufacturing	39.2
	clothing (incl. Footwear)	29.6
Indonesia	manufacturing	154.0
	clothing	812.9
Morocco	manufacturing	135.7
	clothing	332.2
Tunisia	manufacturing	n/a
	clothing	20.1
Romania	manufacturing	20.0
	clothing	33.2
Bulgaria	manufacturing	9.0
	clothing	35.5

Source: ILO (1996) from *Industrial Yearbook Statistics*

these instances, firms were relocating production from such sites to lower cost producers elsewhere in Asia. This relocation plus the demand from Western firms led to rather dramatic increase in countries such as Indonesia and Morocco.

The employment decline (or at the best stagnation) has continued throughout the 1990s in the high-wage countries as import restrictions have been progressively reduced and firms have pursued internal (operational) and external (spatial) restructuring. Declining demand in these markets has also contributed to this trend of falling employment. However, some of these losses might be distorted by the growth of homework in such countries, as employment was shifted to this informal sector – a topic that we shall return to later.

The scale of internal restructuring is reflected in the substantial contraction of clothing employment in the UK, Italy and Germany, where large firms have declined in number and the remainder have downsized operations.[3] In the UK and Italy, large firm contraction has been accompanied by small and medium-sized enterprise (SME) growth in manufacturing. In Italy, mergers and acquisitions have led to horizontal concentration, which is associated with some increase in capital intensity (Belussi, 1992a). In the UK, however, ownership has become more fragmented as a result of substantial SME growth, and these enterprises are generally under-capitalized (Rainnie, 1989; Kasvio,1992; Winterton and Barlow, 1996). In Japan, ownership restructuring has centred on the role of intermediaries in arriving at the patent agreements which are at the heart of the differentiation strategy (Garanto,1987; Nakamura, 1993).

In all of the high-wage countries, clothing manufacture has become more vertically segmented, and sub-contracting, always a feature of the industry, has become more prevalent, taking advantage of SME growth (the UK and Italy), ethnic minority workers (the UK, the USA and Germany), and homeworkers (the UK). The major factor associated with external restructuring has been the continued growth of OPT, which although contributing to import penetration, also means that more value added is retained in the home country. In the UK, OPT still involves sourcing from the Far East, especially Hong Kong and, increasingly, China (Winterton, 1992) although there has been a rise in shipments for tailored goods from Central Europe. In the USA, offshore production mainly involves Mexico, the Dominican Republic and the Far East (Taplin, 1993). In the case of China, Mexico and the Far East, shipped goods typically are of low quality and mass produced. Japan's OPT strategy, which developed relatively late, has predominantly involved China for garment production, rather than Taiwan, Vietnam and Korea, which represent the major sources of imports (Garanto, 1987; McNamara, 1995). Significantly, whereas design operations are normally retained in the high-wage country, Japanese enterprises are also relocating design to Europe because of the global dominance of European designers.

There has also been spatial restructuring within some indigenous clothing industries. In the UK, the growth of SMEs has been predominantly in the inner city areas (London, Leicester, Bradford) having a relatively high proportion of ethnic minority workers (Ram, 1994). In France, Paris's position as the centre of production around a proliferation of SMEs, many of which employ immigrants, continues. Similarly, relocation strategies in the USA have been away from the unionized, high-wage North East towards both the ethnic minority SMEs of the West coast and the non-union firms in low-wage Southern states (Taplin, 1993). In Italy, and to a lesser extent Japan, relocation has centred on the creation of industrial districts and SME networks (Belussi, 1993; Becattini and Bullani, 1993; Bolisano and Scarso, 1995; Brusco, 1982, 1986).

Internal restructuring has involved both process re-engineering and changes in work organization (Bailey, 1993), and this has been common, to varying degrees, in each of the high-wage countries. The vertical segmentation of production described above represented an external response to shorter lead times. An equivalent internal response has involved process re-engineering based on Just-in-Time (JIT) and Quick Response (QR) techniques, at least in leading edge companies (OECD, 1994). Further forms of business process re-engineering have been used to support innovation strategies in Japan (Garanto, 1987), where *kaizen* (continuous improvement) permeates all manufacturing industry, and to a degree in Germany, although there the improvements have been limited by outmoded organization (Adler, 1988;1990).

The adoption of JIT and QR in order to meet shorter lead times (Hammond, 1993), coupled with focused differentiation strategies based on design and product quality, has been associated in all cases with restructuring of work organization. Teamworking and multiskilling have been quite widely introduced in the UK and the USA, but there is little evidence of a departure from Taylorist principles of job design and the emphasis is on work intensification, although the new forms of work organization are generally preferred by work teams (Taplin and Winterton, 1995). A recent study of the Belgian clothing industry found similar evidence of intensification associated with re-organized production in that country (Sels and Huys, 1999). There has been a similar transformation of work methods in a significant number of enterprises in Italy and Germany, where the emphasis is on building competence through vocational training, an approach which is widely perceived as evidence of an emergent flexible specialization strategy (Adler, 1990; Belussi, 1992b; Brusco, 1986). In Japan, there is more ambiguity concerning this restructuring of work organization, which may conform in specific factories with either the Anglo-American or European approaches (Garanto, 1987). Where the emphasis is on productivity, the process is mostly one of work intensification, whereas an emphasis on flexibility through employee development can be construed as a potential flexible specialization strategy.

As many firms have re-focused their core activities on design and marketing, they have shed many of the low skilled jobs that were part of earlier manufacturing processes. With the growing importance of non-cost competitiveness (quality, flexibility and speed of delivery), manufacturers have been forced to pay attention to building quality control into the production process as well as introducing shorter production cycles. Training workers to meet these new mandates has resulted in some skill increases for machinists. Also, more complicated materials handling equipment requires more engineers for maintenance. It is also apparent in the United States and the UK that greater effort is being made by firms to motivate their workers and socialize them into the new 'zero-defects' work culture. In some respects this follows earlier German efforts associated with skill broadening and commitment documented by Steedman and Wagner (1989). Despite evidence of skills broadening and increased discretion by team workers, such changes nonetheless are often embedded in more demanding work schedules (Taplin and Winterton, 1997) and are therefore still a form of work intensification.

Technological innovations and production innovations have often increased the skill requirements of some core workers (machinists) while simultaneously lowering those of others such as cutters. For example, in the USA and the UK, in most cases new technologies have been primarily at the design and cutting stages (CAD and CCC), which have been associated with materials savings and some deskilling (Taplin and Winterton, 1995). In the case of Germany and Japan, many of the 'traditional' lower skilled jobs have simply been transferred to countries with a comparative advantage in low-cost production (ILO, 1996: 59).

One of the features associated with responses to low cost competition has been the growth of atypical employment practices. Of this homeworking is most notable in the clothing industry, building on earlier traditions[4] of such practices whereby women received garments for assembly in the home. As a form of outsourcing, it has become popular again in some countries following labour market de-regulation and as a way of managing the flexibility mandates for production. While official statistics are less accurate on this employment practice than on others, there is plenty of evidence from the popular press that uncovers abuses of this practice to suggest that it is becoming quite widespread.

In Germany, a 1989 report estimated that there were 22,000 homeworkers; in the UK a 1987 government report estimated 35,000. In Italy, meanwhile, where homeworking is virtually indistinguishable from SME production,[5] it has become a crucial part of quick response strategies. It is also a feature of the dual system of structured and informal sectors that exists in Spain (ILO, 1995: 40).

In the United States homeworking was banned in the 1940s, but after 1989 the regulations were relaxed to permit some work at home. Despite strict regulations, however, there is plenty of evidence that homeworking has played an integral part of low-cost production strategies by sub-contractor firms, particularly those who rely upon undocumented workers (Taplin, 1993). Furthermore, its use (and abuse) appears to continue, especially in areas such as New York and Los Angeles, where SMEs rely upon its availability to attain the flexibility necessary to meet quick response needs.

Japan, along with Germany, is one of the few countries that is more rigorous in the monitoring of homeworking. The Industrial Home Work Act of 1970 established strict regulations and required registration of all homeworkers. Although there were 2 million in 1990 such workers, their numbers are falling as wages have risen and Japanese firms shifted production overseas.

Finally, if one had to comment generally on working conditions and payment levels, it would suffice to say that they vary according to sector and labour force demographics. Where firms have sought higher value-added niches, a commitment to quality together with productive flexibility, it has usually resulted in workers earning more but often working harder. This applies to larger firms where the introduction of teamworking has given the illusion of improved work practices (autonomy, less external supervision, etc.). The reality, however, is that even under these circumstances where skill enlargement has occurred, the workpace has increased as workers now engage in a form of 'self-exploitation' (Taplin, 1995). Wages are typically higher in large and medium-sized firms than in SMEs in each of the countries examined.

When lower value-added production is outsourced, it goes either domestically in which ethnic contractors rely upon wage-depressing tactics among immigrant workers to keep their production costs low, or externally to low labour cost countries. In either case, wages and working conditions are less favourable than in the high value-added firms.

In one respect, one could argue that many of the low-skilled, low-cost jobs have moved to areas where their competitive advantage best suits such production techniques. But the growth of SMEs in higher wage countries such as the USA, the UK and even France, has often been predicated upon their ability to compress wages, intensify work and thus re-create a low-cost labour market within a high wage economy.

New technology has also been a mixed blessing for workers in this industry. By allowing automation of pre-assembly stages it has resulted in substantial de-skilling and job reduction for cutters, many of whom were male. It has also enabled sewing machine operators to work faster and improved the inter-changeability of tasks, but this has increased the complexity and intensity of their work. They are also subject to greater micro-electronic monitoring which tracks quality and permits greater accuracy in determining compensation rates. In the SMEs, supervision remains extensive as firms rely upon formal control mechanisms to elicit maximum worker effort.

Piece-rate payment is still the preferred industry norm, despite the growth of quota-based team systems. Managers report a preference for such a system because it regulates the effort bargain in ways that ensure adequate levels of productivity for the firm. This results in a range of earnings for machinists, with the more skilled, older experienced workers, typically earning substantially more than younger, new entrants to the industry.

While it is always difficult to precisely determine the extent of workplace abuses, there is evidence that de-regulated labour markets facilitate if not encourage some illegal practices. The use of child labour might have been curtailed in high-wage economies but it is not entirely absent (cf. recent highlighted problems in the USA). Nor are non-payment for overtime, and below minimum wage payments, or the employment of undocumented workers – all of which can be found in most of the countries under discussion with the possible exception of Japan (ILO, 1995, 1996). And this is in an industry where many of the 'bad' jobs have already been shifted offshore.

Patterns of restructuring

What patterns, if any, exist in the types of restructuring discussed above? At a very general level it is clear that there are two apparently contradictory trajectories, represented by the tendencies towards enskilling and increased value-added on the one hand, and deskilling and wage depression on the other. While one approach is emphasized more than the other in some countries, generally both are present simultaneously. Different enterprises within the same sector in one country can pursue diverse strategies, and some strategies can even contain these internal contradictions.

Increased imports have universally intensified competition on costs and delivery times. As a direct response to market fragmentation, many clothing enterprises have developed strategies of focused differentiation and niche marketing, most successfully in Italy, followed by Germany and Japan, and in some cases in the UK, the USA and France. The relative success of the strategy in Italy is explained by the international acclaim of Italian design, and in Germany and Japan by the quality and status associated with branded garments. The strategy has similarly been adopted in the UK by producers of labels such as Burberry, and in France by firms such as Agnès B. By definition, however, such a strategy is unavailable to the mass producer, which causes problems for such producers of standardized low quality/low-cost items.

The situation is exacerbated in the two highest wage countries, Germany and Japan, by market contraction. External market contraction in Germany is explained by its vulnerability, unique among the countries studied, to the collapse of former Soviet Union markets, while internal market contraction in Germany and Japan is explained by changing patterns of consumer expenditure. The contraction is not a function of the relatively high labour rates, but these constrain the strategic options available to enterprises, which in all countries face difficulties in remaining cost competitive while retaining labour. Labour market de-regulation in Japan has been designed to resolve such difficulties, just as in the UK and the USA it has been designed to stimulate entrepreneurial activity. The German clothing industry, facing a greater product market contraction and more regulated labour market, has divested capacity more rapidly (Adler, 1990).

Market fragmentation introduced two imperatives: a focus on quality and shorter lead times. Import penetration has also increased the importance of delivery times, as well as reinforcing the cost imperative. The intensification of competition can therefore be summarized in terms of the three imperatives: quality, delivery and cost. The diverse strategies identified in the countries considered contribute, in a variety of combinations, to the pursuit of these imperatives. It remains to consider why different strategic responses have been emphasized in particular countries.

The pursuit of quality under a focused differentiation marketing strategy might be assumed to lead automatically to total quality initiatives. In fact, such initiatives are only apparent in those UK and Japanese enterprises that have pursued niche marketing, along with some US firms that have not. In the UK and US cases, however, this still represents a minority of firms. It also suggests that the pursuit of total quality initiatives is often more a consequence of culture than a response to specific market imperatives.

The delivery imperative caused by shorter lead times is more clearly associated with both internal and external restructuring strategies. Internally, enterprises have adopted QR and JIT techniques in most high wage countries. Externally, production has become vertically segmented, leading to increased sub-contracting. The internal strategies have been most prevalent in the UK, US and Japanese enterprises, but sub-contracting has also increased significantly in these countries. In France, Italy and Germany, sub-contracting has been emphasized more, but the internal strategies have also been adopted. Clearly, therefore, the internal and external restructuring strategies are complementary rather than alternatives.

While sub-contracting has become increasingly important in most countries, there are differences in emphasis between sub-contracting to indigenous SMEs and outsourcing in the form of OPT. The SME sector has been most important in the UK, France, Italy, Japan, and to some extent the USA because SMEs are flourishing in these environments. In the UK, and the USA, government policies have encouraged SME growth, while in Italy and Japan, SMEs are thriving in the industrial districts fostered by policy initiatives. Similarly, the use of foreign sub-contracting, or OPT, is common to all the countries considered except for Italy, and the form of OPT is a function of location and tradition. In the UK and USA, OPT involves mainly enterprises in countries which are traditional sources of imported garments, or where preferential trade agreements exist. Germany, meanwhile, is outsourcing to the eastern bloc countries because of its geographic proximity to such low-wage producers. Japan's OPT is also influenced by geographic proximity, although as a longer-term strategy, Japanese enterprises are substituting China for the traditional Far Eastern production sources of imports.

New forms of work organization are clearly associated with the adoption of QR and JIT techniques in all countries, and especially in the more progressive enterprises. The impact of teamworking, modular systems and UPS has been shown to vary significantly between countries, with productivity, work intensification and deskilling emphasized in the UK and USA, compared with quality, competence building and enskilling in Italy and Germany. The difference reflects the dominance of Taylorism in the Anglo-American approach, in contrast with the new European production norm, exemplified by the Social Protocol which is being resisted by the UK government (Lane, 1995). The ambiguities in the case of Japan are of different origin. In Japan, the dominant mode of production is not Taylorist, but seeks to harness workers' tacit skills and knowledge to intensify work (Garanto, 1987).

To the extent that new technology has been adopted in response to quality, delivery and cost imperatives, it is associated with the larger enterprises in the UK, the USA and France, which have access to capital. The adoption of new technologies is more limited in SMEs, which in part accounts for the low innovation potential of Italian clothing enterprises (Antonelli, 1988). In the case of Germany, however, the limited adoption of new technology reflects the industry's crisis of rapid contraction (Adler, 1990). The more extensive technological innovation in Japanese clothing enterprises, including SMEs, is a direct consequence of the role of MITI and the longer-term perspective of the Japanese finance industry (McNamara, 1995).

Sub-contracting and relocation also have wage-depressing effects and the specific focus which these take depends upon the country environment, and especially prevailing labour market conditions. Thus in the deregulated environments of the UK and the USA, sub-contracting to SMEs reduces labour costs more than in the relatively regulated Italian environment (Taplin and Winterton, 1995). Wage depression based on ethnic minority exploitation is a feature of clothing in the UK, the USA, France and Germany because ethnic minority workers are concentrated in local labour markets in these countries (Phizacklea, 1990; Taplin, 1993). Similarly, relocation has a major impact on labour costs in the USA because labour markets are subject to local state, rather than federal, regulation (or deregulation).

Conclusion

From the overview of restructuring in a number of different countries, it is possible to see certain patterns emerge. Furthermore, the differences between the patterns of restructuring of clothing in the high-wage economies are more of degree and emphasis than of fundamental principle. Clothing enterprises in all of the high-wage economies considered face common challenges and have to address the same imperatives. The restructuring strategies have much in common and the diverse combinations reflect variations in the opportunities, constraints and traditions of the different country contexts. While enterprises in some countries provide evidence of the emergence of a new production paradigm, for the most part, the restructuring of clothing in high-wage economies represents merely a reconfiguration of Taylorist production.

It would appear that institutional factors, particular those relating to labour market regulation, predispose firms in certain countries to pursue certain types of strategies. That, and the existence of certain manufacturing traditions (standardized, cost-based versus quality, niche production) can also influence the pattern of restructuring (external versus internal emphasis). Presumably such trends will continue, mediated by product market changes that are often determined by the respective power of retailers in each of the countries.

Given the macro-scope of this study, more firm-based research would be useful, insofar as one could examine detailed managerial responses to uncertainty. How individual firms negotiate responses to market pressures, and position themselves to take advantage of contingent opportunities, would allow one to analyse restructuring at the micro-level and assess the level of fit with the current framework. This, in turn, would enable one to examine whether new production systems at the level of the firm are consistent with what appears to be happening at the industry/sector level or whether generalizations about the latter are masking an embryonic organizational form that is a departure from the Fordist types alluded to above.

Notes

1   In the UK such flexibility was seen both as a route to competitive advantage and as a mechanism for reducing unemployment, especially among young people. See Ashton *et al.* (1990) for more details of this policy agenda.
2   See Hollingsworth and Boyer (1997) for a review of some of this discussion.
3   Substantial data containing details of such changes in clothing employment, establishment and output for high wage economies can be found in Taplin and Winterton (1997).
4   See Mitter (1986) for an extensive discussion of this issue in the UK.
5   The average number of employees in knitting firms in the Prato region during the early 1980s was four. Distinguishing between a small firm and family members who take in work at home becomes extremely difficult.

Acknowledgements

Some of the information for this chapter is drawn from a project we directed entitled 'Rethinking Global Production: A Comparative Analysis of Restructuring in the Clothing Industry'. We would like to acknowledge the help provided by the following colleagues on this project: Ulrich Adler, Michael Breitenacher, Fiorenza Belussi, Annie Garanto, and Antti Kasvio. We also thank Richard Butler, Carola M. Frege, David Hickson, Paul Olk, Andrew Pendleton and an anonymous reviewer for their useful comments on earlier versions of this work.

References

Adler, U. (1988) *Wettbewerb, Technik und Arbeitsgestaltung – neue Tendenzen im Bekleidungsgewerbe?*, Munich: Ifo Institute for Economic Research.

Adler, U. (1990) *Arbeit und Technik in der Bekleidungsindustrie*, Frankfurt: Campus-Verlag.

American Apparel Manufacturers Association (1988) *Flexible Apparel Manufacturing*, Report of the Technical Advisory Committee, Washington, DC: AAMA.

Anson, R. (1992) 'Demise of the MFA', *Manufacturing Clothier*, 73, March: 16–19.

Anson, R. (1993) 'Why Global Sourcing May be the Only Way Forward', *Manufacturing Clothier*, 74, March: 13–14.

Antonelli, C. (ed.) (1988) *New Information Technology and Industrial Change: The Italian Case*, Dordrecht: Kluwer.

Ashton, D., Maguire, M. and Spilsbury, M. (1990) *Restructuring the Labour Market: The Implications for Youth*, London: Macmillan.

Bailey, T. (1993) 'Organizational Innovation in the Apparel Industry: Strategy or Technique?', *Industrial Relations* 32(1): 30–48.

Barlow, A. and Winterton, J. (1996) 'Work Organization and the Restructuring of Clothing Production', in I.M. Taplin and J. Winterton (eds) *Restructuring within a Labour Intensive Industry*, Aldershot: Avebury, pp. 176–98.

Becattini, G. and Rullani, E. (1993) 'Sistema locale e mercato globale', paper presented at the Economia e Politica Industriale in Italia dal 1973 al 1993, conference, Milan, 12–13 November.

Belussi, F. (1992a) *Nuovi modelli d'impressa, gerarchie organizzative e imprese rete*, Milano: Franco Angeli.

Belussi, F. (1992b) 'Benetton Italy: Beyond Fordism and Flexible Specialization. The Evolution of the Network Firm Model', in S. Mitter (ed.) *Computer-aided Manufacturing and Women's Employment: The Clothing Industry in Four European Countries*, London: Springer Verlag, pp. 73–91.

Belussi, F. (1993) 'The Transformation of the 1980s: The Growth of Network Companies, or the Return of Flexibility in Large Business?', *International Journal of Technology Management* 8: 188–99.

Berg, P., Appelbaum, E., Bailey, T. and Kalleberg, A.L. (1996) 'The Performance Effects of Modular Production in the Apparel Industry', *Industrial Relations* 35(3): 356–73.

Blyth, R. (1996) 'Sourcing: The Implementation of Global Strategy through Informed Choice', in I.M. Taplin and J. Winterton (eds) *Restructuring within a Labour Intensive Industry*, Aldershot: Avebury, pp.112–41.

Bolisano, E. and Scarso, E. (1995) 'The International Decentralisation of Production Activities: The Case of the Italian Apparel Industry', paper presented at the Management of Production Systems conference, University of Trieste, 28–31 May.

Brusco, S. (1982) 'The Emilian Model: Productive Decentralisation and Social Integration', *Cambridge Journal of Economics* 6(2): 167–84.

Brusco, S. (1986) 'Small Firms and Industrial Districts: the Experience of Italy', in D. Keeble and E. Wever (eds) *New Firms and Regional Development in Europe*, London: Croom Helm, pp. 184–202.

Dicken, P. (1992) *Global Shift: The Internationalization of Economic Activity*, 2nd edn, London: Chapman.

Garanto, A. (1987) *Nihon no apparel sangyô chosei to gijûtsu kakushin* (The Japanese Apparel Industry: Innovation and Restructuring), Hitotsubashi: Hitotsubashi University.

Groves, G. and Hamblin, D. (1989) *The Effectiveness of AMT Investment in UK Clothing Manufacture*, Cranfield: Cranfield Institute of Technology, Bedford, UK.

Hamel, G. and Prahalad, C.K. (1990) 'The Core Competences of the Corporation', *Harvard Business Review*, May–June, pp. 79–91.

Hammond, J. (1993) 'Quick Response in Retail/Manufacturing Channels', in S. Bradley, J. Hausman and R. Nolan (eds) *Globalization, Technology and Competition*, Boston: Harvard Business School Press.

Hilowitz, J. (1987) Education and Training Policies and Programmes to Support Industrial Restructuring in the Republics of Korea, Japan, Singapore and the United States, Training Policies Discussion Paper No 18, Geneva: International Labour Office.

Hoel, B. (1982) 'Contemporary Clothing "Sweatshops": Asian Female Labour and Collective Organization', in J. West (ed.) *Work, Women and the Labour Market*, London: Routledge and Kegan Paul, pp. 80–98.

Hoffman, K. and Rush, M. (1985) 'From Needles and Pins to Microelectronics: The Impact of Technological Change in the Garment Industry', in S. Jacobson and J. Sigmundson (eds) *Technological Trends and Challenges in Electronics*, Lund: University of Lund, pp. 71–101.

Hoffman, K. and Rush, M. (1987) *Micro-Electronics and Clothing*, New York: Praeger.

Hollingsworth, J.R. and Boyer, R. (1997) *Contemporary Capitalism*, Cambridge: Cambridge University Press.

Hyman, R. (1988) 'Flexible Specialization: Miracle or Myth?', in R. Hyman and D. Streek (eds) *New Technology and Industrial Relations*, Oxford: Blackwell, pp. 48–60.

International Labour Office (1995) *Recent Developments in the Clothing Industry*, Geneva: ILO.

International Labour Office (1996) *Globalization of the Footwear, Textiles and Clothing Industries*, Geneva: ILO.

Jones, B. (1988) 'Work and Flexible Automation in Britain: A Review of Developments and Possibilities', *Work, Employment and Society*, 2(4): 451–86.

Jones, R.M. (1984) 'The Multi-Fibre Arrangement', *Hollings Apparel Industry Review*, 1(2): 21–65.

Jones, R.M. (1994) 'The GATT Agreement 1994', *The Journal of Clothing Technology and Management*, Spring, pp. 46–69.

Jones, R.M. (1996) 'Changes in Regional Employment in the UK Clothing Industry, 1971–1991', in I.M. Taplin and J. Winterton (eds) *Restructuring within a Labour Intensive Industry*, Aldershot: Avebury, pp. 61–111.

Kasvio, A. (ed.) (1992) *Industry Without Blue Collar Workers – Perspectives on the European Clothing Industry in the 1990s*. Working Paper 36, Tampere: Work Research Centre, University of Tampere.

Kern, H. and Schumann, M. (1987) 'Limits of the Division of Labour: New Production Concepts in West German Industry', *Economic and Industrial Democracy*, 8(2): 151–70.

Khanna, S.R. (1994) 'The New GATT Agreement', *Textile Outlook International*, 52 (March): 10–37.

Kurt Salmon Associates (1993) *The Textile and Clothing Industry in the EC Until 2001*, London: KSA.

Lane, C. (1988) 'Industrial Change in Europe: The Pursuit of Flexible Specialization in Britain and West Germany', *Work, Employment and Society*, 2(2): 141–68.

Lane, C. (1995) *Industry and Society in Europe*, Cheltenham: Edward Elgar.

McNamara, D.L. (1995) *Textiles and Industrial Transition in Japan*, Ithaca, NY: Cornell University Press.

Maruyama, M. (1993) 'The Structure and Performance of the Japanese Distribution System – Opportunities and Obstacles, Structure and Practice', in M.R. Czintoka and M. Kotabe (eds) *The Japanese Distribution System*, Cambridge: Probus, pp. 23–41.

Meegan, R. (1988) 'A Crisis of Mass Production?', in J. Allen and D. Massey (eds) *The Economy in Question*, London: Sage, pp. 136–83.

Ministry of International Trade and Industry (1984) *Senshin Koku gata sangyô wo mesashite – Atarashi jidai no sein sangyô vision* (Vision of the new textile industry era), Tokyo: MITI.

Mitter, S. (1986) 'Industrial Restructuring and Manufacturing Homework: Immigrant Women in the UK Clothing Industry', *Capital and Class*, 27: 37–80.

Morishima, S. (1987) 'Quick response wo mesesu apparel sangyô' (The apparel industry and the rapid response system), *Chûsho kigyô Kinyû Kôko Geppo*, 10: 18–33.

Nakamura, Y. (1993) *Apparel Singe* (The Apparel Industry), Tokyo: Nihon jigyô shuppan sha.

National Economic Development Office (1990) *The State of the Clothing Industry*, London: NEDC.

Office of Technology Assessment (1987) *The U.S. Textile and Apparel Industry: A Revolution in Progress*, Washington, DC: OTA.

Organization for Economic Cooperation and Development (1994) *Globalization of Industrial Activities: A Case Study of the Clothing Industry*, Paris: OECD.

Oster, S. (1994) *Modern Competitive Anaylsis*, New York: Oxford University Press.

Phizacklea, A. (1990) *Unpacking the Fashion Industry: Gender, Racism and Class in Production*, London: Routledge.

Piore, M., and Sabel, C. (1984) *The Second Industrial Divide*, New York: Basic Books.

Porter, M.E. (1993) *The Competitive Advantage of Nations*, New York: Free Press.

Rainnie, A. (1989) *Industrial Relations in Small Firms: Small Isn't Beautiful*, London: Routledge.

Rainnie, A. (1991) 'Flexible Specialization: New Times or Old Hat?', in P. Blyton and J. Morris (eds) *A Flexible Future? Prospects for Employment and Organization*, Berlin: Walter de Gruyter, pp. 43–61.

Ram, M. (1994) *Managing to Survive: Working Lives in Small Firms*, Oxford: Blackwell.

Ram, M. (1996) 'Unravelling the Hidden Clothing Industry: Managing the Ethnic Minority Garment Sector', in I.M. Taplin and J. Winterton (eds) *Restructuring within a Labour Intensive Industry*, Aldershot: Avebury, pp. 158–75.

Rothwell, R. (1980) 'Innovation in Textile Machinery', in K. Pavitt (ed.), *Technical Innovation and British Economic Performance*, London: Macmillan, pp. 126–41.

Rush, H. and Soete, L. (1984) 'Clothing', in K.Guy (ed.) *Technological Trends and Employment*: vol. 1 *Basic Consumer Goods*, London: Gower, pp. 174–222.

Sabel, C. (1982) *Work and Politics*, Cambridge: Cambridge University Press.

Scheffer, M.R. (1994) 'Internationalisation of Production by EC Textile and Clothing Manufacturers', *Textile Outlook International* January, 101–23.

Sels, L. and Huys, R. (1999) 'Towards a Flexible Future? The Nature of Organisational Response in the Clothing Industry', *New Technology, Work and Employment* 14(2): 113–28.

Silberston, Z.A. (1993) *The Future of the Multifibre Arrangement: Implications for the UK Economy*, London: Pinter.

Steedman, H. and Wagner, K. (1989) 'Productivity, Machinery and Skills: Clothing Manufacture in Britain and Germany', *National Institute Economic Review* May, 40–57.

Streeck, W. (1987) 'The Uncertainty of Management and the Management of Uncertainty', *Work, Employment and Society*, 22(4): 412–38.

Taplin, I.M. (1993) 'Strategic Reorientations of U.S. Apparel Firms', in G. Gereffi and M. Korzeniewicz (eds) *Commodity Chains and Global Capitalism*, Westport, CT: Greenwood Press, pp. 205–22.

Taplin, I.M. (1994) 'Recent Manufacturing Changes in the US Apparel Industry: The Case of North Carolina', in E. Bonacich and P. Ong (eds) *The Globalization of the Apparel Industry in the Pacific Rim*, Philadelphia: Temple University Press, pp. 328–44.

Taplin, I.M. (1995) 'Flexible Production, Rigid Jobs: Lessons from the Clothing Industry', *Work and Occupations*, 22(4): 412–38.

Taplin, I.M. and Ordovensky, F. (1995) 'Changes in Buyer-Supplier Relationships and Labour Market Structures: Evidence from the United States', *The Journal of Clothing Technology and Management*, 12(3): 1–18.

Taplin, I.M. and Winterton, J. (1995) 'New Clothes from Old Techniques: Restructuring and Flexibility in the US and UK Clothing Industries', *Industrial and Corporate Change* 4(3): 615–38.

Taplin, I.M. and Winterton, J. (eds) (1996) *Restructuring within a Labour Intensive Industry: The UK Clothing Industry in Transition*, Aldershot: Avebury.

Taplin, I.M. and Winterton, J. (1997) *Rethinking Global Production: A Comparative Analysis of Restructuring in the Clothing Industry*, Aldershot: Ashgate.

West Midlands Low Pay Unit (1991) *The Clothes Showdown: The Future of the West Midlands Clothing Industry*, Birmingham: WMLPU.

Winterton, J. (1992) 'The Transformation of Work? Work Organization in the UK Clothing Industry', in A. Kasvio (ed.) *Industry without Blue-Collar Workers*, pp. 273–97.

Winterton, J. (1994) 'Multiskilling, Training and Industrial Relations: Conflict and Consensus in the New Agenda', paper presented at International Sociological Association 13th World Congress, Bielefeld, 18–23 July.

Winterton, R. (1992) 'Restructuring in the UK Clothing Industry: Segmented Production and the Flexible Firm', in A. Kasvio (ed.) *Industry without Blue-Collar Workers*, pp. 27–60.

Winterton, R. and Barlow, A. (1996) 'Economic Restructuring', in I.M. Taplin and J. Winterton (eds) *Restructuring within a Labour Intensive Industry*, Aldershot: Avebury, pp. 25–60.

Womack, J.P., Jones, D.T. and Roos, D. (1990) *The Machine that Changed the World*, New York: Harper.

Zeitlin, J. (1988) 'The Clothing Industry in Transition: International Trends and British Response', *Textile History* 19(2): 211–38.

Name index

Subject index